PUBLIC RELATIONS: CONCEPTS AND PRACTICES

Second Edition

by

Raymond Simon
Professor of Public Relations
Utica College of Syracuse University

Grid Publishing, Inc., Columbus, Ohio

For Lyn, Melissa, Karen, and Lillian
With Love And Affection

Printed in the the United States
1 2 3 4 5   4 3 2 1 0

Library of Congress Cataloging in Publication Data

Simon, Raymond.
  Public relations.

  (The Grid series in advertising/journalism)
  Includes bibliographies.
  1. Public relations—United States. I. Title.
HM263.S533 1980   659.2'0973   79-16160
ISBN 0-88244-193-0

Contents

Preface

When the first edition of this book was published four years ago I stated in the Preface that its basic purpose was to serve as a tool for teachers and students in the one-term, introductory course in public relations.

This second edition aims to serve the same basic purpose. It is not a handbook or history, and it does not aim to set forth innumerable writing, editing, and graphics rules. What I have tried to do is to deal with the essential nature of public relations; its role in American society; the practitioners who manage the function; and the dynamics of the public relations process. Part 1 provides an overview of public relations as it relates to American society; Part 2 explains how the public relations function is managed; Part 3, the core of the book, deals with the dynamics of public relations; and Part 4 is concerned with ethics, professionalism, and careers.

This book is not restricted to business and industry public relations, but rather to public relations in its broadest sense. It's true that public relations is most widely known for its use by business and industry. However, thousands of practitioners work in the field in government, social agencies, hospitals, colleges, and the armed forces. Therefore, in dealing with such key public relations elements as public opinion, research, planning, programming, communication, and feedback, I have have developed the text material as applied to all public relations practice. Given the basics, the student and practitioner can then apply them to a wide variety of situations and organizations.

Teachers who have used the first edition in their classes have provided the author with important feedback and advice. Following their suggestions, for example, I have retained the "minis"—mini-cases, mini-examples, mini-situations, and mini-problems—but have placed them at the end of each chapter rather than within the text. Some of the more classic mini-cases have been included in this new edition, but others have been dropped and new ones substituted in their place. These "minis" are meant to serve as practical illustrations of text material and to raise realistic questions and assignments for students. Intended to bring students face-to-face with reality, the "minis" challenge students to utilize their verbal and writing abilities, to sharpen their perceptions and communication skills, and to form sound judgments and propose reasonable solutions and actions.

Acting on the advice of users of the first edition, I have provided at the end of each chapter a list of recommended readings from other books, articles, talks, and reports. These can be used as the basis for assigned papers or for classroom discussion. Where it has seemed advisable—such as, for example, in considering public relations research and communication—I have added new chapters in order to cover material in more depth. The long new chapter on communication techniques, especially as they relate to publicity, has been provided in response to suggestions from many users of the first edition.

In a field as dynamic as public relations, a four-year spread between editions brings to the fore new concepts and concerns, and these have been treated as new features of this second edition. In this group, for example, one finds such concepts as "issues management," management by objectives, and the use of computers by media and by public relations practitioners. Where necessary, I have updated data so as to make material more timely and relevent.

This second edition, therefore, combines public relations concepts and practices that are tried and true with those that are new. It is my hope that the text material, the "minis," and the recommended readings will provide a learning-teaching experience that will enable students to develop the insights, perceptions, skills, and judgments needed to succeed in public relations practice. Practitioners may also find this book to be a means of refreshing their understanding of the basics of their field and of providing them with description and analysis of some of the field's latest concepts.

I remain deeply indebted and wish to express my appreciation to my wife Lyn and daughters Melissa and Karen for their patience and encouragement; to Ray Hiebert for granting permission to use some of the accreditation study guide material we co-authored for the Public Relations Society of America; and to those former students and to practitioners who graciously granted me permission to use the raw material which made up the mini-cases, examples, situations, and problems.

Utica, New York   Raymond Simon
January, 1980

PART I
PUBLIC RELATIONS
AND THE
AMERICAN SCENE

This introductory section, consisting of three chapters, provides a perspective for viewing the essential nature of public relations and its role in American society.

In order to understand public relations, one must first understand the term itself and the concept. Chapter 1 examines various definitions of public relations; differences between the term and activities that are frequently confused with the term; and questions which arise as a result of assessing alternatives posed by acceptance of the term.

The overview of public relations provided in the first chapter leads to Chapter 2 and its examination of the reasons why public relations exists in American society. Set forth in this chapter are major trends that have brought about the need for public relations and have affected the way in which public relations is practiced.

The increasing concern with the concept known as "social responsibility" and with the idea of "the public interest" is explored in depth in Chapter 3. Differing schools of thought about these two major areas and their connection with public relations practice are presented for discussion and analysis, and questions are raised to induce thought and insight about the kind of problems faced by the practitioner in everyday practice.

1

Public Relations:
An Overview

Three vignettes illuminate some of the problems involved in coming to grips with the real nature of public relations. The first concerns a former United States president, the second a mayor of a large city, and the third a group of public relations practitioners.

Vignette 1

Three years after resigning from office, a former president of the United States writes his memoirs. Admitting that he had misled the American people about his participation in the Watergate cover up, Richard M. Nixon says that his actions were the result of a series of misjudgments and tactical errors. He describes his early reaction to Watergate in the following words:

> I felt sure that it was just a public relations problem that only needed a public relations solution.

Vignette 2

Nettled by a newspaper story, Mayor Lee Alexander of Syracuse, New York, writes a letter to the editor that is subsequently published. Among his observations are these:

> Let me assure you that "public relations" exists neither as a function nor a title. The mayor's office has never had a public relations man assigned to the staff. It does not now. "Public Relations" is a deprecatory term, suggesting self-aggrandizement rather than effective administration. . . .
>
> My most recent appointment is designated as a public affairs coordinator. He is a contact point for both the public and the press

and media representatives. This is an entirely legitimate function. Dissemination of information is a service to the public and the press itself.

Vignette 3

A weekly public relations newsletter reports that many public relations practitioners are seeking a name change because they are increasingly concerned about misuse of and misunderstanding about the term *public relations*. States the newsletter:

> More and more companies are discarding the term "public relations" and substituting "public affairs," "communications," "public information" and other unblemished designations for the corporate executive in charge of PR. This is largely because there is a stigma attached to "public relations," partly as the result of the term's sometimes deliberately improper use in newspaper and magazine columns and by individuals in the news who employ the designation as a shield or a catchall term . . . or because they don't know any better.

In Vignette 1 public relations is viewed as a good fairy whose magic wand turns nasty situations into pleasant ones. The essential problem that faced the President—an illegal break-in condoned at the highest level of government—is given a public relations label. It's no longer a problem of illegal action, but a "public relations" problem. The solution sought becomes a "public relations" solution rather than an admission of wrong-doing and of a massive cover-up.

In Vignette 2 public relations is not a good fairy, but the fox who has gotten into the hen coop. When caught chomping away at the hens, the wily fox calls out, "There's nobody here but us chickens." When the newspaper reports that the mayor's staff includes a public relations man, the mayor says there's nobody by that name in his administration, but rather that there *is* a public affairs coordinator (carrying out what seem to be normal public relations activities).

Little wonder, therefore, that our public relations practitioners in Vignette 3 find there's a stigma attached to public relations and seek to substitute unblemished designations for the term. Unlike Shakespeare's Juliet, these practitioners seem to believe that a rose would smell sweeter if it were called by another name. Whatever we call it, however, we ought to recognize that the proper way to commence a study of public relations is to understand the term, concept, process, and activity known as public relations.

PUBLIC RELATIONS DEFINED

Two decades ago a commonly accepted definition of public relations ran something like this: "Doing good and telling people about it."

Twenty years later, in an increasingly complex world, we have learned this definition could just as well apply to show-and-tell in the first grade. The literature of the field now bears witness to a more thoughtful analysis of the term, and we will try to deal with several definitions, because it's important to understand clearly what we mean by *public relations* as we consider it throughout this book. In analyzing the definitions that follow, keep in mind similarities and differences; do not attempt to memorize the definitions in their entirety, but rather sort out recurring ideas and phrases and come to an understanding of public relations as a *process* and *function.*

"Public relations," state Scott Cutlip and Allen Center in *Effective Public Relations*, "is the planned effort to influence opinion through good character and responsible performance, based upon mutually satisfactory two-way communication."

The above definition sees the process as a *planned effort*—leaving open to conjecture who is responsible for carrying out the activity— that utilizes two-way communication to bring about the end result of influencing opinion. The phrase "good character" is a strange one because it is rather vague, because we generally associate character with individuals rather than organizations, and because, for the most part, we think of public relations as it applies to organizations. Be that as it may, the authors of the definition conceive good character and responsible performance to be essential in influencing public opinion.

In its threefold definition of the term, the third edition of *Webster's New International Dictionary* described public relations as:

The promotion of rapport and goodwill between a person, firm, or institution and other persons, special publics, or the community at large through the distribution of interpretative material, the development of neighborly interchange, and the assessment of public reaction.

The degree of understanding and goodwill achieved between an individual, organization, or institution and the public.

The art or science of developing reciprocal understanding and goodwill; the professional staff entrusted with this task.

The author of Webster's definition of public relations visualizes first the end result sought—*the promotion of rapport and goodwill*— and sees the parties involved as being a person, firm or institution on the one hand and various publics on the other hand. Linkage between the two groups is achieved in three ways: through the distribution of *interpretative material,* the development of *neighborly interchange*— denoting a seeming nostalgia for backyard over-the-fence conversation—and the *assessment of public reaction.* Reference to public relations as an art *or* science is indicative of widespread debate whether there is a scientific base to the activity or whether the practice is a craft. Unlike Cutlip and Center, *Webster's* makes no mention of acceptable performance. Both definitions are silent regarding responsibility for carrying out the public relations function within an organization.

One of the earliest definitions of public relations was developed by the *Public Relations News*, pioneer weekly public relations newsletter, and has stood the test of time as well as changes in the field. John Marston, author of *Modern Public Relations*, added two words—"and communication"—to the *Public Relations News* definition and they are cited in parentheses in the statement below:

> Public relations is the management function which evaluates public attitudes, identifies the policies and procedures of an organization with the public interest, and executes a program of action (and communication) to earn public understanding and acceptance.

Perceptive readers will note the following about the above definition:

1. It places responsibility for the public relations function upon the shoulders of management. The term "management" is used broadly, is meant to cover all managements, not merely business managements, and applies to nonprofit as well as profit-making institutions and organizations.

2. Function and process are tied together in an orderly procedure, and the end result is a definition that provides a step-by-step analysis of public relations in action:

   Step 1: Evaluation of public attitudes

   Step 2: Identification of policies and procedures of an organization with the public interest

   Step 3: Execution of an action and communication program to bring about public understanding and acceptance.

In graphic form, the public relations process described above looks like this:

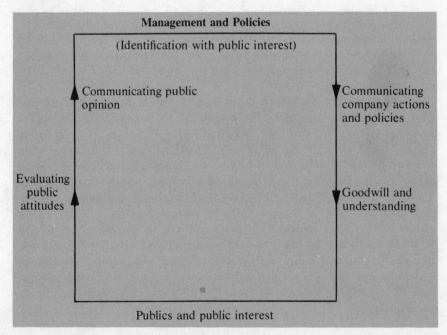

Management and Policies

(Identification with public interest)

Communicating public opinion

Communicating company actions and policies

Evaluating public attitudes

Goodwill and understanding

Publics and public interest

The most recent proof that public relations practitioners are achieving consensus about the nature of public relations was demonstrated in mid-1978 at the First World Assembly of Public Relations Associations. Meeting in Mexico City in August 1978, representatives of various public relations groups and societies from throughout the Western world—including one from the Public Relations Society of America—adopted what they called "The Statement of Mexico." This statement, which follows, is in reality a definition of public relations:

The Statement of Mexico

Public relations practice is the art and social science of analyzing trends, predicting their consequences, counseling organization leaders, and implementing planned programs of action which will serve both the organization's and the public interest.

Thus, in considering all the foregoing definitions, we see that implicit in them is an approach to public relations as a continuous process. The function is carried out by evaluating public attitudes and communicating public opinion to organization leaders or management. Policies and procedures are measured against these public attitudes and opinions, and when necessary these policies and procedures may well have to be changed or modified if they do not meet the public interest. Those responsible for the public relations function then carry out a planned program that includes communication of actions and policies to an organization's publics to bring about good will, understanding, and acceptance.

Frank W. Wylie, Chrysler Corporation public relations executive and a past president of the Public Relations Society of America, has charted the public relations process to show the individual elements and the nature of the process in action (see Figure 1.1). It shows the process starting on the left with "inputs" from various publics, the media, trend data, research, and so forth. These are analyzed and evaluated as they reach management. After discussion and consideration of alternatives, an action program is developed and fed as "outputs" in the forms of stories, speeches, press releases, and so on. The process, a continuous one, then repeats itself with further, continual "inputs."

A SUMMATION

Though they may differ in their emphasis on certain elements, the definitions previously cited have a good deal in common. Public relations, as seen in these definitions, involves the following elements:

1. A planned effort or management function

2. The relationship between an organization and its publics

3. Evaluation of public attitudes and opinions

Figure 1.1

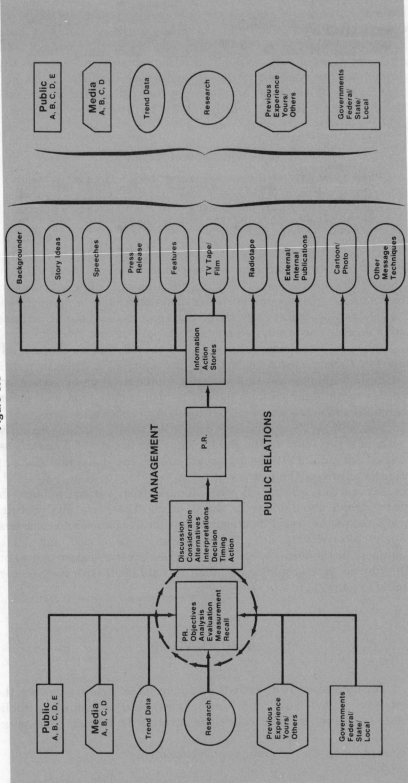

Reproduced with permission of Frank W. Wylie.

4. An organization's policies, procedures, and actions as they relate to said organization's publics

5. Steps taken to ensure that said policies, procedures, and actions are in the public interest and socially responsible

6. Execution of an action and/or communication program

7. Development of rapport, goodwill, understanding, and acceptance as the chief end result sought by public relations activities

Implied in the definitions is the understanding that public relations is a dynamic, continuing *process*, but seldom the neat and orderly one described in the definitions. Those who maintain that public relations is an art and not a science point out that public relations activities and programs do not take place in the controlled situation of the laboratory. Rather, they occur in real life situations amidst constantly changing variables.

A simple example will demonstrate why the dynamics of a situation make it difficult if not impossible to bring about a cause-and-effect laboratory relationship in public relations programming. Practitioner A drafts a carefully prepared message which aims to calm public fears about a shortage in the products of A's organization. The practitioner sends the message to the media in the form of a press release. The day the release is to appear an earthquake occurs, hundreds are killed, and millions of dollars of property lost. The story of the earthquake makes page one news, and the release is lost in the back pages. Natural disasters not only bury people and property, but all other news as well.

Countless other examples abound to prove the point that the best laid (public relations) plans "gang aft a-gley," as Robert Burns noted more than 200 years ago. Within any organization internal in-fighting can often sidetrack sound public relations proposals. Although few nonlegal and nonfinancial personnel would dare to argue the merits of advice and proposals set forth by legal and financial departments, a great many nonpublic relations personnel have little hesitation to contest advice and proposals set forth by public relations departments. Numerous variables outside the purview of public relations practitioners work to scuttle and mitigate programs which are sound in concept, but which fail in execution for reasons beyond the control of the practitioners. Competition for public attention is fierce, and messages aimed at the public often get detoured down unexpected byways. Only the most skillful are able to get their story across in a form and manner to bring about the desired public understanding, goodwill, and acceptance. Achieving desired public relations goals calls for a clear understanding of the fundamental component parts which comprise the public relations process and function. Such an understanding can be brought about in two ways: by recognizing the difference between public relations and terms sometimes mistakenly associated with it, and by raising questions about some of the essential elements of the process of public relations too often taken for granted. The sections that follow will come to grips with both these areas.

TERMS CONFUSED WITH PUBLIC RELATIONS

Because it is a relatively new concept when compared with some functions that have been on the scene much longer, public relations is most often confused with *advertising; sales, marketing, and product promotion; press agentry and publicity*. Public relations, as previously defined in this chapter, at times involves each of the aforementioned areas of activity, but is more than the individual parts.

Advertising is concerned chiefly with the sale of products and/or services and involves the use of paid media space or air time. Advertising may be used in the communications phase of the public relations process, not to sell an organization's product, but to bring about understanding of the organization as an entity. Such advertising is most commonly called "public service" or "institutional" advertising and may be run concurrently with product advertising or by itself. Advertising, when used for public relations purposes, aims to "sell"— using the term in its most direct form—an organization; to communicate specific aspects of an organization's activities; or to deliver, intact as written, special messages that aim to bring about clear understanding by the public.

Sales, marketing, and product promotion are concerned directly with the distribution and sale of goods and/or services. In many cases, because managements do not clearly understand the function, public relations activities and programs are expected to have a direct effect on the sale of goods and/or services. This expectation, of course, does not jibe with the end result sought from public relations: goodwill, understanding, and acceptance. Further, the concept that public relations activity should and can have a *direct* result on sales—to increase sales, of course—is not only a tenuous one, but a dangerous one for the public relations practitioner to propound. Should one expect, for example, that motorists will go out of their way to buy X gasoline because the X Gasoline Company has taken action to reduce pollution? Should one expect that women will go out of their way to purchase Y deodorant products because the Y Toiletries Company has made a special effort to hire more women for managerial positions? How does one prove that a specified number of budgeted dollars devoted to curbing pollution or to employing women have led to a specified increase in sales?

None of this, however, is intended to mean that public relations has nothing to do with sales, marketing, and product promotion. On the contrary, astute use of public relations can be of invaluable assistance to all three, but most often *in an indirect manner*. As a staff function designed to be of assistance to line departments and activities, public relations can and does serve sales, marketing, and product promotion. In some organizations a major share of public relations activity is devoted to product promotion, but the essential goal in most organizations is still the development of goodwill, understanding, and acceptance. Increased sales of goods and/or services will occur, but indirectly.

The distinction between marketing and public relations has been difficult to make because the two functions increasingly overlap in numerous organizations. Professors Philip Kotler and William Mindak note that both are the major external functions of the firm and both share common ground in regard to product publicity and customer relations. At the same time, however, they operate on different levels and from different perspectives and perceptions. The traditional view, note Kotler and Mindak, is that "marketing exists to sense, serve, and satisfy customer needs at a profit. Public relations exists to produce goodwill in the company's various publics so that these publics do not interfere in the firm's profit-making ability." Though the use of the verb *interfere* seems ill-advised, the distinction between the two functions seems clear enough. "No one model will be appropriate for all enterprises," state Kotler and Mindak. "The environmental pressures facing the individual enterprise, as well as its own history, will dictate whether to strengthen its marketing function or public relations function or even whether to start a new pattern of meeting and coping with external opportunities and threats."

Press agentry and publicity are terms that are often used synonymously, but there are differences between the two. Press agentry is chiefly concerned with gaining attention through imaginative—and often rather bizarre—stunts and events which induce media to write about or air them. Press agents have mainly been associated with show business and the entertainment field, either representing organizations associated with the field or individuals who thrive on having their celebrity status kept constantly in the public eye. The philosophy of the press agent's client was probably best summed up by the one who was reputed to say, "I don't care what they print about me so long as they spell my name right."

Publicity, which might well be considered to be the more legitimate son or daughter of press agentry, involves providing information, news, and feature material about an organization or person. Publicity can be and often is linked to newsworthy events, but in a manner generally less bizarre than press agent stunts. Whereas press agents usually work as individuals, publicity men most often operate within the framework of public relations departments and counseling firms. Publicity is used as one of the tools in public relations programming and activity, but it's not unusual to find that entire programs are built on publicity. For the latter reason—that is, because some public relations programs are composed chiefly of publicity—the public frequently confuses the part with the whole and thinks of publicity as being public relations. However, important as publicity may be in the framework of some public relations programs, it should be considered an effective public relations tool, but only a tool.

ASK QUESTIONS

This chapter, which sets the stage for the study of public relations, has included definitions that set forth various public relations verities. The most successful practitioners have reached their place in the sun not merely because of their command of skills but also because they are keen judges of people, know how to operate within organizations, and

ask the right questions of situations. Unless one asks the right
questions, he or she will have great difficulty coming up with the right
answers. Asking questions of public relations verities and discussing
the possible answers can lead to insights that will last a lifetime for
those who hope to make a career in the field.

THE MANAGEMENT FUNCTION CONCEPT

As we have seen, an underlying public relations verity states that
public relations is a management function, but exactly what does this
mean? Does it mean that top management, the heads of organizations
whether profit or nonprofit making, are responsible for carrying out
the public relations function? Or does it mean that the head of the
public relations department should be on a top-management level? If
the former, then why have public relations personnel? If the latter, on
what grounds do public relations practitioners stake their claim for
being on a top-management level?

This last question demands a sound answer because in any large
organization—and public relations departments and personnel are
usually found only in rather large organizations—other functional
areas also stake out their claim to be on a top-management level.
Marketing, legal, financial, and other staff functional people raise the
question: why do public relations people feel they must operate on a
top-management level to carry out their responsibilities and duties? If
the public relations practitioner can't supply the answer, chances are
he won't find himself operating on a top-management level. He doesn't
get there simply because he claims he must be there, but because he's
able to come up with cogent reasons for being in a top-management
position.

Of paramount importance in considering the public relations role
within organizations are the parameters of its authority and responsibility. No matter where public relations fits into an organization it is
generally a *staff* rather than a *line* function. But just what does this
mean?

Briefly, management theorists state that line people are those who
are concerned with the basic objectives of a company. Staff people have
been described as those experts in techniques who aid the line
management to do a better job of reaching an organization's objectives.
One authority sees the line-staff dichotomy in terms of "activities." He
states that the structure of every organization contains "central"
(substitute "line") and "supporting" (substitute "staff") activities.
Central activities in a manufacturing firm are described as those
concerned with engineering, producing, and selling a product, while
supporting activities include personnel, accounting, quality control,
and public relations. Staff positions in a manufacturing firm are not
involved directly with either the production or sale of the organization's products or services. Such positions do not possess command
authority, but are usually classified as advisory, service, or administrative in nature.

Although a staff executive—such as a public relations vice

president—has no authority over the regular line, he does have line authority over his own subordinates. Thus, in a large public relations department, the public relations vice president would have direct-line authority over everyone in his department.

Emphasizing the point, as staff people public relations practitioners have no direct authority over line people but they are expected to assist the line people in carrying out the basic work and purposes of the organization. This assistance applies particularly to those areas of line authority that have a bearing on the organization's relationship with various publics, and obviously this can cover a considerable amount of ground. It also gives rise to some interesting questions and problems.

Take, for example, this simple statement: public relations is a staff function and as such assists the line people in carrying out the work and purposes of an organization. Who takes the initiative in involving public relations with line activities that have bearing on an organization's relationship with its publics? Does public relations wait for line people to come to it? What if a problem develops but is not brought to the attention of public relations until it is too late to do anything except clean up the mess as well as possible? And what if public relations sees the problem developing but is rebuffed when it proffers aid and assistance? If the public relations department has no authority over line departments—and it usually does *not* have this authority— then how can public relations have its advice, counsel, and skills effectively utilized if the line departments don't want to use them? As the monarch said in *The King and I,* "tis a puzzlement," but it's a puzzlement that has to be answered if public relations is to do its job effectively.

POLICIES, PROCEDURES, AND ACTIONS

The model public relations program postulates that after evaluating public attitudes and opinions, the public relations practitioner then checks these against organizational policies, procedures, and actions. If public attitudes and opinions are negative or hostile regarding organizational policies, procedures, and actions, four alternatives present themselves:

Alternative 1:

Public relations can utilize its skills and resources in an attempt to change or modify public attitudes and opinions.

Alternative 2:

Public relations can inform line authorities and top management about the negative or hostile public attitudes and opinions and subsequently utilize its skills and resources in an attempt to change or modify public attitudes and opinions.

Alternative 3:

Public relations can inform line authorities and top management about the negative or hostile public attitudes and opinions; suggest changes or modifications of policies, procedures, and actions so as to conform to public expectations; and subsequently utilize its skills and resources in communicating such changes or modifications to the public.

Alternative 4:

Public relations can inform line authorities and top management about the negative or hostile public attitudes and opinions; play an active role in seeking to change or modify policies, procedures, and actions so as to conform to public expectations; and subsequently utilize its skills and resources in communicating such changes or modifications to the public.

Alternative 1 is based on the concept of public relations as a communication activity whose main purpose is to communicate with an organization's publics. It assumes that words and deeds are not necessarily compatible, and that negative attitudes and opinions can be changed through the skillful use of public relations techniques without need for a corresponding change in policies, procedures, and actions. Indeed, there are on record countless case studies of public relations campaigns based on communications programs that were divorced from actual organizational practices or had but minimal relationship to actual practices. The record in regard to such campaigns actually *changing* attitudes and opinions from negative to positive is a spotty one, however.

Questions related to Alternative 1 come readily to mind. Are words more important than deeds? Are they of equal importance? Does the public buy words separated from deeds? Is not the main purpose of public relations activity to communicate to an organization's public, and are we asking too much of public relations when we ask that it do more than communicate? If there are on record "countless case studies of public relations campaigns based on communication programs divorced from actual organizational practices," then how about citing some illustrations? There should be numerous examples in the literature of the field and in current mass media, and it would be a helpful exercise for you, the reader, to cite and discuss some.

Alternative 2 is based on the assumption that public relations serves as an intelligence-gathering and communicating agency in regard to public attitudes and opinions. It postulates that the basic role of public relations is to gather intelligence and to communicate, but not to be involved with basic policies, procedures, and actions. The alternative does not intend to downgrade the importance of public relations, because it recognizes that evaluation of public attitudes and opinions and subsequent communication with the public are important duties that can best be carried out by public relations. The alternative asserts that, in carrying out these tasks of intelligence-gathering and communicating, public relations has justified its value and existence.

How valid is the above contention? Are there advantages to the practitioner in being satisfied with his intelligence-gathering and communicating role and in not becoming involved with policies, procedures, and actions? What about the disadvantages?

Alternatives 3 and 4 seem initially to be similar, but there is a significant difference between the two. Both assert that public relations has the responsibility to inform line authorities and management about negative or hostile public attitudes and opinions, and to communicate subsequent changes or modifications in policies, procedures, and actions. Alternative 3 proposes that public relations has the responsibility to *suggest* changes or modifications of policies, procedures, and actions. Alternative 4 proposes that public relations should play *an active role* in seeking such changes and/or modifications.

Both alternatives thus see public relations as taking a more active role than the first two alternatives. The philosophical underpinning of Alternatives 3 and 4 is that words and deeds are inseparable. To say one thing and to be doing another, state the alternatives, is to invite public doubts about the credibility of the organization involved. Thus, in order to be credible—and hence effective—public relations must of necessity be involved in some fashion with an organization's policies, procedures, and actions. How involved forms the difference in approach between Alternatives 3 and 4.

Making a choice between the two alternatives seems to boil down to a matter of authorization, areas of responsibility, and competency. Does public relations, for example, have the authority to seek, or merely suggest, changes or modification in policies, procedures, and actions? Who is responsible for the specific policies? Is the area one in which public relations people have competency? Finally, what about jurisdiction and the natural tendency of everyone to guard his own turf?

There are no "right" or "wrong" answers to the questions posed by the four alternatives, and there may be a fifth and sixth alternative. The student who can think of further alternatives is well on his way to understanding why public relations has few eternal verities.

SOCIALLY RESPONSIBLE PERFORMANCE AND PUBLIC INTEREST

In the third chapter, this book will deal at length with social responsibility and public interest, but it's important at this point to deal with these vital considerations briefly. There are very few instances where organizations have *openly* admitted or made it part of organizational policy to be socially irresponsible or to operate in a manner not in the public interest. However, there are numerous instances of organizations adopting and following practices not socially responsible, not acceptable to the public, and not in the public interest. Such instances pose a dilemma for the public relations practitioner because they raise serious ethical and moral problems.

The student who hopes to make a career in public relations should first realize that such problems are not the unique province of the public relations practitioner. Accountants, lawyers, comptrollers, engineers, salesmen, advertising and marketing executives, and production managers are also faced with such problems and dilemmas.

Second, such problems are not the kind to be dealt with frequently (if they were, we'd have to conclude the entire fabric of our society is rotten).

Third, and probably most important in connection with public relations practice, when problems involving social irresponsibility and nonpublic interest do arise, they are especially relevant to public relations practice for two reasons. As already noted, public relations practitioners stress the importance of the activity as a management function, and the ultimate responsibility for actions, policies, and procedures rests on management and on the public relations practitioner who aspires to counsel management. Thus, those who shoulder ultimate responsibility must also shoulder the task of resolving the problems being discussed. The second reason is that practitioners are responsible for relationships that are public, not private, and hence are responsible for the manner in which actions, policies, and procedures will be communicated (or not communicated) to various publics.

At various times in their careers public relations practitioners must face up to the resolution of organizational actions that may be socially irresponsible and not in the public interest. In such instances, do practitioners serve as the "conscience" of their organizations and fight the internal battle needed to have these actions modified or reserved? Do they merely point out possible or probable long and short-range consequences of following such actions? Do they consider themselves strictly as organizational "advocates" whose first, foremost, and perhaps only responsibility is to the organizations they serve? Do they form their judgments about their roles in terms of the magnitude and scope of the particular issue or problem being faced? Is there an imaginary line which the practitioner will not cross when dealing with issues and actions concerning social responsibility, performance, and the public interest? If the answer is affirmative, where does one draw this line and is one willing and able to handle the consequences of not crossing it?

Though many public relations practitioners may never have to deal with the issues and situations described above, the student ought to be aware of them and sensitive to their scope and resolution. For this reason they will be dealt with more fully in a later chapter.

END RESULTS

As has been noted earlier in this chapter, most definitions of public relations stress that the end results sought from public relations activity are goodwill, understanding, and acceptance. These are laudable and sound goals and objectives, but are they sufficient? Do they provide the practitioner with the management support needed to give the function the talent, stature, and budget necessary for carrying out public relations tasks?

Many practitioners question the advisability of phrasing public relations end results in such general terms as the achievement of goodwill, understanding, and acceptance. They point out that other functions of management are more specifically phrased, and they also note that such general phrasing of end results sought makes measuring achievements almost impossible. They ask such questions as these: How does one measure goodwill, understanding, and acceptance? If such end results can't be easily measured, then why should management provide the function with needed resources?

On the other hand, other practitioners assert that public relations does not deal with measurable activities that can be tallied up as easily as the activities of other organizational functions. They stress that other organizational functions are able to control the environment in which they operate — for example, production people have control over raw materials and the manufacturing process — but public relations often has little or no control over the mass media expected to carry public relations messages. Further, they assert, to operate on the premise of such control and to promise specific end results through specific elements of the mass media would be unethical, counter-productive, and sure to bring the practice into ill repute.

The answer to these two schools of thought seems to exist somewhere in the middle of the two sets of perceptives about goals and objectives. The achievement of goodwill, understanding, and acceptance is certainly a sound end result to be sought from public relations activity. Bringing about such results can lead to more sales for an organization, to more students for a college or university, to more funds for a social agency or hospital; however, such achievements will come about indirectly, and very often more direct achievements will be expected and sought from public relations activity. Working out sought-for end results is not a simple academic exercise, but one that must be handled carefully in order to justify the support needed to carry out the function.

QUESTIONS AND PROBLEMS FOR DISCUSSION

1. Cite what you consider to be key points to be covered in a definition of public relations. Explain why you would include the points you consider crucial to a sound definition.

2. Explain the essential difference between public relations and each of the following: advertising; sales, marketing and product promotion; press agentry and publicity.

3. What is meant by the statement that public relations is a management function?

4. On what grounds do public relations practitioners stake their claim for being on a top-management level?

5. What is the difference between a line and a staff function?

6. What kind of problems do public relations practitioners have with line executives in carrying out their staff function?

7. What alternatives do public relations practitioners have in dealing with situations where public attitudes and opinions are negative or hostile to organizational policies, procedures, and actions? Which of these alternatives do you consider the proper one for the public relations practitioner to follow?

8. What kind of ethical and moral problems arise for practitioners when their organizations adopt and follow practices that are not socially responsible, that are not acceptable to the public, and that are not in the public interest?

9. Why do many practitioners question the advisability of phrasing public relations end results in such general terms as the achievement of goodwill, understanding, and acceptance?

10. Why do other practitioners question the advisability of phrasing public relations end results in more specific terms?

11. What is your opinion about the way in which public relations end results ought to be phrased?

PROJECTS, ASSIGNMENTS, AND MINI-CASES

1. PUBLIC RELATIONS AS SEEN BY YOUR PEERS: A MINI-SURVEY

Although college students are not considered to be representative of the general population, they are usually frank and open about their views and opinions of the society in which they live. This project aims to determine what kind of knowledge and opinion your colleagues in other disciplines have of public relations.

The class will be divided into groups of four or five members each. Each group member should interview five students who are majoring in disciplines other than public relations in order to *ascertain their conception of public relations and their opinion about the practice of public relations*. Try to secure in-depth answers rather than one-sentence replies.

Group members should type out their findings and bring sufficient copies of their findings to the next class session. Exchange findings with other group members. Do not use the names of respondents, but do indicate respondents' sex, class, and major. By the following class session each member of the class should hand in a typed report *summarizing the findings of his or her entire group and providing in addition personal conclusions about and reaction to the findings*. (Include the raw interview data as an appendix to your individual report.)

In writing your report, deal with the following points:

1. What seems to be the general view of public relations as shown by the responses?

2. What basic themes or threads seem to run through most of the responses?

3. Why do you think your colleagues in other disciplines perceive public relations as they do?

4. Do you agree or disagree with the views expressed by the majority of the responses? Why?

5. What conclusions can you draw from this mini-survey?

RECOMMENDED READING

William Agee, "The Role of Public Relations," *Public Relations Journal*, September 1978.

Scott Cutlip and Allen Center, *Effective Public Relations*, 5th ed. Englewood Cliffs, N.J.: Prentice-Hall, 1978.

Rex F. Harlow, "Public Relations Definitions Through the Years," *Public Relations Review,* Spring 1977.

Philip Kotler and William Mindak, "Marketing and Public Relations," *Journal Of Marketing,* October 1978.

Philip Lesly, ed., *Lesly's Public Relations Handbook,* 2nd ed. Englewood Cliffs, N.J.: Prentice-Hall, 1978.

John Marston, *Modern Public Relations.* New York: McGraw-Hill, 1979.

H. Frazier Moore and Bertrand Canfield, *Public Relations Principles, Cases, and Problems,* 7th ed. Homewood, Ill.: Richard D. Irwin, 1977.

Doug Newsom and Alan Scott, *This Is PR: The Realities of Public Relations.* Belmont, Calif.: Wadsworth, 1976.

Lawrence W. Nolte, *Fundamentals of Public Relations,* 2nd ed. New York: Pergamon Press, 1979.

Robert D. Ross, *The Management of Public Relations.* New York: John Wiley & Sons, 1977.

Raymond Simon, ed., *Perspectives in Public Relations.* Norman, Okla.: University of Oklahoma Press, 1966.

Charles S. Steinberg, *The Creation of Consent: Public Relations in Practice.* New York: Hastings House, 1975.

Howard Stephenson, ed., *Handbook of Public Relations,* 2nd ed. New York: McGraw-Hill, 1971.

2

Societal Trends and Public Relations

Astute journalists know that the *why* of a story is often more important than the *who, what, when, where,* and *how.* Unfortunately, ascertaining the elusive *why* is so difficult and time-consuming a task that many journalists don't even attempt it.

There are sound reasons, however, for the student of public relations to explore the *why* of his or her chosen field. First, historical perspective serves as a compass: knowing where you've been helps tell you where you are and where you are going. Second, sociological and political perspectives serve as a chart: understanding societal wind and sea currents helps you navigate dangerous waters. Third, placing public relations in proper perspective helps you deal with the general misunderstanding and mistrust of the twentieth-century phenomenon known as public relations.

Is there such misunderstanding and mistrust? Consider for the moment some all-too-frequent and typical comments made about public relations:

Comments and Statements	**Source**
Exhibit A: "Science deals with ultimate truth; public relations deals with falsehoods. Public relations is just a lot of bull served up as a fancy dish."	Observation made by a science major to a public relations major at Multi University.
Exhibit B: "I promise that if elected I'm not going to spend the taxpayers' money on publicity flacks grinding out a bunch of lies and propaganda."	Campaign remarks made by candidate for Congress.
Exhibit C: "No self-respecting newspaper would use the stuff sent to it by PR people. We don't trust public relations men because they're not interested in helping us get at the truth."	Managing editor of a large daily newspaper which is part of a group whose stock is traded on the New York Stock Exchange.

Faced by the above critical barrage, the public relations student is hard-pressed for a rebuttal. One way of answering is to hold a mirror up to the source of the remarks and to suggest the source consider this aspect of the reflection:

Exhibit A:

Science may deal with ultimate truth, but in today's society even the scientific community relies on public relations tactics and skills to make its truths known. Further, both the science and public relations majors were probably drawn to Multi University through the efforts of its long-established public relations department.

Exhibit B:

There is scarcely a single political campaign today that does not utilize public relations tactics and talents. Once elected, virtually every member of congress has at least one staff member assigned to public relations tasks.

Exhibit C:

Every newspaper in America—self-respecting or not—uses material which comes from public relations sources. If you'd like to debate this point, check any issue of your daily newspaper to figure out what stories emanated in some way from public relations. Maybe the managing editor doesn't know it, but his own newspaper has either a public relations or promotion staffer on its payroll.

Forcing the critic of public relations to view his own mirror image is one way of demonstrating that he, too, uses public relations. Much more important, however, is to *recognize the inevitable role of public relations in American society*. Dan J. Forrestal, veteran practitioner, says: "Public relations, in its current concept and nomenclature, was invented simply because a wide variety of organizations couldn't afford not to have it. They recognized that merited understanding and acceptance by their principal constituencies were prerequisite for successful survival. They acknowledged the concept that performance/behavior plus commmunication/interpretation equals reputation. They acknowledged the notion that somewhere in this mix a need existed for specialists with specific skills . . ."

The recognition Forrestal speaks about demands a close look at those facets of society which have brought about the *need* for public relations and which, in turn, have created particular problems for the public relations specialist. These two elements — need and problems, cause and effect — comprise what one might call the climate for public relations in American society.

Long before the term became fashionable, Cutlip and Center linked the term "ecology" to public relations practice in answering the question: why public relations? Biologically, ecology refers to the mutual relationship between organisms and their environment. Ecology in a public relations sense relates to *those aspects of American society which have brought about the need for and the utilization of public relations* in America today and which, in turn, *have created particular problems for the practitioner.* However, before analyzing these societal aspects vis-a-vis public relations, a brief look backward and then to the present will show where public relations stood in the past and where it stands today.

A BRIEF ANALYSIS OF PAST AND PRESENT PRACTICE

Professor Ray E. Hiebert has pointed out that the definitive history of public relations has not yet been and may never be written. He notes, however, that the Foundation for Public Relations Research and Education sponsored a series of lectures by eminent historians "for the purpose of exploring the historical antecedents of what is now termed public relations." The six lectures were reproduced in a special issue of the *Public Relations Review* in its Fall 1978 issue. As such, they provide a fascinating mosaic about the role of public relations in the past 200 years and are recommended reading for public relations students. The discussion of public relations antecedents in this chapter will be brief, but it should provide some understanding of the use of public relations throughout our history.

The use of public relations techniques in America dates back to 1788, one year after the signing of the Constitution. Because the Constitution had to be accepted by Congress and ratified by the States, a massive public relations effort was required. Historians agree that the authors of *The Federalist Papers*—chiefly Alexander Hamilton and James Madison—produced one of the finest public relations documents in history. Declares Allen Nevins: "Obtaining national acceptance of the Constitution was essentially a public relations exercise, and Hamilton, with his keen instinct for public relations, took thought not only to the product but to the ready acquiescence of thoughtful people; and he imparted his views to others." Through their essays and the eloquence of their debating techniques, the Federalists, in Nevins's view, carried out "the greatest work ever done in America in the field of public relations."

More than seventy years after the adoption of the Constitution, the country split in half as the Confederacy and the Union fought a Civil War that Historian Frank E. Vandiver describes as "a war of opinion, a war to win people's approval, a truly public war." As spokesman for the Confederate cause, Jefferson Davis sought indefatigably to present the cause of the South as "the bulwark of constitutional government in America." Speaking just as indefatigably for the Union, Abraham Lincoln used speeches, textbooks, and newspapers to rally public opinion to the Union side. Terming Lincoln as a "master of public relations," Vandiver ranks him as one of "the most effective fashioners of public opinion in American history."

As the above examples show, the major use of public relations in the eighteenth and nineteenth centuries was mainly in the political and government spheres. Business and industry, the major users of modern public relations, were relative latecomers on the public relations scene. The early part of the twentieth century witnessed the first real use of public relations techniques by business in response to the attacks against business by the muckrakers such as Ida Tarbell, Upton Sinclair, and others who exposed some of the more malodorous activities of big business. Most of the public relations activities by business in the period 1900 to 1914 were chiefly defensive in nature. However, one business leader—Theodore N. Vail, president of the American Telephone and Telegraph Corporation—proved to be far ahead of his time in recognizing that sound service to the public, clearly explained to the public, was the road to growth and stability for his company. His organization was one of the first to establish a public relations department—called at the time an Information Department—and to consider that the public interest and the corporation's self-interest were inseparably linked.

Operating as a "publicist" at this time was Ivy Ledbetter Lee, often called the "father of public relations." Lee formed one of the country's earliest public relations firms and also served as advisor to the Pennsylvania Railroad and the Rockefeller interests. In 1906, while representing the anthracite coal interests, Lee wrote his "Declaration of Principles" and sent it to city editors.

Ivy Lee's Declaration of Principles

This is not a secret press bureau. All our work is done in the open. We aim to supply news. This is not an advertising agency; if you think any of our matter ought properly to go to your business office, do not use it. Our matter is accurate. Further details on any subject treated will be supplied promptly, and any editor will be assisted most cheerfully in verifying directly any statement of fact. . . . In brief, our plan is, frankly and openly, on behalf of the business concerns and public institutions, to supply to the press and public of the United States prompt and accurate information concerning subjects which it is of value and interest to the public to know about. . . . I send out only matter every detail of which I am willing to assist an editor in verifying for himself. I am always at your service for the purpose of enabling you to obtain more complete information concerning any of the subjects brought forward in my copy.

Lee, of course, was not the sole practitioner of public relations at the time, and, as Hiebert notes in *Courtier To the Crowd,* "Ivy Lee was never quite sure of the title of his profession, confessing toward the end of his life that even his children did not know what to call him." Others, spurred particularly by the highly successful use of public relations techniques in World War I by the Creel Committee On Public Information, established themselves as independent practitioners or started public relations departments within corporations and other institutions. Some of these pioneers included Edward L. Bernays, John Hill, Paul Garrett, Carl Byoir, William Baldwin, and Pendleton Dudley. By the end of World War II the term "public relations counselor" had come into current usage, and most of the practices now in use today were developed and put into motion.

THE MODERN ERA

In the past three decades public relations has come into its own as a field of activity with recognizable practices, techniques, skills, and boundaries. Not only business and industry—the two prime users of public relations—but *every organization and institution of size has established or should establish public relations as an important staff function to assist management in carrying out its tasks.* We find public relations departments in unions, colleges and universities, social service organizations such as the United Way, religious organizations, governmental agencies, politics, and the courts. In New York City alone close to 800 public relations counseling firms are listed in the yellow pages of the telephone directory, and we find another 300 in Chicago and more than 300 in Los Angeles. Although there are no accurate figures of how many persons in the country are in the field, it has been estimated that there are somewhere between 50,000 and 60,000 public relations practitioners. Scores of colleges and universities offer sequences and majors in public relations, and more than 300 offer at least one public relations course. The Public Relations Society of America (PRSA) was first formed at the end of World War II and by 1979 had grown to a membership of more than 9,000. Chiefly through the initiative of Ohio State University Professor Walter Seifert, the Public Relations Student Society of America (PRSSA) was established in the late sixties, quickly grew to more than 60 chapters, and was formally incorporated into the PRSA a few years later. By 1979 the student group had grown to 82 chapters with a total membership of 3,000. Many specialized public relations groups have affiliated nationally (see Figure 2.1).

There are three weekly newsletters (*Jack O'Dwyer's Newsletter, pr reporter,* and the *Public Relations News*); two well-established periodicals (the monthly *Public Relations Journal* and the *Public Relations Quarterly*); a relatively new journal of research and comment entitled *Public Relations Review*, whose first issue was published by the Foundation for Public Relations Research and Education in Summer 1975; and *A Public Relations Bibliography* by Scott Cutlip, whose second edition published by the University of Wisconsin Press in 1965 contained almost 6,000 entries, and whose third edition by Robert Bishop, distributed through the University of Michigan Press, was published in 1974 and carried an additional 4,000 entries. The fourth and fifth editions, also compiled by Bishop, were published as single-theme issues of *Public Relations Review* in 1976 and 1977. Dr. Albert Walker compiled the sixth edition, published by *PRR* in 1978. New books about public relations have been appearing with increasing regularity each year in the past decade, and there is little doubt that public relations—whether called a field, an activity, or a profession—is here to stay.

Figure 2.1
Major Public Relations Associations

Academy of Hospital Public Relations
418 N. Glendale Avenue
Glendale, CA 91206
(213) 244-4548

Agricultural Relations Council
18 South Michigan Avenue
Chicago, IL 60603
(312) 346-1387

American Association of Minority ,
 Consultants
C/O Charles A. Davis & Associates
2400 South Michigan Avenue
Chicago, IL 60616
(312) DA 6-4140

American Jewish Public Relations
 Society
515 Park Avenue
New York, NY 10022
(212) PL 2-0600

American Society for Hospital
 Public Relations Directors
840 North Lake Shore Drive
Chicago, IL 60611
(312) 645-9467

Bank Marketing Association
309 West Washington Street
Chicago, IL 60606
(312) 782-1442

Baptist Public Relations Association
460 James Robertson Parkway
Nashville, TN 37219
(615) 244-2355

Canadian Public Relations Society, Inc.
Suite 640, 220 Laurier Ave. W.
Ottawa KIP 5Z9, Ontario, Canada
1613-232-1222

Council for Advancement and Support
 of Education
One DuPont Circle, N.W.
Washington, D.C. 20036
(202) 293-6360

International Public Relations Assoc.
Sam Black
50 Pine Grove
Totteridge, London, Great Britain
N20 8LA
(01) 445-5256

International Association of Business
 Communicators
870 Market Street, Suite 928
San Francisco, CA 94102

Library Public Relations Council
C/O Alice Norton
Box 516
Ridgefield, CT 06877
(203) 438-4064

National Association of Government
 Communicators
7204 Clarendon Road
Washington, D.C. 20014
(202) 656-3544

National Investor Relations Institute
1629 K Street N.W.
Washington, D.C. 20036
(202) 223-4725

National School Public Relations Association
1801 N. Moore Street
Arlington, VA 22209
(703) 528-5840

New York Airlines Public Relations
C/O Harvey Berman
National Airlines
219 E. 42nd Street
New York, NY 10017
(212) 697-8181

New York Financial Writers Association
Box 4306
New York, NY 10017
(212) 737-4033

Public Affairs Council
1220 16th Street, N.W.
Washington, D.C. 20036
(202) 872-1790

Public Relations Society of America
845 Third Avenue
New York, New York 10022

Publicity Club of Chicago
1945 N. Hudson
Chicago, IL 60614
(312) 337-1501

Publicity Club of New York
404 Park Avenue South
Suite 1207
New York, NY 10016
(212) 685-8220

Railroad Public Relations Association
American Railroads Building
Washington, DC 20036
(202) 293-4194

Religious Public Relations Council
475 Riverside Drive-Room 1031
New York, NY 10027
(212) 870-2013

Women Executives in Public Relations
C/O Ms. Retha Odom
Shell Oil
50 W. 50th Street
New York, NY 10020
(212 262-6983

Women in Communications, Inc.
8305-A Shoal Creek Boulevard
Austin, TX 78758
(512) 452-0119

FUNDAMENTAL TRENDS IN AMERICAN SOCIETY CAUSING THE PRACTICE OF PUBLIC RELATIONS

Public relations is here to stay because there's a felt need for it. The need is a reflection of fundamental trends in American society that have brought about the necessity of public relations. These trends have made public relations inevitable, and organizations should be and are using public relations as a management function whether they call it by that term or by other terms. In turn, these same fundamental trends have created specific problems for public relations practitioners.

To bring ecology into focus, therefore, this section will discuss and outline the nature of some of these fundamental trends to make clear why they've caused the need for public relations practice.

In a society as complex as America's, there are many major trends which have wide societal significance. Five of them, however, seem to have special pertinence for public relations practice and will therefore be discussed in some detail. They are:

1. Urbanization and suburbanization

2. Large and complex components

3. Growth in the power of public opinion and the swiftness of opinion change.

4. Changes in the technology, role and impact of the mass media

5. Consumerism and environmental sensitivity

URBANIZATION AND SUBURBANIZATION

The first fundamental trend in American society that needs to be understood in considering the ecological nature of public relations is the trend towards urbanization and suburbanization. In causal terms, the ramifications of this trend cannot be overestimated.

In 1910, when there were about 92 million people in the United States, more than 54 percent of the population was classified as rural and 36 percent as urban. By 1970, our population had grown to 203 million people and a drastic shift in habitat had taken place: 73.5 percent now lived in urban areas and 26.5 percent in rural areas.

The chart below, taken from the 1970 census of the population, shows the dramatic change of population in the period 1910 to 1970:

	1910	1920	1930	1940	1950	1960	1970
Urban:	46%	51%	56%	56.5%	64%	70%	73.5%
Rural:	54%	49%	44%	43.5%	36%	30%	26.5%

Equally revealing are the data in Figure 2.2 showing United States population for 1960 and 1970 for central cities, urban fringe of central cities, outside urbanized areas, and rural areas.

Figure 2.2

	1970		1960	
	Population	Percentage of total population	Population	Percentage of total population
Urban	149,324,930	73.5	125,268,750	69.9
Inside urbanized areas	118,446,566	58.3	95,848,487	53.5
Central cities	63,921,684	31.5	57,975,132	32.3
Urban fringe	54,524,882	26.8	37,873,355	21.1
Outside urbanized areas	30,878,364	15.2	29,420,263	16.4
Rural	53,886,996	26.5	54,054,425	30.1

Source: U.S. Bureau of the Census, *1970 Census of Population.*

Of major significance are the changes in population between 1960 and 1970 for those living in central cities and in the urban fringes of these cities. In percentage terms, the population living in the central cities dropped from 32.3 percent in 1960 to 31.5 percent in 1970, but the population living in the urban fringes rose from 21.1 percent in 1960 to 26.8 percent in 1970.

One has to recognize, however, that the United States is a country that produces rapid changes. Although the 1970 census showed a percentage drop in the number living in central cities and a percentage increase in the number living in urban fringe areas, by the end of the 1970s living patterns had begun to change the picture. Professor Franz Schurmann of the University of California at Berkeley, an authority on the problems of American cities, came to the conclusion that an *urban crisis* and an *urban revitalization* was taking place in America at the same time. He predicted that the downtown centers of United States cities would continue to boom, but the poor and the jobless will be crowded into the outer cities and beyond.

T.D. Allman, a *Harper's* magazine contributing editor, perceived in late 1978 the same return to the cities of the rich and the affluent and the displacement of the poor. Urban specialists, he noted, refer to this process as inner-city "gentrification," and he cited as examples Boston and Baltimore, where rebuilt inner-city decaying areas were being turned into much sought-after townhouse developments and high-finance, high-culture centers. The need to keep track of such lifestyle and general living patterns should be apparent to public relations practitioners because of the problems they pose.

Whether we consider the wave of the future as city growth by itself or a combination of city-suburban satellite growth, the trend is obviously towards an urban society. What does this mean vis-a-vis public relations? Compare life in the not-so-distant past with that today (and tomorrow) and the answer becomes a bit more clear.

When most Americans lived on farms or in small isolated communities, life was relatively uncomplicated. People knew their neighbors and were somewhat independent of external forces. There was a sense of community, of belonging. There were problems, plenty of them, but one had the feeling these problems were manageable and within one's ability to solve.

Now that most of us live in cities or suburbs, life is complicated.

Neighbors are often the people who moved in last week (or was it the week before?). We are almost totally dependent today on external forces for mere sustenance. There is little sense of community and a great many maladjusted people. Viewed from this perspective, the movement from rural to urban to suburban sprawl has manifold implications for public relations. In our more leisured, easy-going days the gap of understanding between organizations and their publics was as narrow as the streets of small town America. Today's gap is broad and wide.

By no means should we look upon public relations as a panacea for the better life for all of us, nor as some sort of magical cure-all for the ills of urban life. *But public relations can help bridge the gap of understanding* brought on by the ecological trend towards an urban society. Whether consciously and by plan or unconsciously in random fashion, more and more organizations are utilizing public relations as a means of gap-bridging and the building of goodwill and understanding. They're doing so because the urbanization trend has the causal effect of bringing on the felt need for public relations assistance and practice.

LARGE AND COMPLEX COMPONENTS

A second fundamental trend which needs to be considered in understanding the ecological basis for public relations in American society is the fact that *the chief components of that society are both large and complex.* The Hupmobile and Stutz cars long ago vanished into such giant enterprises as General Motors, Ford, Chrysler, and American Motors. Working men and women have joined together to form the United Auto Workers, the Teamsters, and the United Steelworkers of America. Small state colleges in California and New York have become units of the massive University of California and the State University of New York. Young people may still dream about leading adult lives as individuals controlling their own destinies, but the reality belies the dream. Through large and complex organizations and components most Americans now receive their education, spend their working lives, join together for collective bargaining purposes, are provided with government services, and receive the goods and other services necessary to sustain life. Some randomly selected facts and figures — cited below — prove the pertinency of the above conclusion.

In *industry,* where large firms have taken over small firms and where conglomerates have become commonplace, the giants in January 1978 were General Motors and Exxon, with total gross sales of $54.9 billion and $54.1 billion respectively. Others in the top ten among *Fortune's* 500 largest industrial corporations were Ford ($37.8 billion); Mobil ($32.1 billion); Texaco ($27.9 billion); Standard Oil of California ($20.9 billion); IBM ($18.1 billion); and Gulf, General Electric, and Chrysler, each with over $17 billion.

Sales of such a nature were made possible through the combined efforts of massive numbers of employees, so it's not surprising to find that in January 1978 GM's work force of 797,000 was followed by Ford with 479,000 employees, GE (384,000), International Telephone and Telegraph (375,000), IBM (310,000), Chrysler (250,000), Mobil (200,000), United States Steel (165,000), Exxon (127,000), and Texaco (70,000).

In *labor* we find that the growth of union membership has paralleled the growth in industry. There were 9 million union members in 1940; 15 million in 1950; 18 million in 1960; and 21 million in 1977. Leading unions in 1977 were the Teamsters (2 million), the United Auto Workers (1.5 million), the United Steelworkers (1.3 million), the International Brotherhood of Electrical Workers (1 million), the American Federation of State, County, and Municipal Employees (1 million), the International Association of Machinists (943,000), the United Brotherhood of Carpenters (820,000), and the Retail Clerks (651,000).

The trend toward large and complex components is found not only in industry and labor, but also in many other areas of our national life. *Government* employment at the beginning of 1978 amounted to more than 15 million. *Farming* has seen a steady decrease in the number of farms and a steady rise in average acreage per farm. In 1920 there were 6.5 million farms with an average acreage of 147 per farm; by 1978 there were less than 3 million farms, and the average acreage had grown to 393. In *higher education* at that time 343,000 students were enrolled in the State University of New York, 270,000 in the City University of New York, 128,000 in the University of California, 143,000 in the University of Wisconsin, and 92,000 in the University of Texas. Commenting on the higher education scene, the *New York Times* reported: "Overcrowding has become routine."

The key word in that last quotation is "routine." We accept as routine the fact that large and complex organizations dominate the national scene in industry, labor, government, the military, farming, education, and all other key areas. We also accept as routine the many benefits that size and complexity bring to the average American, but large organizations cannot simply ride with the fact that they bring benefits, because these same benefits bring serious problems that affect all of us.

By their very nature large organizations become bureaucracies, and these in turn cause maladjustments and indifference. Today's highly organized society, says Professor Robert Presthus, has created what he terms "the indifferents" and he describes them this way:

> The indifferents are those who have come to terms with their environment by withdrawal and by redirection of their interests towards off-the-job satisfactions. They have also been alienated by the work itself which has often been downgraded by machine processing and assembly-line methods ... (The indifferents) are found among the great mass of the wage and salaried employees who work in the bureaucratic situation. By a rough estimate we can say that ... just about half the wage-earning labor force now work in big organizations. Moreover, this vast reservoir of potential indifferents is steadily increasing. (*The Organization Society,* Vintage)

Max Scheler, a European social scientist, calls the current condition *ressentiment*. More powerful than just resentment and indifference, *ressentiment* means pervasive, pent-up anger that can best express itself by exploding. Daniel Yankelovich, public opinion authority, states that opinion surveys taken during the Vietnam War and the Watergate crisis revealed national unhappiness with the state of the nation, but he notes that the public was basically able to express its frustrations. More recently, however, polls have revealed that people feel *personally* victimized by institutions over which they have little or no control. David W. Ewing of the *Harvard Business Review* states:

> ... growing numbers of people are not simply disenchanted, irritated, or angry, but they are irrationally afraid of new technologies and business ventures. They want down with computerized plants that threaten them, down with ominous towers, down with the mysterious black boxes, out with toxic substances and gases. They just want to expel, to purify. . . . Whether the protesters are the nuclear power, petrochemical, or cotton industries, the aim and the method are essentially the same: focused, purposive, effective opposition to each industry's present and planned operations.

Thus, we not only have vast numbers of indifferents in today's society, but we've got mistrustful indifferents who are deeply resentful when they perceive they are being ripped off by large organizations and institutions. There is in the American character a traditional, almost ingrained mistrust of size. We value competition because we know that competition is a weapon to cut large organizations down to size and to provide us with some sort of individuality and choice, some way to allow us to exercise a small amount of independence.

Many large organizations take pains to show that they care for the individual. Far too many don't, and the individual reacts accordingly. An increasing number turn to protests. Others see to it that their elected representatives pass antitrust, zoning, and antipollution laws; establish the Securities and Exchange Commission, the Federal Trade Commission, and the Consumer Protection Agency. Astute managements of large and complex organizations call on public relations assistance to measure the national mood, to suggest changes in corporate policy and actions to meet public expectations, and to communicate that size can be trusted (when it *deserves* to be trusted). The causal effect of the trend toward large and complex organizations is the same as the effect of the trend toward urbanization and suburbanization: that is, it has brought about the need for professional public relations assistance and practice.

GROWTH IN THE POWER OF PUBLIC OPINION AND SWIFTNESS OF OPINION CHANGE

A third fundamental trend in American society relates to public opinion. In a later chapter in this book public opinion will be analyzed and discussed in more detail, but our concern at the moment is with two factors: first, there has been a steady growth in the power of public opinion, and second, changes in public opinion can often be swift, sudden, and drastic.

Public opinion in America is a powerful force for the very basic reason that ours, for the most part, is an open society. There are times, of course, when a curtain hides from the general public the policies and actions of important elements of our society. During periods when we are at war, either "hot" or "cold," information is kept from the public while deliberate steps are taken to mold the public's opinion to support the nation's efforts to achieve victory. In peace time the curtain of "national security," sometimes used properly and sometimes improperly, is lowered to prevent numerous government decisions and information from reaching the public and permitting an informed public opinion. In times of negative or bad news and actions, the reaction of many business managements is to hide the news, again because of concern about public opinion.

History teaches, however, that efforts to close off information fail to survive over the long run, and sometimes even in the short run. The reach and impact of mass media is too all-embracing to permit for long the retention of negative news and information. Insiders "leak" information to the media; the press uncovers information on its own; word gets about, and public opinion begins to solidify. Once solidified, whether in a negative or positive direction, public opinion is difficult to change except through some dramatic event or action.

Astute students of the public psyche understand full well the power of public opinion in all elements of American society. Large business organizations that sell consumer products take pains to insure that products sold under their brand names achieve a deserved reputation for reliability. Why? Because about the only guide available to consumers about the worth of the product is in the reliability of the brand. Veteran senators and representatives are reelected not because of their votes on a particular bill, but because the public in their states and districts are of the opinion that they can be relied upon to serve the public's interests. Without having even the slightest knowledge of the kind of education they provide, parents send their offspring to certain institutions of higher education because general public opinion holds that they are excellent institutions. Without the slightest knowledge of the services they provide, millions of Americans support certain health foundations because general public opinion holds that they perform highly valuable services. We vote for certain candidates, buy certain products, and support certain institutions because public opinion holds them worthy of our trust and confidence. Not without reason, then, does one state that public opinion has great power in American life. Achieving favorable public opinion, maintaining it over the years, and solidifying it is the basic reason why such institutions as Harvard and Yale, such corporations as General Electric, General Motors and Ford, and such personalities as Dwight D. Eisenhower and Walter Cronkite have been held in high esteem for decades.

Yet dramatic events and actions can with sudden swiftness change and modify the public's opinion of even the most sanctified institutions and people. Marshall McLuhan makes the following point: "In the mechanical age now receding, many actions could be taken without too much concern. Slow movement insured that the reactions were delayed for considerable periods of time. Today the action and the reaction occur almost at the same time . . . As electrically contracted, the globe is no more than a village." (*Understanding Media,* McGraw-Hill).

McLuhan's "action-reaction" premise is demonstrated by numerous examples. When President Nixon ran for a second term in 1972 he won victory by carrying the electoral vote of every state in the Union except Massachusetts. Yet within a short period of time — chiefly due to Watergate, its cover-up, and subsequent reverberations — public opinion practically reversed itself. Shortly before Thanksgiving in 1959 Arthur S. Fleming, secretary of health, education and welfare, reported at a news conference that parts of the 1958 and 1959 cranberry crop from Washington and Oregon were contaminated by a weed killer. Consumers substituted applesauce for cranberries that Thanksgiving and as a result the nation's cranberry crop, estimated to have a retail value of about forty-five million dollars, turned into a substantial loss. Negative public reaction to President Johnson's escalation of the U.S. involvement in Vietnam was the chief reason he decided not to seek reelection to the highest office in the land.

Accepting the premise that public opinion is all-powerful in American life and that dramatic events and actions can swiftly change and modify opinions, what does this mean for public relations? The answer is that there is a need for experts who have solid insights and understanding of the nature of public opinion, the manner in which it is formed, ways in which to measure it, and realistic means for anticipating its future course. Managements have turned to public relations because its successful practitioners have proved themselves to be experts in the area of public opinion. Dealing with public opinion is as essential to the public relations practitioner as the scalpel is to the surgeon, knowledge of the law to the lawyer, and mathematics to the physicist. The expertise the public relations practitioner brings to the handling of public opinion is one of his chief assets and reasons for existence.

CHANGES IN THE TECHNOLOGY, ROLE, AND IMPACT OF THE MASS MEDIA

Legend has it that when Paul Revere wanted to arouse the Minutemen he got on his horse, rode through the countryside, and shouted at the top of his voice to arouse the sleeping citizenry. Result: a grim band of Minutemen showed up at Lexington commons. Today he would either hold a press conference or telephone the Associated Press and United Press International, the four major radio and the three major television networks; they'd put the story on the air immediately or send it over high speed teleprinters; the news would be all over America in a matter of minutes.

This exemplifies the fourth fundamental trend in American society — the changes that have taken place in the technology, role, and impact of the mass media in the United States. In two of the areas—*technology* and *impact*—the changes have been dramatic; the *role* played by the mass media remains virtually the same as in Paul Revere's day.

Technology *Methods of Communication*

For almost two-thirds of the history of our country the major media force in society was the print media, and for a considerable period of that time, changes in the technology of the print media were of a limited nature. Newsmen wrote their stories by hand, printers set them in type by hand, and slow presses turned the stories into type and printed newspapers. The telephone and Western Union wire speeded up the reporting process; the typewriter speeded up the writing process; and the Linotype and rotary presses speeded up the printing process. Dramatic technological change occurred in the print field in the last decade as newspapers and wire services switched to all-electronic writing, editing, and printing through the use of the cathode ray tube (CRT), the video display terminal (VDT), the optical character reader or scanner, and the master control computer. These technological changes have been designed to reduce errors, facilitate makeup, speed up the entire process, and save money—lots of money. Although newspapers still lag behind the electronic media in the speed race, there's no doubt that the gap has been closed considerably within our own generation.

Speed, of course, is what distinguishes the electronic media. Radio is the fastest way of getting across a message to the largest number of people in the country, chiefly because radio deals only with sound. Within a matter of minutes the radio newsman can gather his news, telephone it into the station or network, and have it heard by millions. Television involves a team effort involving newsman and cameraman, and the latter is the one who poses the problem because his film must be delivered to the station or network before it can be transmitted. However, within a period of years we have witnessed the development of hand-held, portable cameras and the use of satellites high above the earth to bring into our living room events occurring all over the globe. In a short time there will be virtually no gap between the event, the reporting of the event, and its reception by the audience. Further, when the full potential of cable television is finally realized we will see the day when the line between print and electronic media will be erased. We will then be able to turn to channels on our television set that will carry full pages of newsprint (though probably under some fancier name).

Impact

For more than a century and a quarter the daily newspaper served as the primary source of news for the vast majority of adult Americans, but with the advent of the electronic media—especially television—there has been a significant change. The primary source of news, according to continuing trend studies conducted for the Television Information Office by the Roper polling organization, is now television, followed by the daily newspaper, radio, and magazines. The following table tells the story:

Figure 2.3

Response of a national sample to the question: "Where do you usually get most of your news about what's going on in the world today—from the newspapers or radio or television or magazines or talking to people or where?"

Source of most news:	1959	1961	1964	1968	1971	1973	1974	1976	1978
Television	51%	52%	58%	59%	60%	64%	65%	64%	67%
Newspapers	57%	57%	56%	49%	48%	50%	47%	49%	49%
Radio	34%	34%	26%	25%	23%	21%	21%	19%	20%
Magazines	8%	9%	8%	7%	5%	6%	4%	7%	5%
People	4%	5%	5%	5%	4%	4%	4%	5%	5%
Total mentions	154	157	153	145	140	145	141	144	146

Source: Television Information Office.

The data in Figure 2.3 are not surprising. As of January 1978 there were 996 television stations and 8,408 radio stations in the United States; 120 million television sets in 73 million homes (98 percent of all homes); 444 million radio sets (in virtually every home); and a viewing audience of 32 million people for the average successful prime-time television show. The 1,753 daily newspapers in that same year had a total combined daily circulation of 61.5 million. Eleven of these daily papers had circulations of over 500,000; the circulation of the median-sized daily in most states was 13,000; and the circulation of the average-sized daily was close to 37,000.

One has to be cautious in dealing with the above figures and with survey results such as those shown by the survey sponsored by the Television Information Office. For example, a survey sponsored in the late 1960s by a newspaper group, the Newsprint Information Committee, showed that 78 percent of a national sample said they had read a newspaper the day before the survey, 60 percent said they watched one or more television newscasts, and 55 percent said they heard one or more radio newscasts. Note that the Roper question in the television-sponsored survey refers to "what's going on in the world today," and this implies national and international news.

Except in our largest cities where television stations have large and competent staffs with a great deal of financial backing for their news-gathering efforts, local television newscasts don't come anywhere near matching the work of the local daily newspaper. By their own admission, network television commentators such as Walter Cronkite point out they barely scratch the surface with their daily half-hour news show. The newspaper remains the main source of local news and for national and international news and interpretative commentary in depth. For those millions who want the news brought into focus, the three national newsmagazines—*Time, Newsweek,* and *U.S. News and World Report*—are powerful molders of public opinion. Specialized magazines flourish because of their strong appeal and interest to special groups in the population. Ben Bagdikian, author and journalist, sums up the situation: "Even conflicting and competing surveys make clear that there has been no large-scale preemption of one medium by another, that each is used for a different set of reasons.

Certain kinds of news continue to be dominant in print, other kinds in radio and television. In most kinds of news the media seem to reinforce each other—more and more people use both—rather than cancel each other out." (*The Information Machines*, Harper Colophon Books)

Further, the media monitor each other carefully and often feed on each other's output. A local daily in Peoria, for example, runs an unusual feature story. The story catches the eye of the U.P.I. bureau man in a nearby city, and he rewrites it and sends it to the U.P.I. bureau in the state capital. They put it on the national wire. Two weeks later the New York *Times* sends a reporter to Peoria, and after a day or so on the scene he writes his up-dated version of the same feature story. It runs on the front page and is also sent out to subscribers to the *New York Times News Service*. Someone on the *Today* show reads about the story, and as a result the show carries a five-minute segment the following week. Because of one local reporter's curiosity and ability with words, millions of Americans learn about a purely local feature.

Role

From its earliest beginnings in America the role of the daily newspaper has been as a supplier of news, entertainment, and opinion. Radio and television have primarily served as entertainment vehicles, but their role as suppliers of news has become increasingly important. When the unblinking eye of the television camera is focused on an unfolding event—such as happened when television carried gavel-to-gavel coverage of the Senate Watergate hearings—television's role as a molder of public opinion becomes of highly significant importance.

With the exception of the two newsmagazines *Time* and *Newsweek*—which have built their readership through skillful editing and a combination of interpretation and news—the mass media stick for the most part to straight objective reporting and separation of the news and opinion functions. But when a major story or event breaks; when the story carries implications for millions of people; and when it involves controversy and builds momentum, the usual rules go out the window. To the beleaguered organization or individual caught in the vortex of the event, the media assume the role of a thousand Paul Reveres riding about the national countryside arousing the citizenry. A few examples should suffice to establish the point: stories following the Bay of Pigs disaster in the Kennedy administration; stories following the My Lai massacre in the Johnson administration; stories about the major oil companies during the Carter administration; and stories about automobile defects and massive recalls during any administration.

Considering, therefore, the role and effect of mass media in American society, one need not wonder why amateurs should not be entrusted with the task of dealing with the media. *With each passing year as the mass media increase in importance as purveyors of information and molders of opinion, so does it become obvious that organizations and individuals which rely on public support for their very existence turn to public relations practitioners for guidance and assis-*

tance in dealing with the media. It takes skilled public relations professionals to understand and keep up with technological changes in the mass media which require new approaches for those who rely on the mass media to carry messages to the mass public and to special publics. It takes skilled public relations professionals to understand that each of the mass media is unique and has uniquely different advantages and disadvantages in impacting on its audience and fulfilling its role in American society. Dealing with the mass media, in short, is a matter for professionals, not amateurs.

CONSUMERISM AND ENVIRONMENTAL SENSITIVITY

Consumerism and environmental sensitivity—the fifth major trend in American society causing a need for public relations—have been around for a long time, but they assumed heightened significance as recently as the late sixties and early seventies. While in no way meaning to downgrade the importance of the new sensitivity to the environment, this section will deal chiefly with consumerism because of its across-the-board appeal to all segments of the population; its long history as recognized by established government agencies and by newly formed ones; the staying power and strength of broad-based national, regional, state, and local activist groups; and its obvious concern to a wide variety of organizations with direct dealing with the consumer. Further, the term "consumerism" will include concern with numerous environmental aspects of our society as well as concern for the quality and performance of goods and services.

Consumers have always been considered an important public by public relations practitioners, and especially by those whose organizations have had direct contact with consumers. When an organization's chief source of income is through sales to consumers, its relationship with customers is of key importance to profit or loss. With good reason, therefore, such organizations have long-established customer relations departments, and the public relations function has been used in establishing, maintaining, and solidifying good customer relations.

Consumerism, however, is to customer relations what this year's model cars are to the Model T. Just as it would be unwise to try to sell the Model T in today's marketplace, so is it unwise to try to sell the old customer relations platitudes in today's *consumer activist* marketplace. Commencing in the mid-sixties as virtually a one-man movement led by Ralph Nader, consumerism built up an astonishing head of steam in a few short years, and by the mid-seventies had become a force that had to be reckoned with by all major corporations. *U.S. News and World Report,* generally considered to be the most conservative of the three major newsmagazines, described the movement succinctly in a full-page ad in the *Public Relations Journal.* Headed, "A New Breed of Activist Has Emerged in the Seventies," the ad declared in part:

Today's corporation faces a new public interest activism. A new breed of activist has emerged in the Seventies among corporate constituencies which traditionally have looked with favor upon the business community. Skepticism is on the rise, even among shareholders. . . .

Primarily middle class, today's activists bear little resemblance to those of the Sixties. Well above average in income, education and awareness, they speak out for different goals: consumer protection, automobile and airplane safety, pure food, air and water, and (most crucial) corporate accountability. Their radiating influence on the thoughts and actions of millions of others threatens to hit corporations where they live—in the profit and loss statement. . . .

Perceptive analysts of the American scene trace the swift rise of the new consumerism to a combination of factors. In part, it resulted from the general unhappiness with many forms of American life in the late sixties; the political and social activism which found voice in the massive dissent to our continuing involvement in Vietnam; and with what Arthur H. White of the Daniel Yankelovich organization called the "galloping psychology of entitlement." White summed up the essentials of this psychology in the following words:

One of the most boat-rocking social trends in the United States is a phenomenon we have called "the galloping psychology of entitlement," and it has profound implications for the future of American business. It is the psychological process whereby a person's wants or desires become converted into a set of presumed rights.

An American who once said, "I would like to be sure of a secure retirement," now says, "I have a right to a secure retirement." A view expressed not long ago as "my job would mean more to me if I had more to say about how things are run" changes to "I have the right to take part in decisions that affect my job." From "If I could afford it, I would have the best medical care," to "I have the right to the best medical care whether I can afford it or not." From "I hope this cottage cheese is fresh," to "I have the right to know when it was made and how long it will stay fresh."

. . . The consumer movement is a special consequence of the new psychology that is having and will continue to have a profound effect on the way business and businessmen operate in this country. . . .

The consumer movement, as it exists today, has enormous strength. Its public support is massive. In our own surveys and others, an unswerving average of 80-90 percent of the public supports consumerism—virtually a consensus. Furthermore, the support is strongest in mainstream America. It is not a function of liberal politics, but cuts across ideological and class lines. The core of support is the middle and upper middle income housewife—a force to be reckoned with. Of equal significance, the consumer movement has great appeal to political leaders. They see, as we do, that it is an issue people care about . . .

(from an article in the *Public Relations Journal*)

White's emphasis on the broad-based nature of consumerism is particularly important because it was addressed to public relations practitioners, and unfortunately many of them viewed the burgeoning consumer activist movement as being forced on Americans by the government and/or politicians.

This viewpoint was typified in an address given by a leading counselor in the mid-sixties to a group of television advertising executives and summed up in these words:

This country didn't just discover the consumer with the help of Esther Peterson or Betty Furness. We built a successful economy and an unrivaled standard of living on the philosophy that says consumer is king. I argue that business, not bureaucracy, discovered the consumer. And I say that business by and large has served him very well.

And yet business—including your business—is now being told that it can't possibly do the job without a legion of helping hands. Who wants it? Obviously not the consumer.

. . . One thing is sure. If you and I don't speak up, we can't expect others to protect us from the protectors. Even as our fellow consumers, we can be smothered by too much loving attention or drown in the overflow from bleeding hearts. . . .

The difference between White's view of the consumer movement and that of the unnamed public relations counselor cited above is clearly one of perception, but it's a difference that is highly important. White sees consumerism as "the major single cause of erosion of public confidence in business" and involving "the mainstream of American business." The counselor sees consumerism as stemming chiefly from "bleeding hearts" and politicians and being directed at a few dishonest businessmen. It should be obvious that the perception one has of consumerism will affect the response to the movement.

Meanwhile, consumerism has continued to flourish through the various Nader groups; other national and state-wide consumer groups; and such agencies of the government as the Consumer Product Safety Commission, the Food and Drug Administration, the Office of Consumer Affairs, and the Agency for Consumer Advocacy. In a 1978 study the Council on Economic Priorities, a public interest group that makes detailed studies of corporate practices and their impact on consumers, profiled eighty-three major public interest groups. The Council reported that the dominant issue among such groups at that time was energy and the environment. The Council reported that other key issues then were community and consumer affairs, minority rights, fair representation and advertising practices in the media, health and nutrition, and peace and disarmament.

Of special interest has been the growth of the Nader group that by the mid-seventies had become the nation's leading public interest conglomerate. As described by Susan Gross in an article in the *Business and Society Review*, the first Nader organization was the Center for Study of Responsive Law and in the early days the emphasis was on exhaustive investigations and book-length reports. By 1975, however, the emphasis had shifted to litigation, lobbying, citizen organizing, and action-oriented research with most Nader programs concentrated in nine groups in Washington: the Litigation Group, Congress Watch, Health Research Group, Tax Reform Research Group, Citizen Action Group, the Center, Corporate Accountability Research

Group, Public Interest Research Group, and the National Public Interest Research Group. In addition, there were almost two dozen Nader-affiliated student and citizen action state groups and other satellite groups linked to Nader through funding or personnel.

"... Ever since the birth of PIRG in 1970," noted Ms. Gross, "Nader had been increasingly de-emphasizing Center-style massive studies in favor of hard legal and political action. Today the Nader groups rely almost exclusively on lawsuits, administrative agency actions, citizen organizing, and supportive research—while the flow of study groups has slowed to hardly a trickle, leaving the Center in the second rank of the Nader troops."

Through increased governmental and citizen action groups, consumerism by the mid-seventies was here to stay and called for the best talents that public relations could apply. Though public relations practitioners have no direct line authority in regard to consumer products and services, they do have—or should have—*insights* about a trend as persuasive as consumerism. Meeting the justified demands of consumer activists calls for the kinds of intelligence skills, sensitivity, judgment, and communication skills that public relations practitioners are supposed to have.

Some final words are in order about the heightened interest in and sensitivity to the environment. Although environmental factors do not generally have as direct and immediate an impact on the average person as consumerism factors, there is widespread concern and sensitivity about air and water pollution, waste disposal, depletion of natural resources, oil spills, and potential shoreline hazards. This concern resulted in 1970 legislation such as the National Environmental Policy Act, the Clean Air Act, and the establishment of the U.S. Environmental Protection Agency. Within five years the EPA mushroomed into the country's largest regulatory agency by 1975 with 9,000 employees, a two million dollar daily budget, and jurisdictions and responsibilities in air and water pollution, solid waste, noise, pesticides, and radiation. Direct citizen concern with the environment has been evidenced by the strong stands taken by conservation and citizen activist environment groups that fought the Alaskan pipeline project, the building of atomic power plants, and leases for off-shore drilling purposes. When such issues reach the action stage, their handling calls for public relations judgment and skills. In too many instances, however, those handling such sensitive environmental issues have called public relations professionals into play *after* rather than *before* the decisions are made.

Public relations should play the same role in regard to the environment as it does to consumerism, and one of the chief tasks and responsibilities of the practitioner should be to serve as an "early warning system" concerning public attitudes, opinions, and activities relating to environmental factors. When an organization's actions, activities, products, or services have a serious effect on the environment, advice and counsel about expected public relations are clearly needed. No matter what the final decision, communication skills are needed. Thus, at each step in dealing with matters bearing on the environment there is an obvious need for the kinds of skills that public relations practitioners should be able to provide.

FUNDAMENTAL TRENDS IN AMERICAN SOCIETY AND THEIR EFFECT ON PUBLIC RELATIONS PRACTICE

If we want to make an analogy between the ecology of public relations and a phonograph record, then we have heard one side of the record: the causal side. That is, we have heard why certain fundamental trends in American society have brought on the need for public relations. The flip side of the same record tells us why these same trends have brought about difficult problems for public relations practitioners.

URBANIZATION AND SUBURBANIZATION

Urbanization and suburbanization have had several major effects on the practice of public relations.

On the one hand, the movement from a rural to an urban society has brought about a concentration of the population into large urban centers and has thus made it easier for practitioners to reach people through a smaller number of key mass media than if the population were spread evenly throughout the country. Various media in our largest cities reach millions of people, and it is theoretically possible to reach anywhere from ten million to sixty million people by means of a handful of carefully selected media.

On the other hand, however, these media are not simply open to the highest bidder, but are managed by experienced and sophisticated journalists careful to guard their pages and their air time from intrusion by outsiders. Veteran public relations practitioners know they must gear their messages and approaches so that they *first* meet the high demands of the media "gatekeepers," and this means a skillful meshing of one's private interests with the wider public interests serviced by the media managers.

At the same time, the move to the suburbs has brought about a further dispersion of the population and conflict between people's allegiances. Though millions of wage earners *gain* their living from the city, they *do* their living in the suburbs. As a result, conflicts arise in regard to such areas as taxes, municipal and suburban services, and the like. The astute practitioner has to be keenly aware of the nature of one's loyalties in such conflict situations and use judgment in seeking to resolve what may often seem to be irreconcilable differences.

The trend towards urbanization and suburbanization has thus had the interesting effect of concentrating the population and at the same time spreading it out miles beyond the reaches of the inner city. The result has been a significant change in living patterns, social groupings and political affiliations, and attitudes and opinions about a wide variety of issues. All of these call for a wise understanding of the differences existing among people who live and work in our cities; people who work in the city and live in the suburbs; and people who live and work in the suburbs.

LARGE AND COMPLEX ORGANIZATIONS

Any student who attends a large university of 10,000, 20,000, or 30,000 enrollment knows what it means to exist within a large and complex organization. The perceptive student of public relations can immediately recognize the kind of problems that such an organization poses.

One of the first problems is in providing people with some sense of "belonging." A second problem is in attempting to resolve conflicts in needs and demands that inevitably arise in large and complex organizations. When the hourly worker seeks an eight percent increase, he's not really interested in learning that he can't have it because it might mean a decrease in dividends to shareholders. When customers complain about the quality of the products they buy, they're not really interested in learning that it resulted from a deliberate action by disgruntled workers. When students complain about constantly increasing tuition, they're not really interested in learning it resulted in part from a drying up of outside giving. Thus, attempting to resolve conflicts in needs and demands calls for astute and carefully designed explanations, and all too often the explanation will satisfy one constituency but not another.

A final problem facing practitioners who deal with large and complex organizations is the sheer distortion of messages that arises when communication has to move through the many layers that make up such organizations. The problem becomes particularly acute when the central headquarters and its public relations staff is in one city, and the constituency is spread out across the entire country. What seems clear-cut in an office in Chicago's Loop can become cloudy and murky in a plant community in the Deep South. The public relations staffer reporting to the chancellor on the main campus of a multi-university finds it difficult to understand what's really going on at a branch campus several hundred miles away. Maintaining contact, keeping in touch, and understanding the diverse nature, needs, wants, and desires of people existing within large and complex organizations inevitably affects public relations practice and procedures.

GROWTH IN THE POWER OF PUBLIC OPINION AND THE SWIFTNESS IN OPINION CHANGE

Public relations practitioners use primary-direct and secondary-indirect methods in dealing with the vital tasks of assaying and attempting to influence public opinion.

When public relations practice was in its infancy, practitioners relied on relatively primitive methods of measuring public opinion. Just as many small newspapers today measure public opinion by sending a reporter out to do man-woman-on-the-street interviewing, so the early practitioners conducted similar interviews with "average" people and "opinion leaders." Today, however, most practitioners recognize the need for a scientific approach to public opinion measurement and hence turn to national, regional, and state polling organizations to handle both long-range and individually-commissioned, cross-section, in-depth interview polls. These polls—described in more detail in the chapter on public opinion—are carefully designed for a variety of purposes. They're used to measure long-range trends in public attitudes and opinion, to judge consumer reaction to products and services, to ascertain general public or special public moods and attitudes, and to test an organization's reputation among the public at large or among individual publics.

There is also general recognition that a poll is able to measure public opinion only at the time it is taken. Because events and actions can swiftly change the nature of public opinion, practitioners must be cautious in their assessments and constantly alert to the sudden dips in public moods, attitudes, and opinions. This calls for constant monitoring, by means of secondary-indirect methods, of certain weathervanes of opinion change. Long before they become too obvious, changes in public opinion can be detected from trends in news stories and features, articles in national news and opinion magazines and in specialized publications, and books by men and women who have the deserved reputation for sizing up the public scene.

Through such means, practitioners treat the power of public opinion by analyzing it to provide "intelligence" data and information for the organizations they serve. They also use their other skills in attempting to influence public opinion in meeting predetermined public relations goals and objectives. These skills and techniques—described in detail in the chapters on planning, programming, and communicating—make up the core of public relations practice. They've been refined and developed because dealing with public opinion requires the highest degree of public relations competence.

CHANGES IN THE TECHNOLOGY, ROLE, AND IMPACT OF THE MASS MEDIA

Although, as noted earlier in this chapter, there have been technological breakthroughs within the mass media in the past decade, basic concepts about news have remained surprisingly constant. News can be transmitted much swifter than in the past and television has brought instant history into the living room, but the elements that make one story of national significance and another of only local interest remain the same.

Thus, the practitioner should be on top of technological changes in the mass media, but it's more important that the practitioner know when the media will be interested in a particular story or feature. Equally important, the practitioner has to be aware of changes in editorial policy, format, and personnel; to know, for example, the varying deadlines and technical imperatives of differing media; to understand how to ride the crest of the wave of mutual interest shown by all media in certain kinds of stories and events; and to be attuned to the justified criticisms leveled by the media against the amateurs who flood their offices with material that has little interest to readers and viewers.

Practitioners keep track of mass media changes by maintaining personal contact with mass media personnel and by careful reading of publications which reflect developments in the mass media. These include *Editor and Publisher, Broadcasting, Variety,* the *Columbia Journalism Review,* various major city and state-wide journalism reviews, *Journalism Quarterly,* the *AP* and *UPI* internal organs, *ASNE Bulletin,* the press sections of *Time* and *Newsweek,* and the numerous books about the mass media which have been published in increasing numbers in recent years. The hack keeps sending out releases en masse to hundreds of outlets which can have little interest in the material; the skilled practitioner knows the value of keying material to the needs and interests of different media and of keeping abreast of changing media developments.

CONSUMERISM AND ENVIRONMENTAL SENSITIVITY

This trend presents both an internal and external problem to the public relations practitioner. The internal problem arises because the criticisms and complaints of the consumer and those sensitive to the environment are directed at areas of organizational activities which are not directly in the control of the public relations practitioner. The practitioner does not make or produce the products or services or engage in organizational activities and actions which fail to measure up to the expectations of the consumer or the environmentalist. These are the provinces of other functions within organizations: the marketing department which distributes and sells the product through high-pressure methods; the advertising department which extolls products far beyond normal belief; the executive who directs or countenances price-fixing, strip-mining, and carefully "washed" contributions of money to bring about large contracts. Handling and dealing with these internally produced and managed activities and factors calls for the wisdom of Solomon, the patience of Job, and the skill of Moses.

But the external problem connected with consumerism and environmental sensitivity is equally difficult and taxing. When consumer and environmental activists and/or the government target in on an organization's transgressions—or alleged transgressions—the matter becomes one of public interest and display. All too often, in such cases the practitioner is called upon to work some sleight of hand and magically disarm the dragon slayers. Unfortunately, in recent years the shafts and slings of consumer and environmental activist organizations and the government are frequently a justified reaction to products, services, and actions that do not measure up to expectations.

Thus, handling the challenges raised by consumerism and environmental sensitivity calls for ways and means of handling the dilemma posed by the internal-external demands placed on the practitioner. Some basic recommended procedures, organized by Richard A. Aszling of General Foods for PRSA chapter workshops on consumerism, suggest that the practitioner:

Be on top of developments by staying informed about legislative developments and activist actions. Know the literature and the reliable information sources

Seek to provide realistic forecasts of trends and developments

Develop effective communication upwards to boss or client and thus help him stay sensitive and to sort out fact from fancy

Be familiar with the successful programs of response to consumer pressures carried out by other companies

Advise employer or client on effective methods of responding to expressions of consumer dissatisfaction

Develop and carry out effective internal and external communication programs designed to make publics aware of steps taken on behalf of consumers

> from an article by John R. O'Connell in *Public Relations Journal*

By the second half of the seventies there was clear evidence that the public relations field was adjusting itself to handle the challenges of consumerism and environmental sensitivity. One piece of evidence was found in two regular columns appearing in the *Public Relations Journal:* "Environmental Update" by Edward L. Jaffee made its bow in the October 1972 issue, and "Consumer Update" by Ms. Edie Fraser made its first appearance in the June 1974 issue. Both columns have continued to provide readers with vital information about the consumer and environmental movement. The PRSA formed its own National Task Force on Consumerism and another National Task Force on Environment and Energy in the mid-seventies. Both groups have been active in keeping track of consumer and environmental development and in sponsoring such national meetings as The Consumer Conference and White House Briefing, held in May 1975. Consumerism and environmental concerns have been important parts of the programs at recent PRSA national conferences; special consumer and environmental departments and sections have been set up by large national counseling organizations, and industrial and business firms; and there is little doubt that the public relations field has taken steps to deal realistically with the major trends in American society evidenced by consumerism and environmental sensitivity.

QUESTIONS AND PROBLEMS FOR DISCUSSION

1. In what way does ecology, a biological term, apply to public relations?

2. Briefly identify: Theodore Vail; Ivy Lee; the PRSA.

3. Name three public relations publications.

4. Explain some of the ramifications of *each* of the following major trends in American society: (1) urbanization and suburbanization; (2) large and complex components; (3) growth in the power of public opinion and the swiftness of opinion change; (4) changes in the technology, role and impact of the mass media; and (5) consumerism and environmental sensitivity.

5. Explain several ways in which *each* of the above-mentioned major trends in American society have brought about the need for public relations.

6. Explain several ways in which *each* of the major trends has affected public relations practice.

7. When an organization's actions and policies are negative and clearly expected to draw adverse public reaction, is it wisest to communicate nothing, to wait out the resulting adverse public reaction, or to come right out and communicate the negative? Cite any example(s) to demonstrate the wisdom of your choice of action.

8. What steps would you suggest be taken by a large utility to maintain goodwill and understanding when its plan to build a nuclear power plant is vociferously opposed by conservation groups?

9. What would you suggest the public relations practitioner do when his/her organization's policies and actions are profitable to the organization but are viewed negatively by large segments of the population?

10. What would you suggest the public relations executive do when his/her management blames the executive for a loss in sales due to a nationally disseminated story over which the executive had no control?

PROJECTS, ASSIGNMENTS, AND MINI-CASES

1. URBANIZATION AND SUBURBANIZATION AS RELATED TO PUBLIC RELATIONS PRACTICE: A POSITION PAPER

When this chapter was being written the author could discern existing aspects of our urban-suburban habitat that had definite implications for public relations practice. The pace of American life is so swift, however, that new aspects may already have changed the picture, and this ever-changing nature of our society poses challenges to the practitioner.

Consider, therefore, that you work in the national headquarters of a nonprofit social agency that has branches and units throughout the country. You are a research assistant in the public relations department, and you have been given the assignment of exploring the current (at the time you are using this text) extent of the movement from a rural to an urban-suburban society and of setting forth a position paper indicating:

1. How and in what ways the movement affects your organization's basic *programming and activities*.

2. The *special public relations problems* the movement causes for your organization, explaining the problems in some detail.

(Note: In handling this assignment, select a nonprofit social agency you know something about. By all means utilize a variety of resources in researching and handling the assignment.)

2. PREDICTING SOCIAL AND POLITICAL CHANGES: A RESEARCH REPORT

In a 1978 talk to a group of public relations counselors, George Hammond, chairman of Carl Byoir & Associates, Inc., emphasized the need to meet client expectations in the decade of the eighties:

"Our clients know that they're not going to enjoy the luxury of the status quo," Hammond told the counselors. "They want and expect help from us in dealing with large-scale social and political changes that are coming at mind-boggling speed. It will take hindsight and the particular kind of broad experience we bring to the client/agency relationship to spot some of these changes and invent the most effective ways to deal with them."

Among Byoir clients at the time were A&P; The Great Atlantic & Pacific Tea Company; Eastman Kodak; F.W. Woolworth; Hallmark Cards; and Toyota Motor Sales, U.S.A.

Assignment

You are to assume you work for the Byoir organization. Hammond has asked you to select one of the above-mentioned Byoir clients and, through library research, ascertain key data about the company relative to its products, sales, and important publics.

Your assignment is to write the draft of a two- to three-page memorandum, addressed to the client, setting forth some of the major large-scale social and political changes that you predict will take place in the country in the next five years. Try to be specific in assessing these predicted changes in American life and in relating them to the client's major goals and purposes. Wherever possible, cite data from reliable sources to buttress the wisdom of your predictions, insights, and judgment.

(*Note:* Do *not* assume that the five fundamental trends cited in this chapter are *the* answer to this assignment, but rather see them as illustrative of the type of societal and political changes you may want to deal with in your memorandum.)

3. FIVE MAJOR MEDIA DEVELOPMENTS: A RESEARCH REPORT

Each year significant developments occur that involve the ownership, management, operation, and status of the mass media. Such developments, of course, have important consequences for the practice of public relations.

You are to assume that you are on the public relations staff of one of America's largest national corporations. You have been given the assignment of researching and reporting *five major developments* occurring this past year and involving either the ownership, management, operation, or status of one or more of the mass media. Your source can be news stories in the daily press, articles in news and/or trade publications, court decisions, and other such items.

In a memorandum to your department head, cite each development in detail, cite the source for your information, and include an explanation of how each development may affect public relations practice.

RECOMMENDED READING

T.D. Allman, "The Urban Crisis Leaves Town and Moves to the Suburbs," *Harper's,* December 1978.

Ben Bagdikian, *The Information Machines.* New York: Harper & Row, 1971.

Dan J. Forrestal, "Placing Public Relations in Perspective," *Public Relations Journal,* March 1974.

Joe. B. Frantz, "After the Fall—Opportunity: 1918-1945," *Public Relations Review,* Fall 1978.

Eric F. Goldman, "Public Relations and the Progressive Surge: 1898-1917," *Public Relations Review,* Fall 1978.

Ray E. Hiebert, *Courtier To The Crowd.* Ames, Iowa: Iowa State University Press, 1966.

Steven D. Lydenberg, *Minding the Corporate Conscience 1978.* New York: Council on Economic Priorities, 1978.

Marshall McLuhan, *Understanding Media.* New York: McGraw-Hill, 1965.

Allan Nevins, "The Constitution Makers and the Public: 1785-1790," *Public Relations Review,* Fall 1978.

Joseph Nolan, "Watergate: A Case Study in How Not to Handle Public Relations," *Public Relations Quarterly,* Summer 1975.

Robert Presthus, *The Organizational Society.* New York: Random House, Vintage Books 1965.

Frank E. Vandiver, "The First Public War: 1861-1865," *Public Relations Review,* Fall 1978.

Catherine W. Wolff, "Activist Public Relations: Integrity and Respect," *Public Relations Journal,* December 1977.

3

Two Concepts:
Social Responsibility
and
the Public Interest

In their hurry to become overnight experts, some neophytes forget that every top-flight expert first had to master fundamental principles and concepts. If the public relations neophyte is to become more than just an image-builder, he or she has to understand the connection between public relations and an organization's key policies, procedures, and actions. At the core of this relationship are the dual concepts known as *social responsibility* and *the public interest*.

In recent years these concepts have been explored in the professional literature and have become a basic part of public relations practice. However, two men — Edward L. Bernays and Harwood Childs — foresaw their importance as far back as the early twenties and late thirties. In their writings both men developed ideas that were considered innovative and impractical, but time has proved them to be not only provocative and perceptive, but also basic and practical. Decades later, we acknowledge that Bernays and Childs were years ahead of their time.

PUBLIC RELATIONS AS SEEN BY EDWARD L. BERNAYS

Author of a score of books about public relations, Edward L. Bernays had an active career of more than forty years. Starting his professional life as an admitted press agent, Bernays was the first to refer to himself subsequently as a "public relations counsel." He was also one of the first to recognize that the core of the practice is in establishing "a common meeting ground for an entity (whether a business, an individual, a government body, or a social service organization) and society."

Because public opinion is of paramount importance in a democratic society, Bernays said, the public relations practitioner must be alert to changing societal conditions and be prepared to advise modifications in policy in accordance with changes in the public point of view. As he wrote in *Crystallizing Public Opinion:* "Perhaps the chief contribution of the public relations counsel to the public and to his client is his ability to understand and analyze obscure tendencies of the public mind . . . It is his capacity for crystallizing the obscure tendencies of the public mind before they have reached definite expression, which makes him so valuable."

The above statements cover but briefly the Bernays view of public relations, but they are cited specifically to indicate his awareness of the close relationship between public relations and the society in which it operates. Political scientist Harwood Childs of Princeton University amplified this relationship when he delivered a series of lectures in the late 1930s and then expanded his remarks in a book called *An Introduction to Public Opinion.* His views, particularly when analyzed in the light of today's heightened interest in social responsibility, are worthy of careful consideration.

PUBLIC RELATIONS AS SEEN BY HARWOOD CHILDS

Disdaining what he called "the antics, stunts, tricks, and devices by which individuals and corporations often seem to obtain goodwill without actually trying to remove the real cause of ill will," Childs stated that he was not interested in the many ways to win friends and influence people. He foresaw that interest in public relations would continue and increase because, as he put it, public relations reflects one of the fundamental problems of the times. His view of the intrinsic nature of public relations is set forth here:

Public relations may be defined as those aspects of our personal and corporate behavior which have a social rather than a purely private and personal significance.

Childs understood that public relations would gain in importance chiefly because an increasing number of private and corporate activities would have social and public significance.

"Public relations as such," he declared, "is not the presentation of a point of view, not the art of tempering mental attitudes, nor the development of cordial and profitable relations. . . . It is simply a name for activities which have a social significance.

"Our problem in each corporation or industry is to find out what these activities are, what social effects they have, and if they are contrary to the public interest, to find ways and means for modifying them so that they will serve the public interest."

In setting forth this analysis of public relations, Childs stressed that the public relations executive is not primarily a publicist or propagandist. To meet Childs' standards the public relations executive has to be "a student of the social effects of personal and corporate conduct" and has to have a thorough understanding of society from a political, economic, cultural, and sociological point of view. Summed up therefore:

> The starting point in working out a public relations policy is a careful analysis of our personal and corporate behaviour in the light of social change generally. Without knowing the basic economic, cultural, political, and social trends of our times, we cannot ascertain, much less anticipate, the public implications of what we are doing. It is the lag between social trends that gives rise to our problems, and the search for answers must be a search for the reasons why these lags exist, where they exist, and what can be done to synchronize social movement.

> The business of producing and distributing goods and services must be studied in relation to the total situation, the total environment in which we are functioning. Executives of corporations cannot afford to devote all or even the major portion of their energies solely to technological considerations. They must raise their eyes to the level of wider horizons. The public relations counsel must be something more than a publicist, a journalist or a statistician. He must be a social scientist capable of advising management regarding the environment in which it is operating.

OBSERVATIONS CONCERNING THE CHILDS THESIS

A caveat is in order before proceeding with a discussion of the thesis of public relations expounded by Harwood Childs. Most readers of this textbook will be students who hope to make a career of public relations or who hope to use it in other careers where public relations has an important bearing. Young people entering the field will not generally be given an executive position in public relations and expected to serve as elder statesmen. On the contrary, they will most likely be engaged in tasks which Childs claims are not public relations: helping with "the presentation of a point of view" and in "the development of cordial and profitable relations." In time, however, as the neophyte becomes expert in his field he will be given broader and more significant responsibilities and duties. The time to think about and to understand these broader areas is now, for tomorrow may be too late. Consider, therefore, that you were among the business leaders and professionals to whom Childs addressed himself back in the late thirties. Certain observations and questions should then come more readily to mind.

First, a question about Childs' basic premise. Do you agree or disagree with his contention that public relations is "not the presentation of a point of view, not the art of tempering mental attitudes, nor the development of cordial and profitable relations?" What arguments can be raised *against* this viewpoint? Is it possible that in his desire to underscore the importance of the societal approach to public relations Childs may have overstated his case? What do other authorities say about the issue?

Second, what does Childs mean when he says that public relations is "simply a name for activities which have a social significance"? What about activities having a political, economic and cultural significance? Do you think Childs meant to incorporate these three— political, economic and cultural—when he stressed only socially significant activities? How about "societal" as an adjective to describe the activities to which Childs referred?

The word "significance" also brings to mind certain key questions. When is an activity socially *significant,* when is it of moderate importance, and when is it insignificant? Childs does not answer these questions; in fact he leaves the matter up to the individual practitioner. Note, for example, that he states that "our problem" is to ascertain what activities have a social significance, to figure out what social effects they have, and to find ways and means for modifying them if they are contrary to the public interest.

Assuming that Childs' basic premise is correct, we find that he has formulated a conception of public relations which poses innumerable challenges to the competence, wisdom, and judgment of the public relations practitioner. Bernays saw these challenges clearly in 1962 when he told a New York *Times* interviewer that the task of the public relations man should be to study public opinion and social psychology and to "counsel his company on how to adjust to . . . societal forces and to enlist public support for services, products and ideas." One can scarcely counsel if one has little understanding of societal forces. Put another way: "Public relations advice, to be worth anything, must be grounded on a comprehensive knowledge of the past, of trends and relationships in the field of social change," said Childs, and his challenge to the public relations practitioner thus becomes one of being able to cope with the past, the present, and the future of our society.

Coping with the challenge posed by Childs may seem like an academic exercise to some, but relating to problems is a key element in public relations programming. One must first recognize public relations problems before one can hope to solve them. Such recognition comes from understanding past and noting present socially significant activities posing public relations problems and foreseeing future socially significant activities that will bring about public relations problems at some time beyond the present.

Recognition, however, is but one step in the public relations process. What to *do* about these problems is another matter. What to do is often a choice from among three alternatives: what is permissible, what is possible, and what is prohibited. Internal, rather than external, factors generally govern the choice to be made because higher authority in the management of organizations and institutions have the final word over public relations' freedom of action and activity. This is particularly true in the area known as social responsibility.

SCHOOLS OF THOUGHT CONCERNING SOCIAL RESPONSIBILITY

The concept of social responsibility is one that few people dare to challenge. It's akin to God, mother, and apple pie. It takes an agnostic to challenge the idea of God; a Philip Wylie to challenge the institution of motherhood, and a peach pie enthusiast to challenge the virtues of apple pie. Who among us are willing to stand up and say we are socially irresponsible, and what organizations and institutions are willing to contend they are not socially responsible? Everyone, it seems, is socially responsible, but in *varying degrees*. The two major views of thought concerning social responsibility have probably been best expressed by Dr. Milton Friedman and by the Committee For Economic Development.

THE FRIEDMAN VIEW

At one extreme in the debate over social responsibility—particularly as the concept applies to business—is Dr. Milton Friedman, noted professor of economics at the University of Chicago. A staunch defender of the free-enterprise, private-property system, Friedman says that those who contend that business should be concerned not "merely" with profit but also with promoting desirable social ends are "preaching pure and unadulterated socialism."

Friedman's view—set forth in a September 13, 1970, article in the *New York Times Magazine*—reminds us that corporate executives are employees of the owners of their businesses and have a direct responsibility to their employers.

"That responsibility," says Friedman, "is to conduct the business in accordance with their desires, which generally will be to make as much money as possible while conforming to the basic rules of society, both those embodied in law and those embodied in ethical custom."

Friedman observes that the corporate executive is also a person in his own right and as such he may want to devote part of his income to causes he regards as worthy. However, says Friedman, when we talk of the social responsibility of the corporate executive as a businessman we ask him to act in some way not in the interest of his employers. As one example, Friedman says that when we ask the businessman to refrain from increasing the price of his product in order to gain the social objective of preventing inflation, such a decision may not be in the best interests of the corporation. Similarly, he adds, it may be at the expense of corporate profits to ask the businessman to hire "hardcore" unemployed rather than better-qualified workers in order to gain the social objective of reducing poverty.

Professor Friedman sums up his argument in the following words:

There is one and only one social responsibility of business—to use its resources and engage in activities designed to increase its profits so long as it stays within the rules of the game, which is to say, engages in open and free competition without deception or fraud.

THE COMMITTEE FOR ECONOMIC DEVELOPMENT VIEW

Another view of social responsibility was set forth in the seventies in a 74-page statement by the Research and Policy Committee of the Committee for Economic Development (CED), titled "Social Responsibilities of Business Corporation." Addressing itself primarily to the large, publicly owned, professionally managed corporations—though noting its remarks apply as well to smaller enterprises and to businessmen as individuals—the CED cited some negative attitudes toward business expressed by the public in nationwide public opinion polls. It concluded from these statistics that a clear majority of the public believes that corporations have not been sufficiently concerned about societal problems and that "two-thirds believe business now has a moral obligation to help other major institutions to achieve social progress, even at the expense of profitability. . . . Business is being asked to assume broader responsibilities to society than ever before and to serve a wider range of human values. Business enterprises, in effect, are being asked to contribute more to the quality of American life than just supplying quantities of goods and services."

Four basic questions raised by business in response to the above-mentioned demands, said the CED, are as follows:

1. Why should corporations become substantially involved in the improvement of the social environment?

2. How can they justify this to their stockholders?

3. How can companies reconcile substantial expenditures for social purposes with profitability?

4. What are the limitations on corporate social responsibility?

Agreeing that these are legitimate concerns, the CED said the answer to them is found in recognizing that business is a basic institution in American society and has a vital stake in the general welfare as well as in its own public acceptance.

Amplifying Harwood Childs' doctrines, the CED then set forth social responsibilities in terms of self-interest:

There is broad recognition today that corporate self-interest is inexorably involved in the well-being of the society of which business is an integral part, and from which it draws the basic requirements needed for it to function at all—capital, labor, customers. There is increasing understanding that the corporation is dependent on the goodwill of society, which can sustain or impair its existence through public pressures on government. And it has become clear that the essential resources and goodwill of society are not naturally forthcoming to corporations whenever needed, but must be worked for and developed. . . .

Indeed the corporate interest broadly defined by management can support involvement in helping to solve virtually any social problem, because people who have a good environment, education, and opportunity make better employees, customers, and neighbors for business than those who are poor, ignorant, and oppressed. It is obviously in the interest of business to enlarge its markets and to improve its work force by helping disadvantaged people to develop and employ their economic potential. Likewise, it is in the interest of business to help reduce the mounting costs of welfare, crime, disease, and waste of human potential —a good part of which business pays for.

Experience with governmental and social constraints indicates that the corporation's self-interest is best served by a sensitivity to social concerns and a willingness, within competitive limits, to take needed action ahead of confrontation. By acting on its own initiative, management preserves the flexibility needed to conduct the company's affairs in a constructive, efficient and adaptive manner.

Recognizing the cost factor in its analysis of social responsibility, the CED noted that business obviously cannot be expected to solve all the problems of society. The report pointed out that various internal constraints limit corporations in their approach to societal problems. "No company of any size can willingly incur costs that would jeopardize its competitive position and threaten its survival. While companies may well be able to absorb modest costs or undertake some social activities on a break-even basis, any substantial expenditure must be justified in terms of the benefits, tangible and intangible, that are expected to be produced."

The analysis of the two views of social responsibility cited above is obviously a truncated one. On the one hand we have Dr. Friedman's view that the business of business is just business; that management has neither the right nor the qualifications to undertake activities to improve society or to tax its constituents for these purposes, and that society's general welfare is a matter for the government, not business. On the other hand we have the CED view that it's in the self-interest of business to accept a fair measure of responsibility for improving society because "insensitivity to changing demands of society sooner or later results in public pressures for governmental intervention and regulation to require business to do what it was reluctant or unable to do voluntarily."

SOME LAST WORDS BY JOHN W. HILL

In the last year of a long and fruitful life—one that spanned half a century in public relations—John W. Hill summed up in 1977 his views about the erosion of public trust in business. Agreeing that most Americans believe in our economic system, Hill said that there are growing public expectations of business leadership in helping to solve social problems. However, he added, very few corporations have developed effective means of relating their policies to societal expectations and of explaining these policies in forthright and understandable terms.

A major share of the problem, Hill noted, is that corporate leaders have been insulated from the people. Another reason cited by Hill is the public's distrust of all established institutions, including business.

"Even before the post-Watergate disclosures of illegal political campaign gifts," he declared, "a slow-burning resentment had been building up against some companies for shoddy products, careless service, abuse of warranties, alleged foot-dragging in clearing up pollution, and other matters."

In Hill's opinion, every American corporate management faces two tests: to maintain profitability, and to meet the expectations and demands of society. Stating that business must take a closer look at its operations and ethical standards, Hill issued this challenge:

> What is desperately needed is not more money spent on "communications," but a revised philosophy and a new concept of external relations—of social issues—in the minds of corporate managements in this country. Words alone are useless if not fully supported by policies and performance.
>
> . . . Unless corporations are willing to examine their decisions and performance, correct any flaws they find, and adopt a policy of candor on matters of publc interest, they will never regain the public's confidence. And without that confidence and credibility, business can never effectively rebut its militant critics, never successfully defend itself in the court of public opinion.

THE PUBLIC INTEREST

As we have seen, coming to grips with corporate social responsibility is not a simple matter, but it is even more difficult to come to grips with the concept of the public interest. On its face, the public interest concept has the solid ring of immutable dictum and truth. Public relations practitioners continually define their activities in terms of being in the public interest, the literature of the field is replete with references to the public interest, and there exist few if any public relations experts with soul so daring that they would contend their work is *not* in the public interest.

But some disturbing questions come to mind, and they demand answers:

- What is the public interest? Obviously you can't see, hear, or feel it, so how can you tell what it is?

- Can the public interest be measured, weighed, and assessed?

- Who is to be the judge of the public interest?

- What if an organization's policies, procedures, and actions are in the interests of one public but not of another?

- What if an organization's private interests and the public interest are in obvious conflict?

- What if an organization's policies, in order to be in the public interest, can only be modified or changed at an unbearable cost to the organization?

Of course there are answers to the above questions, just as there are answers to almost any question. But the value of the questions is not in their answers, but in the perceptions, insights, and depth of thought that goes into seeking the answers. It is hoped the discussion that follows will assist readers in coping with the questions.

THE CHILDS AND GALLUP VIEW

Harwood Childs defines the public interest in these words:

It is my thesis that *the public interest,* so far as the United States is concerned, *is and can only be what the public, what mass opinion, says it is.* By mass opinion, I mean the collective opinions of the American people as a whole.

Childs cites data from many years of the Gallup poll to support his belief that *over reasonably long periods of time public opinion is as safe a guide to follow as the opinions of smaller and select groups.* He also cites Gallup himself as follows:

The sampling surveys of recent years have provided much evidence concerning the wisdom of the common people. . . . And I think that the person who does examine it (the evidence) will come away believing as I do that, collectively, the American people have a remarkably high degree of common sense. These people may not be brilliant or intellectual or particularly well read, but they possess a quality of good sense which is manifested time and again in their expressions of opinion on present-day issues. . . .

Childs recognized defects in stressing the virtues of mass public opinion as a guide to public interest. In his own words:

The competence of the masses is, of course, conditioned by the environment and by the opportunities they have to acquire information, to listen to different points of view, to discuss and express their opinions freely—and to use their reasoning powers.

Nonetheless, he said, public relations practitioners do have on hand tangible criteria for finding out what the public interest is, and he rests his case by emphasizing that "on broad questions of social, political, and economic policy the opinions of the masses seem to show a remarkably high degree of common sense."

Let us, for the sake of argument, accept Childs' concept of the public interest as expressed in his remarks and those of George Gallup. There will still remain the difficult and expensive task of measuring mass opinion. National polling organizations, such as Gallup's, have a highly creditable record in this area of opinion measurement, but their results are fixed in time. They reveal what mass opinion was at the time opinion was measured. Further, it would be enormously costly, and often impossible, to take a measurement of the public pulse every time a public relations policy, action, or statement is to be put into effect.

LIPPMANN'S VIEW

There are also those who take direct issue with Childs and Gallup. No less an authority on public opinion than Walter Lippmann (*The Public Philosophy*) believes that in normal circumstances voters can't be expected to transcend their particular, localized, and self-regarding opinions. Lippmann adds:

> I am far from implying that the voters are not entitled to the representation of their particular opinions and interests. But their opinions and interests should be taken for what they are and for no more. They are not—as such—propositions in the public interest. . . .

> The Gallup polls are reports of what people are thinking. But that a plurality of the people sampled in the poll think one way has no bearing upon whether it is sound public policy. For their opportunities of judging great issues are in the very nature of things limited, and the statistical sum of their opinions is not the final verdict on an issue. It is, rather, the beginning of the argument. In that argument their opinions need to be confronted by the views of the executive, defending and promoting the public interest. In the accommodation reached between the two views lies practical public policy.

Lippmann's references to the public interest were made in regard to political affairs, but they could just as well apply to corporate and other institutional affairs. His ideas about the public mind will be more fully discussed in a later chapter, but it is sufficient to say at this point that Lippmann felt the public is often misinformed, ill-informed, and poor judges of great issues.

Lippmann doesn't leave us dangling, however, because he provides his own analysis of what is meant by the public interest, as follows:

> . . . The public interest may be presumed to be what men would choose if they saw clearly, thought rationally, acted disinterestedly and benevolently.

Stated another way, Lippmann suggests that if you want to judge whether your organization's policies, actions, or statements are in the public interest then you should view them from the vantage point of men who see things clearly, think rationally, act disinterestedly and benevolently!

HILL'S VIEW

John W. Hill, founder of Hill & Knowlton, one of the country's largest and most respected public relations counseling firms, was so concerned about the public interest he devoted two chapters of his book, *The Making Of A Public Relations Man,* to a discussion of the public interest concept. Where the public interest lies in given circumstances, said Hill, seems to be a matter of opinion and judgment. Hill surveyed fifty leaders in education, government, theology, and labor and came up with these two general answers:

1. A sizeable body of opinion exists that *no precise definition of the public interest is possible.* (One out of three responses).

2. A majority of those who said a definition was possible settled for the clause *"the greatest good for the geatest number."* However, some provided qualifications, and the essential qualification was that *the interests of the minority must be protected.*

From the thoughts about the public interest expressed by his fifty opinion leaders Hill distilled some *criteria* for determining what is in the public interest. The criteria are in the form of questions, and they seem to be sound ones to ask of policies, actions, and statements:

1. How many people will be affected?

2. How many will be harmed?

3. How many people will be benefited?

4. How significant are the effects going to be?

5. What are the probable long-range effects?

PUBLIC RELATIONS PROBLEMS ASSOCIATED WITH THE PUBLIC INTEREST

John Hill's fifty opinion leaders didn't cite answers to the above-listed questions, because the answers depend on the issues under consideration and the many variables associated with these issues. Managements, however, expect answers from their public relations men and women, but it's very difficult to come up with answers when an organization's private interests and the public interest conflict or when an organization is caught in the middle between the conflicting interests of different publics. Consider, for example, the following circumstances and ask what you would do about them:

1. A private four-year college, established 25 years ago in a metropolitan area of 225,000 residents, has been financially and academically successful despite having no endowment. Its revenues have come from tuition and a thriving evening division. Recently a group of community leaders—including local bankers, industrialists and the publisher of the city's two daily newspapers—has mounted a drive to get the state university to establish a four-year undergraduate college in the area. Such a college would, of course, be an economic boon to the area, but because of its much lower tuition it would pose tough competitive problems to the established private four-year college. Suggest the

public relations stance of the private institution where its private interest collides with the public interest.

2. In order to better serve a metropolitan area of one million residents, a large gas and electric utility has announced plans to build a nuclear power plant on the banks of a large lake eighty miles away in a rural area. Since the announcement, two major groups have actively come out in opposition to the proposed plant: a very active conservation group, which claims the plant will destroy plant and fish life in the lake; and a very active citizens' group, led by responsible civic leaders who reside in the towns bordering the lake and who are vehemently and vocally opposed to the nuclear plant. Suggest the public relations stance of the utility caught in the middle between the public interests of residents in the metropolitan area it serves and the public interests of the two groups who oppose the proposed plant.

The two examples cited above are duplicated daily in numerous ways in American society and are indicative of the difficult public relations problems organizations and institutions face when dealing with public interest. In such instances there are no real answers, and very often the questions that astute practitioners raise about circumstances are more important than are the answers. Shooting from the hip may have been the only way to handle a show-down with a gunslinger in a dusty western town. In today's modern society, though, it's usually wiser to avoid that show-down by asking the right questions and by applying sound, professional advice to management caught in the bind of the private-public interest conflict.

T. J. Ross, veteran public relations counselor, sized up the problem in terms of *balance* when he declared:

> In a corporation of size, decisions affecting public interest are often difficult. In striving to carry out its job with public consensus and in the public interest, the best it can achieve is what might be called *an acceptable balance of interests*. It has to deal with a number of groups, each of which seeks something for its own benefit and possibly at the expense of another group within the corporation.

> It is in these areas (balancing of interests) that one role of public relations is performed; namely, that of assisting managements in arriving at policies and practices that will be reflected favorably within the family, in the market-place, in the government, in the press and so forth. ... The other part of our role has to do with communication. ...

Observations about the public interest made by men like Ross, Hill, and other veteran practitioners suggest the following guidelines for public relations in dealing with the public interest:

1. Don't use the term "public interest" loosely. People are not fools, especially when it comes to matters affecting their own interests. Just because an organization claims its actions are in the public interest does not mean that the claim will automatically be accepted by the public. An action that is all-too-obviously a private interest action will be seen as such even though it's wrapped in a pretty package and labeled *public interest*. Use the term carefully, judiciously, and with a sense of discrimination for the nuances of interests.

2. Explain why your policy or action is in the public interest. The public is interested in more than mere labels and would be more likely to support you if you explain *why* your organization's position, proposal, or action is in the public interest. At the same time, however, complex explanations are difficult for the public to assimilate and understand, so keep explanations simple. This, of course, is easily said, but hard to carry out if the issue itself is complex.

This leads to an obvious conclusion: if your explanation has to be so complex that it's hard for the public to understand, then you had better restudy the issue to see if it's really in the public interest. And that leads to the next point:

3. Make sure you're being reasonable and honest. When an action is taken, you should make sure it's a sound one that will be accepted as reasonable and fair under the circumstances. Most people recognize that the primary purpose of an organization is to sustain itself. They can therefore accept the fact that it may not be possible to act in the public interest if, in so doing, an organization's existence or interests will be seriously impaired. What they may not so readily accept is an attempt to pass off one's purely private interests as being in the public interest.

4. Emphasize confluent aspects. There are very few situations that are clearly in the public interest or clearly in an organization's private interests. You can take almost any organization's policy, procedure, or action and chart the degree in which it will be in the public interest and the degree in which it will be in the private interest of an organization. Within a range from zero to ten you will find that one aspect of the situation will rate *two* in terms of being in the public interest and *ten* in terms of being in the private interest of the organization. Another aspect of the same situation, however, might rate *six* in terms of both public and private interests. By all means, therefore, stress the degree of agreement rather than the degree of disagreement:

> Your college decides to raise its tuition by $300 (so what else is new?). The financial aspects of the action would rate *zero* in terms of the interests of the student body and *eight* in terms of the interests of the college. But in respect to being able to maintain and attract an excellent faculty, the action would rate *eight* in terms of the interests of both the student body and the school. In making the announcement, therefore, the public relations department would be advised to emphasize the second point rather than the first.

A cautionary note is in order regarding confluence of interests. When rating interests as they apply to various aspects of a situation, don't overemphasize what is relatively unimportant. It would clearly not be advisable to stress an aspect that is of minor importance within a situation merely because it meshes with both public and private interests.

5. Keep in mind Ross's concept of an acceptable balance of interests. Many times in your professional life you will be dealing with a situation that affects diverse groups. What will benefit one group will not benefit another, and therefore the best that can be achieved is what Ross terms an acceptable balance of interests. Compromise may not be the ideal solution, but it may well be the only realistic solution when trying to mesh public and private interests.

The above guidelines, of course, are predicated on the assumption that your organization's policies, actions, and statements are somehow tuned to the public interest. When they clearly are *not* in said interest, don't try to pass them off as being so. If you are in a position to do anything about them, bring your weight to bear in modifying or changing policies, actions, and/or statements so that they *will* meet the public interest in some degree of importance and will be so perceived by the public. Above all, keep your personal involvement in check when trying to judge the public interest in a given situation. It's usually the disinterested person who can best judge what is and what isn't in the public interest.

QUESTIONS AND PROBLEMS FOR DISCUSSION

1. What does Harwood Childs consider to be the major focus and purpose of public relations?

2. What does Harwood Childs mean when he says that public relations is "simply a name for activities which have a social significance"? Do you agree or disagree with his contention? Why?

3. If we were to grant the validity of Childs' view of public relations, what kind of problems does such a view pose for the public relations practitioner?

4. How does Dr. Milton Friedman view the social responsibility concept as it applies to business executives? Do you agree or disagree with this view? Justify your conclusion.

5. How does the Committee For Economic Development view social responsibility and self-interest? Do you agree or disagree with this view?

6. What is meant by the contention that the prime function of the public relations practitioner is to act as a "mediator" between the corporation and society? Do you agree or disagree with this view? Why?

7. How would you define the term "the public interest"?

8. How is the term seen by Childs and Gallup? By Walter Lippmann? By John Hill?

9. What's your opinion of T. J. Ross's thought that the problem of the public interest is one of achieving "an acceptable balance of interests"?

10. What does the author mean when he advises practitioners to emphasize confluent aspects of a situation in order to best mesh public and private interests?

PROJECTS, ASSIGNMENTS, AND MINI-CASES

1. PRIVATE/PUBLIC INTEREST EXAMPLES: A RESEARCH REPORT

This assignment requires you to clip, paste up, and analyze five stories showing how an organization's private interests—as demonstrated in its reported policies, actions, or statements—either meshed or conflicted with the public interest.

Your examples should come from news stories in the *New York Times,* the *Wall Street Journal,* any other daily newspaper, *Time, Newsweek,* or any other publication. The stories should *deal only with private organizations* or their representatives, not with government or political agencies and/or people.

Your report should contain the stories, neatly organized and pasted up, plus your "expert" commentary. The latter should capsulize the situation or issue as you see it; explain the nature of the private/public interest connection; and analyze its relationship to what you perceive to be the organization's basic goals and public relations objectives. It is expected that each commentary will be at least several paragraphs in length. Provide a summary commentary.

2. CHILDS' THESIS PUT TO THE TEST: A PROJECT

As noted in this chapter, Harwood Childs maintains that a major task of the public relations practitioner is to delineate those policies, activities, or actions of an organization that have societal significance. Listed below is a sampling of some major American organizations and institutions:

commercial airlines	General Motors
hospitals	your favorite con-
private colleges and	glomerate
universities	major oil companies
public colleges and	the television networks
universities	the Red Cross
the United Way	the American Medical
labor unions	Association

For *each* of the above-listed organizations and institutions you are to *cite and briefly describe:*

1. A *past* socially significant policy, activity, or action of said organization or institution that has posed public relations problems for the organization or institution.

2. A *present* socially significant policy, activity, or action of said

organization or institution that has posed public relations problems for the organization or institution.

3. A *future* socially significant policy, activity, or action of said organization or institution that will, in your opinion, pose public relations problems for the organization or institution.

RECOMMENDED READING

Melvin Anshen, *Managing the Socially Responsible Corporation*. New York: Macmillan, 1974.

Edward L. Bernays, *Crystallizing Public Opinion*. New York: Boni and Liveright, 1927.

Daniel Boorstin, *The Image: A Guide to Pseudo-Events in America*. New York: Harper & Row, 1962.

Harwood Childs, *An Introduction to Public Opinion*. New York: John Wiley & Sons, 1940.

David W. Ewing, "The Corporation as Public Enemy No. 1," *Saturday Review*, January 21, 1978.

David Finn, *The Corporate Oligarch*. New York: Simon and Schuster, 1969.

Milton Friedman, "The Social Responsibility of Business Is to Increase Its Profits," *New York Times Magazine*, September 13, 1970.

L. I. Golden, *Only By Public Consent*. New York: Hawthorn Books, 1968.

John W. Hill, *The Making Of A Public Relations Man*. New York: David McKay, 1963.

_____, "Corporations — The Sitting Ducks," *Public Relations Quarterly*, Summer 1977.

"Is Corporate Social Responsibility A Dead Issue?" *Business and Society Review*, Spring 1978.

Walter Lippmann, *The Public Philosophy*. Boston: Little, Brown, 1955.

Organizing for Issues Management — A Public Relations Opportunity. New York: Public Relations Society of America, 1978.

Otto Lerbinger, "How Far Toward the Social Audit?" *Public Relations Review*, Summer 1975.

Robert Lekachman, "A Cure for Corporate Neurosis," *Saturday Review*, January 1978.

Kenneth Rowe and John Schlacter, "Integrating Social Responsibility into the Corporate Structure," *Public Relations Quarterly*, Fall 1978.

Donald K. Wright, "Social Responsibility in Public Relations: A Multi-Step Theory," *Public Relations Review*, Fall 1976.

PART II
MANAGING THE
FUNCTION

Having examined public relations in broad, societal terms, it's now appropriate to focus attention on the men and women who manage the function.

Just as public relations serves as a bridge between organizations and the society in which they exist and operate, so do the practitioners serve as a bridge in this text between the societal aspects of the field and the dynamics of the public relations process. The chapter that follows—the bridge chapter in this text—deals with the two primary groups of practitioners: those working internally within organizations and those working externally in counseling firms.

After a preliminary analysis of the advantages and disadvantages of the two groups, the chapter focuses on the activities, functions, and structure of internal departments and counseling firms.

4

The Practitioners: Internal Departments and Counseling Firms

Public relations, as was emphasized in Chapter 1, is generally considered to be a management function. This means that, in carrying out its job of running sizable organizations that have many publics, management relies in some fashion on public relations principles, talents, and techniques. There are many different ways of achieving public relations goals, but there are chiefly four basic systems for handling the public relations function:

1. Internally, undelegated.

2. Internally, delegated to a department or staff.

3. Externally, delegated to a public relations counseling firm or public relations department of an advertising agency.

4. Through a combination of internal public relations staff and external counsel.

THE FUNCTION HANDLED INTERNALLY, UNDELEGATED

Some managements handle the public relations function without benefit of public relations talents and techniques.
In such instances *someone* in the management hierarchy keeps in mind public relations principles as the organization carries out its primary tasks. The "someone" is usually the chief executive of the organization, and it is expected that he or she will have certain public relations skills that will be used as the occasion calls for them. An example would be the executive director of the local Boys' Club or Girl Scouts, the manager of the town's leading department store, or the president of a local business employing from twenty-five to five hundred people.

It should be obvious that under this system the amount of time and expertise given to public relations will be minimal. Chief executives simply don't have the time nor the expertise to devote to the handling of public relations. The function will therefore be taken care of only in a peripheral sense.

THE FUNCTION HANDLED INTERNALLY THROUGH DELEGATION TO A DEPARTMENT OR STAFF

In most sizable organizations that deal with many publics, the task of utilizing public relations principles, talents, and techniques is entrusted to a department or staff—and sometimes to a single person—specifically empowered and assigned to carry out the public relations function.

In such instances the public relations job is considered important enough and of such magnitude to justify the need for a specialized staff organized into a separate department or integrated with another department. An example would be the public relations department of a large university or business, the public relations staff of a large hospital, or the advertising/public relations department of a large industrial organization or trade association.

It's within this system and the one which follows that most public relations practitioners operate in the United States. The internal staff might be just one person or it might be many people, but the common feature is that the public relations function is entrusted to professionals.

THE FUNCTION HANDLED EXTERNALLY BY A COUNSELING FIRM OR ADVERTISING AGENCY

Large organizations often assign the public relations task, by contract, to a public relations counseling firm or to the public relations department of an advertising agency.

In such instances the managements of large organizations believe that the public relations task can best be carried out by outside firms who represent a wide variety of clients and have proven expertise which may not be possible to achieve through an internal staff or department. An example would be a contract signed with a public relations counseling firm to handle all or certain specific public relations tasks of a national concern whose stock is publicly owned and traded, or a similar contract made with the advertising agency that handles the concern's national advertising and is capable of carrying out specified public relations tasks.

As will be explained later, there are sound reasons why organizations seek outside counsel to handle public relations function. Proof that this arrangement works satisfactorily is found in the fact that numerous large companies have been served by the same public relations counseling firm for many years, some for periods ranging between fifteen and twenty-five years.

THE FUNCTION HANDLED BY INTERNAL DEPARTMENT AND OUTSIDE COUNSEL

Though many large organizations have their own public relations departments, they also retain public relations counseling firms or the public relations departments of advertising agencies. Thus, we have a *combination of the internal staff or department and the outside firm* working together to achieve desired public relations results.

In such instances the managements of large organizations utilize the inside-outside arrangement. An example would be a large midwestern manufacturing concern which has its own public relations department at the concern's headquarters/plant site, but which utilizes a New York City-based counseling firm or ad agency public relations department in an adjunct capacity.

Though one may wonder why organizations with internal public relations departments would also find it advisable to employ outside counsel, the arrangement is a common one. Counseling firms, for example, may be able to provide certain services that the internal department is not geared to handle. An outside firm may be more objective and free from certain political restraints that inhibit the internal staffer. For these and many other reasons, the internal-external combination is on the increase in American public relations activity.

In the ensuing analysis of the systems for handling public relations the internal, undelegated method will not be discussed in further detail because it is based on the philosophy that public relations really does not have to be managed. Rather, the philosophy holds that public relations can be handled as an ancillary activity or some other staff member or department or by management as it does its other tasks. This may be the only feasible or economically sound way to take care of the function in small organizations, but not for sizable organizations with many publics. The other three methods require that the public relations function be *managed*, and the chapter will therefore focus on the way in which the management of the function is carried out under each of the three methods.

Each of the three methods of handling public relations has advantages that the others either do not possess or cannot equal. Yet, given proper circumstances, what may on the surface seem to be an advantage can just as easily turn out to be a disadvantage. It's therefore of value to consider both the advantages and disadvantages of each system.

INTERNAL STAFF OR DEPARTMENT: ADVANTAGES

Although there are many advantages to having the public relations function carried out by an internal staff or department, authorities in the field believe that the three major advantages are:

1. Knowledge of the organization

2. Availability

3. Team membership

Each of these, ranked in no particular order of importance, is discussed below.

KNOWLEDGE OF THE ORGANIZATION

Any competent public relations person working on the public relations staff of an organization ought to have an intimate working knowledge of the entire organization for which he or she works. This should include knowledge of the key *people, products,* and *activities* of the organization; the *"politics"* of the organization; and forthcoming and upcoming *changes* affecting people, products, and activities.

Most organizations publish nice, tidy charts which indicate where everyone belongs and the role assigned to each. But the charts often mask reality, and the astute public relations man or woman should know what really goes on. To do the job properly the practitioner ought also to have advance knowledge of important changes affecting people, products, and activities. There are three basic reasons behind this necessity of having an insider's knowledge:

1. Public relations functions at the optimum when its advice and counsel is sought *in advance,* not after the event.

2. The output of public relations staffs and departments is most effective when it accurately reflects an organization's activities and policies.

3. The public relations department ought to be the department most available to the media when it seeks information about an organization. If the department cannot provide this information or aid the media in securing it, then the media will get its information by other means.

AVAILABILITY

Though a large share of public relations activity involves such routine duties as preparing brochures and publishing periodic newsletters, reports, and magazines, every organization has moments where the unexpected demands immediate public relations action. Being on the spot at such moments is of inestimable value in providing the right kind of advice, suggesting the most effective action, and following through with the proper response.

Sometimes the situation will call only for the giving of advice, but advice given by people who are on the scene has an advantage over advice given from afar. The same applies to the action to be taken and the response to be made. The hospital with its own internal public relations department has a great advantage over one without such a department when a national figure is seriously injured and brought to its emergency room or wing. The college with its own internal public relations department has a great advantage over one without such a department when its students, faculty, or staff suddenly go out on strike. The large research complex with its own internal public relations department has a great advantage over one without such a department when an explosion takes place in one of its laboratories.

Proper timing is so often the key to successful public relations that its role cannot be over-estimated. Timing, in turn, relies on the availability of public relations personnel, and the internal public relations person has the advantage of being always available.

TEAM MEMBERSHIP

The very fact that a public relations department has been established within an organization makes the members of that department part of the management team. Most public relations functions and activities are related to other departments and their activities so the relationship should be cordial, friendly, and cooperative. As an insider who is called upon to interact almost daily with personnel in other departments, the internal public relations man or woman has many opportunities to develop a cooperative working relationship with those in other departments. The more the public relations person demonstrates his or her value and worth to the organization and particularly to other departments in the organization, the more solid becomes the relationship and the more valuable the factor of team membership.

INTERNAL STAFF OR DEPARTMENT: DISADVANTAGES

Two of the three factors which comprise the major advantages of the internal staff or department—availability and team membership—can prove to be dysfunctional in certain circumstances.

There is such a thing as being *too available*. In many organizations there is either no clear understanding of public relations or else there is a tendency to dump on the department many duties and responsibilities which do not belong in the department or which are peripheral to the department's main duties. There is no great mystery about why this happens. Public relations, by its very nature and name, involves relations with the public. Many of an organization's activities do not fall clearly within the province of any single department, but do involve the public. The organization has a public relations department; ergo, dump the matter into the lap of the public relations department.

Availability and interpersonal relationships within an organization have a great deal to do with how much and how often the public relations department will be saddled with peripheral public relations matters. The head of the personnel department, for example, ordinarily wouldn't think of asking ouside public relations counsel to assist in a personal matter that might touch on public relations activity. But he might very well make that same request of the public relations department if it's right in the next office and headed by someone he lunches with every day. If the request is made by the chief executive or other high official of the organization, it's even more difficult to turn it down.

> Responsibility for all social and health agency fund drives carried out in the main plant of a large industrial concern is assigned to the plant personnel department. This year the plant manager has been elected president of the city's United Way organization. He is so busy running the plant he needs someone to do most of his work for the United Way. Both the personnel manager and the public relations manager have more than enough to do handling their own work, but the plant manager asks the public relations manager rather than the personnel manager to help him with his United Way duties for the year. As he explains it: being president of the United Way brings good will to the plant, and the development of good will is a public relations function.

Team membership can be as dysfunctional as availability. *Being a member of the team can cloud one's objective vision,* yet at all times the public relations practitioner needs a clear-eyed view of what's going on. When such a view indicates that one's fellow "teammate" is responsible for product flaws uncovered by an inquiring journalist, what responsibility does the public relations man have to the truth, to his organization, and to his fellow member of the team? When such a view indicates a "teammate's" clear incompetence, which in turn can lead to a loss of public confidence in the organization, it becomes difficult to expose such incompetence within the councils of the organization. The ultimate in professional frustration and dysfunction occurs when top management itself is incompetent but expects the public relations practitioner team member to present the executive to the public as highly competent and able. At such a time the practitioner would gladly trade the so-called advantage of team membership for a job on the assembly line.

THE COUNSELING FIRM: ADVANTAGES

The major advantages of the public relations counseling firm (or the public relations department of an advertisinging agency) are seen by most authorities to be four-fold:

1. Objectivity

2. Wide range of experience and talents

3. Flexibility

4. Economy

Each of these, ranked in no particular order of importance, is discussed below.

OBJECTIVITY

The outside public relations counselor is not a member of the inside organization or team, and this is a virtue because the counselor brings an objective view to public relations problems. The outside counselor calls the shots as he sees them, not as management thinks he *ought* to see them. He is usually retained with the expectation that he will be objective. If he tells some hard truths, gives advice and counsel which causes him to lose the account, the world doesn't come to an end as a result. (That is, unless the counseling firm has only a few accounts and this is a major one.) The outside counselor does not wear rose-colored glasses which cast a euphoric glow over every perceived problem, but bi-focals which enable a realistic, *objective* look at problems.

WIDE RANGE OF EXPERIENCE AND TALENTS

Counseling firms which have been in business for any appreciable length of time have dealt with almost every conceivable type and kind of public relations problems and situations. The longer the firm has been in business, the more its experience in handling a wide diversity of problems and situations can be taken for granted. A new problem to the client has probably been handled by the counseling firm many times in the past.

Further, the well-established counseling firms have on their roster not only account executives with wide experience but also specialists in educational, media, and financial relations; consumerism; pollution; graphics; photography, and a host of other areas. These specialists are there to serve the account executive (and the client) when the situation calls for their expertise.

FLEXIBILITY

Public relations counseling firms have great flexibility chiefly because they can move their personnel around when there is need. At any one time, as the demand requires, these firms can move staff personnel from old Account X to new Account Y or assign an account executive to take on the supervision of a new account as part of her nominal responsibilities.

Flexibility is possible because large counseling firms have a large pool of talent and personnel and a certain amount of client fluidity. Though the firms pride themselves on maintaining a long and continuing relationship with certain clients, they also have other accounts which they are either losing or are at the end of their contractual relationship. Further, when valuable account personnel find themselves temporarily without assignment they can be absorbed into one of the firm's specialized departments until new accounts come into the firm.

ECONOMY

Counseling firms are not inexpensive entities, but they can prove to be economical in certain circumstances. For example, when an organization has a limited but definite amount of public relations work to be achieved it's more economical to utilize a counseling firm rather than to set up a permanent staff with salaries, equipment and supply needs, adjunct salaried personnel, and overhead costs. When an organization runs into a public relations problem which may last only one or two years, again the counseling firm route would be less expensive than to employ full-time staff. Finally, when an organization has certain special needs—such as the need to reach the financial community or the New York City media outlets—it's more economical to utilize a counseling firm rather than hire a financial relations expert or establish a New York City office.

THE COUNSELING FIRM: DISADVANTAGES

Advantages which counseling firms hold can prove to be dysfunctional under certain circumstances.

The outside counseling firm can generally be more objective than the internal practitioner, but it becomes difficult to maintain such objectivity when the counseling firm has had the same account and dealt with the same people for ten, twenty, or thirty years. At such times the nominal outsider virtually is looked upon as a member of the "inside" team.

The larger the account, the more sizable the yearly fee, and the greater the role of a client in the counselor's roster, the more likelihood of loss of objectivity if such objectivity can lead to loss of the account. Counselors have resigned accounts when their objective advice is constantly ignored by the client. However, such account resignations become increasingly difficult and economically painful when the account is a very large one, the yearly fee is very sizable, and the account represents half of the counselor's total yearly billing.

Getting to know you—as the song went in "The King and I"—is a pleasurable experience when one is governess to the king's children. It becomes more difficult to bring about when one is outside counsel to a large and complex organization which has difficult public relations problems. Clients become very edgy in the early stages of the counselor-client relationships. They desire immediate results, but results are not usually brought about until the counselor has a close and intimate grasp of the client's organization, personnel, policies, practices, and problems. Impatience on the part of the client; the geographical distance between the client and the counselor; internal political maneuvering; innate distrust of strangers; unwillingness to give up one's turf—all these provide stumbling blocks as the counselor seeks to obtain a close and intimate grasp of the client's organization, personnel, policies, practices and problems.

Counseling firms provide Cadillac public relations service, but unfortunately most small and medium-sized organizations can only afford medium-priced cars. The most prestigious counselors are located in New York City, Chicago, and other large cities, which means they have to pay high salaries and rent and incur high overhead costs which in turn have to be reimbursed through fees which, though reasonable, are still high to many would-be clients. Though the would-be, relatively small client may not agree, he is fortunate when he is told at the outset by the large, prestigious counseling firm: "Look, you really can't afford to retain us. Why not try Firm X, they're more in your price range."

INTERNAL-EXTERNAL COMBINATION: ADVANTAGES

As has already been noted, certain advantages accrue to organizations having their own public relations departments, and there are certain other advantages to utilizing a counseling firm. It would seem logical to assume that the combination of the two would provide the best of all possible worlds.

In effect, the combination provides a balance, and when the tandem operation is working well it's hard to fault. The internal staff, for example, may be too close to the problem to be objective, but the counselor is sufficiently removed to provide objectivity. The internal public relations director may be too much a member of the "team" to be critical of a colleague when criticism is justified, but the counselor as an outsider is not so bound by organizational politics. In certain situations it may be more economical to use internal staff to handle certain public relations tasks, and in other situations more economical to use the outside counseling firm.

Another advantage of the combination system, not often mentioned because it is mainly psychological and sub-surface, is that the utilization of an outside counseling firm lends weight and substance to the internal department. When the internal director proposes a certain line of action and is backed up by a reputable counseling firm, the proposal seems to gain stature (even though it's still the same proposal).

INTERNAL-EXTERNAL COMBINATION: DISADVANTAGES

The chief disadvantage of the combination system is that it entails additional expenditures for public relations services. Two may be able to live as cheaply as one in popular mythology, but not in the world of public relations. There's no problem when management recognizes or agrees that the additional expenditures are essential and justified. There's a definite problem, though, when management is uncertain whether the additional expenditures are essential in terms of the end results. Legend has it that a newcomer to wealth thought he might want to buy a yacht so he asked J.P. Morgan how much it cost to maintain his yacht. Whereupon Morgan replied: "If you have to worry about the cost you can't afford a yacht." The same might apply to the cost of public relations counsel; if you have to worry about cost, you probably shouldn't retain outside counsel.

THE INTERNAL PUBLIC RELATIONS PRACTITIONER AND DEPARTMENT

The bulk of public relations practitioners in the United States and Canada work internally within organizations rather than in counseling firms. Sizable numbers are found in government, health, social service, higher education, and similar nonprofit bodies. The largest number of internal practitioners, however, work for business and industrial concerns and for trade and professional associations.

The 1978 *O'Dwyer's Directory of Corporate Communications*—described by its publisher as "the most extensive survey of how America's largest companies and trade associations have defined, organized, and staffed their public relations/communications operations"—listed 2,400 companies and 300 of the largest trade associations. This compares with 1,293 companies listed in the first O'Dwyer directory in 1975 and with 2,000 listed in the 1977 edition.

Entries in the 1978 edition included nearly 1,600 large industrial firms, as ranked by *Fortune* and *Forbes* magazines, and the 50 largest companies as ranked by *Fortune* in each of six categories: commercial banking, life insurance, diversified-financial, retailing, transportation, and utilities. According to the directory, approximately 80 percent of the companies had formal public relations/communications titles or departments and they used a variety of means for the public relations function. The directory noted that about 30 percent of the companies carried out the function under the title "public relations"; 20 percent called it "corporate communications" or "communications"; 8 percent termed it "public affairs"; and another 8 percent called it "public relations/advertising." The remaining companies used a variety of other miscellaneous terms.

No matter what the title given to the public relations function, there was clear evidence in the late seventies that the status of the function was increasing in the eyes of management. In a special report in mid-1977, *Dun's Review* concluded that "the seventies have introduced a new seriousness to public relations activities. For the first time, public relations campaigns deal with major public policy issues and are managed on a businesslike basis. And some public relations practitioners believe that sobriety may impel management to accept public relations as an essential business function." The practitioners themselves echoed this sentiment. In its thirteenth annual survey of the public relations profession, the weekly newsletter *pr reporter* in mid-1977 noted that two-thirds of the practitioners responding to their survey reported that the status of public relations in their organizations was either "higher than ever" or "rising."

The common denominator that binds the internal practitioners—profit and nonprofit—is the fact that they serve in a staff rather than line capacity; that is, they provide advice, counsel, and public relations services to facilitate the major purpose for which the organization exists. This section will deal with the internal practitioner's and department's role and place in the organization; activities and functions; structural alignment; relationships with line, plant, and/or divisional personnel; and budgeting.

ROLE AND PLACE IN THE ORGANIZATION

A generally reliable way to ascertain the role of a particular public relations department is by noting to whom the head of the department reports. If the department head reports to top management—whether the president, executive director, or similar functionary; to the chairman of the board or board of directors; or to an executive vice president—the public relations department is a highly regarded staff function. If the public relations department head reports to someone lower down on the organization scale, the public relations department may have difficulty carrying out effectively all of its key staff functions.

The literature of the field—including this book—places great stress on the advisability of having public relations reports as directly as possible to top management. Why? *Because the important functions of the public relations department are of direct concern to top management and because public relations performs most effectively when in a position to provide input into top management decisions.* Obviously, this can best be done when the line between the head of the department and the operating head of the organization is a direct one.

In practice, however, we find many instances where the line between public relations and top management is far from direct. Here are some reasons why this occurs:

1. As organizations grow in size, so do organizational policies. Within large organizations there is as much jockeying for position as there is in the first 100 yards of the Kentucky Derby.

2. As a relative newcomer to the staff field, public relations has to compete with such veteran staff activities as legal, financial, and personnel. The veterans have been there first, hence they occupy choice positions and aren't too likely to open ranks for the newcomer.

3. In order to maintain their sanity, top operating executives restrict their personal contact to as few subordinates as possible. There's little room at the top of the organizational triangle.

4. Some chief executives don't seek or want public relations advice and counsel because they don't consider it important or they consider themselves to be public relations experts.

5. It takes time and *proven* expertise to gain the confidence of top management. Sometimes the opportunity to provide such proof is not given, sometimes it's given but muffed, and sometimes the practitioner is satisfied with his lower management role.

The public relations practitioner who aspires to the role of a valued staff advisor to top management doesn't overcome the above-cited obstacles by mouthing platitudes about the top management role of public relations. He or she secures the role by earning it and by providing valuable advice and service when the opportunity arises.

The opportunity for increasing the role played by public relations is often dependent on external circumstances affecting the role played by top management. This precept was demonstrated in the late seventies when the top managements of many of the nation's largest business and industrial concerns developed a new activist response to outside pressures and trends. In a 1976 survey of 400 chief executives, the Conference Board reported that *their* public relations activities took up 25 percent to 50 percent of their time, a definite increase over the amount of time devoted by top managements to such activities three to five years previously. Clearly, if the chief executive of an organization finds himself devoting increasing time to public relations activities, this provides the opportunity for his public relations department to provide the kind of expert advice, counsel, and services needed to make such activity most effective.

ACTIVITIES AND FUNCTIONS

Though the activities and functions carried out by internal public relations departments will vary—the degree of variance is most often dependent on the nature of the organization—there are certain key tasks common to most internal public relations departments. Authorities generally agree that the following represent the activities and functions considered most important:

Advice and counsel—public relations advice on organizational policies and actions which have public relations ramifications. Given to both top management and to line departments when situations and problems indicate the need for public relations input and expertise.

Publications—a wide variety of publications designed for publics considered important to the organization. These range anywhere from in-plant daily information sheets to four-color internal-external class magazines.

Promotion and publicity—news-making events and activities, press releases, press conferences, and serving as the prime source of an organization's contact with the media. Includes product, corporate, and general publicity.

Relations with publics—two-way communications with those publics deemed important to the organization. Providing public relations input and expertise in regard to an organization's actions, policies, and procedures which have public relations ramifications.

Institutional advertising—those aspects of an organization's advertising which are institutional in nature. Sometimes this is handled in coordination with the organization's advertising department, and sometimes solely by the public relations department.

Miscellaneous—services which do not fall within the scope of any of the above, but which help provide a full range of public relations activities. This sometimes includes the handling of a speaker's bureau; visitor and tour bureau; corporate donations, scholarship and awards program; special convocations and seminars.

Research—chiefly an intelligence-gathering activity and usually concerned with the measurement and analysis of public opinion. Useful in spotting trends, providing supporting evidence for public relations proposals and programs.

Because of variables outside the control of the public relations department there is no reliable way of gauging how restricted or how extensive will be the activities and functions of a public relations department or staff. The reasons may be *historical* (We've always done it this way); *personal* ("The president knows the importance of public relations and supports it fully," or vice versa); *economical* ("We're so small we can't afford a full-fledged department") or *circumstantial* ("We ran into so many problems with so many publics we needed a department large enough and expert enough to handle them").

The Fulmore Company and the Blasted Company both make widgets, have relatively similar total sales and employee forces, and are privately owned.

However, the Fulmore Company's plant is in the inner city of a large metropolis, while the Blasted Company's plant is in a small town in Iowa. Fulmore employees voted down unionization last year, but at Blasted the employees organized, won recognition for their union, and are now part of a large international union.

The public relations department at Fulmore has a director of public relations; a minority affairs manager; a press relations manager; and an internal-external publication. The public relations department at Blasted has a director of public relations, his assistant, and no publications of any kind.

Last year the Fulmore director of public relations spent a considerable portion of his time working out arrangements for a day care center and trying to convince the city council to reroute one of the city's bus lines past the plant. Blasted's director of public relations spent most of his time last year working with the personnel department in the dispute over unionization.

Thus, two organizations of similar nature and size may have public relations departments whose activities and functions differ considerably. For reasons historical, personal, economical, or circumstantial departments will start out emphasizing the same activities but diverge in their approach as time goes on. This does not mean there is no rhyme nor reason to the handling of public relations activities and functions. On the contrary, it means that the handling of such activities and functions is strongly dependent on the dynamics that control every organization's history and growth. The end result sought—attainment of good will, understanding, and acceptance—will remain constant, but the ways of reaching these objectives through the utilization of public relations will vary.

Outside influences, especially broad societal trends and shifts, also affect public relations activities. As *Dun's Review* pointed out in its analysis of public relations practice at the end of the seventies, the focus of public relations activities in the 1950s was on product publicity, in the 1960s on stockholder and financial relations, and in the 1970s on bolstering industry's credibility on issues ranging from product safety and pollution elimination to capital formation and corporate ethics. To help reach their goals, reported the magazine, public relations practitioners used the following approaches:

- Servicing the chief executive in the arena of public debate
- Serving as adjunct in Washington to a firm's lobbying efforts
- Reemphasizing employee communications
- Developing new ways of using television for public relations purposes
- Emphasizing the use of opinion surveys to measure public relations effectiveness and to assess future trends and emerging public issues

As explained in the previous chapter, managing emerging public policy issues loomed as a crucial corporate activity when this second edition was being written at the end of the seventies. Whether it will become a crucial corporate activity in the 1980s and whether public relations practitioners will play a key role in coping with it depends on many factors. Not the least important of these are the competence, judgment, and skills of those who practice public relations within the corporate structure.

The broad scope of the kinds of competence, judgment, and skills needed to practice corporate public relations in today's society was astutely delineated by Harold Burson when he delivered the Garrett Lecture at the Columbia University Graduate School of Business. Here is how the chairman of Burson-Marsteller sees the role of the public relations practitioner today:

The Early Warner—The public relations executive serves as the sensor of social change. He perceives those rumblings at the heart of society that auger good or ill for his organization. And, after detecting the yearnings and stirrings, he interprets the signals for management.

The Conscience—The second role the public relations man must fulfill is that of corporate conscience. You should not infer from this that public relations people behave in ways more moral and ethical or more in the public interest than executives with different titles. Others may possess the same amount or even more of these attributes than the individual responsible for public relations. But being the professional corporate conscience is not part of the job description of other executives. It is part of the job description of the chief public relations officer.

The Communicator—The third major role of the public relations professional is that of communicator—internally and externally. Internal communications must do more than tell or inform. Its primary function is to bring about understanding. The greater the sensitivity of the issue, the more important the need to communicate effectively. The internal communications program must make available to all affected employees the information that will enable them to understand not only what is happening and what they are expected to do about it, but why the new policies have been adopted. Communicating with the public outside the corporation is ann equally critical undertaking. The problem for the public relations man is to convince the public that the corporation is, indeed, being responsive.

The Monitor—The fourth function of the public relations professional is to serve as corporate monitor. Since public relations is involved with public issues, there is a need for constant monitoring of corporate policies and programs to make sure that they do, indeed, match public expectation. If the programs are not functioning or if they fall short of expectations, it is his job to agitate for new programs and new policies. If he fails to do so, he fails to live up to the requirements of his job.

STRUCTURE

There are no definitive guidelines for structuring an internal public relations department, though as a general rule departments are organized in such a manner as to best facilitate the carrying out of their main activities and functions. Where the department is a small one—such as in the case of a social service organization or a hospital—one or sometimes two professionals will be expected to carry out all departmental tasks. As organizations increase in size, so do internal public relations departments; major industrial organizations, for example, have departments with several hundred professional public relations staffers headed almost invariably by a vice president in charge of public relations or of public relations and advertising.

Departments which consist of more than one or two people are usually organized according to one or more of the following:

Publics—consumer relations; stockholder relations; government relations; employee relations; dealer relations; community relations; etc.

Functions—graphics; press and media relations; special events; institutional advertising; internal communications; product publicity; research.

Geography—eastern division manager; Washington office; New York City office; international.

Divisions—western division; corporate headquarters; plastics division; Texas division.

Combination—parts or all of the above, as in the case of large industrial and business organizations.

Though public relations is a staff function, the department itself is managed as though it were a line unit. Reporting to the head of the department will be a limited number of managers; each manager in turn supervises the activities of staffers with skills and experience in the specific area for which the manager is responsible.

In the charts below—showing typical small, medium-sized, and large public relations departments—we note how the line relationship expands as the department expands. In the small public relations department we find only a public relations director and three managers. In the medium-sized department, however, there's a vice-president of public relations, four managers, and scores of specialists reporting to these managers. In the large department the vice-president has an administrative assistant and a plans board to aid him, six managers, and scores of specialists—some at division and plant localities—to carry out the many assignments and tasks needed to fulfill the function in a large and complex organization.

(1) A small public relations department

(2) A medium-sized public relations department

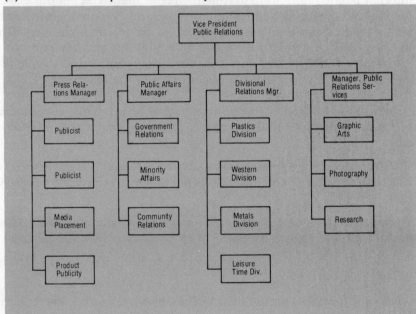

(3) A large public relations department

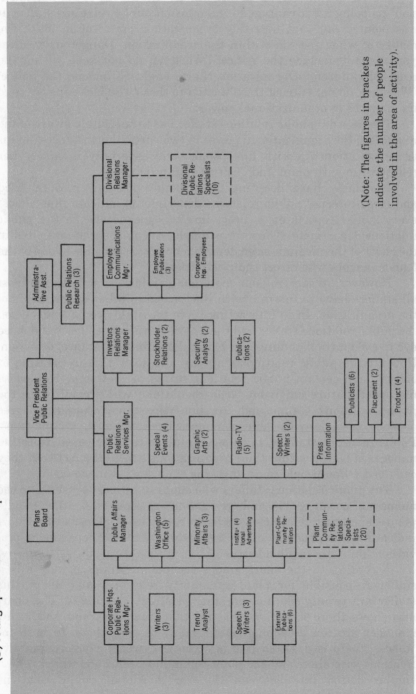

(Note: The figures in brackets indicate the number of people involved in the area of activity).

RELATIONSHIPS WITH LINE, PLANT, AND DIVISION PERSONNEL

Earlier in this chapter in discussing "Knowledge of the Organization" as being an advantage to the internal public relations staffer, it was pointed out that nice tidy organization charts often mask the reality of what goes on within the organization. Dangerous medications usually include the notice: "Warning, do not keep within the reach of children." Organization charts ought to include the notice: "Warning, do not entrust this function to those who lack sensitivity to the nuances of organizational power."

The internal public relations staffer has to be acutely aware of the nuances of the organizational power in two particular instances : in his or her relationship with line people; and especially in his or her relationship with plant and/or divisional people.

The three charts denoting the structure of small, medium-sized and large internal public relations departments indicate that almost every staffer reports on a direct line to someone else in the public relations department. Thus, for example, the staff specialists cited in the chart of the medium-sized department are responsible to one of the four managers who direct their activities.

However, in carrying out these public relations activities, almost all staffers have to interact with line people in other departments of the organization. In so interacting there inevitably come times when the public relations staffer and the line department staffer will not see eye to eye on the handling of a particular situation, stance, or action. How far the public relations staff can and should go in pressing or opting for a certain public relations stance or viewpoint becomes a matter of mature judgment. Who should and will prevail when the public relations staffer and the line department staffer disagree depends on so many variables it's impossible to set down ground rules. Public relations staffers, to be successful, have to be sensitive to the nuances of power within their organizations and to the fact that they can't order line people to do anything they don't want to do.

The public relations staffers who ought to be most sensitive to the nuances of power within an organization are those who either handle plant-community relations or division relations. A glance at the chart indicating the structure of a large public relations department provides a hint why this holds true.

According to the chart, under the public affairs manager is a staffer responsible for plant-community relations, and under this staffer are twenty plant-community relations specialists. The chart also shows there is a divisional relations manager, and under this manager are ten divisional public relations specialists. In both instances, there is a dotted line between the twenty plant-community relations specialists and the plant-community relations staffer, and a similar dotted line between the ten divisional public relations specialists and the divisional relations manager. The specialists in both instances are boxed in by dotted lines.

The English transaction of this chart language means that so far as plant-community and divisional relationships are concerned this organization operates under a *decentralized system.* The dotted lines indicate that the public relations managers responsible for these two public relations staff functions *have only indirect control* over the specialists under them. The plant-community relations specialists are directly controlled by someone in the line organization of the plant-community to which they are assigned. The divisional public relations specialists are also directly controlled by someone in the line organization of the division to which they are assigned.

This arrangement can and often works well but can also lead those involved to ulcer gulch. The public relations staffer most likely to find himself in the direct line of a possible cross-fire between two superiors is the specialist. Further, the same cross-fire can take place if we reverse the situation; that is, if we have ths specialist report directly to the public relations staff manager above him and indirectly to someone in the line organization for whom he or she carries out public relations task.

BUDGETING

Every organization, even the very smallest, utilizes a budget as a means of predetermining what its anticipated costs, income, and profit will be. Within organizations each individual department—such as the public relations department—is asked in advance of the coming fiscal year to provide a financial forecast. As the public relations department is not an income or profit center, its forecast will set forth the expenses it expects to incur in the coming year. This forecast will receive a certain number of checks and changes as it moves up the organizational ladder towards final approval. Once approved, the department's budget is expected to be adhered to carefully. The department which exceeds its approved budget mid-way through the fiscal year is going to run into considerable trouble; in fact, it could well come to a standstill.

Thus, budgeting is more than a game played on a ouija board or the future seen murkily through a clouded crystal ball. Budgeting is the financial plan which the department follows in pursuing and achieving its objectives. When objectives, plans, and programs are carefully worked out in advance, then budgeting is not a particularly difficult task. "Catch-22" becomes commonplace, however, when the unforeseen occurs, because how can one budget in advance for the unforeseen and yet how does one secure the money necessary to meet the unforeseen if one hasn't received budget approval in advance? (As will be soon demonstrated, the wily public relations executive finds answers even to this dilemma.)

In handling his department's budget the public relations executive deals with two essential costs:

Administrative costs—these are costs of salaries of the professionals, secretaries, and clerical workers, plus the benefits they receive and such overhead costs as telephone, space, light, heat, office equipment, and others of a similar nature.

Program costs—these are the costs of carrying out the public relations program, and they include costs for research, publications, special events, films, press conferences and media relations in general, and others of a similar nature.

Program costs, which form the key basis for budget-making, fall within three categories: (1) carry-over or continuous programs; (2) projected or new programs; and (3) the unexpected or contingencies.

Carry-over or Continuous Programs

Unless the head of the public relations department is starting entirely from scratch, he or she has the benefit of past experience in setting up the budget for the coming fiscal year. Further, most departments have programs which are of a continuous and more or less permanent nature, and these will usually form the bulk of the department's total program for the coming year. Budgeting for these continuous programs and activities becomes a matter of projecting expected increases (or decreases in case of a dip in prices) over and above (or below) current costs.

Projected or New Programs

Budgeting for projected or new programs which have been approved for the coming year involves figuring out what the administrative and program costs will be. Arriving at cost figures means researching the expected expenses which will be incurred in carrying out elements of the program, and also figuring out the administrative costs. As a hedge it's also advisable to base cost figures on the "high" side in case prices go up between the time the budget is planned, approval given, and the program put into effect.

Example. Assume the department plans to institute a new external monthly publication commencing with the next fiscal year. To budget for this the department head would need to know the size and press run of the publication; paper and printing costs; and mailing costs. In addition, the department head would have to cover the costs of department staffers and overhead expense. As a hedge, he would be wise to add six percent to the forementioned program costs.

The Unexpected or Contingencies

There are three ways in which a department head can handle the troublesome budget problem of the unexpected or contingencies.

Budget for them—in short, include a specific line item in the budget to take care of the unexpected. Label this item either "contingencies" or "miscellaneous," and keep one's fingers crossed. If the line item is too large, those responsible for approving the budget will probably suggest the line figure be for an approved program item. Most budget approvers have an instinctive dislike for "miscellaneous" line figures, hence it's wise to keep the line figure within reasonable limits.

Use other line items—If management will permit the practice, the department head can use for the unexpected expenses, money which has already been approved but not expended for other line items in the budget. Some managements, recognizing that no one can reasonably be expected to predict the unexpected in advance, will permit the use of unexpended funds from other line items. The problem becomes difficult to solve when this practice is not allowed.

Ask for the funds—when the unexpected or contingencies occur the most direct way to secure money necessary to handle it is to go to management and ask for it. An understanding management knows one can't fight fires without water and one can't handle unexpected developments without money.

THE EXTERNAL PUBLIC RELATIONS COUNSELOR AND COUNSELING FIRM

The closest analogy to the public relations counselor and the public relations counseling firm is the legal counselor and the law firm. Both are retained to give counsel and advice and to provide a variety of services; one does so on public relations matters and the other on legal matters. In both fields there are small, single-member; medium-sized, multi-member; and large counseling firms. In both fields we find counsels situated all over the United States, and in both fields counsels make their living representing a variety of clients.

There are, of course, significant differences between the two. To practice law one needs to be licensed, but you don't need a license to practice public relations. Legal counseling is a much older field of activity, and one finds legal firms—generally single member entities—in even the smallest towns. Public relations counselors are located chiefly in our larger cities because the bulk of their clients are not single individuals but large organizations. Further, the major share of these clients are in business and industry and as their headquarters are generally located in our large cities the public relations counselors find it advisable to locate where the clients and media are.

Small towns and cities are not receptive locations for a public relations counseling firm because there is usually not enough potential business for such a firm. Graduating seniors who have majored in public relations sometimes talk about opening and sometimes do open their own counseling firms in a small town or city, but the chances of succeeding in such a milieu are dim. One might pick up a client or two, but they are generally on the basis of single projects involving a political campaign or the production of print material for a fund drive. To succeed, however, a counseling firm needs clients who are willing to pay for public relations services over a period of time, and such clients are not generally found in small towns or cities.

No one knows for certain how many public relations counseling firms there are in the United States, but the most reliable estimates place the number somewhere between 1,500 and 1,600, ranging in size from one- or two-member operations to the so-called "supermarket" firms with several hundred employees that operate on an international scale. The role and activities, structure, operating methods, and fees of such firms will be discussed in the following section.

ROLE AND ACTIVITIES

Public relations counselors fulfill the same essential role as internal public relations staffers; they provide advice, counsel, and public relations services in order to facilitate the major purpose for which the organization exists. In so doing, the counselor supplies an added dimension in that he is an outsider who may either supplement the insider's staff and work or who is retained because there is no insider staff to carry on public relations tasks.

The Counselors Section of the Public Relations Society of America, comprising more than five hundred consultant firms and individual counselors operating in all areas of the United States and internationally, describes the role of the counselor as follows:

> Public relations consultants work to assess and evaluate opinions held by one or more of the client's publics, and interpret findings to management. The consultant then assists management in formulating plans to change or improve public opinion. Public relations counsel is a partner to management, never a substitute.
>
> The extent and manner of such help provided by the public relations counselor will vary greatly with individual situations. In some cases, the counselor will provide both counsel and will execute a complete action program. In others, the counsel may have a more limited role.
>
> Public relations consultants make their contributions to management and the success of a business endeavor by bringing seasoned experience and specialized skills to the varied tasks of communication. This contribution is strengthened by the consultant's sound judgment in business affairs and by his ability to understand and work sympathetically, constructively and objectively on the problems of the client.
>
> from *Public Relations and Public Relations Counseling,* the Counselors Section, Public Relations Society of America.

Key words and phrases in the above statement are those which stress evaluation of public opinion, guidance and counsel in formulating plans to change or improve public opinion, providing counsel and/or executing a complete action program, bringing seasoned experience and specialized skills to the varied tasks of communication. Without denigrating the role of the internal public relations staffer— in fact, by stressing some of the same activities carried out by the internal staffer—the outside public relations counselor emphasizes his role of complementing the insider's work and provides the added attributes of the outsider.

Note how two large, international counseling firms describe their roles in the following two statements. First, here is how Hill and Knowlton, Inc., the world's largest public relations counseling firm, describes what they do:

We have a strong orientation toward business, industry and the professions.

Though some of us are craftsmen or artists, all of us are business men or women. We think like business people. We act like business people. We strive for businesslike results for our clients—mainly corporations and industry associations.

We program to exploit client opportunities or anticipate problems through specialized departments such as financial relations, federal and state government relations, environmental and consumer affairs, management/employee relations, social issues, and opinion research.

We conduct studies involving business relationships internally and externally, and we stand ready to execute programs resulting from them.

We serve immediate and long-term client needs through our account management teams, working with departments specializing in publicity, marketing services, women's interests, creative writing and graphics, education, and training in radio, television, and public speaking.

We are nearly universal. Hill and Knowlton operates in the United States, Europe, Japan, Southeast Asia and Australia through thirty-six wholly-owned domestic and foreign offices and twenty-six domestic associates. We serve clients in Canada and elsewhere in the world through ten foreign associates with thirty-five offices.

> from an advertisement in the 1978
> edition of *O'Dwyer's Directory Of
> Public Relations Firms*

Second, here is how Ruder & Finn, Inc., sees the role of the public relations consultant:

As we look ahead to the end of the 1970s and the beginning of the 1980s, we recognize that the responsibilities of public communications are becoming increasingly demanding.

Stockholders, customers, employees, students, citizens want to know more than they have in the past about the institutions which have so much influence on the condition of our society. Public confidence in a corporation, university, government agency or professional group cannot be secured by previous norms of performance. Integrity, openness, concern for human welfare, respect for the problems of future generations must be clearly demonstrated if credibility is to be achieved.

Today's manager is learning the value of a continuing alertness to the expectations of his various constituencies. He is also recognizing the importance of opening up entirely new channels of communications to transmit and listen to new kinds of messages.

The task of public relations counsel in these years is to help further the interests which are shared by institutions and their varied audiences. We see ourselves as an external public relations staff, capable of rendering a detached, objective opinion about the value of these alliances. We are a group capable of assisting an internal staff in times of crisis . . . an outside force able to foresee possible pitfalls or dangers inherent in a course of action or point of view. Sometimes the function is one of cutting through the complexities and overlays of ambiguity which surround an issue, of encouraging reflection, of stimulating debate, of presenting the other side of a question. . . .

As a management communications resource to corporations, governments, associations and institutions, Ruder and Finn provides counsel on major policy decisions. We are involved with planning for the future and helping to identify and evaluate the long-term consequences to corporations and institutions of developments within our society. . . .

from *The Ruder & Finn Review,*
1978

Of interest about the two counseling firms' self-description are their points of similarities rather than differences. Both stress the special virtues of outside counsel—objectivity and depth of experience and talents—and the ability to deal with the kinds of tough problems facing all large organizations today. Elaboration of the outside counsel's role is provided in the following description of typical counseling activities compiled by the Counselors Section of the PRSA:

Establishment and definition of short-range and long-range public relations goals.

Support of the marketing program including product or process publicity—news releases, feature articles, case studies, audio visual aids, press, radio, and television coverage.

Stockholder and financial relations—annual, quarterly or interim reports to shareholders, special releases to financial news media, assistance with the annual meeting, liaison with security analysts, investment dealers, and the professional investment community.

Employee and internal communications—company publications, information programs for employees on profits, the economics of industry, quality control, and over-all company operations.

Community relations—counsel on public relations policies at the local plant or branch office level, liaison with local news media, assistance in establishing policies of corporate giving, staging special events such as "open houses" and plant tours.

Government relations—international, federal, state, and local public relations counseling and liaison with agencies or officials whose policies influence and affect the operations of the client.

Evaluation and measurement—analysis of the effectiveness of public relations programs, application and use of budget, and attainment of identifiable objectives.

> from *Public Relations and Public Relations Counseling*, the Counselors Section, Public Relations Society of America, Inc.

The above list, developed before it became important, makes no mention of the role played by public relations counselors in spotting and assisting in the management of emerging public policy issues. The speed with which the counseling firms moved to deal with this new force in American society proves the flexibility of such firms in adapting to changes in corporate goals.

Further, although the list does not make the point directly, a key role of the public relations counsel is in *problem-solving*. Counseling firms build their reputation—and their business—on their ability to *provide counsel on problems in public relations areas and to develop programs to meet these problems*. The firms that have been the most successful are the ones that have proven their ability to handle the most difficult, not the easiest, public relations problems. Illustrative of this point is the following random selection of some fairly typical situations handled by a variety of counseling firms:

- Helping to secure landing rights in the United States for the supersonic transport Concorde

- Communicating management's story during an extended strike

- Guiding a company and its top management through a congressional committee hearing

- Helping a corporation fight a takeover bid and assisting others to develop plans to avert such tender offers

- Preparing chief executives to articulate their views more effectively in public on controversial issues

- Publishing daily reports and monitoring hearings for possible legislative and regulatory changes that affect a client corporation

Crises problems don't happen every day, and counseling firms don't solve them all when they do happen. However, enough of them exist, and the firms have compiled a sufficiently good problem-solving average to justify their role and function on the American public relations scene.

STRUCTURE

Counseling firms are basically organized according to (1) *the size and scope of their operations*, but their structure is also affected by (2) *the accounts they service* and by (3) the *kinds of services they emphasize*.

Items 2 and 3 are not major reasons for the structuring of counseling firms, but they occur often enough to warrant explanation.

At times a counseling firm will handle a major client that requires a specific type of servicing, and if the client is retained a sufficient length of time this service department becomes a feature of the firm's operation. Given sufficient time to prove itself, the service department attracts other clients and becomes a permanent part of the firm's structure.

At one time in its past a major counseling firm had a client that needed assistance in its relationship with the world of education. This need was of sufficient scope to justify the setting up of an education department in the counseling firm. Other clients came along with need of similar assistance, and by this time the education department had proven its worth. The department today is considered one of the most valued service arms of the counseling firm.

Some counseling firms have found it advisable and profitable to concentrate on special areas of public relations competence. Rather than expand into full-service firms they prefer to maintain their limited size, capitalize on their special expertise, and prove thereby that size alone doesn't make for success. A few firms, for example, concentrate on straight counseling and very personalized service, hence keep themselves deliberately small. Others specialize in the nonprofit field or in financial or labor relations.

The major share of the counselors, however, opt for full-servicing, and the distinguishing factor among them is size. As with internal departments, these firms are divided among small, medium-sized, and large firms, size being dependent on the number of clients served.

An indication of the relative size and approximate percentage of counseling firms in each category was revealed in a survey of firms made in 1974 by Walter V. Carty, senior vice president of Hill and Knowlton. Responses from 173 or 40 percent of 445 firms surveyed showed that 61 or 35 percent of the 173 had 6 or less professionals and were termed by Carty as small; 76 or 44 percent had 7 to 25 professionals and were termed medium; and 36 or 21 percent had more than 25 professionals and were termed large. Carty's survey shows that the bulk of the firms are in the small and medium-sized categories.

Carty, of course, set up his own parameters in citing small firms as those with six or less professionals, medium firms as those with seven to twenty-five professionals, and large firms with more than twenty-five professionals, but his survey does give a good indication of the percentage of firms in each of his designated categories. A developing trend at the end of the 1970s was the large-firm purchase of those medium firms with between twenty-five and seventy-five employees. Some of the larger firms continued to rely for full service on so-called "national networks" by setting up cooperative arrangements with smaller regional counseling firms, but others found it more advantageous to buy out other firms and set them up as wholly-owned subsidiaries. The larger firms with multinational clients either set up cooperative arrangements with foreign counseling firms or else purchased them outright.

Jack O'Dwyer, publisher and editor of the weekly newsletter bearing his name, compiles an annual list of the largest United

States-based public relations operations. O'Dwyer's listing, which includes independent counseling firms and advertising agencies with public relations departments, ranks firms by net fee income (which does not include production costs or out-of-pocket expenses) and includes total employees (see Figure 4.1).

The 1979 *O'Dwyer's Directory* listed basic data on 905 firms, including the firms' clients—who totalled 6,000—and a ranking of the 50 largest firms. According to the directory, net fee income of the 50 largest public relations operations jumped 14 percent from $127 million in 1977 to $145 million in 1978, and this represented the second straight year of rapid growth for the leading firms.

A total of 33 firms had 1978 net fee income of more than $1 million, topped by Hill and Knowlton with net fee income of $22,558,248 and by Burson-Marsteller with a net fee income of $22,190,900. The two were almost tied in terms of employees, with Hill and Knowlton having 672 and Burson-Marsteller 670.

The number of employees a firm has is a good indication of its state of business activity. It's therefore instructive to compare the number of employees of the top ten firms on O'Dwyer's 1978 list with the number these same firms had a year earlier. As noted in Figure 4.2, the total employee force of the top ten firms increased from 2,590 in 1977 to 2,876 in 1978, and in individual cases the employee force increased significantly.

Though almost every counseling firm stresses its individual virtues, there is a great deal of similarity in the way firms are structured. In the small firm where there are a limited number of professionals, members of the professional staff serve as both account executives and specialists. Each member of the professional staff is expected to advise and counsel and also to handle the myriad of specialized tasks demanded by the nature of client accounts. This would include writing releases, handling press conferences and media contacts, conducting studies, writing and preparing publications, and similar tasks.

As firms grow in size and take on more accounts and employees the structure of the firm takes on added dimensions. At the top of the structure will be the senior members of the firm: the chairman of the board; president; one or more senior or executive vice presidents. Each senior member of the firm takes under his wing a group of account executives, and usually these will be given vice president status after suitable service with the firm. If an account is large enough, the account executive vice president will have one or more professionals working with him on the account. In a large number of instances account executives will be handling more than one account unless an account is of sufficient substance and billing to warrant the full-time attention of one account executive.

To provide quality control and integration of talents, skills, and judgment, counseling firms add various forms of committees or boards to the above basic structure. Some firms call these a plans board, audit review committee, program review committee, or account performance review committee. Such groups provide a pooling of talents and resources which are called upon either at the onset or during a client relationship, and they serve to assist in planning and programming for

Figure 4.1

50 Largest U.S. Public Relations Operations, Independent and Ad Agency Affiliated
(Based on Documentation Submitted To The
1979 O'Dwyer's Directory of PR Firms)

		1978 Net Fee Income[1]	Total Employees
1.	Hill and Knowlton	$22,558,248	672
2.	Burson-Marsteller*	22,190,900[2]	670
3.	Carl Byoir & Assocs. unit of Foote, Cone & Belding*	12,457,000	408
4.	Ruder & Finn	7,762,000	240
5.	Harshe-Rotman & Druck	4,855,000	165
6.	Daniel J. Edelman	4,682,044	164
7.	Manning, Selvage & Lee	4,671,038	111
8.	Doremus & Dompany*	4,323,391	130
9.	Ketchum, MacLeod & Grove*	3,578,300	116
10.	J. Walter Thompson Company PR Department*	—	200+[3]
11.	Sydney S. Baron & Company	3,450,400	46
12.	Rogers & Cowan	3,246,884[2]	71
13.	The Communications Board	3,221,633	102
14.	Booke and Company	2,933,934	69
15.	Rowland Co., The	—	80
16.	Bozell & Jacobs Public Relations*	2,441,209	75
17.	Robert Marston and Associates	2,437,000	44
18.	Creamer Dickson Basford*	2,063,393	62
19.	ICPR	1,958,740	58
20.	Underwood Jordan Yulish Associates	1,919,000	37
21.	Dudley-Anderson-Yutzy	1,906,234	64
22.	Ayer Public Relations Services*	1,564,000	40
23.	The Rockey Companies	1,540,184	50
24.	Fleishman-Hillard	1,512,530	38
25.	Aaron D. Cushman and Associates	1,510,000	35
26.	Hank Meyer Associates	1,427,000	22
27.	Golin Communications	1,300,000	39
28.	Gibbs & Soell	1,262,195	38
29.	Padilla and Speer	1,209,331	33
30.	Barkin, Herman, Solochek and Paulsen	1,139,039	32
31.	Edward Howard & Company	1,057,650	25
32.	Anthony M. Franco	1,041,000	27
33.	The Softness Group	1,000,000	25
34.	Lobsenz-Stevens	945,000	28
35.	Grey & Davis*	865,000	20
36.	Richard Weiner	760,900	24
37.	Cunningham & Walsh Public Relations*	742,050	22
38.	Kanan, Corbin, Schupak & Aronow	733,215	16
39.	Gross and Associates/Public Relations	728,500	25
40.	Selz, Seabolt & Associates	719,104	26
41.	Public Communications Inc.	711,617	26
42.	Zigman-Joseph-Skeen	695,918	26
43.	Anna M. Rosenberg Associates	676,000	13
44.	Fraser Associates	666,814	9
45.	Woody Kepner Associates	644,317	20
46.	Sontheimer and Co.	638,635	13
47.	P/R Associates	611,270	12
48.	Gray & Rogers*	606,716	17
49.	Bob Thomas & Associates	502,221	16
50.	Paluszek & Leslie Associates	465,000	14

*Advertising agency PR department or partner.
1 For the 12 months ended June 30, 1978, unless otherwise indicated.
2 Year ended Sept. 30, 1978
3 Approximately 90 employees are in U.S. offices

Figure 4.2
Comparison of Employee Force of Top Ten Firms

	Total Employees in 1978	Total Employees in 1977
1. Hill and Knowlton	672	602
2. Burson-Marsteller	670	605
3. Carl Byoir & Associates	408	293
4. Ruder & Finn	240	240
5. Harseh-Rotman & Druck	165	146
6. Daniel J. Edelman	164	148
7. Manning, Selvage & Lee	111	111
8. Doremus & Company	130	118
9. Ketchum, MacLeod & Grove	116	95
10. J. Walter Thompson, PR Department	200+	232
Total	2876	2590

the client or to measure, assess, and improve performance by those primarily responsible for the account. (see Figure 4.3)

Thus, the medium and large counseling firms have the senior executive and account executive tier to handle accounts, and various committees or boards to backstop the primary, front-line team. The third element in the firm's structure is provided by the specialized departments common to all medium-sized and large counseling firms. These departments are not responsible for accounts as such, but are available for use by all account supervisors as the occasion warrants. If the account executive handling Client A, for example, decides to hold a press conference he calls on the publicity department to help him plan and run it. If the account executive for Client B decides to produce a four-color brochure he calls on the graphics department for assistance. At any one time, each specialist department could be providing assistance for a wide variety and number of clients retained by the firm. How many and what kind of specialized departments the counseling firm will have varies with the firm. Figure 4.4 exemplifies the specialized departments of three major firms.

The final structural element of the medium-sized and particularly the large firms is geographical in nature. In order to provide on-the-spot national and international service these firms either establish their own offices in major cities in the United States and abroad or work out arrangements with other U.S. and foreign counseling firms. Through such arrangements the larger firms are able to provide local, regional, national, and international service when such service is needed. Hill and Knowlton, for example, has regional, subsidiary, and affiliate offices in Los Angeles, San Francisco, Dallas, Seattle, and Chicago, and in addition has exclusive reciprocal working agreements with public relations firms throughout the country. To serve clients abroad H & K has offices and facilities in London, Geneva, Paris, Brussels, the Hague, Milan, Rome, Frankfurt, Madrid, and Tokyo, plus affiliates in Australia, Southeast Asia, the Middle East, Latin America, Scandinavia, Austria, Greece, and other major world markets. Ruder & Finn has branches in Chicago, Washington, Dallas,

Figure 4.3

Plans Board at Carl Byoir & Associates meets to discuss new ways to address a client's problem. Byoir also has a Creative Task Force that helps account staffs develop new short-range programs. Membership of the two units comes from among the agency's account executives, specialty department managers, regional office directors, and the firm's executive staff.

Courtesy of Carl Byoir & Associates

Executive group at Ruder & Finn meet in the firm's conference room to discuss a client's problems. Heading the group is David Finn, one of the firm's founders.

Courtesy of Ruder & Finn. Photo by Amy Binder.

Figure 4.4
Specialized Departments of Three Large Counseling Firms

Firm A	Firm B	Firm C
Design	Creative services	Audio visuals
Financial relations	Editorial services	Creative services
Fine arts	Graphic services	Editorial services
Public affairs	Environmental	Government relations
Product publicity	and consumer affairs	Graphics
Research and forecasts	Financial relations	Investor relations
Creative services	Publicity	Media placement
Films	and marketing services	Production
Photographic services	Program research	Research
Public speaking	Research	
Shopping center	and library services	
promotions	State and government	
Television and radio	relations	
	Youth and education	
	Urban affairs	

Houston, Los Angeles, and San Francisco, and in addition operates a network of affiliate public relations companies in major areas of the country. To service its clients abroad, R & F has offices and affiliates in Toronto, London, Australia, Stuttgart, Paris, Israel, Milan, and Tokyo. Similar national and international branch and network affiliations are in effect at Carl Byoir & Associates, Harshe-Rotman & Druck, Burson-Marsteller, Infoplan International, and other large counseling firms.

METHOD OF OPERATION

Clients who retain public relations counsel can be assured hey are buying a service tailored to their measurements. In fact, public relations counseling firms operate very much like custom tailors. When you have a fine suit made to order by a custom tailor you don't go into his shop and pick your suit off the rack. Rather, you'll be greeted by the owner of the shop, have your measurements taken, shown some swatches of material, come to agreement about the kind of suit you want, come back another time or two to try on the suit while it is being made by skilled craftsmen, and finally end up with a garment that meets your objectives and is fit only for your frame.

Counseling firms work in similar fashion. Most counselors do not sell pre-packaged programs, but rather get to work tailoring a program only after the client has agreed to retain counsel. The "swatches" the client is shown are usually testimonials from other clients who have recommended the counseling firm. Most counseling firms do not sign lengthy, formal contracts with their clients but rather have relatively simple letters of agreement and, in some cases, verbal agreements. These outline the general nature of the work to be accomplished, the basic elements of the fee involved, and the stipulation that either party can terminate the contract by giving 30, 60, or 90 days' notice. (A typical letter of agreement is cited at the end of the chapter)

The counselor "measures" his client by conducting a careful and systematic study of the client's organization, policies, strengths and weaknesses, competitive position, needs and problems. The account team responsible for handling the client then gets to work in the back shop setting objectives and goals and developing an overall public relations plan and budget to meet them. Some counseling firms then have the plan and budget reviewed by standing or special review committees within the organization before it is submitted to the client for approval. Once the client approves the program, the account team puts it into effect utilizing the members of the team, senior management, and the specialized departments. Further, in order to insure quality control during the contract period many firms conduct periodic account reviews or "audits" to check on account team performance, measure the program's effectiveness, and make revision when necessary.

The operating procedures described above are illustrated in actual practice by Ruder & Finn and by Carl Byoir & Associates in the brochures published by both firms. In stating "How We Work," Ruder & Finn explain their method of operation as follows:

Ruder & Finn is a firm of generalists and specialists.

It is a flexible organization in which account teams are organized to work on specific programs under the supervision of senior management. Advice and counsel are contributed by a variety of specialists within the firm.

With each new client, public relations points of view and needs are analyzed. The environment in which a corporation or institution operates is examined, audiences are identified and appropriate communications techniques proposed.

A comprehensive program is developed by the account team, detailing both short-term and long-range goals. The program serves as a blueprint for action prepared with time-tables, staff resource allocations and line-by-line budgets.

The firm's partners participate actively in the implementation of client programs. Frequent creative sessions involving staff members with varying skills help spark new ideas and approaches in carrying out different elements of the plan.

The Account Performance Review Committee, comprised of staff specialists and members of senior management, examines client programs at regular intervals to provide fresh ideas to the account team and to ensure that high performance standards are maintained.

. . .

from *The Ruder & Finn Review*

Carl Byoir & Associates describe "The Byoir Systems Approach" as follows (see Figure 4.5 on page 108):

> Just as successful businesses today rely on a complex and orderly organization of systems . . ., public relations, as we view it, must be responsive to similar discipline.
>
> In any area, an efficient and effective system is one in which all elements are related to each other and to stated objectives. And that characterizes the Byoir systems approach to public relations.
>
> In developing a comprehensive program, it is our practice to work in close, daily contact with a client in undertaking a series of methodical steps:
>
> 1. Systematic study and analysis of all elements of the company's present situation, including its management's policies, relationships with various publics, organizational attributes and opportunities, competitive position, outside trends (social, political, environmental) and goals (financial, marketing, social).
> 2. Planning and programming of a system of specific projects and actions, related to each other and to goals determined by the preceding analysis.
> 3. Implementation of the program through systematic application in all communication media to achieve the stated objectives with maximum impact.
> 4. Regular review to measure the program's effectiveness, with revisions to meet any change of conditions or objectives . . .
>
> . . . The most important result of the Byoir systems approach is: (a) to identify a company's true objectives and (b) to help it achieve them by projecting a strong, clear and consistent picture of the company's activities to its various publics. Another result, though less important, is to increase the efficiency of the money spent by the company on its public relations.
>
> from *The Byoir Way*. Reprinted with permission of Carl Byoir & Associates.

FEES

In the early days of public relations counseling there was so little mention of fees in the professional literature one might have concluded that a fee was some sort of social disease not to be mentioned in polite company. In the past decade, on the other hand, there have been so many confusing articles about fees one might just as well concluded that a fee is one of the mysteries of the Far East.

Boiled down to its bare essentials, a fee is what the counselor charges the client in order to cover the following four elements:

1. The cost of servicing the client

2. The counselor's overhead costs

108

Figure 4.5
Typical Systems Flow
Carl Byoir & Associates

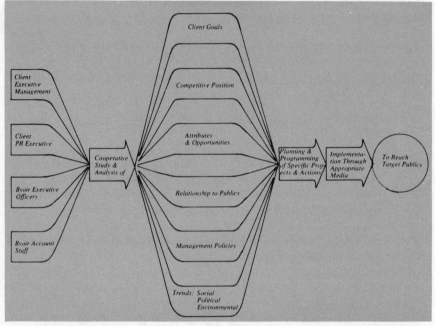

Courtesy of Carl Byoir & Associates

3. The counselor's margin of profit

4. Reimbursement for the counselor's out-of-pocket expenses

To cover the *cost of servicing the client,* the firm's billing system must provide for the salaries of everyone working on the account, and this includes reimbursement for top-level management, professional, and secretarial staff time spent working on the account.

Overhead costs include the client's share of the firm's total overhead items including rent, telephone, heat, lighting, and so on.

As for *profits*, most counseling firms aim for a target gross profit before taxes of 25 percent of gross billings less out-of-pocket costs. Such a 25 percent gross profit will normally produce a net profit of approximately 5 percent to 6 percent after provision is made for annual contribution to employee profit sharing and federal and state income taxes.

Included in out-of-pocket expenses—which are almost always billed separately—are the cost of printing, postage, messenger service, press clippings, radio and television reports, travel, and entertainment expended by the firm in servicing the account.

There are various systems of billing the client, but the most common is to bill monthly in advance to cover an agreed-upon minimum fee or retainer, and to bill at the end of the month for all out-of-pocket and other expenses. It is still common for counseling forms to charge out-of-pocket expenses at cost. However, many firms now apply an additional percentage—usually 15 percent or 17 percent—for handling such out-of-pocket expenses as printing and artwork.

The basic difference in charging systems involves the minimum monthly fee or retainer and charges for staff people who work on the account. In some firms, the monthly retainer is an all-inclusive fee covering not merely the services of the top executives of the firm but also all others servicing the account. In others, the monthly retainer only covers consultation, planning, supervision by the executive officers, and overhead and profit. In addition, the client is also charged for the salaries—usually two and a half to three times their hourly rate—of the account executives and staff working on the account. Work performed on the account by the special services departments are also charged separately on the same basis of two and a half to three times the hourly rate of those in the departments.

A survey of counselors conducted in 1976 by Anthony M. Franco, a Detroit counselor, demonstrated the variety of charging systems in use. A total of 33 percent of the counselors reported they have a straight hourly charge system; 30 percent said they charge a monthly retainer; 25 percent said they charge a retainer plus hours charged for actual staff time spent on the account; and 12 percent reported they charge a service fee, billed monthly, for staff time spent on the account. Of significance is that 90 percent of the larger firms and 61 percent of the smaller firms said they use cost accounting in setting their fees and charges.

The examples that follow explain the fee systems of three counseling firms. Figure 4.6 explains the charging system of Carl Byoir & Associates; Figure 4.7 is a typical letter of agreement used by Harshe-Rotman & Druck; and Figure 4.8 is an explanation of the fee system of Gibbs & Soell.

Figure 4.6
The Byoir Fee System
How We Charge

We offer two plans of payment for our services. Plan A is our basic plan utilizing a retainer fee, and we feel it provides the most satisfactory service to the majority of our clients and the best utilization of the money they wish to spend. Plan B makes our services available without retainer fee by charging for time used on a formula basis.

Plan A

For services in the United States our clients pay us a standard annual fee which covers consultation, planning, supervision by the executive officers, overhead and profit. Contracts are written for a minimum of one year.

All direct expenses incurred in the conduct of the program are billed net to the client.

These expenses that we bill without adding commission or overhead charges include:

Salaries of the account executive and the staff assigned to the account and their payroll taxes.

Travel, telephone and telegraph, entertainment in the client's behalf, stationery, postage and supplies utilized in news releases, photography mats, printing, art work, stenographic service and all other outlays connected with publicity or promotions.

Uniform per diem or hourly charges for work performed by Byoir's special services departments, domestic regional offices and field men.

For the time and counsel of the executive officers of the Byoir organization there is no charge beyond the retainer fee except for travel and communications incident to these services.

At the time a plan of action is being worked out, an estimated annual budget for expenses is agreed upon. Expenses are then projected in advance for each month throughout the year subject to approval of the client. They are based on the activities that we recommend be carried out, and the client has the prerogative of deciding whether or not to undertake recommended projects. There is no contractual obligation on the client's part beyond the fee.

The client is billed monthly for the fee and for expenses incurred during the preceding month.

For programs conducted outside of the United States separate contracts are negotiated, fees and costs depending upon the geographical area and the nature and extent of the projects.

We make no commissions on services or materials purchased for the client's account, and there are no extra charges for overhead. Our only interest in the size of the budget is that it be adequate to implement the programs mutually agreed upon. We pride ourselves upon careful budgeting to obtain for the client the maximum result for every dollar of expense.

Plan B

Under this plan clients pay us a monthly minimum charge on an annual basis. For actual services rendered and manpower used, we bill with a percentage markup of the actual salaries and per diem costs of employees involved. These billings are applied against the monthly minimum with any excess added on. Out-of-pocket expenses are billed as under Plan A with no markup.

Reprinted with permission

Figure 4.7
A Typical Letter of Agreement

HARSHE-ROTMAN & DRUCK INC. PUBLIC RELATIONS

NEW YORK   CHICAGO   LOS ANGELES   MEMPHIS   DALLAS

300 E. 44TH ST.   NEW YORK, N.Y. 10017   PHONE (212) 661-3400   TWX 710-581-5312

Date

Mr. John Doe
President
Client Corporation
000 North Michigan Avenue
Chicago, Illinois 60600

Dear Mr. Doe:

In accordance with our oral understanding, we are submitting the following
as a letter of agreement covering our relationship.

(1) Effective (date), Client Corporation has retained Harshe-Rotman & Druck,
     Inc. as its public relations counsel.

(2) Public relations services to be provided under terms of this agreement
     include: analysis of public relations objectives; creation, planning,
     and execution of programs designed to achieve agreed-upon objectives;
     counseling; preparation of written and other public relations materials;
     representation of Client Corporation to the public, as its agent; and
     periodically reporting on progress and achievements in a manner to be
     mutually agreed upon.

(3) Harshe-Rotman & Druck, Inc. will be paid for its services at the annual
     rate of $_____, billable in equal monthly installments, in advance, of
     $_____. Billing will be on the first day of each month, and payment
     will be due during that month.

(4) The established fee is determined by the nature of the program and
     personnel necessary to implement it. If additional service is required
     beyond that initially contemplated, we will present a budget for this
     for approval in advance. Financial public relations work is not included
     in the fee covered in this agreement.

(5) Services provided by Harshe-Rotman & Druck, Inc. subsidiaries
     or affiliates are not covered by this agreement unless specifically
     included and budgeted for. At any future date such services are
     available on a special project or hourly charge basis.

(6) Out-of-pocket expenses incurred specifically as part of the Client
     Corporation program, which are not part of our overhead, will be
     billed monthly as incurred. Expenses to be billed at our cost include
     communications (telephone, teletype, telegraph, postage); transportation
     and other travel expenses; restaurant and other entertainment charges
     for business meetings and press conferences; fees of specialized
     individuals hired for a Client Corporation project, such as models
     and free lance writers; clipping services, and such other items as are
     not mentioned below. In accordance with normal agency procedures, the
     following expense items will be billed at our cost plus 17.65 per cent
     service charge: printing, typography and artwork; photography, films,
     and recordings. No major expenditures will be incurred without prior
     approval. The expense budget is to be $_____ for the year.

(7) Client Corporation agrees to deposit with Harshe-Rotman & Druck, Inc.
     the sum of $_____ to be used as a revolving credit against which
     approved out-of-pocket disbursements may be paid. Client Corporation
     agrees to reimburse this fund each month in the amount of such out-of-
     pocket charges. Harshe-Rotman & Druck, Inc. agrees to refund promptly
     to Client Corporation any unspent balance remaining therein at the
     completion of this agreement or extension thereof.

Figure 4.7 (Cont.)

(8) It is agreed that Client Corporation shall and does hereby indemnify Harshe-Rotman & Druck, Inc. against any damages, costs, and expenses, including reasonable attorney's fees, incurred in defending against any action arising out of the release of materials previously cleared and approved for and on behalf of Client Corporation, and Client Corporation does hereby expressly hold Harshe-Rotman & Druck, Inc. harmless from any such damages, costs, and expenses.

(9) At any time after the first three months of this agreement, the agreement can be cancelled by either party on 90-days advance notice in writing.

If this statement of our working relationship is agreeable, will you please sign and return one copy to us, keeping one copy for your files.

Cordially,

Harshe-Rotman & Druck Officer
Title

ACCEPTED BY:

CLIENT CORPORATION

Date: _____

Reprinted with permission of Harshe-Rotman & Druck, Inc.

Figure 4.8

GIBBS & SOELL. INC.

126 East 38th Street
New York, N. Y. 10016

FEES -- EXPENSES

Professional Service Fees

Fees for counseling and program implementation are billed either on an hourly or monthly retainer basis. Monthly retainers are agreed upon in advance for services to be rendered. Special projects or services by affiliated agencies in other cities are billed separately.

Hourly Rates

The agency's hourly rate ranges from $50 for the two agency principals to $35 for some production and junior account personnel. The average hourly rate of all account personnel is approximately $39.50.

Manpower

With the exception of secretarial and administrative personnel, the agency assigns 140 billable hours per month to every account person. Time is recorded daily and compiled twice monthly. For fixed fee accounts, the agency provides a quarterly report on time expended -vs- fees billed. For time input accounts, the agency bills the hours expended on the first day following each month of activities.

Expenses

All out-of-pocket expenses incurred on a client's behalf are billed monthly with no markup for handling. These include art, printing, photography, messenger and delivery service, postage, long distance and message unit telephone, release and photo reproduction, enter-tainment of media contacts, travel and local transportation costs. All supplier invoices are paid by the agency and detailed in the monthly invoice. The invoice is due and payable upon receipt.

Documentation

The end result of agency effort, whether it is a corporate press briefing or a feature article placement, is the only true method of evaluating the quality of performance -vs- dollars expended. With each invoice, however, the agency provides a monthly activities report, detailing all work performed during the preceding 30 days.

Reprinted with permission

QUESTIONS AND PROBLEMS FOR DISCUSSION

1. Explain the four basic systems whereby the public relations function is carried out.

2. Explain some major advantages and disadvantages of having public relations handled by an internal staff or department.

3. Explain some major advantages and disadvantages of having public relations handled by a counseling firm.

4. Explain some major advantages and disadvantages of having public relations handled by a combination of an internal department and a counseling firm.

5. In what respect is it possible to ascertain the role of a particular public relations department by noting to whom the head of the department reports?

6. Public relations practitioners contend they can best perform their function when they report directly to top management. What are some of the factors which make this difficult to achieve?

7. What are some key tasks common to most internal public relations departments?

8. Explain the various ways in which public relations departments are structured, and cite an example to illustrate each of these ways.

9. In a large organization where there is a central public relations staff and divisional public relations staff at various locations through the country:

   a. What kinds of problems are involved when divisional public relations staffers report directly to division managers and indirectly to central public relations?

   b. What kinds of problems are involved when divisional public relations staffers report indirectly to division managers and directly to central public relations?

10. Why is it possible for a young lawyer to open his own firm and succeed in a small town or city, but it's usually not possible for a young public relations counselors to do the same?

11. Explain the various ways in which counseling firms are organized.

12. Explain the various ways in which counseling firms charge for their services.

PROJECTS, ASSIGNMENTS, AND MINI-CASES

1. WALTER DRAGO ASSESSES HIS AVAILABILITY: A MINI-CASE FOR DISCUSSION

Upon graduation with a degree in public relations, Walter Drago was given a job as director of public relations of a local manufacturing concern with an employee force of 980 in a city of 54,000. The position was a new one and the president of the firm told Drago that his chief responsibility would be to write, edit, and produce a semimonthly internal publication of six to eight pages. Drago was given to understand there would be other duties, but the nature of these was not clearly defined. As the president explained: "Of course, I expect that you will be doing other public relations things, but we'll see about them as they develop. I'm mainly interested in having you produce a fine publication."

Drago found little difficulty in producing the first issue of the new internal publication because there was a backlog of material available for the initial issue. Commencing with the second and third issues, however, he found that a good deal of his time was taken up not only with writing and editing, but with gathering news and exploring story ideas with various department supervisors. Drago began putting in ten hour days and shortly found himself hard put to meet his publication deadline.

As he reviewed the situation in his own mind two months after starting work as director of public relations, Drago set down on paper some of the activities—other than those connected with the publication—in which he had been engaged. They consisted of the following items:

1. Two days spent helping the personnel manager, at his request, produce four advertisements designed to attract much-needed trained machinists for a government contract project the company had suddenly secured.

2. Serving as a tour guide, at the request of the president, when four Japanese industrialists inspected the plant as part of their two-day trip sponsored by the United States Department of State.

3. At the request of the company's vice-president, writing a story announcing the engagement of his daughter to a member of one of Virginia's most prominent families.

4. Answering a variety of inquiries originally directed to various managers of the company and re-routed by them to Drago for reply. The inquiries came from a college student assigned to write a term paper and requesting detailed information about the company; a long complaint letter from a disgruntled customer; the local newspaper which was planning a special industrial edition

and which asked for a 1,000-word story about the company; and ten members of a sixth grade class, each of whom said he or she was entered in an essay contest entitled, "What Industry Does For Our Community," and would appreciate information about Drago's company.

In reviewing the above activities, Drago found they had substantially interfered with his major responsibility of producing the semimonthly internal publication, but he was not sure what, if anything, he should do about the situation. He asked himself questions such as these:

Am I too available, and is this good or bad?

Which of the things I've been doing are public relations activities?

What should I do at this point?

2. A MATTER OF FEDERAL GUIDELINES: A MINI-CASE FOR DISCUSSION

Joshua Mouldoon is a plant-community relations specialist working for a large national corporation which has its public relations headquarters in Boston. Mouldoon reports indirectly to Walter Cragnolin, manager of plant-community relations for the corporation, but he actually works at the Peachtree Plant of the company in a rural Georgia community. His direct supervisor there is Rip Sturgiss, director of personnel at the plant.

At the yearly meeting in corporation headquarters of all plant-community relations specialists, Mouldoon is brought up to date on recent developments in the company affecting his work. Among other things, Mouldoon and the other specialists are told by Cragnolin that the company is particularly sensitive about meeting new federal non-discrimination guidelines in hiring and promotions. Cragnolin warns the group that since the company has many federal contracts it is imperative that the federal guidelines be met. He says that the plant-community relations specialists are being involved in the compliance matter because the company recognizes that compliance will be a sensitive matter in some plant locations. Finally, he asks that the specialists send him a report in two weeks advising him what they've done since returning to their plants.

On his way back to Georgia, Mouldoon reflects on the fact that although the Peachtree Plant has 400 blacks out of a work force of 1,200, only two are in a supervisory position and 60 percent of them are in the lowest pay category. He also knows that about 40 of the black employees are college graduates.

The day after Mouldoon gets back, Sturgiss calls him into his office and asks him what he's learned at Boston that might be of some help. Mouldoon thereupon advises Sturgiss about Cragnolin's talk about federal guidelines and suggests that something ought to be done at Peachtree to meet them.

"Listen, Josh," says Sturgiss, "we're in the middle of Georgia, not in Boston, Massachusetts. Why don't you start working on that United Way report and just let me take care of the hiring and promotions, right?"

Questions for Discussion

1. What factual data or information about the people or the situation cited above would you like to have before coming to a decision about the case?

2. Assuming you now have the factual data and information you seek, what do you suggest that Mouldoon *say* in response to Sturgiss? What do you suggest he *do*? What do you suggest he say in his report to Cragnolin?

3. GETTING TO KNOW YOU COSTS MONEY: A MINI-CASE FOR DISCUSSION

A medium-sized Pennsylvania firm seeking to expand its market regionally retained a major New York City counseling firm at a monthly retainer fee of $5,000 plus out-of-pocket costs. The letter-of-agreement was signed after two exploratory sessions between the executive head and public relations director of the client and the president and executive vice president of the counseling firm. It was agreed that the $5,000 retainer fee would be paid monthly in advance, and out-of-pocket expenses would be billed at the end of each month in which they were incurred. Each party to the contract had the option of cancelling out by giving thirty days' notice.

On September 1, the first month of the contract, the client PR director was billed for $5000 and subsequently paid the bill. On September 10 he was visited by P. Brigham Broughton, an account executive whom he had briefly met at an exploratory session in New York City. Broughton made another visit on September 20, and on September 30 he sent the client a five-page program proposal.

On October 1, the second month of the contract, the client was billed for $5,000 and subsequently paid the bill. Along with the payment the client's director of public relations sent a detailed letter of response to the five-page program proposal citing serious reservations about some of the proposed ideas and projects. The client also expressed some concern because, as he put it, he hadn't seen any "action on the account," and he suggested that the account executive concentrate his activities at the moment on the handling of an upcoming trade show. On October 14 he received a reply from the counseling firm, signed by Joseph Tenney and notifying him that Broughton was being replaced on the account by Tenney but assuring him of immediate service and attention to the trade show project. A telephone call from the client brought Tenney to the client's headquarters where he spent the day getting acquainted with the client and its director of public relations.

On October 31 the client received a revised proposal from Tenney and Tenney's ideas about handling the trade show. Attached was a bill for $850 for out-of-pocket expenses for the months of September and October. The next day, of course, the client received his retainer bill of $5,000 to cover the month of November. Two days later the client notified the counseling firm it was exercising its thirty-day option and cancelling the contract.

Question for Discussion

What seems to have gone wrong here, could it have been anticipated, and what could have been done to prevent it?

4. A COUNSELOR EXPLAINS HIS FEE SYSTEM: A MINI-EXCERPT FOR DISCUSSION

When counselors write proposal letters—whether they be general letters outlining the counselor's competence or more specific letters outlining the proposed program—they usually end up discussing their fee. Here is how one counseling firm explained the proposal fee:

Our fee for professional services is $48,000 annually. This covers the professional side of the budget in New York City., which would be the center of account activity.

At this point we can only estimate the 'out-of-pocket' part of the budget for such things like publications, travel, telephone calls, photography, and so forth. We're sure we'd be well covered if you would budget $25,000-$30,000 for the year for these items. With the exception of petty cash items, disbursements from this fund would be made only with your prior approval.

We would also like to suggest that you set aside a contingency fund of $10,000 so we could have on-the-spot support for the market-by-market program from our regional offices located in Los Angeles, Washington, Chicago, and Houston and supplemented by our Field Network in the next 25 most important cities in the country. We can use the regional office people as we need them for specific support of special promotions.

Thus, the total cost should be in the neighborhood of $83,000-$88,000 for the year. We would want a firm one-year agreement, cancellage either was thereafter by sixty days notice. . . .

Questions for Discussion

1. In what way does the above fee system protect the counseling firm? The client?

2. If you were the client-to-be, what questions might you have about the above fee system?

3. If you were the counseling firm, what answers would you give to the questions?

RECOMMENDED READING

William Agee, "The Role of Public Relations," *Public Relations Journal,* September, 1978.

Sue H. Bell and Eugene C. Bell, "Public Relations: Functional or Functionary?" *Public Relations Review,* Summer, 1976.

Allen Center, *Public Relations Practices: Case Studies.* Englewood Cliff,s N.J.: Prentice-Hall, 1975.

"Fourteenth Annual Survey of the Profession," *pr reporter*, September 11, 1978.

Anthony M. Franco, "Counseling Fees: It's a Matter of Cost Consciousness," *Public Relations Journal,* August, 1976.

George Hammond, "Meeting Client Expectations," PRSA East Central District Seminar, Detroit, May 16, 1978.

Rex Harlow, "Management, Public Relations, and the Social Sciences," *Public Relations Review*, Summer 1975.

Arlene Hershman, "Public Relations Goes Public," *Dun's Review*, September 1977.

Edward Langley, "The CEO and the Practitioner," *Public Relations Journal*, March 1978.

Philip Lesley, "The Place and Function of the Public Relations Counsel," in *Lesly's Public Relations Handbook,* 2nd ed., ed. Phil Lesly. Englewood Cliffs, N.J.: Prentice-Hall, 1978.

Phyllis S. McGrath, *Managing Corporate External Relations: Changing Perspectives and Responses.* New York: The Conference Board, 1976.

Jim Montgomery, "The Image Makers," *Wall Street Journal,* August 1, 1978.

O'Dwyer's Directory of Corporate Communication. New York: J. R. O'Dwyer Company, 1978.

O'Dwyer's Directory of Public Relations Firms. New York: J. R. O'Dwyer Company, 1978..

Charles H. Prout, "Organization and Function of the Corporate Public Relations Department," in *Lesly's Public Relations Handbook,* 2nd ed., ed. Philip Lesly. Englewood Cliffs, N.J.: Prentice-Hall, 1978.

Public Relations and Public Relations Counseling. New York: Public Relations Society of America.

Irwin Ross, *The Image Merchants,* Garden City, N.Y.: Doubleday, 1959.

Raymond Simon, *Public Relations Management: Cases and Simulations,* 2nd ed. Columbus, Ohio: Grid Publishing, 1977.

PART III
THE DYNAMICS OF
PUBLIC RELATIONS

The basic premise of this book is that public relations is a dynamic process involving a series of interlocking elements constantly interacting with each other. In the preceding chapters we have analyzed the broad nature of public relations and discussed its role as a function of the management ofprofit and nonprofit organizations. We have also described how public relations relates to American society and we have discussed the role and nature of its major practitioners.

The chapters in this section deal with the elements that comprise the dynamics of public relations in action. To achieve a clear understanding of the process, we have treated each key element separately, but the reader should keep in mind that as an action process public relations is constantly in motion. This section, forming as it does the core of the book, describes, discusses, and analyses the following key elements:

PUBLIC OPINION

Prerequisite to all public relations activity is an understanding of the nature of public opinion. Analyzed in detail here are publics, attitudes, morés, stereotypes, opinion formation, and public opinion guideposts.

RESEARCH

In dealing with research we first provide an overview of research by discussing its meaning, benefits, and use in public relations programming. The audit as a research tool is described, and the environmental and social audit is discussed as a means of dealing with emerging public issues. A second chapter concentrates on the application of research techniques, particularly public opinion polling, as a means of aiding the public relations process.

PLANNING AND PROGRAMMING

Though public relations in action is not always an orderly procedure, there are certain steps that should be taken in programming public relations activities. These steps are set forth to provide a blueprint for action.

COMMUNICATION

Communication, which is considered by many to be the basic skill of the most proficient public relations practitioners, is treated in two chapters. The first sets forth some basic elements and theories of communication and then dissects a communication model. The second emphasizes communication techniques, stressing media relations, publicity, and institutional and advocacy advertising.

FEEDBACK: REPORTING, MEASUREMENT, AND EVALUATION

Feedback by means of reporting, measurement, and evaluation closes the public relations circle. This chapter explores the various ways in which the practitioner measures progress and reports the results of public relations activities.

Some words of reminder are called for at this point. Dynamics refers to forces in motion, hence the reminder that the public relations process is not static but continuously in action. At any one time the busy practitioner may be planning a new program while carrying out an old one. The practitioner may also be involved in several steps in the public relations process at the same time. An orderly discussion of the dynamics of public relations should be a first step in understanding the whole as well as its parts.

5

Public Opinion

SCENES FROM A TELEVISION PLAYLET

Scene 1: The plaza in front of the administration building at Roscoe College. Students mill about as a group of thirty faculty members with hand-painted signs walk up and down in front of the main entrance chanting, "No Contract, No Teaching." The signs tell us that the faculty is on strike.

Scene 2: The president's office in the same building. The president is reviewing the situation with her top assistants: the strike is one week old; no classes are being held; students are tossing Frisbees and planning a rally; a score of students have packed up and gone home; the bursar reports a potential loss of $90,000 in tuition income. The president tells the group that the trustees refuse to reopen negotiations. She turns to her director of public relations and asks: "Just how strong is faculty feeling on this strike business? Do you think they're united and behind their leaders? What about the students, how do they feel about all this?"

Scene 3: The office of the director of public relations, a half an hour later. He is being interviewed by the education writer for the local newspaper. The writer asks: "How do the trustees feel about the strike? Will the students support the faculty? How solidified are the teachers?"

Our brief television drama ends with a close-up shot of the director of public relations. He is peering at a little crystal ball that he keeps on his desk, and at the same time he is playing with a ouija board he keeps within easy reach. He looks like a man who hopes to find the answers to the questions about public opinion that have been directed at him by the president and the education writer, but he knows that neither the crystal ball nor the ouija board will be of much help. He also knows that he doesn't have the time—given the situation—to conduct a scientific poll of public opinion. Finally, and most important, he's aware that because he's the director of public relations the president expects him to know the state of student and faculty opinion. It's obvious to the director, as it should be to those reading this book, that his ability to assess public opinion is directly linked to his ability to function as a public relations practitioner.

Exactly how important is public opinion to public relations practice? Socrates would probably answer that question with some questions of his own: How important are the lungs to breathing? How important are the ears to hearing? How important is the nose to smelling?

The answers to the questions are self-evident. Without an understanding of the nature of public opinion and how it operates there can be no meaningful public relations practice. It's with good reason that the word "public" is an integral part of both terms; in the one case we are dealing with the *opinions* of the public and in the other we are dealing with *relations* with the public. Thus the tie that binds the two is the public, and it's the public's opinion with which the practitioner is concerned when he or she plans and carries out a public relations program. The details of the program, in turn, depend on the specific concern the practitioner has with public opinion. Is he concerned merely about the *essence* of public opinion? Does he want simply to *measure* public opinion? Does he want to *create* favorable public opinion? Does he want to *neutralize* unfavorable public opinion? These are some of the basic questions which have to be faced and answered by the practitioner.

DIFFERING PERSPECTIVES

Dealing with questions and answers to public opinion first involves recognition of the relative place of public relations as compared to other, more firmly established, fields of study, standing, and research. Public relations practitioners are relative newcomers to the study of public opinion and hence have relied on the findings of other disciplines, primarily political science, sociology, and psychology. As one goes through the literature of the three fields he discovers studies dealing with the formulation of basic theories of public opinion as well as empirical studies describing research in public opinion formulation. Some authorities have gone so far as to formulate so-called rules of public opinion, but a close analysis of these "rules" reveals that they hold true only under certain circumstances. Unfortunately, these circumstances have a disconcerting tendency to occur only once in their pristine state and are not much help.

Analysis of the theories of public opinion and the empirical studies also reveals that there is not a great deal of agreement among the political scientist, the sociologist, and the psychologist when it comes to public opinion. This is due partly to the fact that the authorities in each of the three fields approach public opinion from the unique perspective of their specialities. The political scientist is primarily concerned with public opinion in the framework of politics and governance; the sociologist's primary concern is in the framework of society;

and the psychologist approaches public opinion in the framework of the individual. There is nothing wrong with each of these concerns—but the fact remains that each perceives only part of the picture.

There's a final significant difference between the approach to public opinion taken by the public relations practitioner and that taken by the political scientist, the sociologist, and the psychologist. The practitioner is concerned with *practical* aspects of public opinion whereas the other three are concerned chiefly with theoretical and academic aspects. In no way should we consider theory and academic perspectives to be inferior; on the contrary, it's from them that most of what is practical in today's world is derived.

If the practitioner were dealing with tangible objects his search for answers would not be so difficult. Public opinion, however, is not a tangible object. We know that it exists, we know that it's all-powerful in a democratic society, but our problem is in defining it, measuring it, trying to influence it, and above all, understanding it. This chapter aims to examine these problematic aspects of public opinion and to relate them to the practice of public relations. As a preliminary warm-up for this examination the student should consider the questions which follow and discuss them in dialogue with his fellow classmates.

1. Under what circumstances would the public relations practitioner be concerned merely about the *essence* of public opinion? About the *measurement* of public opinion? About wanting to create *favorable* public opinion? About wanting to *neutralize* unfavorable public opinion?

2. How would you rate the four public opinion goals or concerns in terms of their degree of difficulty of achievement? Justify your selections.

3. Why do you think it's so difficult to *define* public opinion? To *measure* public opinion? To *influence* public opinion? To *understand* public opinion?

4. Can you cite any organization which has little or no need to be concerned about public opinion? Justify your selection.

5. How do you think students feel about the college in which you are enrolled? How about the alumni? How about the public at large? What's the reason(s) for the similarities or differences in these views? Justify your conclusions.

6. How well do you think you are able to judge the opinions of your classmates about the kind of job the president of the United States is doing? A little experiment should give you the answer.

   In advance of actual measurement, jot down on a piece of paper your assessment of the percentage of the class who you think judge the president as doing an excellent, good, fair or poor job. The instructor will now have each of you jot down your own judgment of the job the president is doing, and the total percentages will be tabulated. Now compare your prior estimate with the actual percentages.

7. In his editorials dealing with public issues the editor of a daily newspaper in a city of 125,000 invariably concluded with the remark that "rank and file Americans" or "rank and file residents" felt thus-and-thus about the particular issue. What's your reaction to this usage of public opinion?

THE PUBLIC

From Roman times to the present the phrase *vox populi* has been used as a way of saying that the people have spoken. The Romans used the phrase to mean "the voice of the people," and today *the public* is used to mean anything from the entire United States population to an alderman's ward constituency. Two parties in a conflict, taking opposite sides of an issue, frequently base their claim to legitimacy on the allegation they are doing so because this is what the public wants. No term should be used so loosely, and certainly not by public relations practitioners who claim expertise in the area of public opinion. Clarification rather than obfuscation should be the goal of those who deal with the opinions of people, and one way to achieve such clarification is to recognize the following key ramifications about the word *public*:

1. There is no such entity as "the public" because "the public" is a myth.

2. There is not one, but many publics.

3. Issues create their own publics.

4. The nature of an organization usually dictates its publics.

"THE PUBLIC" IS A MYTH

Politicians, news and editorial writers, columnists, and others refer constantly to the mass audience as *the public*, but they do so because necessity is the mother of invention. Plainly stated, there is no such entity as the public, even though the term seems to suit the needs of those who use it indiscriminately. Sometimes they do so because of ignorance. More often, they do so because it's convenient and helpful to contend that their point of view has the support of the American public. Reality, however, tells us that the so-called American public is made up of innumerable subpublics, some of whom may support organizations strongly, some weakly, and some not at all. Two examples should suffice to demonstrate misuse of the term:

> The American public firmly believes that our military establishment should be second to no one. I support the new super carrier because the public demands that we be Number One.
>
> —A United States Senator

We are building this nuclear plant because the American public demands we meet the energy challenge and because the American public insists that we be less dependent on foreign oil imports.

—Utility executive

The important point to keep in mind is that only in exceptional circumstances can one speak of an American public united in its views on an issue. For the most part, the American public is amorphous, transitory, ever-changing, and virtually infinite in numbers. To lump together 213 million people under the umbrella term *the public* is to misconstrue and oversimplify the term.

THERE IS NOT ONE, BUT MANY PUBLICS

All of us, at one and the same time, belong to an almost infinite number of publics. At this very moment you may well be a Protestant, union member, Elk, youthful, a voter, football fan, bird-watcher, and a Democrat. Or you may be a Catholic, an entrepreneur, Knights of Columbus member, chess player, hunter, and a Republican. If you want to complicate matters, consider that you and your neighbor are Protestants but you are a Methodist who goes to church every Sunday and your neighbor is a Congregationalist who only attends church on Easter Sunday. First and foremost you're Methodist and Congregationalist; second, regular and irregular church-goers; and third, members of that vast body of people who call themselves Protestants.

For the sake of convenience, practitioners prefer to deal with publics in broad, general terms by referring to the employee, stockholder, customer, and community publics. Harwood Childs, however, warns against the danger of such easy generalizations. He points out that if you want to analyze a firm's actions on employees you should examine not merely broad publics but sub-publics. In seeking to predict employee reactions to company actions it's important to distinguish between employees who belong to unions and those who don't; employees who have been in the work force for decades and those who have but recently been employed; employees who hold two jobs and those who hold but one.

Further, to be successful in reaching people one must be cognizant of the fact that *the multiplicity of publics to which all of belong can cause internal conflicts of loyalties not easy to resolve*. Examples of those who face loyalty conflicts due to multi-public membership are the professor who believes firmly in independence of mind and in professionalism and yet joins with his colleagues in a union; the young Catholic mother who is an ardent believer in feminist rights, including the right to abortion; the son of a Marine colonel who is torn between duty to country and fighting in an undeclared war which he believes is immoral. Sorting out primary loyalties for such individuals becomes a soul-wrenching experience, and should teach all of us to heed the road sign which reads: warning, publics ahead, proceed with all due caution.

That road sign should serve as a warning that the large public is always a combination of smaller publics, that individuals usually belong to different publics simultaneously, and that one of the most difficult tasks in the world is to figure out which public has an individual's loyalties when two or more of his publics are in a collision course.

ISSUES CREATE THEIR OWN PUBLICS

Though members of a public are usually not in direct physical contact with each other, there are times and circumstances when such members get together to form an audience. There are also times when a loosely organized public is activated by an issue which is of prime importance to those making up said public. At such a time, when an issue activates a public, the effectiveness of such a public as an action group becomes a matter of real concern to the public relations practitioner. Individuals who previously had an unstructured relationship to each other may join together or tie themselves to other groups with a more institutionalized structure. The result is a public which has found its voice to make its weight felt, and in such instances attention must be paid.

Issues which are perceived by members of a public to be of key importance to them are the ones which trigger a public to coalesce into an action group. Unfortunately, there is no magic means whereby the practitioner can predict with certitude that such-and-such issue will activate a hitherto nascent public to become an active public. Nor is there any magic method of predicting the degree of intensity of feelings which an issue can arouse in a particular public. The astute practitioner:

1. Keeps careful watch as issues arise.

2. Tries to anticipate which individuals in society are affected by issues.

3. Notes whether these individuals are either in an organized grouping or are in the process of becoming an organized grouping.

4. Takes steps to deal with statements or actions that he or she anticipates to be forthcoming from that particular public.

5. Provides answers to questions that people may have but that they may often not express.

THE NATURE OF AN ORGANIZATION USUALLY DICTATES ITS PUBLICS

Probably because he didn't have to deal with the public, Thomas Carlyle was able to be rather cavalier in dismissing the public as "an old woman"—his words, not this author's—who should be left alone to "maunder and mumble." Organizations in today's society can't afford Carlyle's suggested treament, but instead they need to view their publics carefully. The nature of an organization usually dictates its publics, but there are distinctions that have to be made by each organization. Five major distinctions, applied to the nature of organizations and their publics, are as follows:

1. Organizations with similar goals and purposes usually have similar publics.

2. The unique nature of an organization can often make its publics different from organizations that seem similar to it.

3. There's a pecking order among publics as well as among chickens.

4. Publics shift as organizations shift.

5. Latent publics have to be handled with special care.

Organizations with similar goals and purposes usually have similar publics. All colleges exist for the purpose of educating students, hence the student public is a basic college public. All appliance manufacturers exist by selling their products to consumers, hence the consumer public is a basic appliance manufacturer public. Every daily newspaper in the country exists by attracting readers and advertisers, hence the reading and advertising publics are basic publics for daily newspapers. However . . .

The unique nature of an organization can often make its publics different from organizations which seem similar to it. Yes, it's true that all colleges exist for the purpose of educating students, but some colleges only admit women, some only admit men, some admit both men and women, some draw students from their immediate area, and some draw students from the entire country. In each case, though all colleges exist for the purpose of educating students, the college in question may have a public vastly different from the others.

There's a pecking order among publics as well as among chickens. All men and women are created equal, but some publics are much more important than others. Pin-pointing publics in order of importance is a crucial matter for the public relations practitioner, and shouldn't be handled routinely. Consider, for example, a 100-year-old, private university which has an alumni body numbering more than 100,000 and compare it with a 10-year-old public college which has an alumni body numbering less than 5,000. Obviously, the first-named institution's alumni are a public more important to it than the alumni of the second-named institution.

Keep in mind that publics shift as organizations change. Because we live in a fast-changing world organizations are in a state of flux. Today's small private college is liable to become a part of a state university tomorrow. Today's manufacturer of widgets is liable to become a part of some vast conglomerate tomorrow. Yesterday's March of Dimes to combat infantile paralysis is today devoted to combating birth defects, and who can tell what will need combating tomorrow? As organizations change in nature and purpose, so do their publics change; an outdated list of publics is about as worthless as last year's calendar.

Beware the latent public. Keeping track of such major publics as customers, employees, and the like is generally not a difficult task. Remember, however, that there are publics within publics and many of these are hidden from view and in a latent state. As issues arise which are important to them, these latent publics begin to stir, to write letters to editors, to become organized, and to surface and cause innumerable problems if their presence is not detected beforehand and steps taken to handle them. Many a school budget has been defeated because school administrators and boards of education didn't realize until too late that a pocket of dissatisfied residents would turn out in force when the budget came up for approval. The time to treat a latent public is before, not after it becomes an overt one.

The need to keep a careful watch on latent publics is exemplified in the story below:

In the summer of 1978 there were clear indications in many states and communities that taxpayers, especially property owners, were unhappy with rising taxes at all levels of government. A striking illustration of taxpayer unhappiness was the passage in California of Proposition 13 which placed a strict limit on property taxes.

As it did every year, early that summer the Board of Education of the Darwin Central School District in a midwestern state mailed to Darwin taxpayers a four-page flyer explaining the school budget for the coming year and bearing a projected tax increase of $4.70 per thousand dollars of assessed valuation. Also, as usual, two weeks before the vote the board held a public hearing on the new school budget. A total of 30 residents—in a district of 22,000 households—showed up for the hearing and asked a few desultory questions which were easily answered by board members. Satisifed that there was no strong opposition to the budget, the board did nothing more to publicize the budget or "sell" it to the voters.

Because there were no letters to the editor in the local daily and no public indication of voter sentiment, the board was much surprised when the residents turned down the budget by a vote of 1,200 against and 1,180 in favor of passage. Because the vote was so close and believing more yes voters would turn out for a second vote, the board submitted the same budget to a second vote to take place two weeks later. Again, the board did nothing to publicize or "sell" the budget. There was a larger turnout this time, but this time 1,532 voted against the budget and 1,120 voted for it.

What lessons do we learn from this illustration? First, you can't take chances when dealing with a gut economic issue. Second, in school budget voting there's always a subpublic of older residents with no school-age children who are ready to vote no if the budget increases their living costs. Third, simply because sentiment is nascent and subsurface doesn't mean it is nonexistent. Fourth, it's the board's responsibility to take positive steps to get out the vote of those most likely to support the budget—in this case those parents with school-age children.

NO MAN'S LAND: THE GAP BETWEEN PUBLIC AND OPINION

Lying somewhere between "public" and "opinion" is a vast no man's land made up of morés, stereotypes, and attitudes. Virtually unexplored except by the social scientists, this land is an important link between public and opinion. Anyone who hopes to understand public opinion must first understand the morés, stereotypes, and attitudes which exist between and link public and opinion.

Morés (more-rays) are *deep-rooted, customary ways of looking at and doing things in a society*. They are persistent, nonreflective, deeply ingrained, and taken for granted as being the ground rules of daily existence within a society.

Morés, which have also been termed folkways, are compelling and rigid in nature, accepted as right, true, proper, and necessary for the proper functioning of the society in which they exist. Unfortunately for the public relations practitioner, morés and folkways are largely *unwritten and are endemic to the society in which they exist.*

The student reading the above two paragraphs is undoubtedly less worried about the practitioner than about the problem of finding out about a term which describes the unwritten ways of doing things in a society. A few examples may light up the darkness:

Whistling in America is a means of indicating either contentment (e.g., while one works) or fear (e.g., while walking past a cemetery on a dark night). Whistling in Europe is a way of showing disapproval at a soccer match.

When Erskin Caldwell's "Tobacco Road" opened on Broadway New Yorkers were shocked when one of the male characters in the play strolled out of his shack, turned his back to the audience, and urinated. New Yorkers, used to the amenities of urban life, didn't realize they were observing a Deep South rural moré in action.

Circa John F. Kennedy an all-persuasive moré of American political life was that no Catholic could become president of the United States. That particular moré became extinct with Kennedy's election to the highest office in the land.

The last example illustrates two important aspects of morés. One is that morés are persistent and deeply ingrained. The second is that morés are subject to change, though the change is as slow-moving as the advance of a glacier. Because morés are so persistent and nonreflective, it is difficult to resist or try to change them. A person or organization runs grave risks when taking a stand or action which is contrary to public morés, hence the necessity to know when one is dealing with public morés or with public opinion.

The morés of Puritan America regarding sex were light years removed from general American sexual morés of today. At the same time, however, in certain sections of the country views about sex are still not far removed from those of Puritan America, and it's imperative to understand how strongly and to what degree morés govern thought and action in rural and urban America, in Appalachia, in the Northeast, and throughout the entire country.

Stereotypes are conventional labels or preconceptions which are acquired from the culture. Psychologist William Albig reminds us that stereotypes may be counterfeits of reality, but they are also psychological realities. Stereotypes, like morés, are generally unwritten ways of viewing things and people, but they can become embellished through the written word.

The concept of stereotypes was first enunciated by Walter Lippmann in his 1922 book, *Public Opinion,* in which he described the world of the 1920s as one that was "out of sight, out of mind." He meant that for most Americans of that period the world was that of Sinclair Lewis's Sauk Centre, Minnesota, or of Chicago, Illinois, but certainly not that of Germany, Russia, Japan, or China. Not only was the world far removed to the average American, said Lippmann, but the average American was too busy with his own life to pay much attention to what was going on thousands of miles away.

Lippmann further noted that there were major factors that limited access to the facts about the wider world beyond America, and he cited them as follows:

1. Artificial censorship

2. The limitations of social contact

3. The limited amount of time available in each day for paying attention to public affairs

4. Distortions arising because events have to be compressed into very short messages

5. The difficulty of making a small vocabulary express a complicated world

6. The fear of facing those facts that would seem to threaten the established routine of people's lives

Despite these barriers to a true understanding of the wider world, Lippmann said, the American nonetheless made for himself "a trustworthy picture inside his head of the world beyond his reach," and all too often this picture was a stereotype, or what Albig referred to as a "counterfeit of reality."

Do we still stereotype our vision of the world when today television brings the world right into our living room? To a disquieting extent, the answer is yes. Some examples to prove the point:

Many Americans still see the Russians as uneducated peasants (until we learn they've put up as many satellites into the sky as we have).

Many American manufacturers believed there was nothing like Yankee manufacturing ingenuity (until the Japanese and German auto makers entered the American market and made a huge dent in it).

Many Americans considered American military might to be invincible (until we fought an undeclared war in Vietnam and 56,000 of us died).

One might logically conclude that the world of today is very much unlike that of the 1920s when Lippmann listed six major factors that limit access to the facts about the wider world beyond America. After all, we now have radio and television, more social contact and free time, and we are now better educated and supposedly have better vocabularies. But we still manage to hang on to our stereotype impressions and ideas of the wider world beyond America and within America as well. A study conducted in the late 1970s by the Council on Interracial Books for Children proves this point all too well:

Reviewing 75 widely available children's picture books, the Council reported that in these books American Indians are still depicted today as fierce, violent, tomahawk-brandishing fancy dancers.

Among the numerous misconceptions, said the Council, are beliefs that "Indians always wear feathers and headdresses, frequently brandish tomahawks, live in teepees, are fierce and violent, lurk behind trees, spend much time dancing on one leg and live in a mystical past."

The Council concluded that the main perception that non-Indian children gather from their picture books dehumanizes the Indian people, degrades their culture and distorts non-Indian children's perceptions of Native Americans.

"In an effort to debunk the stereotypes," said the Associated Press in its story about the study, "the non-profit Council has produced a film strip and teachers' handbook for non-Indian elementary school children."

The lesson is all too clear: we have to understand the extent of stereotyped thinking that exists today, and we ought to do what we can to ensure that the pictures in people's heads conform to reality. As communicators, however, we also have to understand the difficulty in seeking to deal with such thinking. Producing a filmstrip and a teacher's handbook is one way of combatting children's stereotyped views of the American Indian, but they're small slingshot stones to toss at the Goliath of stereotyping.

Attitudes are the *predispositions, thoughts, or feelings of people toward issues that have not yet materialized in a specific way.* Attitudes have been described as the sum-total of one's feelings, inclinations, notions, ideas, fears, and convictions about any specific topic or issue. As such, they represent a tendency to act in a particular manner. They form what Daniel Katz terms the raw material out of which public opinion develops, and hence understanding the nature of individual and group attitudes is critical to understanding the nature of public opinion.

Attitudes and opinion are so closely intertwined it's often impossible to ascertain any distinction between the two terms. It is generally agreed that, with certain exceptions, opinion is usually consistent with attitude. (One such exception, for example, would be the verbal response or opinion given by a bigoted person to a racial question; under social pressures, such a person may well state an opinion which is inconsistent with his or her attitude). Because of the close connection between attitude and opinion a fuller discussion of the roots of attitude and opinion will be held in abeyance until later in this chapter.

OPINION

Opinion is to attitude what the hand is to the arm. One is an extension of the other.

Simply defined, an opinion is *an expression of attitude*. Some authorities contend that opinion is a *verbal* expression of attitude, and although verbal means are the most common way of demonstrating expression, a person can express opinion by nonverbal means. A grimace or a gesture may often express better than words the opinion held by a person. This nonverbal method of expression must, however, be capable of being readily translated into words.

> One of history's most famous examples of a nonverbal expression of attitude which showed opinion is that of Winston Churchill's "V for Victory" expression of determination and faith in England's ability to defeat Hitler Germany.

> A less famous but nonetheless clear indication of a nonverbal expression of attitude which showed opinion was given by Governor Nelson Rockefeller (N.Y.) in mid-1970 when he was heckled by some young people in the midst of a speech he was giving. Rockefeller's response was to hold high his right middle finger. The picture made front pages all over the country, and there was no need for a caption to make clear Rockefeller's response to the heckling.

The hand serves in many ways to indicate nonverbal expression. The raised thumb indicates approval or victory; the thumb held down indicates disapproval. The forefinger held high indicates "We're Number One," the clenched fist indicates power to us, and the nose held between thumb and index finger means something is rotten in the state of Denmark (or wherever one happens to be).

Whether verbal or nonverbal, *an opinion is always the opinion of a person, not a group.* By expressing his or her opinion a person may *suggest* that he or she is speaking for a group, but it's misleading to think in terms of a "group mind," because public opinion always refers to a collection of individual opinions. This point will be explained in more detail after a brief analysis of the dimensions of an opinion.

The characteristics or dimensions most commonly used to describe an opinion are *direction, intensity, stability,* and *latency.* Each of these is discussed in the sections that follow.

DIRECTION

Describing an opinion in terms of its direction means to state whether a person approves or disapproves of something. In the pioneer days of opinion measurement this approval-disapproval was indicated via a pro-con dichotomy, but as techniques of measurement became refined the simple pro-con description has been complemented by finer distinctions of opinion.

Simple pro-con, for-against, yes-no measurements of direction all too often conceal wide gradations of opinion. Asking a woman whether she is for or against the death penalty could easily produce statistics which are misleading. A person may be for the death penalty in certain circumstances, but not under other circumstances. A simple for-against or pro-con expression of opinion would obviously provide an insufficient measurement of the direction of opinion about the death penalty.

Scaling, which means providing a choice ranging from one extreme to the opposite extreme, is used to set forth more accurately the direction of opinion. The opinion of an individual can be located at one of many points along a scale, and thus sets forth a better estimate of public opinion direction than was possible through the earlier pro-con method.

> V. O. Key cites the difference between the pro-con and the scaling methods of measuring direction in the following example: "A division of people who support and oppose government ownership of industry does not provide a useful indication of the nature of public opinion on the question of government policy toward economic activity. Views on economic policy may be arranged along a scale from the extreme left to the extreme right. The opinion of an individual may be located at any one of many points along such a scale. One person may favor governmental ownership of all the means of production; another may be satisfied with a large dose of governmental regulation; still another may prefer only the most limited control of the economy; and others may wish to abolish whatever controls exist."

National opinion polls utilize both simple pro-con measurements of direction and scaling to provide gradations of direction. First, here's an example of a question asking for a simple pro-con response:

> Now I'd like you to tell me if you agree or disagree with the following statement: The government should help a poor woman with her medical bills if she wants an abortion.
>
> from CBS/*New York Times*, 1978

Second, here's an example of a question providing for a scaled response:

There's been a lot of discussion about the way morals and attitudes about sex are changing in this country. If a man and a woman have sex relations before marriage, do you think it is always wrong, almost always wrong, wrong only sometimes, or not wrong at all?

> from National Opinion Research
> Center, General Social Surveys,
> 1972, 1975, 1977

Finally, here are two different ways—simple pro-con and scaled—of asking the public to assess the way the president of the United States is doing his job:

Do you approve or disapprove of the way Carter is handling his job as president?

> from American Institute of Public
> Opinion (Gallup) 1978

How would you rate the job President Carter is doing as president— excellent, pretty good, only fair, or poor?

> from Louis Harris and Associates,
> 1978

(Note: Although the problem of devising public opinion poll questions will be explored in the next chapter, it would be of some value at this point to analyze the wording of the four questions. Do they seem free from bias? Are they clear? Can you think of an alternate way of wording the questions?)

INTENSITY

The intensity of opinion describes the *strength of feeling* existing in that opinion. Certain issues may induce strong feelings of opinion among people while other issues may be of little importance. In dealing with people's opinions the public relations practitioner would be wise to know which issues arouse or are likely to arouse opinions of high intensity and which arouse or are likely to arouse opinions of low intensity.

Political Scientist Key suggests that we use common sense in seeking to distinguish between high and low intensity issues. This may well be too generalized a guideline for those who seek a more scientific way of prejudging the expected intensity of opinion about issues, but it makes sense to anyone who keeps abreast of social, economic and political issues in the country.

> In the late-seventies issues which aroused a high intensity of opinion were abortion; busing; foreign policy as it applied to the Mid-East and Southeast Asia; and inflation. Issues which aroused a low intensity of opinion were foreign policy as applied to Afghanistan, South America and Europe; civil rights; and boxing.

The same strictures apply to the the measurement of intensity of opinion as apply to the measurement of the direction of opinion.

Scaling, rather than the simple pro-con method of measurement, provides distinctions which ensure a more accurate assessment of opinion. Scaling indicates not merely the low and high of intensity of opinion on an issue, but gradations in between.

During the debate in the late 1970s over the Panama Canal treaty between the United States and Panama, the national opinion polls ran numerous questions at periodic intervals to measure various dimensions of opinion. One such dimension was intensity of feeling about the treaty, and the CBS News/*New York Times* poll in October 1977 used this question to measure the intensity of feeling of those who said they either approved or disapproved of the treaty:

> Do you feel strongly enough about the way your senators vote on the Panama Canal treaty to change your vote because of it when they run again?

Commenting on opinion about the treaty, Professor Everett Ladd stressed the importance of the intensity factor in this commentary: "The surveys . . . indicate that the more informed Americans are about the treaties, the more likely they are to favor them. But if better informed Americans are generally more supportive, the intensity factor is on the side of the opposition: many more foes than supporters say they feel so strongly about the issue that they would vote against a senator who joins the other side."

Some words of caution are in order. Polls only measure how people feel about an issue at the time they're polled. Whether people with strong feelings about an issue at one point in time will have the same feelings some years later is uncertain. Fortunately for senators, they come up for reelection only once every six years. Today's strong feelings may well be weak ones tomorrow, provided that by "tomorrow" we mean some years from now.

STABILITY

Whether an opinion has stability is of concern to the public relations practitioner because it indicates the degree of commitment to the issue in question. Opinions which have a high degree of stability are not easily changed. They demonstrate that the individual having that opinion has held to it for a long period of time, considers it important, and is not likely to alter it readily. Low stability or unstable opinions, on the other hand, are not important to those holding them and may readily be changed given the proper circumstances.

Public opinion polls taken over a long period of time that ask the same questions at varying intervals show that on certain issues there is a high degree of opinion stability. Over a period of many decades the majority of Americans have been consistently negative in their opinion about communism and consistently firm in their feeling that America should maintain a strong military establishment. Opinions about the job being done by the president, however, have been highly unstable, and it doesn't seem to matter who happens to be the president. According to the Gallup Poll, President Truman's approval rating during his first fifteen months in office ranged from a high of 87 percent to a low of 43 percent, and similar sharp swings in approval were shown for succeeding presidents. The unstable nature of presidential popularity is shown in the chart below, which shows the highest and lowest approval ratings during the first fifteen months in office of presidents from Truman through Carter. The percentages represent approval responses to the question: "Do you approve or disapprove of the way (name of the president) is handling his job as president?"

Highest/Lowest Approval Ratings During First 15 Months

	Highest	Lowest
Truman	87%	43%
Eisenhower	75%	59%
Kennedy	83%	71%
Johnson	80%	69%
Nixon	68%	53%
Ford	71%	37%
Carter	75%	39%

Source: Surveys by American Institute of Public Opinion (Gallup), most recent in 1978.

Although there has been a high degree of instability of opinion regarding personalities, as a general rule there has been a high degree of stability of opinion concerning matters of basic concern to most people. Pollsters Charles Roll, Jr., and Albert H. Cantrill report that the major concerns of the American people "continue to be good health, a better standard of living, peace, the achievement of aspirations for one's children, a good job, and a happy family life." Political scientist Alan D. Monroe suggests the following reasons for the relative stability of public opinion on most substantive issues:

1. People resist changing their minds, and social factors such as economic status, race, and religion reinforce this tendency.

2. Personal contact reinforces stabilization of opinion because people tend to talk to other who hold the same views.

3. The political system also works against change. Parties, political leaders, and loyal followers tend to hold to the same positions over the years.

4. Individual changes of opinion largely cancel each other out.

The optimists among us will be cheered to note the stability of self-happiness reported over the years. Measuring the degree of happiness over a thirty-year period, the Gallup Poll reported that Americans are either "very happy" or "fairly happy" with their lot. As reported in *Public Opinion* magazine (May/June 1978), the chart below shows responses to the Gallup Poll question: "In general, how happy would you say you are—very happy, fairly happy, or not happy?"

	Very Happy	Fairly Happy	Not Happy
1947	38%	58%	4%
1970	44%	49%	6%
1973	52%	45%	3%
1977	42%	48%	10%

Source: Surveys by American Institute of Public Opinion (Gallup), most recent in Nov. 4-7, 1977.

LATENCY

Latent opinion, according to V. O. Key, is "really about the only type of opinion that generates much anxiety" in the practice of politics and government. He suggests the following kinds of questions should be asked of latent opinions: "What opinion will develop about this prospective candidate? What opinions will be stirred by this legislative proposal? What opinions, anxieties and moods will be generated by this event or by that action?"

Key's questions certainly apply to policies, statements, and actions of all, not merely political, organizations and institutions. The college mulling the size of a tuition increase should ask: "What opinion will develop about this prospective increase?" The trade association advocating a fair trade law should ask: "What opinions will be stirred by this legislative proposal?" The company trying to decide whether to close a plant and move it elsewhere should ask: "What opinions, anxieties, and moods will be generated by this event or that action?"

Key suggests that in considering latent opinion we should distinguish between latent opinion of the "attentive public" and the "great inattentive public." As examples of the attentive public he cites the American Medical Association, the National Association of Manufacturers, and the AFL-CIO, and he says that over the short run the latent opinions of such groups can be anticipated because, as he puts it, "these attentive publics have their patterns of reaction that serve as bases for predictable response." The inattentive public, on the other hand, poses a much more difficult problem and situation. The problem, Key says, results from "uncertainties about whether mass attention will be mobilized or whether it will remain indifferent and uninformed."

Handling latent opinion, then, becomes a matter of predicting and sensing when public response to an issue or event will be temporary or more than just of the moment. It would be wise to view latent opinion as one might view a sleeping German shepherd dog. Because it's dormant doesn't mean it's dead; because it's sleeping doesn't mean it can't be aroused; because it seems so peaceful doesn't mean it's not powerful once aroused.

Estimating latent opinion involves the estimation of three elements:

1. Those sectors of society—the various publics and subpublics— affected by the issue.

2. The nature of the event or issue.

3. The intensity of feeling one might expect from the aroused latent opinion.

All three elements are interrelated, so the practitioner must use careful judgment in assessing and dealing with them. However, the nature of the issue or event seems to be the crucial factor in trying to assess its impact on latent opinion. Some issues and events are of such a universal nature that they're bound to command a wide audience and arouse strong feelings in that audience. Others will be perceived as being of minor significance and will impact only on a small number of people. Not to be overlooked is the fact that issues and events are in competition with themselves for public attention; an issue or event that might normally be expected to arouse strong feelings among many segments of society may pass unnoticed because it takes place at the same time as a far more profound issue or event.

Is there a guideline for attempting to assess the impact of an issue, event, or statement? Key makes the following suggestion:

> An action that clearly conflicts with a widely held attitude may be expected to stir up controversy if it comes to public attention; an action patently within the limits of the firmly held norms may pass unnoticed or arouse only mild approbation. Many governmental actions attract little attention because they raise questions within the permissive limits fixed by latent opinion. The excoriation of cancer, the idealization of the American mother, and the condemnation of sin never get a politician in trouble . . .

PUBLIC OPINION

In attempting to define public opinion the social scientists have had as much trouble as the poets and philosophers have had in attempting to define beauty. To John Keats, "Beauty is truth," and if that doesn't help he proposes that "truth is beauty" and advises us that it is all we know on earth and all we need to know. Taking the safer approach, philosopher George Santayana tells us in one breath that beauty is indescribable and he then proceeds to describe it as "a pledge of the possible conformity between the soul and nature. . . ." Kahlil Gibran conceives of beauty as "eternity gazing at itself in a mirror." Those who seek to capture the essence of beauty by relying on the poets and philosophers have been given some fascinating choices; they can either find it in truth, the indescribable, or eternity.

Though they are considered to be a more practical lot than the poets and philosophers, the social scientists have been equally obtuse in trying to define public opinion. Their attempts to pin down the term range from the simple to the complex, from the tentative to the definitive, from being so describable as to be virtually unfathomable.

This conclusion is evident from Floyd H. Allport's article in the very first issue of the *Public Opinion Quarterly* in which he described public opinion as follows:

The term public opinion is given its meaning with reference to a multi-individual situation in which individuals are expressing themselves, or can be called upon to express themselves, as favoring (or else disfavoring or opposing) some definite condition, person, or proposal of widespread importance, in such a proportion of number, intensity, and constancy, as to give rise to the probability of affecting action, directly, or indirectly, toward the object concerned.

If you're adventurous you might try playing Allport's definition your flugelhorn, but it won't be of much help if you try to use it to deal with public opinion in a practical situation. Allport's definition is important, however, because it indicates his tortuous attempt to cope with the many contingencies which involve public opinion. All too often those defining public opinion do so from the vantage point of their special interest. Note, for example, the connection (in italics by the author) between the specialist and the definitions cited below:

Political scientist V. O. Key defines public opinion as "those opinions held by private persons which *governments* find it prudent to heed."

Lucien Warner, writing about *public opinion surveys*, describes public opinion as "people's reactions to *definitely worded statements and questions under interview conditions.*"

James Bryce, one of the earliest writers of the *government process,* saw public opinion as "the power exerted by any such view, or set of views, when *held by an apparent majority of citizens.*"

Sociologist G. A. Lundberg described public opinion as "that opinion though it be the opinion of a *single individual* in which the public in question finds itself for any reason constrained to acquiesce."

Social Psychologist L. L. Bernard considered public opinion to be "any fairly uniform collective expression of *mental or inner behavior reactions . . .*"

Harwood Childs felt it necessary and important to cut through the verbiage and to eliminate the specialist's approach. His simple definition, which this author believes sufficient for the purposes of this book, states that public opinion is "*simply any collection of individual opinions designated.*" Though he admits his definition is a very broad one, he believes it's applicable to public relations because both "public opinion" and "public relations" are very broad in meaning and assume validity when they relate to paticular publics. Noting that an opinion is always that of a person, Childs stresses that public opinion always refers to a collection of individual opinions and hence *if we want to ascertain a given state of public opinion we have to ascertain the opinions of individuals.*

Childs is also critical of those who set forth certain principles of public opinion or who would narrow the meaning of the term to include only those collections of opinion which have a specific degree of uniformity. In his view *there are no public opinion principles which are applicable under all circumstances.*

"All principles," he notes, "hold true only under certain circumstances. Given the conditions, the principles will apply. But the conditions must be stated. This is what makes the study of public opinion and public relations so difficult. Conditions vary; publics differ; the relations between groups are always changing. Generalizations regarding human behavior and human relations are peculiarly hazardous to make."

As for the alleged need for the existence of a degree of uniformity, Childs points out that this is a matter of investigation not an a priori condition of public opinion. As he puts it: "The degree of uniformity is a matter to be investigated, not something to be arbitrarily set up as a condition for the existence of public opinion."

Summed up, then, public opinion is a general and inclusive term. It always refers to a collection of individual opinions. It can be studied with some degree of significance when related to a particular public and to specific opinions about definite subjects. The source for the opinions of individuals and an analysis of how opinions are formed will be examined in the section that follows.

THE FORMATION OF PUBLIC OPINION

Of crucial importance to the student of public relations is not merely understanding the nature of publics, opinion, and public opinion, but also understanding how public opinion is formed. Unfortunately for those who dote on pat answers that can be highlighted by multi-colored markers, there are no pat answers to the process of opinion formation. So many factors are involved in the process of opinion formation that it is well-nigh impossible to state with certainty that this factor, that factor, or a set of factors cause opinion to develop in a certain way. At best, one can seek the answer to the quandary of opinion formation only in very broad, general terms. Stated in such terms, the two major elements in the process of opinion formation are the *person* and the *environment*.

THE PERSON

When we look at the individual we should recognize that the list of tangible and intangible attributes that can be used as factors to explain personality, attitude, and opinions are endless. Some authorities concentrate on such factors as perceptions, habits, complexes, frames of reference, and values. Others cite self-esteem, loyalties, moods, and drives. Still others cite traits such as introverts, extroverts, and inner-and-outer directed. The list of personal attributes of the individual is infinite and impossible to weigh and assess with any degree of certainty.

Though it may not be possible to weigh personal attributes accurately, their importance in the process of opinion formation cannot be denied. Our physiological, biological, and psychological traits and make-up undoubtedly play a role in the way we view issues, actions, and events. Thus they form an integral share of the mix that results in the formation of our opinions. Consider the following situation:

A few weeks after the United States withdrew from South Vietnam in the Spring of 1975 an unarmed American freighter named the Mayaguez was seized in disputed waters in the Gulf of Siam and forced to anchor off a tiny crescent island called Tang. After briefly trying via diplomacy to secure the liberation of the ship and its crew of 39, President Ford ordered the use of force: U.S. planes blasted five Cambodian vessels out of the water; the marines boarded the Mayaguez and assaulted Tang Island; American fighter-bombers blasted an oil depot and air base on the Cambodian mainland. The crew was subsequently rescued, the Mayaguez retaken, and the event became a minor footnote of history.

However, in the first days of the operation the outcome remained uncertain and there was the possibility that the United States could again become involved militarily in Southeast Asia. Other factors aside, consider the probable initial reaction of two different personalities to the unfolding situation. Mr. Shy is an introvert, inner-directed, fearful, cautious and timid. Mr. Bold is an extrovert, outer-directed, fearless, impetuous and aggressive. Given these traits—and for the sake of argument omitting all other factors—there is little doubt that Shy's opinion of the president's action would be essentially negative and Bold's would be essentially positive.

The example cited above is a set-up situation, of course, because people don't come to their opinions solely on the basis of their personality traits. These traits come to grips with issues and events within the vortex of other factors mainly environmental in nature.

THE ENVIRONMENT

As with personality traits, there is no end of environmental factors affecting the process of opinion formation. Some are general and some specific; some are remote and some proximate; some are stable and some changeable; some are large and some small. The list includes economic, religious, and political institutions; physical, biological, and sociological factors; demographic, climatic, and topographical features; professional, peer, ethnic, and special purpose groups; the government and mass media of communication. Mind-boggling in its array and diversity, the list is of great importance because each element can play a vital role in the formation of public opinion.

The dubious reader may cast a jaundiced eye on some of the previously mentioned environmental factors, but consider the answers to the following questions.

Re climate: Would the cold climate of the frozen north cause an Eskimo to have a different opinion on certain issues than that of an Amazonian who lives in the torrid climate of the equator?

Re demography: Would a woman, age 76, have a different opinion of Social Security than a young woman, age 21?

Re profession: Would a doctor have a different view of malpractice insurance than a trial lawyer?

Re sociology: Would an inner city mother have a different view of busing than a suburban mother?

The answer to all fours questions is yes, chiefly because of environmental factors influencing the people concerned. Of course, the factors have been posed here within the context of situations to which they are directly related. In most cases, however, such a connection between environmental factors, situation, and opinion formation is much more tenuous. Those factors which are significant and those which are insignificant in the formation of opinion usually cannot be sorted out.

In the early formative years of most people three environmental factors—the family, church/religion, and the school—are considered to be of paramount importance.

The *family* is the source of one's first impressions, early habits, likes, dislikes, prejudices, and goals. The family has a direct influence on the selection of childhood companions and on attitudes towards a wide variety of subjects. Because the family isolates the small child from other countervailing forces, it has a great influence on his character, motivation, personal habits, and ideals.

The *church and/or religion* begins to make its influence felt at a very early age and for many people continues throughout a lifetime. In addition to providing the basis for beliefs and opinions relative to God, life after death, salvation, and other tenets, the church and religion influence opinions about sin, sex, tolerance and intolerance, economic, social, and political matters.

The *school*, and especially the public school, commences the process of socialization which continues throughout a lifetime. Traditions, learning, and skills necessary to maintain a society are transmitted through the schools. The range of information about public policies increases in direct proportion to the amount of schooling an individual has. On economic and political matters, the school tends to reflect family and community attitudes. Observes V. O. Key: "In the largest sense the educational system is a great mechanism for *conserving* the values, the institutions, the practices of the political order, as it inculcates from the primary school even through college the memories, the unities, and the norms of the system."

As the child becomes the youth and the youth the adult, other key environmental factors come into play and either reinforce or subvert the early influences of family, church/religion, and the school. By the manner in which they funnel information, entertainment, and opinion the media provide the means whereby the individual ascertains facts, perceives and identifies issues and problems, and becomes aware of alternative solutions. Peer, professional, and interest groups exert a modifying influence on individual opinions, and in some cases profoundly shape such opinions. Even the issue itself—the time it takes place and its setting—becomes an environmental factor influencing opinion formation. All these factors play roles in the opinion formation process. Trying to ascertain the relative importance of each factor becomes a task worthy of a Solomon, who might not even be up to handling it.

THE FORMULA APPROACH

In attempting to bring order out of the chaos of the many factors involved in the process of opinion formation, some authorities have evolved tidy formulae to describe the process. They usually imply or directly contend that opinion formulation is an orderly, rational procedure with debate pro and con followed by some form of agreement or consensus.

For example, here is how one book describes the process of opinion formation:

1. A number of people recognize a situation as being problematic and decide that something ought to be done about it. They explore possible solutions and do some fact-finding.

2. Alternative proposals for solving the problem emerge, and these are discussed back and forth.

3. A policy or solution is agreed upon as best meeting the situation recognized as problematic. Agreement and a decision to promote its acceptance lead to group consciousness.

4. A program of action is undertaken, and this is pressed until the requisite action is obtained or the group becomes weary of the battle and its members turn to other projects and other groups.

Another author has a shorter version of the opinion formation process: "A treatment of the dynamics of public opinion formation must concern itself with at least three major phases: (1) the rise of the issue; (2) the discussion about the issue and proposed solutions pro and con; and (3) the arrival at consensus."

The major problem with the above-mentioned formula approaches to the opinion formation process is that they either seem to be taking place in some sort of apolitical vacuum or else they're describing how organizations supposedly debate alternative solutions to problems. Properly labelled, they may well describe "How Insiders Debate An Issue and Decide On Action To Be Taken."

But *public* opinion, which is the subject being discussed, is not arrived at so tidily, nor is the public usually privy to the discussion and the pro and con that may well take place before some organization decides on a policy or action. Further, the public is not some sort of neat entity which by some means or other goes through a series of steps to reach a decision on an issue. To visualize opinion formation as a standard pattern is to engage in a set of generalizations which can lead only to the illusion of reality but which reality itself belies. The members of publics and sub-publics may well form opinions about issues and events, but they are seldom in the position to have a direct influence or part in the actions taken by authorities and organizations. V. O. Key sums up the criticism of the tidy formula approach to the process of opinion formation in the following words:

> More is lost than is gained in understanding by the organismic view of the public. Occasionally, in relatively small communities, citizen concern and involvement over an issue may be widespread and community consideration may move in close articulation with the mechanism of authority to a decision that can realistically be said to be a decision by public opinion. At far rarer intervals great national populations may be swept by a common concern about a momentuous issue with a similar result. Yet ordinarily a decision is made not by the public but by officials after greater or a lesser consideration of the opinion of the public or parts of the public.

In summation, the following can be said about the process of public opinion formulation:

1. The factors involved in the formation of public opinion relate to the *person* and the *environment* but they are so numerous it is impossible to state which are paramount and which secondary.

2. The influence on opinion of the family, church/religion, and the school are considered to be of paramount importance in the formative years. Thereafter, other key environmental influences begin to be felt.

3. There is no pat formula to describe the process of opinion formation. The process is too full of variables; untidy rather than tidy; often irrational rather than rational.

NEWSOM'S PUBLIC OPINION SIGNPOSTS

Seekers of truth, wandering among the public opinion thickets, will be helped along the way by four signposts erected by veteran counselor Earl Newsom.

Newsom notes that many carefully conceived and executed campaigns designed to "educate the public" subsequently fail because of myopia about the intended audience of these campaigns. All too often, says Newsom, the sponsor of an idea, point of view, or opinion fails to ask this simple question: "Does it clearly help toward the solution of a problem which worries those I am addressing?" If the answer is yes, the sponsor of the idea has correctly read Newsom's first signpost which is cited below.

THE IDENTIFICATION SIGNPOST

"People will ignore (or won't support) an idea, an opinion, a point of view unless they see clearly that it affects (in a positive way) their personal fears or desires, hopes or aspirations."

Self-motivation—the id and the ego that possesses all of us—is a powerful force. "What's-in-it-for-me?" asks the recipient of a message. In too many instances the sender is too busy composing his message to consider the recipient, and there are far too many cases where the sender is so inconsiderate he sends the message "to whom it may concern." Sending messages without careful consideration of a specific audience and of the desires, hopes, and ambitions of its members is like blowing dandelion seeds into the wind.

To reach people, to influence their opinions, a first necessity is to *appeal to their personal interests,* to show them clearly that your words or actions *identify with their present and pressing problems.*

This is often more easily said than accomplished. It *presumes* that the sender of an idea, opinion, or point of view has knowledge and understanding of the personal interests of the recipient. But if the sender and the recipient live in different social and economic worlds— as is most often the case—the gap between them serves as an effective barrier to knowledge and understanding. On a clear day one can easily see the South Bronx from a window high up on a Madison Avenue office building. On any weekday that same Madison Avenue public relations writer or advertising copywriter rides past block after block of crowded inner-city housing on his or her way to life in the "safe" suburbs. But sight and proximity do not equate to real knowledge and understanding, and that's one reason why many public relations messages and advertising commercials are either laughed at or ignored by their intended audience.

Being able to identify with your audience is even more difficult when the audience is not in sight nor close by. And yet, as you read this text, hundreds of public relations practitioners in New York, Chicago, Los Angeles, and other large cities are composing messages beamed at people living and working in the so-called hinterlands. At worst, practitioners blithely assume that messages exist in some sort of limbo land where life is uncomplicated and people are so unsophisticated that they don't know what is in their own self-interest. At best, practitioners at least *recognize* the identification problem and attempt to solve it through observation, reading, research, and careful monitoring of audience mood, interests, and opinion.

THE ACTION SIGNPOST

"People do not buy ideas separated from action—either action taken or about to be taken by the sponsor of the idea, or action which people themselves can conveniently take to prove the merit of the idea."

We tend to reject words which are divorced from actions. An organization's words and its actions must be compatible if the words are to be believed. In forming their opinions about organizations, individuals base their judgments as much on what organizations *do* as on what they say. And if what they "do" is contrary to what they say, the public will generally base its opinions on the doing rather than the saying.

Modern-day life abounds with illustrations—usually in the negative—of the action guidepost. There's the corporation which touts the free enterprise system in its advertising but which engages in price-fixing and other anti-competitive activities. There's the legislator who promises to cut down on unnecessary government spending but then votes himself a hefty salary boost. There's the United States of America which is dedicated to democratic principles but which at times provides economic and military aid to totalitarian regimes.

Eliza Doolittle spoke for the cockney in all of us when she shouted, "Show Me!" in response to a torrent of words, words, words about love. We seek to be shown by actions, not merely by words, and our opinions tend to be positive when we perceive that the actions of organizations are those which affirmatively affect our important personal interests.

Summed up, the action signpost warns that words are insufficient by themselves to engender favorable public opinion. Taken together, words and actions support themselves if they are compatible, honest, and appeal to people's self-interests.

THE FAMILIARITY AND TRUST SIGNPOST

"We the people buy ideas only from those we trust; we are influenced by, or adopt, only those opinions or points of view put forward by individuals or corporations or institutions in whom we have confidence."

Simple ideas sometimes have profound meanings, and this third Newsom signpost teaches an important lesson about the formation of public opinion in the twentieth century.

The world is too much with us yet, as William Wordsworth reminded us in the eighteenth century. Wordsworth was able to retreat from his world by turning to nature, but modern men and women retreat by turning off the world. Wise in the knowledge that the world is too complex and complicated to understand, the individual today must nonetheless have opinions and judgments. Wisely or not, the individual relies on the opinions and judgments of those he trusts.

Very often these "trustees" of opinion and judgment are newspaper columnists and editorial writers, radio and television comentators, political figures, teachers, doctors and priests, rabbis and ministers. Or, on a smaller scale, the trustees may be certain key people among the many groups to which we belong. To the leader who rise up to serve our needs, we entrust our opinions, our judgments and our decisions.

"Our every act," says Newsom, "is the voicing of a preference. We 'vote' when we pick our grocery store, our gas station, our doctor, our college, the movie we go to, the radio program to which we listen, the charities to which we send our checks."

Is our vote based on intimate knowledge of the store, the gas station, the doctor, etc.? Scarcely, because we haven't the time to acquire this knowledge. We give them our vote because we've learned at some time or another to have confidence and trust in them; once we lose this trust and confidence we cast our vote elsewhere.

Wise practitioners recognize the importance of Newsom's third signpost. They know that the building of trust is not an overnight matter, but one that takes years to achieve. They also know the value of "trustee endorsement," and they therefore cultivate those people, groups, and institutions in whom people have a great deal of trust and confidence. A few words of endorsement from a trusted source are of far greater value than a torrent of words from a relatively unknown, distant, or untrusted source.

THE CLARITY SIGNPOST

"The situation must be clear to us, not confusing. The thing we observe, read, see, or hear, the thing which produces our impressions, must be clear, not subject to several interpretations."

The American landscape is unfortunately littered with statements which are obtuse, unclear, confusing, and open to varying interpretations. On the presidential level there's the press secretary's use of the word "inoperative" to explain away his own crossed signals. On the professional level in almost every field there's the use of jargon, circumlocution, and obfuscation in phrases which talk about:

maximization of profits   empirically derived taxono-
delimitation of debts   mies
cancellations   normative sanction patterns of
factor analysis by means   causative behavior
  of chi square deviations   the limited channel capacity of
                                the perceptual system

Reading the above, one wonders what's happened to the English language. Organizations can't expect others to understand them if they can't explain their actions clearly and without equivocation. The basic trouble seems to reside in the fact that the truth of an action or statement, simply and clearly stated, seems to be an insurmountable barrier among organizations which are afraid to trust the people with simple, unvarnished truths. But if we can't trust people with the truth, then we don't deserve their support.

Newsom's fourth signpost is predicated on the premise that the action point of view being clarified is one that reflects favorably on the organization or individual taking the action or advocating the point of view. There are two circumstances, however, where the action or point of view reflects unfavorably on the proponent and yet is illuminated with such blinding clarity as to remain indelibly fixed in the public mind.

The first of these two unfortunate circumstances most often occurs on impromptu occasions and usually results from off-the-cuff remarks or from hasty responses to press inquiries. The thoughtless statement which triggers unfavorable public reaction almost never occurs as a result of carefully designed and written statements because these are usually edited with care and foresight. Rather, it's the quick response that brings about the negative reaction, and it takes place in interviews; at question time following press conferences; on radio and television talk shows; and at impromptu sessions during political campaigns. There's little the public relations specialist can do about such situations except to brief his client or spokesman in advance or to batten down the hatches and try to repair the damages once the winds blow.

The second of the two unfortunate circumstances involving clarity occurs when remarks are stated clearly but subsequently are either wrongly reported or simply distorted. Public relations men and women are, of course, not responsible for the manner in which statements and remarks are handled by the media. However, it is their responsibility to monitor press treatment of statements and/or actions and to suggest appropriate and, hopefully, judicious response and reaction. The response, of course, may well be a decision not to respond. The decision whether to respond or not to respond becomes a matter of professional judgment, experience, and thoughtful assessment of expected public reaction.

Whether the fault lies in the one who makes the statement or in the media handling of the statement, Newsom's clarity signpost holds true and should be a steadfast guide: the situation must be clear . . . not confusing. The more clear the situation, explanation, or statement, the less likely it will be misinterpreted. Even though we identify with our publics, even though we have their trust, and even though our words and our actions are compatible, we don't gain public approval or understanding unless we explain ourselves clearly.

QUESTIONS AND PROBLEMS FOR DISCUSSION

1. Why is it misleading to speak of *the public* as an entity?

2. Cite some examples—other than those mentioned in this chapter—of individuals who face loyalty conflicts due to multi-public membership.

3. Take any current issue of importance to groups of people and explain the various publics it affects.

4. List, in order of importance, the publics which are of major concern to your college or university. In what way(s) would this list differ, if it does differ, from any other college or university you care to select for comparison?

5. Select any organization which has had a major shift in purpose and/or goals and explain how this shift has brought about a shift in its major publics.

6. Explain some current student-life mor és which exist on your campus.

7. Using the next week's issues of the daily newspaper clip, paste up, and comment on five to ten examples of stereotyped thinking or writing.

8. Explain the meaning of an opinion in terms of its *direction, intensity, stability,* and *latency.*

9. What current or recent major issue of national or local concern illustrates how latent opinion became active? Explain your choice.

10. Selecting any major issue of national or local concern, explain which specific environmental factors played a vital role in the formation of public opinion concerning the issue.

11. In what respects has your family, church/religion, and education affected your attitudes and opinions about specific issues?

12. Why is the so-called formula approach to opinion formation open to criticism?

13. What examples can you cite to illustrate each of Newsom's four public opinion signposts?

PROJECTS, ASSIGNMENTS, AND MINI-CASES

1. THE PRESIDENT OF OTIS ELEVATOR DELIVERS A TALK: A MINI-CASE FOR DISCUSSION

Not many weeks after the Alexander Smith Carpet Company moved its mills from Yonkers, New York, to a new location in the South, President Le Roy A. Petersen of the Otis Elevator Company delivered a talk to an invited audience of over 2,000 employees and Yonkers city officials. (The same talk was given to employees of Otis in Harrison, New Jersey.)

At the time (January, 1955) Otis had been part of the industrial base of Yonkers for 101 years, had a local yearly payroll of more than ten million dollars, and was one of the community's major taxpayers. The talk was given at 9 a.m. and the setting was the Brandt Theatre in Yonkers.

President Petersen began his talk by citing the loyalty of the 2,000 Otis men and women who had received service pins the previous year for service records ranging from 25 to 55 years with the company. Stressing the fine reputation of the company in the design, manufacture, and installation of elevators and escalators, Petersen discussed the large number of competitors who had entered the field in the past decade.

"These statements," he said, "should not be interpreted as indicating that the Otis Elevator Company has ceased to be a profitable company or is on the verge of becoming an unprofitable one. On the contrary, it is anticipated that, since our income is derived from a variety of sources, including a substantial service business and extensive operations throughout the world, the annual report for 1954 will show an increase over the previous year in sales and earnings. In addition, it is believed that our backlog will assure a profitable level of operations in 1955.

"However, the Yonkers Works is primarily engaged in the manufacture of equipment for new elevators for domestic use and has relatively little to do with service or foreign operations and its performance must be judged solely by the quality and cost of the products it makes. . . .

"The Otis Elevator Company has prospered and has been a source of employment in Yonkers for moe than a hundred years because it has continued to manufacture high quality product at a cost sufficiently low to permit it to be sold with a fair profit at a competitive price.

"Unless we can continue to do this, we will cease to be a prosperous company and will also cease to be a source of employment. It is, therefore, my duty and obligation as president of this company to take such steps as may be necessary to maintain Otis quality and still reduce costs to the point where we can continue to secure the necessary volume at a profitable price."

Stating that an extensive study had been conducted to ascertain how the needed reduction in cost best be accomplished, Petersen said:

"Of particular interest to you, however, is the result of the study relating to manufacture, and this study indicated that an annual saving in manufacturing costs of several million dollars could be secured by building a single plant to replace the Yonkers and Harrison plants, and that this plant should be located in the middle west near the geographical center of our elevator market. . . .

"A further careful study has, therefore, been made which indicates that about half of the savings that are attributable to a new mid-western plant could be accomplished in our present plants, providing we secure the enthusiastic and understanding cooperation of our employees and of the city authorities.

"With the purpose of preserving as many as possible of your jobs with Otis in Yonkers and a local payroll amounting to about ten million dollars per year, we are willing and anxious to make every effort to continue the operation of the Yonkers plant providing we are able to accomplish, with a minimum delay, the reduction in cost which we believe is reasonably obtainable in this location.

"A definite decision to take such steps as are necessary to reduce costs substantially has already been made, and the only question remaining is which of the known methods will be chosen. If we are unable to bring about these reductions in cost in our present plants, we will have no choice but to transfer our manufacturing, as soon as possible, to a new midwestern plant—and will not hesitate to do so if it becomes clearly necessary. . . .

"Kindly note that our plans for reduced costs are not based upon any change in our past policy of paying all who work for Otis at least as much as is paid by other reputable and comparable companies for similar jobs, both in the form of wages and salaries and in supplementary benefits. It is still our desire to keep the Yonkers Plant not only a place in which to work, but a *good* place in which to work.

"Rather, our ability to secure reduced costs here and now is dependent upon our receiving your active cooperation in eliminating avoidable and unjustifiable expense and in reducing lost time and motion, in increasing the efficient use of existing equiment and in utilizing to the utmost the production capacity of such new equipment as may be warranted in installing. We will welcome your suggestions.

"In seeking to accomplish our objectives, we propose, of course, to work with and through the unions which you have selected as your bargaining agents and to solicit the active cooperation of their officials. . . .

"I trust that you will clearly understand that this is not an attempt to persuade you to do anything that you do not want to do or which you do not recognize as being clearly in your own interest.

"It should be apparent that the Yonkers Works has, in effect, become a community enterprise. The Company, because of its earnest desire to retain its present organization and to continue to provide good jobs for its loyal employees, has indicated its willingness to forego some of the larger savings obtainable by other methods and to continue to operate the Yonkers Plant as long as it can afford to do so. It cannot afford to continue to operate it under present conditions—but is offering you an opportunity to create the conditions under which we could afford to continue its operation.

"We could, of course, have decided to go ahead immediately with the building of a new central plant, basing ou decision solely upon the outcome of the study which clearly showed savings sufficient to justify the investment, the cost of transfer and the loss on existing plants.

"We could, and some may say that we should, have done this without prior discussion with you. I trust that you feel, as I do, that in fairness to you and to the City of Yonkers, this prior general discussion is desirable.

"I also trust that you realize that we are trying to help you retain your jobs with Otis and that we hope that, together, we will be successful in doing so.

"Next week, we will present to your union officials concrete proposals outlining the conditions which we consider reasonable and essential for continued future operations in Yonkers.

"We sincerely hope that these proposals will be recognized as consistent with the interest and welfare of our Yonkers employees and that agreement will be reached for their early adoption.

"We are prepared to make substantial additional investment in the Yonkers Plant, if such investment appears to be clearly justified. We will do our best to further improve our methods. We will look to the city authorities for fair treatment on taxes and for a disposition to help in all other ways consistent with the welfare of thg city as a whole.

"The rest is up to you, and we hope that you will give the problem careful consideration."

The day following Mr. Petersen's talk, the New York *Times* reported it in a front-page story with the headline:

OTIS ULTIMATUM
GIVEN IN YONKERS

City Officials and Employees
Told Costs Must Be Cut or
Elevator Company Moves

The lead paragraph stated that "The Otis Elevator Company issued an ultimatum today to 2,000 employees and city officials. It said: 'Cooperate to cut costs or the company will move to a new plant in the Midwest.'"

After reporting the essence of Petersen's talk, the story continued:

"Members of the audience sat throughout the talk quietly. There was scattered applause when the company president walked from the wings to a mid-stage lectern. There was no interruption of his speech and no visible reaction at its conclusion. His listeners filed quickly and silently from the big theatre."

The story quoted the union representing the Yonkers plant employees as calling attention to the following points:

'The Otis Elevator Company has averaged over $9,400,000 net profit for the last eighty years. This represents a return of 18 percent of net worth. Most companies regard 8 percent as a high return. A few shorts months ago Mr. Petersen in reporting to the stockholders of this corporation stated that the outlook for the future was for increased business. He also reported a record for bookings.'

"The existing contract between Otis and the union," the story continued, "does not expire until next June. In 1947 the company closed its Buffalo plant, employing 1,000 and transferred operations to the Yonker and Harrison works. The move was attributed to 'changes in the elevator industry and the plant's obsolete equipment.'

"Last month Mr. Petersen announced an extra common stock dividend of 50 cents a share. At the same time a regular quarterly dividend of 62½ cents was declared. Dividend declarations for 1954 came to $3 a share, or 25 cents a share more than in the previous year. The net income for the first nine months of 1954 was $6,689,057. For the same period in 1953 the net was $6,179,807.

"Charles Curran, Yonkers City Manager, when asked for comment on Mr. Petersen's appeal for 'fair treatment on taxes and for a disposition to help in all other ways consistent with the welfare of the city as a whole,' declared:

" 'We certainly don't want to lose Otis. We'll give them all the cooperation we can.' "

Questions for Discussion

1. What's your judgment of Mr. Petersen's talk—its contents, circumstances of delivery, and reported audience reaction—as it relates to the four signposts of Earl Newsom? That is, evaluate the speech in terms of Newsom's signposts for achieving favorable public opinion.

2. Assume that you are public relations counsel to the Otis Elevator Company. You have been shown a draft of the speech prior to its delivery and have been told when, where, how and to whom it will be given. You are asked to provide your professional advice about the speech and its projected delivery. Please do so, and justify your conclusions.

3. What questions would you ask and what kind of information about the Otis situation would you want to know about which have not been given in the case description?

4. Comment on the following release which was sent out by public relations counsel to the company:

FOR: OTIS ELEVATOR COMPANY
FROM: (Name, address, and
             phone number of PR
             counsel)

NOT FOR RELEASE BEFORE 12:00 NOON
SATURDAY, JANUARY 15, 1955

(*Note:* Copy which follows
       was double-spaced)

At a meeting held today at the Brandt Theatre in Yonkers, New York, L. A. Petersen, President of Otis Elevator Company, told over 2,000 employees of the Otis Yonkers Works and a group of city officials that sales and earnings in 1954 were expected to exceed those of 1953 and that satisfactory operations were anticipated in 1955.

He pointed out, however, that the number of competitors had more than doubled during the last eight years to a present total of 262 and that substantial reductions in cost were necessary to retain the company's competitive position.

Mr. Petersen stated that an extensive study had indicated that a saving of several million dollars could be secured by establishing a single midwestern plant to replace the present plants at Yonkers, New York, and Harrison, New Jersey, but that, in consideration of the hardship that would be imposed upon present employees, every effort would be made to secure a sufficient reduction in costs in the present plans to avoid the necessity for moving to a new central plant.

Mr. Petersen emphasized that the plans for reducing cost were not based upon any change in the past policy of paying all who work for Otis at least as much as is paid by other reputable and comparable companies for similar jobs, both in the form of wages and salaries and in supplementary benefits, but that such plans were based upon eliminating avoidable expense, upon improved methods and upon the efficient use of new and existing equipment.

He expressed the opinion that the success of these efforts would depend upon the cooperation received from employees and union officials.

A similar meeting was held later on today at the Otis plant in Harrison, N.J.

—30—

5. In response to a request by the author, the account executive of Otis's public relations counsel sent the above news release and a copy of Mr. Petersen's remarks. He closed by stating: "I am sure you will understand how delicate a matter this is and that it requires the utmost fairness and tact. Mr. Petersen approached the problem and the employees in this spirit."

What is your reaction to his statement?

2. PROFILING AN ETHNIC SUBPUBLIC: A RESEARCH ASSIGNMENT

The fascinating thing about sub-publics is that they can exist virtually unknown within the lager American public, and that they often come into being in a short period of time. In the first half of the seventies a sub-public of close to 50,000 Korean immigrants settled into a two-mile stretch of Olympic Boulevard in Los Angeles, and in short order came to be known as Koreatown.

According to a *Newsweek* report by John L. Dotson, Jr. (5/26/75), 200,000 Koreans settled in America after the Korean War, most of them coming between 1965-1975 and with the largest concentration in Los Angeles. By 1975, reported Dotson, there were 1,400 Korean-owned businesses in Los Angeles and these included 58 restaurants,

150 grocery stores, two hospitals, five newspapers, two radio stations, and two UHF television stations that operated on weekends.

Thus, in 1975 Koreatown represented a sizable sub-public smack in the middle of sprawling Los Angeles, yet to most Americans the mere existence of this sub-community must have been unknown until they read about it in *Newsweek*.

That sizable sub-publics of similar nature exist in every city of even medium size in America is a fact of American life. It merely takes some on-the-spot research to prove this fact, hence the following assignment.

1. Read John Dotson's *Newsweek* profile of Koreatown on page 10 of the May 26, 1975, issue.

2. Research a similar ethnic subpublic existing within any large or medium-sized city of your choice.

3. Write a 600- to 700-word Dotson-type profile of this subpublic.

3. SOME BASIC RULES FOR RELATING TO BLACKS: A MINI-CASE FOR DISCUSSION

Concluding a four-part series dealing with public relations and the black community Frank M. Seymour, president of Seymour & Lundy Associates, Inc., of Detroit, cited eight basic rules for dealing with blacks on an individual and community level. The precepts, previously published in a Seymour & Lundy booklet called "What *Not* To Say to a Black American," were carried in a supplement to the *pr reporter* and are reprinted below with permission:

1. DON'T attempt to show an affinity for black people. ("One of my best friends is black.") More often than not, the best "friend" has never once been invited into the speaker's home or his social circle.

2. DON'T attempt to show an understanding of the black person's experience. ("I know exactly how you feel.") We doubt if whites know how it feels to be called "nigger," stared at, cursed and spit upon by persons whom you've never met nor harmed; to have been ridiculed and scorned as a chid simply because you had "kinky hair," thick lips, or were noticeably "different"in color; to grow up with the erroneous and fallacious illusion that "your kind" is more animal than human, intellectually inferior and doomed to the most despicable conditions in a ghetto existence.

3. DON'T stereotype. ("All blacks drive big cars" or "Show me the latest dance.") It's interesting how many whites can drive through the ghetto, with dilapidated dwellings, unclothed and hungry children and notice only a big, shiny new car (which could belong to a hustler, which all societies have, or a black man who too often sweats long hours in a hot foundry to make the payments on the highest dream his country offers him) and remark: "You see, they really love to drive big cars and waste their money, so why should we listen to their complaints?"

4. DON'T misunderstand the black person's problem—"You have a chip on your shoulder." Probably so, and you can expect many more "angry young men" as today's youth, with new interest in black history, learn more and more about the black man's experience in America; as they learn that their fathers and grandfathers were not necessarily stupid and lazy, but were until recently literally barred from most professions and still are today in many trades.

5. DO be honest. Admit you may be prejudiced and, of course, you don't "know" how it feels to be black. Explain, however, that you accept the fact that blacks are people, and as such are entitled to the same rights, privileges and freedoms as any other human beings.

6. Do avoid asking how *all* blacks feel about anything! This question automatically tells the listener you consider all blacks to be alike. Remember, there are over 22 million of us in the U.S. alone, and only God knows how many in the world—a lot of room for variation.

7. DO speak to blacks in the same tone and tongue you would to anyone else. Don't try to emulate black speech or mannerisms. Blacks may peceive this is an attempt to ridicule, to "make fun," not friends.

8. DO discard the popular retort: "Maybe blacks did have it bad in the past, but things have *changed*." It is unfair to expect anyone, black or white, raised under ghetto conditions to instantly forget the mental and physical hardships of such an environment. And remember, moral behavior cannot be legislated. Change has to come from the heart.

Questions for Discussion

1. As a white (or black) student, how do you personally feel about Mr. Seymour's eight rules for relating to blacks?

2. Under what specific circumstances can you conceive of the eight rules being (or having been) of value to a public relations practitioner?

3. What rules would you (as a member of another minority group) draft for dealing with those in your group?

   Note: This question is addressed to those in the class who belong to other minority groups. It would be instructive to have the rest of the class give their personal reactions to the rules set forth.

RECOMMENDED READING

Lloyd A. Free and Hadley Cantril, *The Political Beliefs of Americans, a Study of Public Opinion*. New Brunswick, N.J.: Rutgers University Press, 1967.

Harwood L. Childs, *An Introduction to Public Opinion*. New York: John Wiley & Sons, 1940.

_____, *Public Opinion: Nature, Formation, and Role*. Princeton, N.J.: D. Van Nostrand, Co., 1965.

Robert Dahl, *Who Governs?* New Haven, Conn.: Yale University Press, 1961.

Louis Harris, *The Anguish of Change*. New York: Norton, 1973.

Bernard C. Hennessy, *Public Opinion*, 2nd ed. Belmont, Calif.: Wadsworth, 1970.

V. O. Key, *Public Opinion and American Democracy*. New York: Alfred Knopf, 1961.

Everett C. Ladd, Jr., "Traditional Values Regnant," *Public Opinion*, March/April 1978.

Robert E. Lane and David O. Sears, *Public Opinion*. Englewood Cliffs, N.J.: Prentice-Hall, 1964.

Philip Lesly, "Winning Public Opinion," *Public Relations Review*, Summer 1976.

Walter Lippmann, *Public Opinion*. New York: Macmillan, 1960.

Seymour M. Lipset and William Schneider, "How's Business? What the Public Thinks," *Public Opinion*, July/August 1978.

Alan D. Monroe, *Public Opinion In America*. New York: Dodd, Mead, 1975.

Robert D. Novak, "What's Happening Out There?" *Public Opinion*, September/October 1978.

Charles Roll, Jr., and Albert H. Cantrill, *Polls*. New York: Basic Books, 1972.

Richard M. Scammon and Ben J. Wattenberg, *The Real Majority*. New York: Coward McCann & Geoghegan, 1970.

Daniel Yankelovich, *The New Morality: A Profile of American Youth in the Seventies*. New York: McGraw-Hill, 1974.

6

Research: Vital Public Relations Tool

Research is an intriguing word because it conjures up different images for different people. If you mention research to the average person, he or she pictures someone in a white smock peering through a microscope or mixing chemicals in a test tube. The Ph.D. in literature envisions research as a search through the library stacks. The scientist recognizes that research begins with a search through the literature followed by countless hours in the laboratory.

Most public relations practitioners reflect the existing uncertainty and ambivalence about research. As we learned in an earlier chapter, *Webster's New International Dictionary* defined public relations in part as "the art *or* science" of securing reciprocal goodwill and understanding. As a so-called artist, the public relations practitioner conceives of himself or herself as a creative person endowed with a certain degree of imaginative skills and attributes that defy orderly measurement. However, he or she is in a managerial world—whether he or she works for a profit or nonprofit organization—where managements expect each function to operate in an orderly (scientific) fashion and to be capable of measurement and of being measured.

Although public relations practitioners tend to be uncomfortable with techniques that are scientific in nature, they certainly need—and many use—research and the scientific method as much as any scientist. To assist the reader in meeting this need, this chapter aims to strip the mystique from research and show how its usage aids and abets public relations practice.

RESEARCH AND THE PUBLIC RELATIONS PROCESS: MEANING AND BENEFITS

Professor Edward J. Robinson provides a simple definition of research when he describes it as "methods used to obtain reliable knowledge." He further points out that everyone uses reliable knowledge merely to function as human beings and that the major difference between the scientist and the nonscientist is how this reliable knowledge is achieved.

The nonscientist, says Professor Robinson, depends on his own judgment, intuition, hunches, and previous experience in attempting to solve problems. The extent of his use of reliable knowledge is personal and nontransferable. The scientist, on the other hand, makes his decisions on the basis of knowledge gained from scientific research and according to a set of rules or steps. There is no agreement about the number and kind of rules involved, but Professor Robinson cites nine steps in the scientific research process: (1) statement of the problem, (2) narrowing the problem to manageable size, (3) establishing definitions, (4) searching the literature, (5) developing hypotheses, (6) setting the study design, (7) securing data, (8) analyzing the data, and (9) interpreting and drawing conclusions about the results and reporting them.

Professor John Marston conceives of public relations research as "*planned, carefully organized, sophisticated fact finding and listening to the opinion of others.*" The connection between the Marston and Robinson descriptions of public relations research are apparent. Both stress the collection of data—one terming it "sophisticated fact finding" and the other "reliable knowledge"—and both stress the need to apply the scientific approach.

No matter how one approaches the public relations process, the need for research is paramount.

In Chapter 1 we described the public relations process as involving the evaluation of public attitudes and opinions; counseling management on policies and actions to ensure they're socially responsible and in the public interest; and executing an action and communication program to secure public understanding and acceptance. In an ensuing chapter programming will be described as a series of steps ranging from a preliminary study to communication and evaluation. As a continuous process—no matter how it's viewed—public relations in action is circular in motion. If we were to compare the public relations process to a wheel, research is the center core with spokes to the outer rim at all key points (see illustration on page 165).

There are six major benefits derived from research support of the public relations "wheel":

1. Research provides input about public attitudes and opinion.

2. Research provides factual input for programming.

3. Research serves as an "early warning" system.

4. Research serves to secure internal support for the public relations function.

5. Research increases the effectiveness of communication.

6. Research lubricates the public relations machinery.

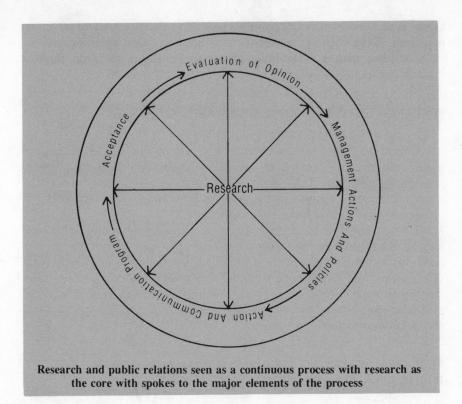

Research and public relations seen as a continuous process with research as the core with spokes to the major elements of the process

RESEARCH PROVIDES INPUT ABOUT PUBLIC ATTITUDES AND OPINION

Research, primarily opinion-survey research, is the means whereby the practitioner is able to use the scientific method to ascertain public attitudes and opinions. As Professor Robinson points out, this form of research is the most prevalent type of research utilized by public relations practitioners. Surveys of attitudes and opinions may be initiated at the onset of a program, while a program is in process, or after a program has been carried out. They may be used to spot trends or for short-range, more immediate purposes. They may be self-produced by the practitioner or assigned to professional organizations which specialize in such research.

RESEARCH PROVIDES FACTUAL INPUT FOR PROGRAMMING

Ascertaining public attitudes and opinions enables the practitioner to pinpoint with some degree of accuracy the relative standing of his organization vis-a-vis its important publics and sub-publics. Given this raw material, the practitioner is then able to fashion a program designed to solidify or improve that standing.

Research also serves the valuable purpose of providing *data* useful in subsequent programming. Through library sources and a search of the literature the practitioner is able to make a preliminary study of the organization as an entity and as part of the larger body of which it is a unit. Programming undertaken without supportable data will be superficial in nature; reliable data, gathered through research, makes it meaningful.

RESEARCH SERVES AS AN "EARLY WARNING" SYSTEM

Countless hours of time, effort, and talent are wasted handling public relations problems after they arise. Research, which can serve to spot problems *before* they arise, enables the practitioner to use his time, effort, and talents to purposes more productive than solving problems which could have been prevented.

Using research to keep abreast of those developments in our society that have consequences for organizations served by public relations is crucial to effective handling of the function. Gathering information and data about such developments is similar to the role intelligence-gathering serves with the military. Such research helps spot long-range trends in society and short-range trouble spots which can develop into festering sores.

RESEARCH SERVES TO SECURE INTERNAL SUPPORT FOR THE PUBLIC RELATIONS FUNCTION

As a relative newcomer to the management of organizations, public relations often finds itself at a disadvantage when matched against legal, financial, and marketing departments. When a problem arises in which there are differences of opinion among these departments and the public relations department, the others often win out because they rely on factual data and evidence to support their point of view.

Research provides the means whereby the public relations practitioner gains support for his/her point of view by evidence secured through scientific methods. Research replaces hunch with facts and data and thereby strengthens and supports the counsel and advice put forth by the practitioner. Research is thus not merely of value because of its substantive aid, but also because of the manner in which it builds and sustains status.

RESEARCH INCREASES THE EFFECTIVENESS OF COMMUNICATION

Studies which explore the communication process provide important lessons for those practitioners who seek scientific evidence about the effectiveness of the various forms and means of communication. Such studies are reported in articles and books and are readily available to those practitioners who seek to mine this valuable resource.

Research aimed at measuring the effectiveness of communication can also be used by the practitioner himself as part of an on-going program. A limited number of practitioners have used before-and-after studies to measure the effect communication has had on various audiences, while others utilize communication research on a regular basis as part of the total public relations program.

RESEARCH LUBRICATES THE PUBLIC RELATIONS MACHINERY

All machines, including the public relations machine, need periodic lubrication. Research is often the lubricant needed to oil all parts of public relations programming: at the commencement of a program; at various intervals during the program; and after the program has come to a halt.

When there is uncertainty about public attitudes and opinions, ← 4 Para research can be applied to find out what motivates the public. When there are doubts about steps to be taken in programming, research can be applied to resolve these doubts. When there are concerns about the effects of program activities, research can be applied to ascertain effects.

> The use of survey research by the Bethlehem Steel Corporation in conjunction with its corporate advocacy (public relations) advertising campaign in the late seventies illustrates some of the multi-benefits stemming from such research.
>
> At the time Bethlehem's advocacy advertising in 13 magazines concentrated on three issues considered important to the company. To determine the impact of such advertising and "to provide a new road map for copy and media plans," the company carried out three surveys. One was an attitude survey of subscribers of the magazines. A second was a benchmark reader awareness study of Bethlehem's corporate advertising. The third was a follow-up study to measure the impact of the company's advocacy advertising.
>
> Of interest is to note how many of the benefits of research are exemplified in the following conclusions drawn by William A. Latshaw, Bethlehem's manager of advertising:
>
> "The benchmark study and follow-up established two points of interest to us: 1) awareness level of Bethlehem Steel; and 2) awareness of our efforts and agreement or disagreement with our views.
>
> "The benchmark gave us a base from which to build. The follow-up, conducted after our . . . advocacy campaign, showed a positive result. And the attitude survey told us where our audiences lay, while providing a tool to buy media for our corporate ad campaign more intelligently, selectively, and efficiently.
>
> "With this background and reinforcement, our management agreed to our corporate advertising proposals for 1977 and approved a budget increase of 50 percent to enable us to carry out their programs."
>
> from *Public Relations Journal,*
> November 1977

MAJOR WAYS RESEARCH IS USED

A convenient way to deal with research and the public relations process is to consider the major ways in which research is used. They range from the carefully designed public issues screening procedures developed by some of America's largest industrial corporations to the simple screening of the local daily newspaper by small companies. Some cover the entire spectrum of the public relations process, while others are involved only with the listening phase. No matter what its scope or degree of sophistication, public relations research usage has one major goal: it is designed to obtain reliable knowledge and thus to facilitate the public relations function.

In no particular order of importance, our discussion of major ways in which research is used will center on the following:

1. Accumulating knowledge: the basic fact file

2. Auditing public relations

3. Auditing environmental and social problems, including emerging public issues

4. Assessing attitudes and opinion

5. Evaluating program effectiveness

The first three items cited above will be explored in this chapter. Item 4 will be discussed in detail in the next chapter, and Item 5 will be discussed in a subsequent chapter.

ACCUMULATING KNOWLEDGE: THE BASIC FACT FILE

As depicted in far too many movies and novels the typical public relations practitioner solves organizational problems by uncovering his trusty typewriter and dashing off a fast press release. In reality, the work done by the responsible practitioner is the result of long hours of careful research and fact-finding, just as the case presented in court by the trial lawyer is the result of similar long hours of research and preparation. Both the public relations practitioner and the trial lawyer may *seem* only to have a glib command of language, thought, and expression, but this is merely the surface appearance of the hard preparation which preceded the public presentation.

There are sound reasons for this preparatory fact-finding on the part of the practitioner. First, the public relations department should be the natural source of information about the organization. Unless the organization has a library and information department of its own—and only the largest organizations have such libraries and information departments—queries directed to the organization by the public, media, and by others in the organization will normally be referred to the public relations department. Such queries can best be answered when files of reliable material are available.

Second, no respectable and responsible public relations practitioner would dare practice his profession without recourse to authoritative facts and data. Because the practitioner's work deals with every aspect of the organization, it is the practitioner—more than anyone else—who has to be an authority about the organization. He has to know its history; key personnel; objectives; operations; products and/or services; and its role and place in the field and in society. In his dealings with publics and sub-publics, the practitioner will find daily need to call upon the resources of his fact-file of information and data. Compiling, maintaining, and keeping this fact-file up-to-date becomes one of the prerequisites of sound public relations practice.

Though there are many ways one can compile, maintain, and keep a fact-file current, there are two essential elements to the process. One is to establish a library of basic reference books, and the other is to establish a basic system of compiling and maintaining data.

The public relations department's *basic library* cannot, of course, be expected to rival that of the average public or university library and will obviously be limited by available space, money, and the special needs of the organization. At a minimum, the following basic library is recommended:

Britannica Book of the Year. Encyclopedia Britannica, Chicago, Illinois (Annual update of the *Encyclopedia Britannica*)

Census of Population, U.S. Government Printing Office, Washington, D.C.

Columbia Encyclopedia. Columbia University Press, Columbia University, New York, N.Y. (Latest Ed.)

Facts on File. Facts on File, Inc., New York, N.Y. (Weekly)

New York Times Index, New York *Times*, New York, N.Y. (Bi-Weekly)

Official Congressional Directory. U.S. Government Printing Office, Washington, D.C. (Annual)

Statistical Abstract of the United States. U.S. Government Printing Office, Washington, D.C. (Annual)

U.S. Government Manual. U.S. Government Printing Office, Washington, D.C. (Latest Edition)

Vital Statistics of the United States. U.S. Government Printing Office, Washington, D.C. (Annual)

Who's Who in America. Marquis Co., Chicago, Illinois (Latest edition)

World Almanac and Book of Facts. Newspaper Enterprise Association, New York, N.Y. (Annual)

Webster's Third New International Dictionary of the English Language, Unabridged. C & C Merriam Co., Springfield, Mass.

Whether one uses an alphabetical file or simply places material into compartments, there must be a *basic system of compiling and maintaining data.* The following alphabetical classification system should suffice to cover public relations source material for fact-file purposes:

Background material on the organzation, including historical, statistical, and legal material

Biographies of key personnel in the organization

Competitor and opposition literature and data

Government agencies, committees and hearings related to the organization

Legislation: pertinent bills, laws and regulations

Organizational communications: public relations ads, press releases, feature stories, speeches, and the like

Press clippings from newspapers, magazines, and trade publications

Public opinion studies relevant to the organization

Reference materials dealing with the organization's special field

Trade association literature

Setting up the above system is a relatively simply task; much more difficult is maintaining and keeping it current. Such files tend to get out of hand quickly, but as public relations departments learn to use computers, data banks, and terminals, more sophisticated retrieval systems are being developed and put to use. When background material and data are needed in a hurry—as they usually are—there's no reason why they can't be conjured up by the push of a button. For those organizations which have far-flung, dispersed public relations operations there's even more reason for the use of terminals connected to a central data bank installation. But whether maintained by hand or by means of computers, the use of a central repository of facts and data relevant to the organization is vital for research as an aid to effective public relations.

K. L. Bevak, a consultant for the Arthur D. Little Organization, notes that information gathering is so important and difficult today that only the most sophisticated and careful methods can be successful. He cites the *literature search*—described as an inventory of published and unpublished information on a given topic—as one of the most productive ways of providing data that can be used to serve public relations activities. The Little Organization, he reports, conducts its literature search with the help of over 100 computerized data bases that ferret out material from technical and scientific journals, conference proceedings, unpublished research, government documents, newspapers, and magazines. An example he cites shows how literature research can be useful in public relations planning:

As public relations director of a pharmaceutical company, you call for a scan of scientific and medical journals and the popular press for items relating to your company's products. In one of the monthly reports, you spot test results suggesting that one of the ingredients used in an adult cold remedy sold by your company could be harmful to children if the dosage directions are not strictly followed. Five months later, another research team presents similar findings, but a third test on the suspect ingredient concludes that there is no cause for alarm. Further investigation reveals that the ingredient is not among those under the Food and Drug Administration (FDA) review. Yet, over the months, the debate, still confined to professional journals, continues.

At this point, you are uncertain whether you have the germ of an explosive issue or a topic for scholarly debate. But, clearly, the onus is upon you not only to continue to watch the data, but also to seek advice from key members of your organization who could help place the conflicting studies in perspective. . . .

Technical, economic, and strategic assessments of alternatives are also part of the internal search. From the public relations perspective, it may seem that the social benefits gained by taking immediate action . . . outweigh all other considerations. Perhaps. But all of the implications of any plan of action must be considered. For example, do the benefits of a product . . . outweigh potential hazards? What will the effects be on employees and their job security if products are suddenly taken off the shelves and market positions lost? Could these results be softened by phasing actions over a period of time? Few public relations practitioners have the capability to answer these and similar technical questions, but you have the responsibility to raise them. With the opinions gleaned from literature and the insight gained by looking within your organization, you can alert top management to a potential problem and present thoughtful recommendations on handling the situation. . . . By arming yourself with the facts before the problem evolves into a public issue, you gain time to consider alternative actions. . . .

from the *Public Relations Journal,* February 1979

PUBLIC RELATIONS AUDIT

Professor Otto Lerbinger of Boston University describes the public relations (or PR) audit as "the most widely used form of public relations research." Although no empirical study has proved this claim, there is no doubt that the public relations audit serves as a valuable means of assessing public relations strengths and weaknesses and is in widespread use by public relations counseling firms in the early stage of a client relationship.

The public relations audit, as defined by Joyce F. Jones of Research and Forecasts, a wholly-owned subsidiary of Ruder & Finn, is a "broad-scale, loosely structured research study exploring a company's public relations both internally and externally." Carl Byoir & Associates describe the public relations audit as follows:

The Public Relations Audit . . . involves a comprehensive study of the public relations position of an organization; how it stands in the opinion of its various publics—stockholders, employees, customers, suppliers, investment community, thought leaders and the public at large.

It points out public relations strengths and weaknesses . . . public relations assets and liabilities. It analyzes specific problems, sharpens objectives and evaluates the adequacy of the methods used to gain goodwill and patronage.

In short, the public relations audit is a research tool used specifically to describe, measure, and assess an organization's public relations activities, and to provide guidelines for future public relations programming. The methods used in carrying out an audit vary widely, but they usually include comprehensive interviews with knowledge-able people both within and outside of the organization; various forms of public opinion surveys; a careful analysis of the organization's current public relations practices, procedures, and personnel; and recommendations for future programming.

As a general rule, the key elements of a public relations audit include a careful delineation of the publics considered to be of most importance to the organization being audited; an analysis of how these key publics rate the organization; issues considered by key publics to be of major concern; a description and analysis of current public relations programming; and the auditor's view of opportunities for future public relations programming.

It should be apparent why the public relations audit is most successful when carried out by an outside counseling firm in the early stages of a client relationship. The major purpose of a public relations audit is to provide an honest, skillful, and candid assessment, and most counselors have the capability to do just that. Lerbinger reminds us that "the whole purpose of the public relations audit is to study the public relations position of an organization so that communications plans can be drawn." That purpose is achieved when skilled resear-chers provide the client with an honest assessment and a plan for future public relations programming based on research findings. The use of research through the public relations audit is explored further in Chapter 8 in the preliminary study stage of program planning.

The term "communications audit" is sometimes used interchange-ably with the term "public relations audit," but the former is more narrowly conceived. A communications audit concerns itself mainly with internal and external communication means and methods utilized by an organization—not with the entire public relations process. To carry out a communications audit, the researcher generally relies on readership surveys, content analysis, and readability surveys.

The *readership survey* utilizes survey techniques to measure readership patterns of a particular publication, most often by means of a questionnaire.

A *content analysis* is a means of measuring and codifying the way a publication handles various stories and issues. A *readability study* is a method of measuring the ease with which stories and articles can be read.

ENVIRONMENTAL AND SOCIAL AUDIT: EMERGING PUBLIC ISSUES

Commencing as a small blip on public relations radars in the late 1960s, a new activity of interest and concern grew so fast that by the late 1970s it was called "the fastest growing area of public relations research." In fact, it grew so fast that practitioners were even uncer-tain about what to call it. Some termed the activity *environmental monitoring*. Others labeled it *social auditing*. Many preferred to term it *emerging public issues management*. Not wanting to slight any of the three, we've put them under one heading.

In actuality, the new activity that engaged the close attention of practitioners in the late 1970s had its genesis when Bernays and Childs first emphasized the need for practitioners to be concerned about vital societal trends and issues. Four decades later, the concept of emerging public issues management became a "hot" topical item in professional public relations circles. At its national conference in 1977, the Public Relations Society of America selected as its theme "Identifying and Examining Four Major Public Policy Issues." Nationally known speakers led discussions about institutional credibility, government regulation, the individual and society, and balancing natural and human resources with needs. Speakers at the Corporate Section meeting at the same annual conference described techniques of dealing with issues management employed by corporations of varying size. The Conference Board, a prestigious business management research and study group, became involved a year later in a major study exploring "how business firms are attempting to address emerging issues which are pertinent to their corporate concerns." At regional and sectional conferences, in supplements to national public realtions newsletters, and in articles in the professional journals, veteran public relations practitioners sought to come to grips with research and managerial problems involved in dealing with public policy issues.

In dealing with the problems of emerging public issues management it is probably wise to start at the beginning and come to some agreement about what we mean by the term. As already noted, such agreement is hard to achieve. Societal issues have been referred to in terms of being "emerging issues," "strategic issues," "public policy issues," "emerging public policy issues," and the like. Robert H. Moore, the Conference Board's emerging issues coordinator, seems to have best described an "emerging public policy issue" when he explained it as being one that:

1. has arisen/rearisen, or recombined with other issues, but definition and interest positions are still evolving; and

2. is a matter in which affected private institutions (such as business, labor, higher education, foundations) can and should participate in the public policy process concerned; and

3. is or is likely to be an active subject within a rolling three-year time frame.

> from a talk given at a 1978 conference sponsored by the PRSA's National Capital Chapter

The above definition clearly provides wide latitude for those who deal with public policy issues. But it has the virtue of seeing issues in terms of those that are evolving, that affect a variety of institutions, and that are likely to become a matter of public concern and policy within a three-year span of time. Of key importance to public relations practitioners is recognition of the need to foresee public policy issues in advance rather than after they've become a pressing problem. Richard Mau, Sperry Rand's vice-president of corporate communications, points out that public issues reach into every aspect of the corporate organization, reflect broad causes and broad effects, and therefore are a total management responsibility. At the same time, Mau points out, the growing pressure of issues creates the best environment for the public relations practitioner to set up the kind of relationship with top management that's needed to "pre-act" to influence from outside the corporation.

Mau's use of the verb "pre-act" rather than "react" is well advised, because reaction has all too often been management's response pattern in the past. William Durbin, chairman of the Hill and Knowlton counseling firm, characterized this response pattern as follows:

> Business habitually waits until it can no longer ignore an issue. Public relations has historically been putting out fires, rebutting charges, explaining positions. . . . By being on the defensive the corporation convinces even the uninvolved there's an antagonist-protagonist struggle. Because of this polarized universe on seemingly simple issues like clean air or financial disclosure, business is seen as opposed to clean air, in favor of secrecy. . . .

> from "Managing Issues Is Public Relations Responsibility," *tips and tactics, pr reporter.*

Durbin and other veteran practitioners concerned with issues management suggest that public relations departments enlarge their traditional activities and devise a systematic, organized approach to public policy and emerging issues. He feels that the public relations department should select a relatively small number of issues affecting the business and, with the help of operating management, develop issues positions and ways of acting on these positions. Harold Burson, chairman of the Burson-Marsteller counseling firm, also visualizes an active role for public relations in respect to social issues:

"In assessing and responding to social change," Burson wrote in the *Burson-Marsteller Report*, "the public relations function must play a central role. It is the responsibility of the public relations professional to convince his management that there is, indeed, a ground swell of public opinion sufficiently significant to lead to social change. And it is his responsibility to participate in the policy determination that will lead to an effective response."

Burson considers that a prime function of the public relations practitioner is to act as a "mediator" between the corporation and society. In carrying out this function, says Burson, the practitioner has the following four responsibilities:

1. He serves as the sensor of social change. He perceives those rumblings at the heart of society that augur good or ill for his organization. He provides a qualitative evaluation of those movements and trends.

2. He must formulate policies that will enable the corporation to adapt to those trends. In so doing, of course, he must exercise good business judgment. At the same time, he must fulfill the role of

"corporate conscience." This does not mean that a person must be a public relations professional to be sensitive. It does mean that acting the role of "corporate conscience" is not part of the job description of other executives. It *is* part of the job description of the chief public relations officer.

3. He must communicate corporate policies in two directions: internally and externally. (Burson adds here that the corporation must truly be responsive.)

4. The public relations professional must serve as corporate monitor. He must constantly monitor corporate programs to make sure they match public expectations. If the programs are not functioning or if they fall short of expectations, it is his job to agitate for new policies and programs. If he fails to do so, then he fails to live up to the requirements of his position.

Whether public relations is given the responsibility of handling emerging public policy issues or whether the responsibility is assigned to others, it should be clear that Durbin's suggestion for a form of systematized approach is necessary. One such approach is the one devised by Howard Chase, past president of the PRSA and a pioneer in issues management teaching. He describes the process components as issue identification, issue analysis, issue priority setting, and task force issue management. Others break down the procedure into two or three parts, but general consensus seems to favor a four-step approach along the following lines:

1. Identifying issues
2. Ranking issues
3. Relating issues to the organization
4. Developing action alternatives

Identification of issues may sound like a simple matter, but it's more complex than it seems on the surface. Moore, for example, reminds us that there's a fundamental problem of distinguishing between what he terms "strategic issues" and "public policy issues." He describes the former as "those environmental forces and trends which may be demographic, sociological, resource related, technologically related, political, economic, or what have you, that have a bearing on how a company does business, and therefore have a bearing on that company's survival and success." On the other hand, he says, public policy issues are "those questions or problems in the public domain which corporate management believes it should take a stand on, even though they do not appear to be vital to the company's survival or success and, thus, are not of primary relevance to its planning." He reports that some senior public affairs officers claim they can tell you in ten minutes what the major emerging issues are for their organizations. Others, he notes, may well view the list of events and trends as almost endless. In its study, he notes, the Conference Board focused on the following ways of establishing issue identification systems:

1. The chief executive officer designates the issues.

2. Senior executives, through informal discussion, draw up a list of issues.

3. Through structured polling, senior executives establish a list.

4. A staff unit is charged with the specific responsibility of developing an issues list for senior management's collective consideration and refinement.

5. Issues are developed initially by division or profit center heads.

6. A formal "exploratory planning process" is established to develop a list that goes well beyond the typical three to five years' limits of "the strategic plan" that many companies employ.

7. Issues are identified by a cadre of volunteers who scan a wide variety of publications.

The above are not all-inclusive because there is no right way to research and identify emerging public issues. Public relations practitioners must not only be aware of this elementary fact, but also of the probability that many others within their organizations may be involved in the issue identification process. Moore therefore suggests that it's necessary to know the answers to the following questions: What is the corporate planning unit doing? the legal department? the people in market research? those in research and development? The old saying holds true: the right hand ought to know what the left hand is doing, and this applies to issue identification just as it does to playing the old shell game.

Ranking issues calls for a winnowing process. Issues come in all sizes, shapes, and forms. So do organizations, and that's why Issue A may be of vital importance to Organization X but of little importance to Organization Y. Furthermore, issues do not exist in laboratory isolation, but are deeply related to the social, political, and economic environment in which they arise and flower or wither and die. What may have been a low priority issue yesterday could well be today's high priority issue. Note, for example, this statement by Anthony G. DeLorenzo, former vice-president for public relations of the General Motors Corporation:

> Sometimes we have to shift gears on our priorities. For example, the energy issue was in our 1973 Plan, but well down on our priority list because there just wasn't great public concern about it at the time. It got a sudden promotion when the oil embargo struck that fall.

DeLorenzo provides a clue to one method of bringing down to manageable size the usually large number of issues that make up an original list; *establish a time frame.* Clearly, some issues will be immediate, others intermediate, and still others long-range.

Another method is to *decide which issues are of direct and which of indirect importance* to your organization. Although the oil embargo had important consequences for most American organizations, it certainly was more important to General Motors than to a manufacturer of Frisbees. Equal rights and facilities for women athletes has more importance for a large coeducational university than for a small, all-women's college.

A third method is to *group issues according to relative overall significance.* In the overall scheme of things, the issue of nuclear power for nonmilitary purposes is more significant than the issue of sex education in kindergarten. (Obviously, this is an example of card-stacking. It would be more difficult to decide which is a more significant issue: nuclear power for nonmilitary purposes or sex education in junior high school.)

The above three methods are certainly not the only ways to handle ranking of issues, but whatever method is used it should serve the basic purpose of cutting issues down to a manageable level. Matching issues to your organization becomes the next step in the process.

Relating issues to the organization calls for further refinement of issue ranking, and in many instances the two steps can be carried out concurrently. As previously explained by Moore, there are certain strategic issues that have a distinct bearing on an organization's survival and success, whereas public policy issues are not of primary relevance to that same organization. But, Moore reminds us, what may be simply a public policy issue for one company may be a strategic issue for another. To illustrate this point, he explains that a national energy policy would probably be a strategic issue for most manufacturing concerns, but not for most companies in the publishing industry. Deciding the relevancy of issues thus becomes a matter of careful judgment. One must deduce whether and to what degree the issue affects the organization and whether the organization can do anything about it.

Developing action alternatives, the final step in the care and handling of emerging issues, presents thorny problems for the public relations practitioner. When Moore addressed the Washington Chapter of the PRSA in mid-1978, he was asked to offer the group a provocative listing of some emerging issues for the 1980s. The last of his laundry list of twelve emerging issues was described as follows:

> For individuals in your line of work, a major emerging issue will be to present the output of issue identification systems in "actionable" terms. Management generally doesn't want just to know that a particular trend is likely to reach a crucial turning point in 1985. Management wants to know what the consequences are of the paticular trend and what specifically management should do about it. And as you know better than I, this is a dilemma to which there is no ready solution.

It would be wise to read that last statement twice. Moore is perceptive of realities when he tells public relations practitioners that an emerging issue *for them* is the need to develop alternative methods of handling all the other emerging issues they've decided are important to the organizations they represent. True, public relations provides valuable input to management when it calls attention through research to key public policy issues that are emerging in importance.

Equally true, public relations is even more valuable when it comes up with alternative ways of *dealing* with or reacting to such issues.

How effective the public relations practitioner can be in carrying out the vital fourth step in issues management will depend on the answers to the following kinds of questions:

1. What kind of skills and attributes does the practitioner have? Is he or she capable of analyzing societal trends and of perceiving the direction in which society is moving? Is he or she similarly capable of devising creative action alternatives to meet the challenges of societal trends?

2, How does management view the public relations function? If public relations is seen chiefly as a *communication* function, it can have little impact on emerging issue *action* policies.

3. Where does public relations stand *vis-a-vis* the other powerful functional areas in large organizations? Will public relations be able (given the chance) to make its voice and counsel heard and heeded at the highest levels of the organization?

4. Finally, does management really want to *do* anything about emerging social issues, or is it satisfied to be chiefly *informed* about them?

The questions above explore in a tentative way the many dimensions of the "actionable" dilemma to which Moore refers. The answers depend on the unique nature and qualities of each public relations practitioner and each organization.

The perceptive reader will have noted that this chapter's discussion of three major ways in which research is used deals with the employment of research in the early or "listening" phase of the public relations process. One should not conclude that the use of research is restricted to this phase, for such is not the case. Research is also utilized in the evaluation stage of the public relations process, but a detailed discussion of such usage will be provided in the chapter concerned with evaluation.

QUESTIONS AND PROBLEMS FOR DISCUSSION

1. How would you distinguish between scientific and nonscientific research?

2. Would you consider public relations research to be scientific or nonscientific? Justify your conclusion.

3. What is meant by the statement that "public relations in action is circular in motion"?

4. Why does the author place research at the center core in comparing the public relations process to a wheel?

5. Explain some major purposes or benefits of public relations research.

6. What is meant by the statement that "research is of value because of its substantive aid, but also because of the manner in which it builds and sustains status"?

7. What is a public relations audit?

8. How is such an audit carried out?

9. What's the difference between a public relations audit and a communications audit?

10. What is meant by the term "emerging public policy issue"?

11. Name and explain the four major steps in handling emerging public policy issues through a systematized approach.

12. Explain the difference between "strategic issues" and "public policy issues."

13. Explain the kinds of internal problems that face public relations practitioners in dealing with emerging public policy issues.

PROJECTS, ASSIGNMENTS, AND MINI-CASES

1. TREND-SPOTTING AT GENERAL MOTORS: A MINI-CASE

Today's complex and changing public issues require that corporate executives be informed promptly of problems and trends that affect their operations.

At General Motors, this task is the responsibility of the public affairs section of the public relations staff, which is headed by A. V. Gagliardi, Manager of Public Affairs. With a staff of seven, and buttressed by libraries and staff in Detroit and New York, GM's public affairs section devotes its time to:

- Reading and reviewing a broad selection of newspapers, magazines and books

- Pinpointing trends emanating in academic and scientific circles

- Sponsoring and monitoring public opinion studies relating to issues that affect the auto industry

- Preparing and distributing reports and digests to GM management

The material reviewed includes well-recognized publications such as *Fortune, The Atlantic, Harper's*, the national weekly magazines and the *Harvard Business Review*. The section also covers ecology newsletters, technical publications, political publications, and television and radio programs that relate to the automobile industry. The more specialized material is covered by staffers with engineering and economics backgrounds.

The reports that are distributed to management vary in format. They may be a single page digest of a speech; a brief memo of an article in *Nature* magazine; or a lengthy analysis of an important book on economics. The writers strive to be concise and readable, aware that their work must compete with the many other reports the average auto executive lugs home.

Distribution of public affairs reports usually begins with the chairman and extends down to middle management.

Questions for Discussion

1. What qualifications do you think someone would need to work in GM's public affairs section?

2. What are some other publications this section might review?

3. Do you feel this activity would increase or decrease in importance in the future? Why or why not?

4. What do you perceive to be some major problems involved in the public affairs work described in the case? How would you handle them?

5. In addition to air pollution and automotive safety, what other issues do you feel GM might be following? Why?

Assignment

Assume that you are a researcher on Gagliardi's staff. Your assignment is to research and summarize two articles that have appeared in national publications in the last six months and that, in your opinion, seem to have important consequences for General Motors. The articles should *not* be about General Motors itself, but about problems and trends that could conceivably affect the corporation. Each of your two summaries should be about two typewritten pages long.

2. PUBLIC RELATIONS EXTENDED PLANNING: A MINI-CASE

Harshe-Rotman & Druck, veteran international public relations counseling firm, offered in 1975 a new service called PREP, or "Public Relations Extended Planning." The service was announced by various means, including a brochure which was distributed in the fall of that year. Details of the service were spelled out in this brochure in the following description of the program:

PREP

In an era of unprecedented, monumental, and accelerating change, public relations professionals have an added and demanding dimension to their jobs: They must be able to alert the rest of their top management group of these changes before they happen or while the changes are in the early stages of development. Failure to act until changes have matured and almost run their course often can be disastrous.

Harshe-Rotman & Druck offers a new service that it has been developing for about a year, from elements that go back several years, a specialized, four-part program to help top management in public affairs planning.

Harshe-Rotman & Druck, a 44-year-old international public relations firm, developed the program to allow public relations professionals to present, in an organized and well-documented way, potential or evolving public affairs issues deserving top-level management attention.

Called PREP (an acronym for "Public Relations Extended Planning"), the program is tailored, based on specialized research, to the needs of the company or other groups, such as associations or nonprofit organizations, contracting for it.

The program is a four-part presentation that requires one to two days, depending upon the complexity of the group to which the presentation is being made.

Part I—A broad overview of what's gone before in areas of public opinion.

Part II—What's ahead during the next year or two that could affect the specific audience hearing the presentation.

Part III—What might happen during the next two to ten years.

Part IV—What the audience can do to accelerate or slow down potential changes.

I. The presentation begins with a review by a spokesman from National Opinion Research Center, University of Chicago, which has been conducting nationwide public opinion studies for 34 years. The NORC representative describes attitudes, especially those affecting the business community, that have changed dramatically during past years and those that have held relatively constant. While the NORC spokesman does not try to predict from past studies, he does provide a backdrop for the rest of the presentation and suggests which opinions are likely to be relatively constant and which are likely to change.

II. The next part of the presentation is made by John Naisbitt, chairman and president of Urban Research Corporation and publisher of the *Trend Report*, a specialized publication that is subscribed to by such companies as Bank of America, Xerox, General Motors, General Electric, Squibb, and Celanese. Naisbitt outlines developments that are likely to evolve during the next year or two and have a substantial impact on the group hearing the presentation.

III. Dr. John G. Keane, president of Managing Change, Inc., a company that specializes in what Keane calls "anticipatory intelligence" for major corporations, then describes developments that can affect the group two to ten years into the future.

IV. The fourth part of the presentation is by a representative of Harshe-Rotman & Druck. He describes what public relations techniques can be used to accelerate or combat evolving trends. Presentations tailored to the group contracting for them require about $4,000 in time for a one-day presentation to a company with a relatively uncomplicated product line. Other presentations, dealing with more complicated structures, require appropriately more time for preparation. Not inexpensive, but valuable.

Top management groups that have heard elements of these presentations speak extremely highly of them. If you're interested and would like to see some of their comments, please contact one of the seven U.S. offices of Harshe-Rotman & Druck.

Reproduced by permission.

Questions for Discussion

1. What is your opinion of the PREP program as spelled out in the brochure?

2. What changes, if any, would you suggest be made in the PREP program?

3. What is your opinion of the way in which Harshe-Rotman & Druck presented the program in its PREP brochure? Cite specific elements of the brochure which you approve or disapprove.

Assignments

1. Assume that you have been given the responsibility for "selling" the program. In a memorandum to A. R. Roalman, executive vice-president of H-R & D, explain how you intend to merchandise PREP.

2. Assume that you are director of public relations of a national firm that manufactures and sells a wide variety of major appliances. The president of the firm has received a copy of the PREP brochure and she sends it to you with this notation: "This looks interesting. What do you suggest?" Reply to the president in a memorandum.

3. ROBERT MOORE'S LITTLE LIST: A MINI-CASE

When Moore addressed the Washington Chapter of the PRSA in May 1978, he was asked to provide the group with a list of some emerging issues for the 1980s. He told the group that it's "not possible to satisfy the request in any sensible way because one company's emerging issue may be another's chronic problem." However, an obliging guest, Moore proceeded anyway to offer a list of a dozen issues that he felt might well affect many in the audience in the years ahead. Following are the first ten of the twelve issues as described by Moore:

1. Consider the issue of demographics. The trend toward smaller families means more disposable family income and, for an airlines for instance, this means more pleasure air trips. Thus, demographic projections will be built into airlines' demand forecast.

2. The changing ramification of EEO programs. Today it is women and blacks who are at the forefront of attention. Tomorrow it may be the Vietnam veterans, the aging, and the handicapped. Some believe there have been more changes in the last five to eight years in employment practices than in the previous century and the changes are by no means all at the federal level.

3. The declining ability of high school students to read, write, and compute properly.

4. The growing unwillingness of junior and middle-age executives to relocate. This reflects a sharply growing concern in American society with the quality of life, and in the long run such trends could have a severe impact on the personnel policies of corporations.

5. The increasingly politicized nature of American society. Thus, if one's basic premise is that public attitudes are sooner or later sure to be translated into legislation, then the resulting issue identification system will be highly sensitive to political concerns.

6. For the diehard futuristic, I offer volcanic eruptions which are apparently creating problems in some agricultural areas due to the ensuing blockage of sunlight. This in turn affecting matters such as planned reclamation, fertilizer applications and runoff problems, as well as the need to develop other growing areas.

7. Consider that the post-World War II economic and political stability of Europe may be severely tested in the next decade by a juxtaposition of events that would separate U.S. interests from those of Western Europe. These may include an energy shortage, at least partially successful efforts of European Communist parties to achieve power, and a U.S.-U.S.S.R. confrontation under conditions of nuclear parity when, this time, we may "blink" first because we have less at stake in Central Europe than does the U.S.S.R.

8. Migration to the "sunbelt" states will continue. Population problems will increase in the southeast and southwest while declining population in the northern states will cause political and economic problems.

9. We may reach a crisis in water quality. Only now are we beginning to discover some of the exotic chemicals contained in surface water, rivers, and streams, and their health effects are not clearly defined.

10. The long-term impact of the deferred cost of retirement programs including Social Security, state, local and Federal Civil Service and military retirement programs. Private pension programs are also a problem in some instances but the biggest risk centers around the many government programs.

Reprinted with permission of
Robert Moore.

Assignments

1. You are to assume that you are considering Moore's list as of the time you are reading this text. Decide which five items on his list are, in your opinion, of *lesser* importance than the other five. Then draw up a new list of five issues you feel should replace those you've eliminated, and briefly explain why you've selected each of the items on your substitute list.

2. You are to assume that you are a public relations counselor who has three major clients: General Electric, Stauffer Chemicals, and Burger King. You are to consider each item on Moore's list as of

the time you are reading this text and to rate the items in terms of what you believe to be their comparative importance to *each* of your three clients. A suggested rating system for each item and each client: very important, important, not very important. Briefly justify each of your ratings for each item and each client.

RECOMMENDED READING

K. L. Bevak, "Literature Search and Analysis: Key to Vital Information," *Public Relations Journal,* February 1979.

Gler M. Broom, "Coorientational Measurement of Public Issues," *Public Relations Review,* Winter 1977.

Burson-Marsteller Report, May 1973.

Howard Chase, "Public Issues Management: The New Science," *Public Relations Journal,* October 1977.

William A. Durbin, "Managing Issues Is Public Relations Responsibility," *tips & tactics* supplement to *pr reporter*, May 15, 1978.

Barrie Jones and W. Howard Chase, "Managing Public Policy Issues," *Public Relations Review,* Summer 1979.

Joyce F. Jones, "Audit: A New Tool for Public Relations," *Public Relations Journal,* July 1975.

William A. Latshaw, "Target Group Research: New Tool for Advocacy Advertising," *Public Relations Journal,* November 1977.

Otto Lerbinger, "Corporate Use of Research in Public Relations," *Public Relations Review,* Winter 1977.

_____, "How Far Toward the Social Audit?", *Public Relations Review,* Summer 1975.

Walter K. Lindemann, "The Missing Link in Public Relations Research," *Public Relations Review,* Spring 1979.

John Marston, *Modern Public Relations.* New York: McGraw-Hill, 1979.

Robert Moore, "Spotting Emerging Issues," talk given to the National Capital Chapter, PRSA, Washington, D.C., May 9, 1978.

"Organizing for Issues Management—A Public Relations Opportunity." New York: Public Relations Society of America, 1978.

Robert Van Riper, "The Use of Research in Public Relations," *Public Relations Journal,* February 1976.

Edward J. Robinson, *Public Relations And Survey Research.* New York: Appleton-Century-Crofts, 1969.

Claire Selltiz, ed., *Research Methods in Social Relations,* rev. ed. New York: Holt, Rinehart and Winston, 1962.

Carlton E. Spitzer, "Where Are We Getting All This Information and What Are We Doing With It?" *Public Relations Journal,* February 1979.

"The Corporate Image: PR to the Rescue," *Business Week,* January 22, 1979.

James F. Tirone, "Education, Theory, and Research in Public Relations," *Public Relations Review,* Spring 1979.

7

Research Techniques:
Reading, Viewing,
Observation, Public
Opinion Polling

As noted in the previous chapter, public relations research is used to accumulate knowledge and to carry out public relations, environmental, social, and emerging public issues audits. Four basic techniques are utilized in achieving these purposes. The most common are reading, viewing, and observation (to be discussed briefly in this section), and public opinion polling (to be discussed more fully in the section that follows).

READING, VIEWING, AND OBSERVATION

The three research tools of reading, viewing, and observation are at the disposal of almost anyone who cares to use them. All of us read, view, and observe to some extent. However, the difference between the public relations researcher and "almost anyone" is that the researcher uses the tools in a purposeful way. The researcher, for example, not only tries to spot societal trends, but he or she *seeks to make reasonable assumptions and judgments about probable influence of these trends on public relations practice.* Thus, the chief purpose of reading, viewing, and observation is to use the results for public relations purposes. One such purpose is to provide intelligence data. Another is to provide information and data for public relations planning. A third is to establish warning signals about impending changes in public attitudes and opinion. Thus, through research uses and techniques, the public relations practitioner is able to carry out his or her function in a planned rather than in a random fashion.

READING

One of the first lessons that the public relations graduate learns when he gets his first job in the field is that the reading he's done in college is just a prelude to the reading he will have to do for the rest of his professional life. Others may read for pleasure or not read at all, but the public relations graduate reads because reading is the lifeline to a successful career.

Purposeful reading is an important research tool because the printed page reflects the facts, ideas, and opinions about the society in which we live. At a minimum this reading should include the daily newspaper(s) published in the city where one works; the nearest metropolitan newspaper of national stature; either *Newsweek* or *Time* or both; *Variety, Broadcasting, Editor and Publisher*; trade and specialized publications; and nonfiction books related to one's special field or which provide insights about important trends in American life.

The local newspaper(s) will provide timely intelligence about local affairs, but may print a minimum amount of state, national and international news. The nearest metropolitan newspaper of national stature fills out the daily intelligence diet by the volume and quality of nonlocal news it carries. Considered to be papers of national stature are the: Boston *Globe*; New York *Times*; Washington *Post*; Miami *Herald*; Chicago *Tribune*; Des Moines *Register* and *Tribune*; St. Louis *Post Dispatch*; Denver *Post*; Los Angeles *Times*. If your public relations activities concern business or industry, then the *Wall Street Journal* would also be required daily reading.

Newsweek, Time, or both not only serve to bring together into a single weekly package the loose ends of daily national and international news, but their many special sections are guides to the entire spectrum of American life.

Because the public relations practitioner is so dependent on mass media, he must be aware of what's happening with the media, and *Variety, Broadcasting* and *Editor and Publisher* serve this purpose. Trade and specialized publications are indispensible as information sources about the fields they cover.

VIEWING

Motion pictures and television are not merely powerful media of communication but molders of national life styles, manners, dress, and customs. Prior to the advent of television—particularly in the twenties, thirties, and forties—motion pictures were *the* trend-setter in depicting the so-called American way of life. The fact that the movies of that period were more fantasy than reality is less to the point than the fact that they set trends in dress, style, manners, and morals.

In the fifties, television replaced motion pictures in the trend-setting department. Excluding its coverage of news and live events, the bulk of afternoon and prime-time television in 1979 was devoted to fantasy in the form of "soaps", game, detective, and sit-com shows.

Although none of these can be considered reality, they set trends, and the avid TV watcher can keep up with trend changes by watching.

Whether motion pictures and television initiate or mirror trends is less important than the fact that both have enormous influence on the viewing public. Successful movies and television shows attract audiences numbering in the millions. The public relations practitioner can make movie and television viewing productive by assessing it in terms of spotting the trends depicted in each medium.

OBSERVATION

Whether the research is that carried out by the scientist in the laboratory or that followed by the public relations practitioner in real life situations, the need to observe pertinent phenomena is a paramount concern. The phenomena that the practitioner observes is the current scene. Such observation is open to everyone, of course, but most people are casual observers; the practitioner is, or should be, a purposeful observer. If he travels widely throughout the country he notes local, regional, and national aspects of American life, manners, and style. At all times he keeps in touch by recognizing that there is more to the country than the route he travels from his home or apartment to his office.

Keeping in touch becomes more difficult as the practitioner's income and status rise. In fact, the more successful he becomes the greater the distance between him and the rest of the country. Trying to observe how most Americans live is almost impossible when the observation post is a first class seat on a 707 flying at 32,000 feet between New York City and Los Angeles. Because America itself is the practitioner's laboratory, the practitioner must observe American life on the ground where it exists. From time to time he should travel by subway instead of taxi, by car instead of plane, through cities instead of around them on super highways; visit Disney World instead of London; eat at McDonalds instead of the Four Seasons; shop at Sears instead of Count Charles; go to baseball games instead of the opera; in short, mingle with and observe the majority of his countrymen on their home turf.

Observation as a research tool comes in varying degrees of difficulty. Such life-style appendages as dress, public behavior, work and play habits, and manners can be observed with the naked eye. More difficult to discern and chart are mores, private behavior, reactions to major institutions and their actions and policies, and similar covert aspects of life-styles. Impossible to discern and chart through mere observation are attitudes and opinions, and to cope with trends in these areas the practitioner turns to more sophisticated techniques. Survey research is such a technique.

PUBLIC OPINION POLLING

Survey research in the form of public opinion surveys and polls is the most scientific and prevalent form of research used by public relations practitioners. Its techniques—particularly those developed by such national polling organizations as the Harris organization, the American Institute of Public Opinion (Gallup), Opinion Research Corporation, the Yankelovich organization, the Roper organization, and others—have been refined and honed to the point where they are universally accepted as scientifically proven ways of measuring public opinion. National organizations with large public relations departments use their own resources to carry out public opinion polls, but the more common practice is for public relations departments and counseling firms to contract for surveys with professional polling organizations.

Depending on the degree of refinement desired, public opinion polls and surveys consist of a series of steps or procedures. At a minimum these include the following: (1) *defining the purpose*; (2) *identifying the population*; (3) *selecting the research method*; (4) *selecting the sample*; (5) *constructing the questionnaire*; (6) *interviewing and processing data*; and (7) *analyzing, interpreting and reporting the data*.

DEFINING THE PURPOSE

Defining the purpose is as important and crucial a step in public opinion surveying as defining the problem is in public relations planning and programming. Taking a survey without a clear understanding of the reasons for the survey can lead to no end of trouble and can be a sheer waste of time, money and talent.

On the surface, there seems to be no problem involved in defining the purpose of a survey. After all, isn't a survey conducted to ascertain public opinion? The answer is "yes, but" with public relations becoming the "butt" when results turn out to be negative instead of positive.

All too often when managements approve the commissioning of a survey of public opinion they do so on the assumption that said opinion will be favorable. Unduly sensitive managements tend to consider negative public opinion to be a personal affront to their competence—which it sometimes is—and although they may seem to approve an impartial survey they really expect the mirror on the public opinion wall to show them to be the fairest of them all. When it doesn't, public relations is blamed for the bad image the mirror reflects.

Thus, one of the first steps to take when surveying public opinion is to find out if management really and honestly wants to ascertain public opinion or only go through the motions of a survey but really doesn't want to face up to any negative findings. Securing the answer to this question is no simple matter, but the practitioner must settle the problem of purpose—whether directly or by circumlocution—before the survey has been taken.

Assuming that management does seek honest answers, the practitioner must decide just what he wants to know about such opinion. Does he seek to find out what people *know* about his organization? Does he seek to find out what people *think* about his organization? Is he seeking public reaction to *specific organizational actions, policies and/or plans*? Does he want to measure and assess the *impact and effectiveness of the organization's public relations program* or specific aspects of said program? Is he attempting to assess *trends* in public opinion? Is he seeking to assess *probable public reaction to projected* organizational and public relations actions and programs? Each of these purposes is a valid target and goal of survey research, but each calls for a specific and special set of questions. Such questions cannot be devised unless the purpose or purposes have been clearly established in advance.

IDENTIFYING THE POPULATION

People, not animals, form the audience for public opinion surveys, but that's about the easiest distinction that can be made. *Who* forms the population becomes a matter of setting parameters and eliminating the noninvolved.

Assume your firm has been asked to conduct a survey to ascertain who will be elected alderman in Ward 10 of a city of 80,000 population. First, forget about the entire city and concentrate on Ward 10. Second, eliminate all those under 18 years of age. Third, eliminate those of voting age but not eligible to vote. Fourth, try to screen out those most likely to stay away from the polls. Those remaining form the true population for your survey.

Another example. The Calcium Chloride Institute has budgeted between $5,000 and $9,000 for a survey of attitudes and opinions about the use of calcium chloride to keep down dust on Iowa roads in the summer and to clear ice off roads during the winter. Accepting the assignment, you have an initial interview with the CCI and learn that county highway engineers and county supervisors have responsibility for highway maintenance and the purchase of appropriate highway clearance agents. Your population is not the adult population of Iowa but the county highway engineers and county supervisors.

These are two examples of problems connected with the determination of the population to be surveyed in public opinion polling. Similar problems arise in all surveys, whether you are surveying *employees* (all employees, hourly employees only, division employees, field employees only?); the *college* community (all students, full-time students only, dormitory residents, faculty, administration?); the *community* (adults only, everyone 16 years and older, opinion leaders, everyone except those in nursing homes and hospitals?); and similar general groupings of people. In each case a clear distinction must be made of the exact population to be surveyed.

SELECTING THE RESEARCH METHOD

There are a variety of ways to describe and discuss the major survey research methods available to public relations practitioners, but the simplest is to consider them as *structured* or *unstructured*.

Unstructured

The *depth interview* is the most common and widely used form of the unstructured survey and is best described as informal in nature and lasting from a half hour to an hour. The interviewer usually compiles in advance a series of "probe points," but these are not set up in the form of carefully designed and worded questions but rather as general areas to be explored with the interviewee. The basic idea of the depth interview is to explore in depth the respondent's ideas, attitudes, opinions, knowledge, and expertise on a series of subjects.

The depth interview has plus and negative factors. On the plus side is the fact that such an interview provides a more intensive reading of the respondent's mind and thinking than is possible from a structured questionnaire interview. The relatively free-wheeling atmosphere of the depth interview often brings out information, ideas, and opinions not anticipated by the researcher. Because the interviewee is not restricted by the confines of specific and carefully worded questions, the interviewee is able to express his or her intrinsic and honest thoughts, attitudes, opinions, and feelings.

On the other hand, few interviewers have the talents required for depth interviewing and such interviews are costly because of the time and talent involved. Furthermore, tabulating, codifying, assembling, analyzing, and reporting the results are extremely difficult tasks. Because such interviews are free-wheeling, long, and involved, the answers to "probe questions" are also free-wheeling, long, and involved. Yet for purposes of reporting the results, answers have to be compressed, analyzed, and put into final report form and this inevitably leads to editorial tinkering and interpretation. Finally, because of the time, talent, and cost factors already cited, depth interviews cannot economically be used for large samples or where respondents are widely dispersed. Because of these limiting factors, depth interview surveys are seldom representative of total populations but represent the views of a limited number considered to be unusually well-informed about the areas being surveyed.

Structured

The most common form of the structured public opinion survey utilizes a questionnaire as its basic tool. Such surveys are carried out in three major ways: by personal interviewing, by mail, and by telephone. The best method to use is dependent on a variety of factors: the subject of the survey, the population to be surveyed, the geographic location of the population, the length and complexity of the questionnaire, and the time needed for and the cost of the study.

Personal interviewing was once the most prevalent of the three forms, but increasingly it is sharing popularity with telephone interviewing. A major advantage of the personal interview is that it permits flexibility in regard to the type and kind of questions that can be asked. Researchers consider that complex questionnaires are best administered by personal interviewing. Scaling can be used to permit respondents to indicate the dimensions of their responses. Questions can be placed on cards, and respondents can be given the chance to read the question and choose their responses from a list. Complex questions can be read out and repeated, and interviewers can probe and secure explanations when desired.

National polling organizations have refined their sampling techniques to the point where they're assured of a true representative sample in national surveys with totals of between 1,500 and 2,000 respondents. By using callbacks they're usually able to obtain completion rates from 90 percent of the designated sample, and their record of accuracy in predictions measured against final results in voting surveys has been generally excellent.

In recent years, however, personal interviewing has encountered serious difficulties for polling organizations for a number of reasons. Because of the national concern with crime, many people refuse to open their doors to strangers. Because of the increasing number of women entering the job market, the problem of "not-at-homes" has intensified. In many urban areas personal interviewing has become almost impossible to carry out:

> When an agency of the government reports problems in gathering data for its decennial census count, you can be sure private polling organizations are encountering similar problems in urban areas.
>
> Reporting to a House subcommittee about their inner-city experiences in a "dry run" prior to the 1980 census count, three young crew chiefs stressed the considerable difficulty they've had in gaining public cooperation in certain areas of New York City. They reported that their enumerators had met with widespread hostility toward the government and a reluctance to answer questions about income and housing.
>
> from *New York Times,* March 31, 1979

There are other reasons for the declining use of personal interviewing by national polling organizations. Personal interviewing is the most costly of the three methods and also the most time-consuming (other than small studies carried out in one or a few locations). Other drawbacks of personal interviewing relate to the kinds of questions that can be asked and to the interviewers. Because of the face-to-face nature of personal interviewing, interviewers claim that questions of a personal nature cannot easily be asked. It is also claimed that an interviewer can bias results by the manner in which he or she handles the interview and the questions.

Mail surveys are far less costly and time-consuming than are personal interviews, and they have a special advantage when the population to be surveyed is widely dispersed or is situated in hard-to-reach rural or inner-city areas. Interviewer bias is eliminated because there are no interviewers. The questionnaire can be answered at the convenience of the respondent, not at the convenience of the interviewer. Because mail surveys are handled from a central office, there is no problem with controls and checks. Because the respondent has the questionnaire in hand, there is less problem with complex questions than there is in personal or telephone surveys.

Mail surveys have certain drawbacks inherent in their basic nature. Such surveys have to be drawn from lists, and in certain circumstances there simply isn't an available list. For example, there is no readily available mailing list for a probability sample of the national population. In some cases lists do not represent a true sample of the universe to be surveyed, and in other cases the list is incomplete, old, or unreliable.

Another drawback of the mail survey is in regard to the length and nature of the questionnaire. In very few instances are respondents willing to complete a questionnaire of more than four to six pages. If the questionnaire is not carefully designed—so that easy-to-answer and noncomplex questions come first—the survey document won't be returned. Because no interviewer is involved, the questionnaire and its covering letter must stand on their own without chance for amplification, explanation, or motivation by a third party.

The final drawback of mail surveys concerns both the response rate and the representative nature of the response. Because almost all surveys involve sampling from a list representing the universe to be polled, an estimation must be made in advance as to the expected response rate. Paul Erdos, authority on mail surveys, says that "no mail survey can be considered reliable unless it has a minimum of 50 percent response, or unless it demonstrates with some form of verification that the nonrespondents are similar to the respondents."

The Advertising Research Foundation recommends 80 percent as a standard for mail surveys. To reach these levels generally requires at least one, and sometimes more than one, followup mailing. This, of course, takes time and adds to the cost of the survey.

Whether the responses are representative of the universe being probed can best be proved by the inclusion of demographic questions in the questionnaire and by measuring answers, when possible, against the known demographics of the total universe probed. Erdos suggests the following simple rule:

"No mail survey can be considered reliable unless it has a high percentage of return, or unless some kind of verification proves that the response actually received is representative of the entire sample."

The answer to the question of a "high" percentage of response, says Erdos, is found in the degree of reliability the researcher expects from the survey. This in turn depends on such factors as the nature of the universe and whether one is seeking general patterns or accurate projections.

Those interested in exploring specifics about mail surveys are referred to Erdos's *Professional Mail Surveys,* cited among the list of recommended books at the end of this chapter.

Telephone surveys, although not as versatile as personal surveys, have become the most often-used type of public opinion survey because of several factors. With the introduction of Wide Area Telecommunications Service (WATS) it is now possible to conduct a national survey from a central location at far less cost and with far more speed than it is possible to conduct a personal interview survey. The fixed line rental makes it possible to conduct a large survey in a short period of time. The fact that 95 percent of American homes now have telephones has also been a major reason for the use of surveys by telephone. Refinement of techniques, such as drawing the sample by means of random digit dialing (RDD), is a further reason why the major polling organizations have turned to telephone interviewing. (The method of drawing a sample from a table of random digits is described on p. 199.) Random digit dialing, in effect, is a means of compensating for the fact that unlisted telephones have been on the increase and hence would not normally be included if a telephone survey were to be based on a sample drawn from telephone directories. Klecka and Tuchfarber describe the RDD system as follows:

> This method requires the identification of all working telephone exchanges in the target geographical area. A potential telephone number is created by selecting an exchange and then appending a random number between 0001 and 9999. Subsequent numbers are created by repeating these two steps. Nonworking numbers, nonresidential telephones, and households outside of the geographical area are excluded during the interviewing process. Households with more than one telephone number are downweighted accordingly.

There are many advantages to telephone surveys. As already noted, two main advantages are speed and lower cost. If properly planned, a national survey of public opinion can be conducted immediately after an event, and the results can be reported shortly thereafter by the use of computers. Because the interviewing process can be controlled and monitored from a central location, the quality of information obtained tends to be better than that achieved from personal interviewing. Although telephone surveys encounter the same not-at-home and refusal problems as do personal interviews, repeated callbacks can be more easily made by telephone, so a higher response rate can be achieved. The problem of hard-to-reach respondents, encountered increasingly in personal interviewing, is minimized by telephone surveys because telephones are so widely in use today.

Blankenship, in his authoritative book about telephone surveys, says that one of the characteristics of such surveys is that frankness of response is facilitated because the respondent does not see the interviewer or the interviewer's reactions. He reports that controversial topics can be covered best by telephone for the same reason, and he notes there is less interviewer bias and cheating.

Telephone interviewing has its disadvantages, and a major one is the fact that a telephone survey cannot be too long. Replies also tend to be shorter, it is more difficult to probe, and there is a tendency to give neutral replies. Open-ended questions are usually limited because respondents become impatient while waiting, on a seemingly dead line, for the interviewer to write down the responses.

Despite its drawbacks, telephone surveys have become the major means of measuring after-event public opinion. An example of telephone survey use was a survey carried out for the *New York Times* and CBS News the day after President Carter announced in December 1978 that full relations would be opened with China. Here is how the *Times* described the survey procedure:

> The latest survey by the *New York Times* and CBS News was conducted Dec. 16-17 after President Carter's speech announcing the establishment of diplomatic relations with China. It is based on telephone interviews with 1,011 adult men and women.

Telephone exchanges were selected by computer so as to insure that each region was represented in proportion to its population. For each exchange, telephone numbers were formed by random digits, permitting access to both listed and unlisted numbers.

The results have been weighed for household size and to adjust for variations in the sample relating to region, race, sex, and education.

In theory, in 19 cases out of 20, the results based on the sample differ by no more than 3.5 percentage points in either direction from what would have been obtained by interviewing all adult Americans. An additional margin of error results from the practical difficulties in taking any survey of public opinion.

Of major interest is the speed with which the survey was taken and reported. A story citing the results appeared in the *Times* on December 19, just four days after the president made his announcement. That, by any assessment, is proof of the speed and timeliness of telephone surveys of national public opinion!

Recommended for its detailed description and analysis of telephone surveying is Blankenship's *Professional Telephone Surveys,* cited among the list of recommended books at the end of the chapter.

SELECTING THE SAMPLE

Polling a sample of the population or universe rather than the entire population or universe is a basic feature of virtually all public opinion polls today, yet the concept of sampling seems to be least understood by the lay person. In their national pre-election polling and predictions the polling organizations work with samples ranging between 1500 and 2500 adults of voting age, and these numbers inevitably cause doubters to question how such minute samplings— when compared to the total number of pesons of voting age—can be considered representative of the entire universe of voters. The answer is found in an explanation of sampling theory, practice, and procedures.

The first important point to understand about sampling is that *the size of the sample is far less important than representativeness.* The key to proper and effective sampling is to use a system of sample selection which gives each individual in the universe an equal opportunity to be selected in the sample polled. If improperly drawn, a sample of one million cannot be considered a true indicator of the universe it supposedly represents. Properly drawn, a sample of 1500 can be considered a true indicator of the opinion of millions.

Random or Probability Sampling

To make sure that the sample polled is representative of the universe, the major polling organizations draw a random or probability sample. Such a sample means that it has been selected in such a manner that *each element* in the universe has an equal or known chance of being in the chosen sample. The term "random" should not be taken to mean that selection has been obtained willy-nilly, but rather that the sample has been obtained without bias and by a carefully designed process. Further, probability sampling enables the pollster to specify the degree by which the sample is representative of the universe. Here is an explanation by the Gallup Organization of the manner in which it designed the sample for a national survey:

> The design of the sample is that of a replicated probability sample down to the block level in the case of urban areas and to segments of townships in the case of rural areas.

> After stratifying the nation geographically and by size of community in order to insure conformity of the sample with the latest available estimates by the Census Bureau of the distribution of the adult population, about 320 different sampling locations or areas were selected on a strictly random basis. The interviewers had no choice whatsoever concerning the part of the city or county in which they conducted their interviews.

> Approximately five interviews were conducted in each such randomly selected sample point. Interviewers were given maps of the area to which they were assigned, with a starting point indicated, and required to follow a specified direction. At each occupied dwelling unit, interviewers were instructed to select respondents by following a prescribed systematic method and by a male-female assignment. This procedure was followed until the assigned number of interviews was completed.

> Since this sampling procedure is designed to produce a sample which approximates the adult civilian population (18 and older) living in private households in the U.S. (that is, excluding those in prisons and hospitals, hotels, religious and educational institutions, and on military reservations), the survey results can be applied to the population for the purpose of projecting percentages into number of people. The manner in which the sample is drawn also produces a sample which approximates the population of private households in the United States. Therefore, survey results can also be projected in terms of number of households when appropriate.

> Reproduced by permission of The
> Gallup Organization

Size Versus Representativeness

A comparison of the ill-fated *Literary Digest* straw polls of the thirties and the modern-day Gallup, Harris, and Roper national pre-election polls illustrates the matter of sample size and representativeness. In the decade preceding the 1936 presidential election the *Literary Digest* conducted its straw polls by mailing out millions of postcard ballots to persons listed in telephone directories, on lists, or who were owners of automobiles. Despite the fact that such lists numbered in the millions they did not represent the entire American electorate, and were particularly deficient in lower income representation. The *Digest's* straw poll hut came tumbling down in 1936 when it mailed out ten million postcard ballots and received a return from two million persons who marked their choices. The *Digest's* final pre-election poll showed that Landon would win by 57 percent and Roosevelt would lose with 43 percent of the popular vote. The actual vote was 62.5 percent for Roosevelt and 37.5 percent for Landon. The 19 percentage-point error was one of the largest in polling history.

By comparison, using proper representative techniques and relying on a sample of less than 1,500, the Gallup Poll predicted a 55.7 percent vote for Roosevelt and a 44 percent vote for Landon. The Gallup organization was on target in its prediction of the winner, though it erred by 6.8 percent in its predicted percentage of the vote that would go to Roosevelt. That 6.8 percent error, by the way, was the largest error in Gallup Poll predictions in the period from 1936 through 1974. Gallup has correctly predicted the winners in all but one (1948) of the elections held in the years between 1936 through 1974 and has come remarkably close to the actual vote figures with the exception of the 1948 election when Gallup, and all the other national polling organizations, failed to conclude polling close enough to election day. (The Gallup Poll record of accuracy in pre-election polling is shown in the following table):

Record of Gallup Poll Accuracy in National Elections

Year	Gallup Final Survey* %		Election Result* %		Error on Winning Candidate or Party, Based on Major Party Vote %	
1936	55.7	Roosevelt	62.5	Roosevelt	−6.8	Roosevelt
1938	54.0	Democratic	50.8	Democratic	+3.2	Democratic
1940	52.0	Roosevelt	55.0	Roosevelt	−3.0	Roosevelt
1942	52.0	Democratic	48.0	Democratic	+4.0	Democratic[1]
1944	51.5	Roosevelt	53.3[2]	Roosevelt	−1.8	Roosevelt
1946	58.0	Republican	54.3	Republican	+3.7	Republican
1948	44.5	Truman	49.9	Truman	−5.4	Truman
1950	51.0	Democratic	50.3	Democratic	+0.7	Democratic
1952	51.0	Eisenhower	55.4	Eisenhower	−4.4	Eisenhower
1954	51.5	Democratic	52.7	Democratic	−1.2	Democratic
1956	59.5	Eisenhower	57.8	Eisenhower	+1.7	Eisenhower
1958	57.0	Democratic	56.5	Democratic	+0.5	Democratic
1960	51.0	Kennedy	50.1	Kennedy	+0.9	Kennedy
1962	55.5	Democratic	52.7	Democratic	+2.8	Democratic
1964	64.0	Johnson	61.3	Johnson	+2.7	Johnson
1966	52.5	Democratic	51.9	Democratic	+0.6	Democratic
1968	43.0	Nixon	43.5	Nixon	−0.5	Nixon
1970	53.0	Democratic	54.3	Democratic	−1.3	Democratic
1972	62.0	Nixon	61.8	Nixon	+0.2	Nixon
1974	60.0	Democratic	58.9	Democratic	+1.1	Democratic

*The figure shown is the winner's percentage of the Democratic-Republican vote except in the elections of 1948 and 1968. Because the Thurmond and Wallace voters in 1948 were largely split-offs from the normally Democratic vote, they were made a part of the final Gallup Poll pre-election estimate of the division of the vote. In 1968 Wallace's candidacy was supported by such a large minority that he was clearly a major candidate, and the 1968 percents are based on the total Nixon-Humphrey-Wallace vote.

[1]Final report said Democratics would win control of the House, which they did even though the Republicans won a majority of the popular vote.

[2]Civilian vote 53.3, Roosevelt soldier vote 0.5 = 53.8 Roosevelt. Gallup final survey based on civilian vote.

Reprinted by permission of The Gallup Poll

The Gallup Poll, and the other polling organizations dealing with nationwide polling, draws its sample by dividing the population into strata according to the size of the locality in which the people live. A specified number of interviews are then conducted after specific geographical areas are selected by a systematic, random basis. Those interviewed are chosen for the sample on a chance basis, and the result is the closest approximation of all characteristics of the universe being surveyed.

The same procedure can be used for *lists* provided the lists include everyone in the universe and are up to date. For example, assume we want to survey student opinion in a college with 10,000 students. If we determine to use a sample of 200, then we would first divide 200 into 10,000 and thus arrive at intervals of 50. By random selection we would choose a starting point within the first 50 on the list. If the choice falls on the 25th person, then that person would be the first to be interviewed and the next person would be the 75th on the list. The resulting 200 interviews would comprise a probability sample reflective of the key characteristics of all 10,000 students.

The list procedure can also be used in drawing a probability sample of a town or city, though in such a case we would want to deal with addresses rather than individuals. Using an up-to-date city directory we would first number every single household address, including apartments, in the city. (We do this because people move, but houses and apartments don't.) If the last numbered address turns out to be 30,000 and our designated sample is 300, we would divide 300 into 30,000 to arrive at an interval of 100. Again, by random choice we would select a starting number within the first 100 addresses and then interview at intervals of 100.

Instead of using intervals and drawing every nth name from a designated list, another way to select a sample is to utilize a table of random digits. Such tables are sometimes found in the appendix of a statistics textbook; a valuable source is The Rand Corporation, *A Million Random Digits with 100,000 Normal Deviates*, the Free Press, 1955. Each page of such published tables of random digits contains a large number of random digits divided into blocks of five for the sake of convenience. The digits can be read in groups of two, three, or more to produce two, three, or more digit numbers. The starting point is selected haphazardly. Following is an excerpt from a table of 10,000 random digits:

Line No.	1-5	6-10	11-15	16-20	21-25	26-30	31-35
0	10097	32533	76520	13586	34673	54876	80959
1	37542	04805	64894	74296	24805	24037	20636
2	08422	68953	19645	09303	23209	02560	15953
3	99019	02529	09376	70715	38311	31165	88676
4	12807	99970	80157	36147	64032	36653	98951
5	66065	74717	34072	76850	36697	36170	65813
6	31060	10805	45571	82406	35303	42614	86799
7	85269	77602	02051	65692	68665	74818	73053
8	63573	32135	05325	47048	90553	57548	28468
9	73796	45753	03529	64778	35808	34282	60935

To use the above table the first necessity is to number every name (or address) on the list representing our universe. The next step is to decide on the size of the sample, and then to draw the sample from the table of random digits. As an example, assume the last number on our universe list is 2,530 and we want to draw a random probability sample of 200. We have chosen as our starting point line 2, column 3. Reading four digits across and then down, our first eight four-digit numbers are 4226, 0190, 8079, 0657, 0601, 2697, 5733, 7964. Because they're under 2530, the first numbers to be included in our sample would be 0190 (190), 0657 (657), and 0601 (601). Continuing to draw from the table, our next numbers would be 2533, 4805, 8953, 2529, 9970, and so on running down columns six, seven, eight and nine. Of the five numbers, only 2529 would be included in the sample selection because it's the only four-digit number that is lower than our 2530 limit. We would continue our selection of four-digit numbers ranging under 2530 until we had reached a total of 200, the size of our sample.

Thus, in choosing a sample from lists we can either use a procedure of selecting every nth number or make our selection by means of a table of random digits. The remaining questions about sampling concern the way in which we can calculate the chances that our sample is representative of the universe, and this is done through the statistical concept known as "sampling error."

Sampling Size and Error

Samples are used in polling public opinion because it is usually impossible to poll the entire population, and even if it were possible, the cost would be prohibitive.

The same two reasons apply when we consider how large a sample must be to secure a truly representative reading of public opinion. Deciding on the size of the sample is a matter of achieving a balance between the cost of the survey and the degree of precision needed. The end goal is to use a sample that will produce results within *acceptable margins of error*, and it is important to understand that in dealing with probability sampling reasonably accurate findings can be achieved with surprisingly small samples.

Professional polling organizations operate on what is known as a 95-confidence level, and this means in effect that in an infinite number of similarly designed and executed surveys the percentage results would fall within a given margin of error in 95 percent of these surveys. Thus, the Gallup Poll estimated margin of error at the 95-confidence level is three percentage points for a sample of 1,500; four percentage points for a sample of 1,000; five percentage points for a sample of 600; and six percentage points for a sample of 400. If a Gallup Poll survey of 1,500 interviews shows the president having the support of 50 percent of the population he might actually be supported by as few as 47 percent or as many as 53 percent. If the sample consisted of 400 interviews that 50 percent support could be as high as 56 percent or as low as 44 percent.

Table of Suggested Tolerances for the Gallup Poll

The table below provides the suggested sampling tolerances for the Gallup Poll's standard sampling unit on the basis of procedures presently in use. The figures take into account the effect of the sample design upon sampling error. They show the range, plus or minus, within which results can be expected to vary with repeated samplings under exactly similar conditions.

In Percentage Points
(at 95 in 100 confidence level)*

	Sample Size						
	1500	1000	750	600	400	200	100
Percentages near 10	2	2	3	3	4	5	7
Percentages near 20	2	3	4	4	5	7	9
Percentages near 30	3	4	4	4	6	8	10
Percentages near 40	3	4	4	5	6	8	11
Percentages near 50	3	4	4	5	6	8	11
Percentages near 60	3	4	4	5	6	8	11
Percentages near 70	3	4	4	4	6	8	10
Percentages near 80	2	3	4	4	5	7	9
Percentages near 90	2	2	3	3	4	5	7

*The chances are 95 in 100 that the sampling error is not larger than the figures shown.

To use the table above, these directions should be followed. Suppose a reported percentage is 33 for a group that embraces 1500 respondents. Since 33 is nearest 30 in the table, look in row 30 under the column headed 1500. The number in the table is 3, which means that the 33 percent figure obtained in the survey is subject to a sampling error of plus or minus 3 percentage points. Another way of saying this is that very probably (95 times in 100) repeated samplings of this size would yield figures ranging between 30 and 36, with the most likely figure being the 33 percent obtained.

It should be noted that the table deals with the normal sample unit now employed by the Gallup Poll. Many surveys of this organization embrace a far greater number of persons, usually multiples of 1500 unit.

Reprinted by permission of The Gallup Poll

Roll and Cantril raise an important question that relates to the suggested tolerance of error shown in the preceding table. They ask: "Would it be worth nearly doubling the cost of a survey by increasing the sample size from 750 to 1,500 in order to reduce the expected sampling error from plus or minus four percentage points to plus or minus three percentage points?"

The answer would be "no" when considering most surveys carried out for public relations purposes. If our survey reveals that 60 percent of those surveyed think poorly or highly of our organization's policies and actions, it really doesn't make that much difference if the percentage were 56 percent or 64 percent. The important consideration for the practitioner is to make sure that the sample is a carefully drawn random-probability sample which is broadly representative of the universe and which has given every individual an equal opportunity of being selected. Sample size is certainly crucial when polls are used to predict election results, but not for other public opinion assessment purposes. Carefully drawn, samples as low as 200 to 400 are adequate to reveal public attitudes, opinions, and knowledge concerning organizational policies, actions, programs, and standing.

CONSTRUCTING THE QUESTIONNAIRE

The major tool used in structured random-probability survey research is the questionnaire. Designing the questions to be asked and arranging them in proper order requires the most careful attention on the part of the researcher. There is a definite knack to question design, as Stanley Payne implies by the title of his book (*The Art of Asking Questions,* Princeton University Press), and this art will be discussed in respect to the placement, form, and wording of questions.

Placement

Unless one is willing to have the interviewing terminated early in the interview, difficult or challenging questions should not be among the first questions asked. The initial questions should be the kind that are easy for the respondent to answer. They should not challenge the respondent's intelligence or knowledge, but should be of such a nature as to put the respondent at ease. Preferred as opening questions are those which can be answered with a simple yes or no, will give the respondent confidence in himself, and are not of a sensitive or embarrassing nature.

There should be a logical arrangement of the questions, and this is best achieved by grouping them so that the conversation leads logically from one question to another. Thus, questions relating to a specific area of concern should follow one another and not be spread throughout the questionnaire. When posing general and specific questions, ask the general ones before asking the specific questions. If this is not done, the respondent is likely to answer the general questions in terms of the specific ones asked earlier. Avoid grouping sensitive questions, but rather intersperse them with neutral ones. If a question poses some long or involved alternatives, put these on cards which can be handed to the respondent. The interviewer then reads out the question and asks the respondent to make his choice from the card.

Form

There are three basic forms of questions with many varieties of each form. Only the basic forms will be described here.

Dichotomous questions are those which provide two options. Examples of dichotomous questions are those which pose a choice between yes and no, approve and disapprove, good and bad. Proper procedure is to provide also for a third response, such as don't know, no opinion, or neither. If the third possibility is not provided then the question may force respondents to make a choice which they would not really want to make.

On the positive side, dichotomous questions are simple, easy to pose, understandable to the respondent, and easy to tabulate.

On the negative side, such questions may force respondents to make a choice they do not want to make. Opinions about many subjects do not fall readily into a simple yes-no choice, but may fall in between the two extremes.

Multiple choice questions in a variety of styles provide alternatives not available in dichotomous questions. Such questions are most often phrased to provide three-four and five-point rating scales. Examples of three-point scales: above average, average, below average; higher, the same, lower. A four-point scale would be excellent, good, fair, poor. Some five-point scales: much greater, somewhat greater, equal, somewhat less, not at all; strongly approve, approve, undecided, disapprove, strongly disapprove.

A refinement of the verbal multiple choice rating scale is the graphic rating scale in which the respondent is asked to show strength of opinion on a line of numbers. Highest approval might be a plus five, middle would be zero, and lowest would be a minus five.

The virtue of multiple choice, rating-scale questions is that they allow degrees of opinion to be expressed. On the negative side is the fact that such questions tend to be long and place a heavy burden on the respondent's remembrance of the choices.

Open end questions make up the third major form of questions. Instead of providing preconceived response choices they permit the respondent to answer the question freely and allow wide latitude for his answers. Their major virtue is that they pick up the full flavor of a response and often reflect unanticipated opinions. Their major problem is that they are hard to categorize and often have to be forced into a mold for tabulation purposes.

Wording

Though the wording of questions seems to be a simple matter, it actually requires a great deal of care and skill. The following major guidelines are suggested:

1. Use simple rather than complex words. Aim questions so they're understood by those with a tenth grade level of education.

2. Be precise and absolutely clear. Payne suggests the following six-point test of a proposed question:

    a. Does it mean what we intend?

    b. Does it have any other meanings?

    c. If so, does the context make the intended meaning clear?

    d. Does the word have more than one pronunciation?

    e. Is there any word or similar pronunciation that might be confused?

    f. Is a simpler word or phrase suggested?

3. Cover only one point at a time, not two or more in one question. Asking "Do you like the taste of wine and cheese?" assumes that everyone considers the two in combination with each other when judging their taste. It's possible for someone to like the taste of wine and dislike the taste of cheese, but the question does not permit such an answer.

4. Avoid leading questions. Any question that is likely to produce a biased answer can be considered to be a leading question.

Leading questions lead to misleading answers. Unless the surveyor is deliberately trying to secure predetermined answers, he should avoid phrasing the question to bring about desired answers.

5. Make sure the question will elicit the exact information sought. Questions which are not explicit enough will often produce answers which can't be combined for data reporting. For example, asking employees to estimate how much profit their company makes can bring answers in dollar figures, percentages, and gradations ranging from "a lot" to "not much." If you want the figure to be in dollars, specify dollars in the question. Further, does the question mean "net profit" or "gross profit"? If the surveyor is not sure what he means than he can't expect the respondent to be sure.

6. Frame alternatives carefully and honestly. Provide the same number of alternatives for each side of a question. Recognize that the more alternatives, the less likely respondents will favor the extremes. Try to phrase alternatives realistically the way people think and feel about problems and issues. Do not combine issues and partisan arguments. Balance the wording of alternatives so as to avoid biasing the results.

INTERVIEWING AND PROCESSING DATA

Good interviewers are basically good listeners rather than good talkers. Interviewing requires the ability to be at ease in social situations and to be able to adapt easily to one's surroundings. Above all, interviewers must be reliable, honest, and able to work on their own. Although interviewers have to go through a preliminary training session, thereafter they work independently and hence must be trustworthy.

Professors James Mullen and Michael Bishop ("Clinical Interviewing in Public Relations Research," *Public Relations Quarterly*) consider the field work aspect of public opinion polling to be an area of real concern. They cite laziness and dishonesty as two human failings with which all organizations must do constant battle. "When just a little of either creeps into an interviewing organization," they state, "accuracy in survey research is no longer possible. Given large doses of either or both, the value of a survey is totally destroyed."

Guarding against bias or inaccuracy resulting from interviewing failures is a constant problem for polling organizations. The national ones rely on checking and supervision to weed out undesirable interviewers, but checking is difficult when interviewers are widely dispersed and work independently, as all interviewers do. Finding good supervisors is even more difficult.

Handling survey data is done chiefly through machine processing and has reached a stage that cannot be described in detail in a textbook of this nature. The major polling organizations use skilled punch card and data processing operators and machines for sorting, compiling, and storing the survey data, and this calls for a preliminary coding of responses. In small surveys this work can be done manually, but the task is a tedious one that calls for the utmost care and attention to detail in handling data and percentages.

Robinson describes the steps in preparing data for analysis:

> Translation of raw data into analyzable form requires a number of steps, some comparatively simple and others much more complex. Easiest is the straight forward tabulation of the various direct questions (age, income, and so forth) that were precoded beforehand and which require only a checkmark or a circle on the part of the interviewer. The open-ended questions and the various indirect data collection techniques require more elaborate rate procedures. Generally these questions elicit answers that range from a few words to hundreds of words, depending upon the question and the purpose of the survey. In order to make sense out of these thousands of words, they must be analyzed and put into response categories that *reflect* the content of the answer in manageable form. This process is known as *content analysis*. Essentially, it is a technique which permits a systematic, objective, and exhaustive analysis and classification of the responses or "thought units" obtained from all of the interviewees in a given survey into response categories that sum up their replies to a certain question or series of questions. . . .

> After the raw data have been prepared for analysis (by simple tabulation or content analysis), they are generally expressed in terms of tables, which pull together all of the replies to a given question and enable the researcher to make his interpretations. . . .

> from *Public Relations and Survey Research*, p. 97

ANALYZING, INTERPRETING, AND REPORTING DATA

If wrapping up the results of survey research were only a matter of presenting the data in tabular form, life would be relatively uncomplicated. The facts could speak for themselves. However, as Robinson warns, there is no such thing as a fact standing by itself. Raw data has to be reassembled into some form of logical order and interpreted to those for whom the survey is designed. One way to achieve such meaning is to *apply percentages* to the findings. A second is to *describe* the findings by means of adjectives and adverbs, and a third is to apply some interpretation to the findings.

Percentages are important because they widen the narrow focus of the sample figures and make them applicable to the universe. Let us say we used a sample of 100 respondents and the universe is 2,000 people. A response to a question shows that 75 out of the 100 are "very much" in favor of a particular action. Widening this finding we can say that 75 percent of the universe are "very much" in favor of the action.

Stating this same finding in descriptive words we can say that "a high proportion" or "three-quarters" or "more than seven out of ten" people favor the particular action.

Thus, by the use of percentages and descriptive words we're able to express the findings in a variety of ways and at the same time to place them in perspective. Relatively dull figures take on life through such techniques, but description and interpretation should honestly reflect the figures on which they are based. Unfortunately, managements often either expect interpretation to gloss over deficiencies or else don't want to face up to negative findings. The positive ones are always easy to handle; the negative ones can be the moment of truth for the public relations practitioner.

RESEARCH, ONLY THE BEGINNING

In concluding this chapter on research it's appropriate to cite this reminder by Professor Robinson: ". . . a research study, survey or otherwise, seldom tells the practitioner what to do." Through the use of fact-finding, trend study, and public opinion survey research, the practitioner gains valuable information for subsequent public relations programs and activities. Ways of making the most intelligent use of research findings will be explored in the chapters that follow.

QUESTIONS AND PROBLEMS FOR DISCUSSION

1. What seven basic steps are the minimum ones involved in public opinion surveying?

2. Why may it be necessary at times to use indirect rather than direct methods to ascertain management's reasons for approving a public opinion survey? If circumlocution seems called for, specifically how would you go about ascertaining management's reasons?

3. List and explain some valid goals of public opinion surveying for public relations purposes.

4. What are some of the problems which arise in identifying the population of a public opinion survey?

5. Explain the major advantages and disadvantages of depth interviewing.

6. Under what circumstances would one prefer to conduct a mail and/or telephone rather than a personal interview public opinion survey?

7. What is meant by a random/probability sample, and what steps need to be taken in drawing one?

8. What is meant by the statement that "the Gallup Poll estimated margin of error at the 95-confidence level is three percentage points for a sample of 1,500?"

9. What are the differences among dichotomous, multiple choice, and open end questions? What are the advantages and disadvantages of each?

10. Explain some major guidelines for wording questions, and draw up some survey questions to illustrate each guideline.

11. Why should survey data be expressed in percentages?

12. Beginning in 1959, the Television Information Office has commissioned the Roper Organization to design and conduct a survey of national public opinion towards television and other mass media. The first question in all the surveys was worded as follows:

> First, I'd like to ask you where you usually get most of your news about what's going on in the world today—from the newspapers or radio or television or magazines or talking to people or where?

Do you think the wording of the question is fair to all media or do you think it is worded in such a way as to result in responses favorable to one or more media? Explain your conclusions.

PROJECTS, ASSIGNMENTS, AND MINI-CASES

1. THE PROFESSOR DESIGNS A QUESTIONNIARE: A MINI-CASE

A college professor decided to measure student opinion about the area's local daily newspaper. He therefore designed the following questionnaire for students to complete. (The paper was an afternoon daily; the average issue ran to twenty-eight pages; the editorial page usually contained several editorials, three national columns, and letters to the editor; the front page always contained only national and international news from the Associated Press.)

Questionnaire

1. Do you read the Gazette? Daily_____ Frequently_____
   Seldom_____ Never_____

2. Do you read any other newspapers? Yes_____ No_____ Which
   ones? (1)_____ (2)_____ How often? Daily_____ Occa-
   sionally_____ Sundays only_____

3. What part of the newspaper do you usually read first?
   Comics _____Front page stories_____
   Sports_____Advertisements _____
   Editorials _____Obituaries_____
   Local news _____Other _____
   Favorite_____
     columnist_____

   What do you read next?_____

4. Do you read the editorials? Daily_____ Frequently_____
   Seldom_____ Never_____

5. Are there some parts of the paper you never read? Yes_____
   No_____ Which parts? (1)_____ (2)_____ (3)_____

6. Which candidate in the current presidential campaign does your
   newspaper support? (Check one)
   Ford_____ Carter_____

7. Do you feel that your newspaper is giving fair news coverage to
   both major candidates?
   Yes_____ No_____ Don't know_____ If not, who is more favored?_____

8. Do you think the editorials deal fairly with both candidates?
   Yes_____ No_____ Don't know_____

9. Do you think the columnists deal fairly with both candidates?
   Yes_____ No_____ Don't know_____

10. Do you think both the Republican and Democratic viewpoints are presented by the editorials and columnists in your newspaper?
Yes_____ No_____ Don't know_____
Do you approve of this? _____
Why? _____

Questions for Discussion

1. In your opinion, which questions need rewording? Specifically, what is wrong with the questions which you think need to be reworded?

2. Rewrite the questions which the class found unacceptable.

2. REPORT OF AN INNER-CITY SURVEY: A MINI-CASE

A 1970s client of Carl Byoir & Associates was the Children's Television Workshop, producer of the much-praised program, "Sesame Street." To measure inner-city attitudes about the program and about viewing habits, the firm commissioned the Daniel Yankelovich survey firm to conduct a personal interview survey in the Bedford-Stuyvesant area of Brooklyn. In reporting to the Byoir account executive responsible for the Children's Television Workshop account, the Yankelovich firm underscored the care taken in handling survey methodology. The report stated:

> This is to report to you on the extremely encouraging and outstanding results for "Sesame Street," which we found in our recent study, conducted among ghetto households in the Bedford-Stuyvesant area of Brooklyn, New York.

> Indeed, the results are so outstanding that we feel it is important to first state the methodology, sampling methods, field interviewing procedures, and validation techniques used to guarantee that these results are completely reliable and projectable.

> 1. *Qualifications of Respondents:* In order to qualify for the interview, a respondent had to have either children between the ages of 2 to 5 who were neither in day care or nursery schools during the day, or to care for other children of this same age group on a regular (five day a week) basis. All interviewing was done during the daytime to guarantee that the mothers or babysitters were at home during these hours and could speak from first hand knowledge. The second qualification was that there had to be at least one television set in working order in the household.

> 2. *The Sampling Procedures:* The sample was designed to insure maximum representation of the entire Bedford-Stuyvesant area, and minimize any bias due to either the clustering of the interviews or possible interest generated by the appearance of the interviewers in the area. A total of 40 sampling points were used. In each sampling

point, an interviewer was given a starting point, and a route to follow. When it was necessary for the interviewer to return to the sample point for a second day to complete her assignment, she was given a second starting point and routing. Listing sheets were kept to account for not at home, ineligibles, and refusals.

In order to obtain the 500 completed interviews, a total of 1676 households were contacted. The results broke down as follows:

Total Contacts	*1676*
Completed Interviews	502
Eligible Respondents—Refused to be interviewed, language problems, etc.	42
Ineligible Respondents	
No child 2 to 5	1037
Eligible on child 2 to 5 qualification/no working television set	22
Refusals/before eligibility could be ascertained	73

Both the recovery rate and the low incidence of refusal, we believe, are exceptionally good.

3. *Field Interviewing:* All interviewing was conducted by black interviewers living within or immediately adjacent to the Bedford-Stuyvesant area. No one interviewer was assigned more than two sampling points. Almost all of the interviewers had had previous interviewing experience. Despite this, each interviewer assigned to the project was personally trained for this assignment.

4. *Validation:* Close to 100 percent validation was made of all completed interviews. Respondents were asked whether or not they had been interviewed, and the subject of the interview. In addition, direct questions were asked about the viewing of "Sesame Street" and the demographic characteristics of the household.

Each of the completed interviews was also carefully read and checked by the project director as a final validity check.

Reprinted with permission

Questions for Discussion

1. What do you consider to be of significance about the qualification of respondents? About the sampling procedure? About the field interviewing? About the validation?

2. Why do you think the Yankelovich organization stressed that "indeed, the results are so outstanding (etc.)"?

3. Do you think there would be special problems in polling in Bedford-Stuyvesant? If so, why and what do you feel they would be? If not, why not?

4. What do you think of the relative merits of a telephone survey rather than the personal interview survey used in this instance? How about a mail survey?

3. REPORTING RESULTS OF AN EMPLOYEE SURVEY: A MINI-CASE

To measure and evaluate employee knowledge, attitudes and opinions a large manufacturing company contracted with a professor of industrial relations to prepare a questionnaire and personally supervise the polling of employees on company time. The results were presented in a 15-page printed report which was divided into sections dealing with areas such as pay, profits, opportunity, etc., and distributed to employees. Each section contained the questions, responses in percentages, some typical comments, and an interpretation in the form of a "management comment." Following is the first section of the report dealing with pay:

Pay:
(1.) How do you feel your pay compares with that paid in other companies for similar type of work?

Lower 31%

The same 52%

Higher 16%

Employee Comments:"Skilled experienced workers are paid too low in comparison with production workers. . . . For what we have to know, they're too low. . . . Pay isn't everything when you like the company and work. . . . I have checked with other companies and wages are higher. . . ."

(2.) Do you feel you are paid what you are worth to the company?

Much less 11%

Somewhat less 43%

About worth 41%

More than worth 2%

Employee Comments:"If a company paid employees what they (the employees) thought they were worth, no company could stay in business today. . . . Starting wages are too low. . . . I could use some more money. . . ."

Management comment: We were most interested to see that on the vital subject of pay, more than two-thirds of you felt that you were receiving the same or higher pay than in other companies for the same work. Our policy is to try to make our pay scales higher by helping and encouraging you to operate with higher efficiency. This is the only way higher than average pay can be permanently maintained under our competitive system. We believe our pay scales as well as our efficiency are generally higher than average today, and we hope we can progressively increase them.

About half of you feel you are worth more than you are paid. That's human nature. It was once remarked that there were only two classes in society: Those who get more than they earn, and those who earn more than they get. The other fellow, naturally, is the one who gets more than he earns, while we are the folks who are earning more than we get. A certain amount of dissatisfaction on this score is healthy and necessary, for we would have no ambition if we were entirely satisfied on this point.

We have been conscientious in making periodic reviews of pay and job classifications and making adjustments wherever and whenever they seem fair. We shall continue that policy.

As the business expands, we employ more people. However, in most departments, and often in branch office, clerical and service departments, a given amount of work may be done by fewer people at higher pay—rather than by more people at lower pay. In other words, if we can find ways to increase our efficiency and productivity, we naturally open the way for advancement and higher pay.

Questions for Discussion

1. What is your opinion of the wording of the two questions about pay? If you were to change them, how would you reword them?

2. What is your opinion about the "employee comments" cited at the end of each set of results?

3. What is your opinion about the "management comment?" Discuss in terms of content, tone, length, and wording.

4. If you were to change the "management comment," how would you change it?

4. CLINICAL INTERVIEWING: A MINI-CASE

Professors James Mullen and Michael Bishop presented a strong case for depth interviewing—they term it "clinical interviewing"—in an article they wrote for *Public Relations Quarterly*, Spring, 1975. They cite the following example to demonstrate the value of such interviewing:

One study concerned the use of bank credit cards. The organization behind the card had a number of unanswered questions concerning the acceptance, use, and nonuse of its card. Among the questions were these: (a) Who is a good prospect for a bank credit card? (b) Why do some people keep a bank card but fail to use it? (c) Is there a difference in perception of bank card credit vs. other types of credit among users? (d) Why do some people use these cards only for "big ticket" items while others use them for anything *but* such items? (e)

How have various bank public communications (personal contact, letters, media advertising) been received by users and prospective users?

Such "why" and "how" questions as these have represented a prime source of difficulty for those using regular survey research. One can't be certain about what constitutes the universe when dealing with such a diversity of questions. (To include everyone who should be involved in *one* part of the study would mean that large numbers of people could be included who should *not* be involved in *other* parts.) Using the clinical method, any person interviewed would contribute only to those sections of the study where his contribution is relevant.

In order to obtain answers to these questions using quantitative survey methods, it may have been necessary to draw three or four separate samples and prepare a specific questionnaire for each. Instead, the authors were able to obtain useful results with just one small sample and no questionnaire. They conducted all 75 interviews themselves (in three states, in communities of varying size, with old and young, rich and poor, black and white). They were able to stop with 75 interviews as they found they were getting little new information and were largely confirming what they had already learned.

The project cost much less than would have a series of quantitative studies, and all parties concerned were convinced that the results (while not projectable) were reliable and therefore useful. Three years after the study was completed, its conclusions are still being employed as a basis for guiding successful corporate communications.

Questions for Discussion

1. What's your opinion of the study and the authors' conclusions about its effectiveness?

2. Do you agree or disagree with the author's contention that finding answers to the six questions would have required three to four samples and surveys using quantitative survey methods?

3. What criticism, if any, do you have about the composition of the 75 interviews?

4. What questions do you have about the selection of the sample of 75?

RECOMMENDED READING

A. B. Blankenship, *Professional Telephone Surveys.* New York: McGraw-Hill, 1977.

Leo Bogart, *Silent Politics: Polls and the Awareness of Public Opinion.* New York: John Wiley and Sons, 1972.

214

Harper W. Boyd, Ralph Westfall, and Stanley F. Stasch, *Marketing Research,* 4th ed. Homewood, Ill.: Richard D. Irwin, 1977.

Paul L. Erdos, *Professional Mail Surveys.* New York: McGraw-Hill, 1970.

George H. Gallup, *The Gallup Poll: Public Opinion 1972-1977.* Wilmington, Del. Scholarly Resources, 1978.

———, *The Sophisticated Poll Watcher's Guide.* Princeton, N.J.: Princeton Opinion Press, 1972.

James Hanson and Herbert I. Abelson, *Persuasion: How Opinions and Attitudes Are Changed,* 3rd ed. New York: Springer Publishing, 1976.

Matthew Hauck and Michael Cox, "Locating a Sample by Random Digit Dialing," *Public Opinion Quarterly,* Summer 1974.

William R. Klecka and Alfred J. Tuchfarber, "Random Digit Dialing: A Comparison to Personal Surveys," *Public Opinion Quarterly,* Spring 1978.

Walter K. Lindemann, "Opinion Research: How It Works; How to Use It," *Public Relations Journal,* January 1977.

Maxwell McCombs, "The Agenda Setting Function of Mass Media," *Public Relations Review,* Winter 1977.

Harry W. O'Neill, "Survey Research as a Public Relations Tool," *Public Relations Review,* Fall 1977.

Donald C. Orlich, *Designing Sensible Surveys.* Pleasantville, N.Y.: Redgrave Publishing Company, 1978.

Edward J. Robinson, *Public Relations and Survey Research.* New York: Appleton-Century-Crofts, 1969.

Charles Roll, Jr., and Albert H. Cantril, *Polls.* New York: Basic Books, 1972.

Claire Selltiz, ed., *Research Methods in Social Relations.* New York: Holt, Rinehart, and Winston, 1962.

8

Planning and Programming

Observations about planning and programming made by a veteran public relations counselor and by a neophyte illustrate the complexities of this crucial step in the public relations process.

Counselor Jack R. Nowling, after two decades of experience preparing programs for clients and would-be clients, states:

> Program writing tests our intelligence, our experience, and our creativity in a special way, almost a unique way. It forces us to survey our mission in its totality. It compels us to rationalize our goals, to establish our priorities, to organize our activities—and then, as the ultimate booby-trap, it demands that we project the results.

And here's what a neophyte—General William C. Westmoreland (Ret.)—told his supporters following his sound defeat in a Republican gubernatorial primary in South Carolina:

> I was an inept candidate. I'm used to a structured organization and this civilian process is so doggone nebulous. . . .

Both Nowling and Westmoreland are talking about ways of reaching and motivating publics, but they draw opposite conclusions about the process. Nowling sees planning and programming as a carefully organized procedure. Westmoreland found it to be so nebulous and different from the organized planning he was accustomed to as a military man that it made him an admitted inept candidate. Actually, both men are correct in their assessment of public relations planning and programming, even though they come to different conclusions about it.

In actual practice—just as in the military—the seasoned practitioner uses both planning and instinct/experience in carrying out public relations programming. Of necessity the most detailed planning preceded the allied invasion of Normandy in World War II, but once

215

the troops landed improvisation took over. In similar manner, the public relations practitioner can draw up the most detailed plan but improvisation takes over simply because so many ingredients necessary for successful completion of the planned program are *out of the control of the planner*. Most public relations projects involve a combination of events, people, and media, and though the practitioner has control over his own events and his own people, he certainly has no control over other events which affect his project; no control over most of the people affected by his project; and certainly no control over the mass media. Therefore, through long experience the seasoned practitioner develops a program which starts with a plan but which recognizes the inevitability of the unplanned taking place.

David Finn of Ruder & Finn notes there are two schools of thought about public relations programming:

1. *The inspirational school,* which operates on the assumption that sound programming is at best a matter of keen intuition and that the practitioner is most effective when he is alert to problems that arise from day to day.

2. *The planned school,* which operates on the assumption that working on the basis of a carefully chartered program is the only way to be businesslike and to enable management to know clearly what the practitioner is doing at all times.

Recognizing there is merit to both approaches, Finn feels the solution is found in a *balanced* program.

"The key to balanced service," he says, "may be program development not as a schedule of activity to be followed but rather as a thoughtful document setting forth the major direction which public relations effort should take."

Finn is undoubtedly correct when he contends that programming involves part planning and part inspiration. The experienced chef follows a set routine in preparing a souffle but uses instinct and judgment in deciding the exact moment to take it out of the oven. The experienced practitioner follows certain routines in carrying out public relations activities but also uses instinct and judgment in deciding when the activities are half-baked or well done and in dealing with day-to-day problems that require creative thinking. Whether baking a souffle or carrying out public relations activities, one is advised to start with a plan.

Three of the major advantages of public relations planning are as follows:

1. The thinking that goes into planning helps clarify the problem(s).

As has been emphasized several times in this book, public relations practitioners are problem-solvers, but the problems they deal with generally do not come in convenient, prepackaged shapes. Public relations problems are most often untidy and amorphous and must be clarified long before the attempt is made to solve them. The thinking that goes into planning helps induce such clarification.

2. The plan provides a blueprint and a working schedule.

Public relations problems are more often complex rather than simple. The more complex the problem, the more the need for an operational blueprint to enable activities to proceed in an orderly and predetermined fashion. Plans will often be subjected to sudden changes, but the blueprint and working schedule serve to provide *direction* and guidance.

3. The creation and approval of a plan prevents misunderstandings.

Public relations is such a relatively new field and management tool that there is need to ensure understanding of its essential nature and thrust. In almost all but the very smallest organizations, most plans involve rather large groups and require the cooperation and understanding of other departments. As a "support" function, public relations itself needs internal support. Further, when approved, the plan provides the practitioner with needed authority and serves as a "document of record."

Counterbalancing the advantages of planinng are some common pitfalls, and Finn cites the following three:

1. Overprogramming

Public relations people, like advertising men, often are guilty of "running it up the flagpole," which is a euphemistic way of suggesting as many ideas and projects as one can conceive to see if they'll be "saluted." The trouble with saluting is that it can turn into a mindless exercise, and the trouble with overprogramming is that the plan will contain too many projects to be carried out successfully. Having projects which do not meet basic objectives is as mindless and unproductive as oversaluting.

Overprogramming can be especially dangerous when a department is undermanned. Inevitably in such circumstances there will be counterpressures on staff members, and as a result one or more programs will suffer. In recognizing this dilemma, a Byoir staffer offers this tip:

> Even Robinson Crusoe couldn't get everything done by Friday. Set achievable timetables, and if slippage occurs, be sure the client knows it early—not when you have to show up at deadline with empty hands. When the workload surges and you find yourself over-extended, get help. Don't try to do everything yourself, which is a classic public relations syndrome. Be sure the client knows the situation and accepts it. Most management people are reasonable and will accept legitimate explanations for unexpected delays or derailments.

2. Undue program rigidity

The Byoir staffer's warning about unexpected delays or derailments applies particularly to the common pitfall knwn as undue program rigidity. In two circumstances of the unexpected—one labelled *opportunity* and the other *crisis*—program rigidity can lead to program rigor mortis. When unexpected opportunities or crises arise, the practitioner must be prepared to deal with them, even though this might well mean temporarily abandoning a planned program or project.

Such situations are akin to following a road map while on a trip. When taking a long trip it's helpful to have a detailed road map, but when you come to a detour that is not on the map, it's better to obey the dictates of the detour rather than the map. When the unexpected happens—as often occurs in public relations activity—it's wise to discard the plan and take care of the unexpected.

3. Losing faith in the approved plan

The fact that detours do show up from time to time does not mean that all road maps are obsolete. Following a planned public relations program is often as difficult as driving a car with three backseat drivers shouting, "Turn right!" "Turn left!" "Go back to that last crossroad!" There are many backseat public relations "experts" in every organization, and the practitioner has to have sufficient faith in his or her own ability and judgment to disregard well-intentioned, but unwise, advice from the backseat drivers.

However, having faith in one's ability and judgment is only part of the problem in dealing with managements. The other part, equally as important, is in securing management's faith in the practitioner's ability and judgment. As another Byoir staffer explains the problem:

> Today, many professional managers are running companies and this trend can be expected to become the rule in the future. They are a different breed than the old entrepreneurs who had great seat-of-the-pants instincts. The new CEOs want to apply computer analysis and zero based budgeting to public relations as they do to any other company function. They listen to counsel, but are likely to pull in several opinions. They like consensus and are much harder to reach with warning flags. The public relations counselor of the future, in my opinion, will have to win the confidence and support of the entire management team to have his ideas listened to at the very top.

Given the positive aspects and the pitfalls of programming, we find that public relations programming can be divided into two broad groups. One consists of daily, on-going activities carried on from year to year, and the other consists of special, planned projects, events, and activities meshed into a blueprint for action. The former will be discussed briefly in the section that follows, but the major part of the rest of this chapter will be devoted to the latter type.

DAILY, ON-GOING ACTIVITIES

In many organizatios the public relations function has become so routinized it seems to exist like the gyroscope spinning in its own orbit impervious to outside forces. This is particularly evident in those organizations where public relations is handled by one or two professionals who provide public relations advice (when asked) and also produce public relations "hardware." The latter could take the form of news releases, feature stories, some internal publications, and brochures. As the organization grows in size, or as new public relations activities are called for, additions are made to the public relations staff to handle them and in time these new activities become routinized and are carried on from year to year.

There seems to be little planning and programming in the above situation, but this does not mean the public relations function is being handled poorly. So long as the staff's activities are geared to meet specific public relations objectives and goals, the fact that formal planning and programming hasn't taken place does not automatically imply a failure on the part of the public relations staff.

Furthermore, even in large organizations where there is formal planning and programming there are always certain public relations tasks and activities which are so obviously necessary there is no need to plan for them. At some point in time someone responsible for the function had to make a decision to carry out the activity and that decision became part of the regular program of the department.

The important point about programming in this type of arrangement is that it consists chiefly of daily, on-going activities carried on from year to year, and these involve both counseling and public relations "hardware" such as releases, internal publications, etc.

SPECIAL PLANNED PROJECTS, EVENTS, AND ACTIVITIES MESHED INTO A BLUEPRINT FOR ACTION

This second major type of public relations programming is that referred to by David Finn when he speaks of "balanced service," and it is the kind of programming most often developed and followed by counseling firms. Internal public relations departments also follow the same general procedure, although not as frequently as counseling firms because there is usually not the same need for internal departments to develop broad new programs. However, when a counseling firm takes on a new account, there's an imperative need to present the client with a plan and a program, and in essence to provide a blueprint for action.

Such programming involves a series of steps or procedures. These are not institutionalized to the extent that every public relations department and counseling firm always proceeds from Step A to B to C, etc., but the approach is common enough to provide a blueprint for programming. The pattern provides a logical means of handling public relations problems via the following steps:

1. Making a preliminary study

2. Defining the problems

3. Establishing objectives and goals

4. Defining the audience

5. Establishing a theme

6. Initiating action and activities: projects, tactics and timing

7. Communicating and evaluating

MAKING A PRELIMINARY STUDY

Folklore has it that the public relations practitioner is a magic medicine person with secret potions to cure organizational ills. Actual practice is far removed from this stereotyped impression. The experienced practitioner knows that it's impossible to carry out an effective public relations program without having intimate knowledge of the organization he or she represents.

When a counseling firm is retained, almost inevitably the *first action taken does not involve public relations per se,* but research concerning the organization and its environment, policies, people, publics, problems, and reputation. How does the counselor go about conducting such research? Very much like a veteran reporter assigned to cover an involved story. Interviews are held with key personnel within the organization and with outsiders who are most likely to have knowledge about the organization. If the client is a business or industry, then important sources of information are editors of business, trade, and financial publications; key suppliers, dealers, and customers; trade association executives; and any others who are most likely to be knowledgeable about the client. Valuable sources of print material—such as annual reports, brochures, publicity files, etc.—are also consulted. Like the investigative reporter, the counselor probes to find weaknesses and strengths, to become intimately aware of almost every conceivable facet of the client organization. The end result of the investigative reporter's probing will be an article or series of articles; the end result of the counseling firm's probing will be a written report which forms the foundation for subsequent public relations activities.

Reading the above paragraph has probably taken about a minute or two, but compiling data for a preliminary study and writing a background report can take a month to six weeks. It takes time and skill to interview key personnel and editors, conduct library research, gather facts and data about an organization's history, facilities, products, people, et cetera. Into the preliminary study goes much hard, unglamorous but extremely valuable work which, as one practitioner declares, serves three functions: (1) *it provides a logical foundation for the program;* (2) *it enables the account executive to secure a solid grounding in the client organization;* and (3) *it demonstrates to the client that the counseling firm has the proper background and experi-ence to interpret the client to its publics.* From a substantive point of view the first function served by the preliminary study—that is, providing a logical foundation for the program—is most important. Without a logical foundation based on data and facts about the organization, a public relations program would be like a house built on hot air—supportable for a limited amount of time only.

Thus, if the preliminary study or background report is to be solid enough to support the superstructure of the public relations program, it has to be built with this superstructure constantly in mind. No two studies will, or should, be exactly alike, but at the minimum they should encompass the following elements:

1. *Facts and data about the organization* as they relate to the organization's public relationships. For example, if the organiza-tion is a business, what are its products, gross sales and net profits; employee force; customers; rank and place in its industry; dealers; suppliers; past history; future possibilities?

2. *Reputation and standing.* What do others—especially those in a position to know—think about the organization? Is it held in generally good or ill repute and why?

3. *Personnel.* What kind of management does the organization have? Who are the key people? What do they think about public relations and what is their level of sophistication about the public relations function? What's the relationship between management and its employee force?

4. *Past and present public relations practices.* What has the organiza-tion done in the past about public relations and what is it now doing? What changes ought to be made, and what seems to be the climate for acceptance of proposed changes? What should be retained and/or modified?

5. *Weaknesses.* What, if any, activities or policies of the organization are causing unfavorable opinions about the organization? Will the organization be receptive to suggested changes or modifications of these activities and policies?

6. *Strengths.* What, if any, activities or policies of the organization are causing favorable opinions about the organization, and has the organization sufficiently capitalized on these? Are there any unique or unusual activities or policies which can be emphasized in future public relations programming?

7. *Opportunities.* Is there anything about the present climate or the situation of the organization which provides opportunities for creative use of public relations?

8. *Obstacles.* Is there anything about the present climate or situation of the organization—including personnel and "politics"—which would cause obstacles to public relations programming?

9. *Conclusions and judgments.* Is the background report factually

correct, will it sustain careful scrutiny and criticism, and does it convey the proper analytical and professional tone?

Each of the above elements is amplified by questions for a specific reason: no public relations textbook can provide instant answers to public relations problems. However, in going through the process of asking proper questions of a situation the practitioner finds that complex problems narrow down. The answers to the right kind of questions suggest a focus for future public relations programming, but before any programming can begin the questions have to be posed and answered.

DEFINING THE PROBLEMS

Practically every organization of size has public relations problems, and these range in scope and intensity from those which can be safely ignored to those which demand immediate attention lest they get out of control. The preliminary study, like a medical check-up, will uncover many problems. Many of them can either be cured by simple treatment or can be dismissed as being relatively inconsequential. Others will need action taken to check their development, and finally a number of them will be so deep-seated and dangerous as to call for surgery.

It should be obvious that immediate, pressing problems are the least difficult to define because they seem to shout for attention and resolution. Though such problems may not be the most important to an organization, time dictates their immediate solution.

If, for example, a small college finds in May that its fall semester entering class is 30 percent short of expectation, the public relations department will probably be asked to drop everything and put its energies, resources, and skills into attracting more entering students. The immediate problem of declining enrollment may well be due to a variety of basic factors that should have been remedied years ago, but there's time to work at these factors after college commences in the fall. Thus, although the immediate problem may not be the most important to the organization, time dictates an immediate solution.

The small college public relations staffer is undoubtedly fortunate because he will probably be cognizant of the enrollment problem. In large organizations he or she may not have this advantage. As one counselor points out:

> Given adequate notice, and full input from the client, we can anticipate problems and, at times, turn a potential negative into a positive. But, if given last-minute notice and sketchy details, the public relations practitioner's performance is hampered.

> The public relations professional is like the navigator in a plane. He can tell you where you are, where you're going and when you'll get there; but not if he's blindfolded.

The skilled practitioner, like the skilled internist and navigator, is able to make *distinctions* about problems. Public relations problems come in all sizes and shapes. Some are internal and some are external; some are temporary and some are permanent; some are on the surface and some are deep-rooted. Recognizing, dissecting, and handling them calls for skills born out of years of experience.

"One of the greatest shortcomings of public relations programs, and of the planners who write them, is *failure* to understand the problem," states H. Zane Robbins, director of communications, Arthur Andersen & Co. "Most public relations men and women can tell you in 25 words or less: 'The company's basic problem is . . .' But that doesn't mean they really understand the broad implications of that problem. There's a wide gap between enunciating a problem and comprehending it."

The gap that Robbins cites can be bridged by applying a four-fold approach to problems: (a) ask the right questions, (b) recognize that problem identification is largely a result of assumptions, (c) get rid of nonessentials, and (d) establish an order of priorities.

Ask the Right Questions

As in the preliminary study stage of programming, it is essential to ask the right questions about a situation. Asking the right questions doesn't necessarily mean that the right answers will be immediately forthcoming, but start with questions to come up with answers. Fools rush in with answers; wise men ask questions. Note the emphasis which the late Earl Newsom put on questions in a talk he gave at the New School for Social Research:

(There) is an implication that we are the white-haired boys who have easy answers to everything and are responsible for all the good deeds of our clients. That isn't true, of course. The facts are much less dramatic and, I am afraid, not nearly so complimentary. This kind of thing is much nearer the truth: somebody in some department of management finds himself with a problem—or a potential problem—that cuts across the interests of large groups of people. He calls us up and says, "We would like to talk to you about this." He might also quite properly bring in the head of the company's public relations department or the officers of other departments that might also be involved. So we sit down and consider the situation. It might be, for example, a threatened strike. Primarily, of course, this is a problem of industrial relations. But it becomes a problem of public relations because not only are the employees an important part of the company's public, but in moments of tension of this kind the whole situation is apt to become a public matter.

I hope you don't get the notion that we hurry into such a meeting and say, "Well, what you should do is this." Such problems are complicated and many things have to be considered besides what the public will think. How will actions that the company might take affect the industry as a whole? How do they relate to national policies as set in Washington? What do polls show about trends of public thought? What do economists have to say about the future? What is the wise thing to do about this? In those discussions our voice is no louder than our judgment, or the opinion of our client on how good we are in matters we are supposed to be good about. . . .

. . . Or another kind of thing. Somebody in Washington on the floor of the House may get up and say something that is untrue or misleading about a client corporation. A first question is,"How important is this?" Who made the statement? Why did he make it? Should we do something about it? So we're apt to get together and talk about it and present our ideas. Perhaps the president of the corporation should telephone or telegraph the Congress and ask to be heard. If so, facts have to be gotten together and help given in assembling them.

Those are problems that are apt to come up. You can't do business without stepping on the toes of people and the problem is to deal with it as best you can. . . .

Newsom's questions, it should be noted, aim to broaden one's view to extend beyond the seemingly narrow scope of the problem. Perceptive questions expose the ramifications which exist within most public relations problems and enable the practitioner to get to the real crux of a situation. Asking the right questions, in short, is where one starts to define the problem(s).

Recognize That Problem Identification Is Largely a Result of Assumptions

In developing a conceptual framework to analyze the public relations function, Professor Edward J. Robinson stated that one of the key factors in isolating or identifying problems is the assumptions that the practitioner brings to the problem-solving situation (*Communication and Public Relations,* Charles E. Merrill Books). He points out that in dealing with a problem all of us make certain assumptions, even though we may not be consciously aware of doing so. These may be true or untrue, but the important thing is that *assumptions influence the way we look at the problem and then attempt to solve it.* If our assumptions are correct this can help clarify the problem, but if they are incorrect they can lead us down many a wrong path. Robinson therefore suggests that the practitioner ask himself continually:

What are my assumptions?

What have I assumed to be true (or false) in this particular situation?

What implicit assumptions have I made about the *human* element—i.e., What convenient generalization have I made about human behavior?

The relationship that assumptions have to problem viewing is similar to the relationship that a cataract has to sight. We "see" because light rays move freely through the lens of the eye to reach the retina:

$$\text{Light rays} \rightarrow \text{lens} \rightarrow \text{retina} = \text{clear vision}$$

However, when the normally transparent lens of the human eye becomes clouded by a cataract, clarity of vision is lost because the rays are blocked from moving through the lens to the retina:

$$\text{Light rays} \longrightarrow \text{cataract} = \text{loss of vision}$$

Substitute "assumptions" for the lens of the eye. If one's assumptions are correct, then the light rays thrown on the problem will move freely through the lens of correct assumptions of the retina of possible answers to the problem:

$$\text{Light rays} \longrightarrow \text{lens of correct assumption} \longrightarrow \text{retina}$$
$$= \text{clear perceptions of the problem}$$

However, if one's assumptions are incorrect, then the light rays thrown on the problem will be blocked by the lens of incorrect assumptions and will result in opaque perceptions of the problem:

$$\text{Light rays} \longrightarrow \text{lens of incorrect assumptions} =$$
$$\text{cloudy perceptions of the problem}$$

If we are to view problems with clear vision we must be vigilant about the assumptions we bring to problem-solving situations. In today's fast-moving world, it is particularly important that our assumptions about people and society are in tune with the times; in trying to cope with problems, attempts based on outdated and false assumptions are almost certain to flounder.

Counselor George Hammond provides an excellent illustration of the relationship between assumptions and programming in the following remarks:

When The Road Information Program hired us, their first instructions were for us to develop a nationwide publicity program in support of a second system of interstate highways. That's what they wanted. It would mean lots of business for the roadbuilders.

But we asked for time and used that time to conduct a survey of attitudes among the press and the public. What we found out was that the public didn't want a second interstate system. What they wanted was an easier commute, lower operating expenses for their cars, safer transportation to school for their kids, lower food and fuel costs, and so forth.

So we went back to the organization's board of directors—a tough-minded group of 20 highway builders—and told them we'd have to do it differently, that people wouldn't buy new highways but that our surveys showed that the best appeal we could make was to the values that people already embraced about prices and the ease of living, and that new values such as new highway systems were almost impossible to sell.

Now we're deeply involved in a program that translates road improvement into the values most people already hold dear, and the roadbuilders support it vigorously. In fact, we've been able to win millions of dollars in government funds for the kinds of projects we have proposed. It's a striking example of how a public relations agency can change the direction of an entire industry by demonstrating, through a trusting relationship with its client, a new and profitable pathway to growth.

Hammond's example is also an excellent illustration of how assumptions can cloud one's vision and how research can be used to check the validity of assumptions and at the same time to point out directions for future programming. That same research, it should be noted, also provided the means for meshing an organization's private interests with public interests, resulting in clear benefits for all concerned.

Eliminate Nonessentials

Problems, like grapes, tend to come in clusters and one of the difficult tasks of the practitioner is to eliminate from the cluster of problems what the late Verne Burnett called "nonessentials." In his view handling public relations problems calls for a process of elimination.

> For instance, a trade group asked a public relations firm to get the general public conscious of twelve facts about an industry. All of these facts seemed important to the trade group. There was an ancient law suit, but the public would have no interest in that. There had been some involved labor negotiations several years ago. Again the public wouldn't bother to learn the details. One by one the twelve points were whittled down until there were three to which the public might pay attention. Finally the three, which were closely related, were condensed into one. Thus it was possible for the public relations worker to concentrate all efforts on explaining a single idea, with considerable success.

Burnett's advice to whittle down problems is echoed by most veteran public relations practitioners. They realize that the public finds it difficult, or doesn't have the interest, to grasp a mass of information too extensive or complex. Given a set of problems, the practitioner strips away the relatively unimportant ones and by a process of elimination tries to focus on those that are primary and essential. The process is simple when the major problem is obvious, but requires sound, objective judgment when the major problem is obscured by a host of other problems. Since almost every public relations problem situation is unique, the process of defining the key factor by stripping away nonessentials is always a challenge, but one that must be met before further action is taken.

Establish an Order of Priorities

Whether done by design or accidentally, the act of defining the problem will culminate in establishing an order of problem priorities, which will lead in turn to a similar order of solution priorities.

The usual way of establishing priorities is to decide which problems are immediate and which are long-range. Put another way, which problems should be handled today and which can be taken care of over a period of months or years? Another method is to rank problems in order of importance, though the end result is usually the same because of the general assumption that immediate problems must be most important because they must be taken care of at once while long-range problems aren't as important because their handling can be delayed.

Such an assumption—as with many assumptions examined superficially—has to be scrutinized carefully. While it is true that practitioners tend to concentrate on immediate problems—chiefly because practitioners can't very well ignore their existence—these are not necessarily the most important problems facing an organization. In fact, one of the fatal flaws of many public relations programs is that they tend to be "fire-fighting" efforts aimed at dousing the flames caused by immediate problems. Because the practitioner is so busy trying to solve immediate problems, long-range problems are ignored even though they may be more important.

The sensible way of insuring that proper attention will be given to all problems is to establish a realistic order of problem priorities and put it in writing. If it's possible to rank problems, then the ranking ought to be in terms of most important, next most important, and so on down the line to those considered least important. If an immediate problem turns out to be the most important problem then the practitioner has a perfect match. However, if an immediate problem is not the most important one but still has to be handled immediately, the practitioner must remember that the most important problem still exists and must be treated at some time. The practitioner may still handle the immediate problem at the moment it faces him, but he shouldn't put the most important problem on the back burner indefinitely.

ESTABLISHING OBJECTIVES AND GOALS

The act of establishing public relations objectives and goals is a logical follow-up to the problem-definition stage of programming because of the close affinity between problems and objectives. If, for example, it has been decided that an immediate major problem facing a publicly financed organization is virtual ignorance about the organization among financial analysts, then an obvious immediate public relations objective and goal would be to inform these analysts so they will recommend its stock as a good buy.

The example is illustrative of several important criteria of sound public relations objectives and goals: (a) they should be directly related to the basic objectives of the organization, (b) they should be specific rather than general, and (c) they should be set forth in order of importance and time.

Public Relations Objectives Should be Related to the Basic Objectives of the Organization

There is no utility value to public relations objectives with little relationship to the basic objectives of the organization they supposedly serve. It is, at times, very tempting to set forth a public relations goal that can be achieved through some dramatic and imaginative program activity or event, but if the goal has little relationship to the basic goals of the organization the result will be a meaningless waste of time, money, and manpower. There's little point in trying to increase applications to a prestigious law school when that school already has so many applications it can accept only 10 percent of those who apply. It makes little sense to aim your public relations efforts at establishing among citizens in Plant Community A that your firm's plant there is a strong, stable one if management has already decided to close the plant a year from now. If a public relations program is to keep in step with reality, the objectives of that program and the objectives of the organization must march to the same tune.

The previous paragraph seems to imply that it's the responsibility of public relations to keep in step with the organization of which it's a part. There are times, however, when the preliminary study and setting forth of problems show that the policies and actions of an organization, not public relations, are clearly out of step with public opinion, the public interest, and commonly accepted standards of behaviour. Knowing this to be so, does the practitioner continue to march along with his plans and programs or does he come to a parade rest?

Those who have read the earlier chapters in this book ought to know the answer to that last question. If an organization's basic policies and actions are clealy counter to the public interest and to commonly accepted standards of behaviour, it's the responsibility of the practitioner to use his influence to modify or seek changes in policies and actions. In the short run it is conceivable—and it has happened—that clever use of techniques might camouflage shoddy organizational policies and practices, but in the long run they will be shown up for what they are. The time to align organizational and public relations policies, actions, and objectives with the public interest and in accordance with commonly acceptable bounds of behaviour is before, not after programming has begun.

Public Relations Objectives Should be Specific Rather Than General

Though public relations, as a general concept, aims to bring about the end result of "goodwill, understanding and acceptance," programming objectives must be stated in more specific terms if they are to be meaningful and acceptable to management. Particularly in business and industry, but also in other areas of human endeavor and activity, managements expect, demand, and receive specific inputs and goals from the various main functional areas of organizations. These are then measured against end results. The sales department doesn't project a general increase in sales, but rather a 2 percent or 5 percent or 10 percent increase. The production department doesn't project a general increase in production, but rather a 2 percent or 5 percent or 10 percent increase. The admissions director of a college doesn't project a general increase in the freshman class, but a 2 percent, 5 percent or 10 percent increase. In each instance the responsible executive is held to account if end results fail to measure up to forecasts. Public relations, though involved with factors more difficult to measure than the production and sale of products and the admissions of students, should expect to be held to thorough measurements and management expectations.

Unfortunately, many public relations objectives and goals are fuzzy in conception and much too general in nature. Note, for example, the following "seven objectives of a representative gas utility," and decide which are specific and which are general:

1. To establish the company as a valuable citizen

2. To make all personnel more PR-minded

3. To offset competition

4. To cultivate and maintain good will of customers, editors and key citizens

5. To devise new ways of interpreting modern gas service to the public

6. To strengthen private management of utilities

7. To educate the public on need for adequate utility earnings

John F. Budd, Jr., of Carl Byoir & Associates cites a different kind of objectives when he discusses public relations objectives for Republic Aviation:

A 31-page program analysis and recommendations for Republic Aviation opened with five specific public relations objectives. One, "to report and reiterate the technological expansion and new capabilities of the company." Two, "to emphasize the financial soundness of the company." Three, "to find ways to dramatize the mission of the F-105." Four, "to improve impressions of corporate management and to introduce the new sales and engineering heads." Five, "to restore community confidence in the company's future."

H. Zane Robbins of Arthur Andersen & Co. contends that objectives should not only be specific, but measurable as well. Although measurement of public relations activities and results is both difficult and expensive, Robbins feels that management is justified in expecting and demanding specificity and measurement of public relations activities. He makes his case as follows:

Here are some fairly typical public relations objectives:
    To enhance the image of the company.
    To win greater acceptance of our boll weevil extractor.
    To attract more college graduates to our training program.
    To win the favor of the professional financial community.

You can guess the sort of projects that as dre med up to go along with goals of that type. Usually they are as ill-conceived, as fuzzy, and as poorly executed as the goals themselves.

Nowhere can good, effective opinion research be more useful than in planning the public relations program. If you're going to "enhance the image of the company" or "win greater acceptance for the boll weevil extractor" or do anything else, you must first know your starting point.

What percentage of your audience—which also must be clearly and specifically defined—has a favorable impression of the company right now? Of those who don't like the company, what influences their attitudes? What is the size of the market for boll weevil extractors? What percentage of this market do you now have? Why have you been unable to sell your product in some areas?

Research can answer those questions. Research can show you not only how your company ranks in an absolute sense, it also can show how you rank in a relative sense—compared to similar companies in your field. Research can tell you what businessmen like or dislike about your company. Research can tell you why customers buy or don't buy your product. And research can tell you where you stand today—in numerical terms—in any market or in the opinion of any audience.

If you have that sort of benchmark, you can rewrite your objectives in a meaningful way. Instead of citing a meaningless goal such as "to enhance the image of the company," you might state it this way:

> To improve attitudes toward our company among business managers, cotton farmers and members of the professional financial community. Our objective is to increase favorable response from 12 to 25 percent in the first category, from 15 to 25 percent in the second category and from 9 to 30 percent in the third category over the next two years.

Now that is a meaningful objective. It's specific. Management can understand it. And your success in attaining those goals can be measured simply and inexpensively by followup research.

> from remarks made at a Public Relations Society of America seminar

Robbins would undoubtedly approve of the public relations objectives set forth by the Silverman and Mower agency of Syracuse, New York, in its proposed program for the New York Racing Association. To reverse declining attendance at the association's three thoroughbred racing tracks at Belmont Park, Aqueduct, and Saratoga, the agency proposed a "Newcomer's Program" to attract new customers through special group and individual sales activities. Here's how Silverman and Mower phrased the program's objectives:

> Obviously, the general objectives for a Newcomer's Program is to increase attendance at the track. This is both a short-term goal for next year and a long-term goal for years to come.

However, more specific objectives are proposed:
1. Increase overall track racing attendance.
2. Attract 1,000 newcomers per week to the track.
3. Increase group sales activity to a documented 10 percent of total attendance during first full year of implementation.

4. Document a 20 percent return of newcomers and group members on their own within one month.

In addition, two other factors should be kept in mind:

1. There must be a quantifiable way of measuring the Newcomer's Program after one year of implementation; and

2. The first year is a developing year, a building year, in which the program is honed and sharpened but not quite ready for full capacity.

For a variety of reasons, most practitioners do not "lay it on the line" as directly as do Silverman and Mower, but few would argue the wisdom of being specific rather than general. The value of specificity applies particularly to the matter of relative importance of objectives and the time frame in which they are set.

Public Relations Objectives Should be Set Forth in Order of Importance and Time

As with problems, public relations objectives and goals should be set forth in order of their importance and the time period within which they are expected to be reached. In effect, this means setting priorities for objectives and goals.

Some objectives are so clearly important and immediate there is no question about the need to meet them at once. Others, while important, can await their solution over a longer period of time. When Whitaker and Baxter, for example, took on the assignment of handling The American Medical Association account two decades ago they defined their objectives in this manner:

> The first objective was an uncompromising immediacy: to stop the Compulsory Health Insurance legislation then pending (in Congress).

> The second objective, longer-range and more constructive, was to establish firm proof with the majority of the people that the American medical system not only is the finest in the world's history, but that it can meet the medical needs of the people by voluntary means and without Government control.

Depending on one's views, one might argue the merits of the issue, but no one can argue about the specific nature of the campaign's objectives. They were direct, to the point, and included both short and long-range goals. In effect, they provided the client (or management) with a timetable and a way to judge whether the program was proceeding according to schedule.

Management by objectives (MBO) is a technique that has been adopted by public relations departments to meet managerial demands for accountability and measurement. Time and space preclude a full discussion of MBO, but the basic elements can be explained briefly.

MBO calls for the establishment of organizational and departmental goals; the development of objectives to meet these goals; the establishment of deadlines and target dates; and a means of evaluation

232

and revision. Goals under MBO are general guides for action, while objectives—set for both the department and for individuals within it—are measurable targets set within a time frame. For measurement purposes, terms should be set qualitatively and quantitatively.

Anita H. Thies of Pennsylvania State University explains goals and objectives as follows:

> By definition and purpose, an objective is a statement that is specific, single-purpose, measurable, set in a time frame, and achievable.

> Objectives grow from goals and help determine progress toward the accomplishment of ideas set forth in goals. Goals are broad, general statements, usually neither quantifiable nor set in a time frame, and usually not attainable as stated.

As an example of the above, Thies notes that one of Penn State's public relations goals is to achieve more recognition for the university. In targeting staff objectives to meet this goal, she explains, one objective is to have each news bureau writer produce two or three "statewide" stories per week; another is to have the Speakers Bureau arrange an average of one speaking engagement per day; and a third is to have each staffer ask faculty menbers to write monthly opinion pieces for the editorial pages of target newspapers.

In warning about the dangers of overquantifying when writing objectives, Thies puts her finger on the major reason why MBO is not used more extensively by public relations practitioners. She points out that overquantifying may misdirect staffers to play a numbers game, and it also takes up a considerable amount of staff time in following intricate measurement systems. Finally, she notes, the real measurement of performance in public relations involves a judgment of quality that cannot be quantified. As she puts it: "While we try to quantify wherever possible, we also know that a story's importance to an institution isn't necessarily measured by its length or newsplay."

One might well add this reminder about timetables: too rigid a timetable can be dangerous because public relations practice calls for flexibility. Unless one provides for flexibility in setting objectives and programs, there will be too many instances of missed opportunities and of programs outdated by unforeseen events. By all means be specific and work according to a timetable, but don't be inflexible.

DEFINING THE AUDIENCE

All public relations programs are aimed at some group or groups in our society, and therefore the audience should be precisely defined and delineated *before* a program is charted and put into effect. Usually this process is a matter of simple, logical deduction. As the practitioner goes through the process of defining an organization's essential public relations problems and objectives, the audience for the ensuing public relations programming should come into focus. Problems arise because of relationships with *people*; objectives deal with goals concerning *people*; to meet these objectives one must first zero in on the *people* to be reached.

Charting the audience can be achieved in a variety of ways. Audiences can be defined as *primary, secondary* and *tertiary,* and obviously such a delineating implies that the main effort of the program will be directed first at the primary audience and later at the secondary and tertiary audiences. Or, the audience can be divided into *internal* and *external* groups with specific programming aimed at each or both groups. Audiences are often divided into *local, regional* and *national* groupings and again subsequent programming can be charted for each group.

As a simple example, let us assume that the Boy Scouts of America are having difficulty attracting inner city youngsters to scouting. The problem results from the fact that inner city youngsters of scouting age feel that scouting has little relationship to their lives. The objective of the public relations program is to demonstrate that modern-day scouting bears a close and direct relationship to the lives of inner city youngsters. Logical deduction tells us that a public relations program designed to attract inner city youngsters to scouting ought to be directed specifically at inner city youngsters and not at youngsters living on farms.

However, research reveals that inner city youngsters have such a deep-seated suspicion of the so-called Establishment they reject the usual type of appeals stemming from the Scouting Establishment. Further research reveals that well known professional athletes are looked at with awe and respect by inner city youngsters of scouting age. These athletes might become the primary audience and the conduit for a public relations program aimed at attracting inner city youngsters to scouting.

Thus, though audience-projection is often a matter of simple logical deduction, circumstances may indicate that a straight line may not be the most effective way of moving from Point A to Point B. Consider, for example, the previously cited program that Whitaker and Baxter carried out for the American Medical Association. The objective, as noted, was to head off pending national health insurance legislation. Such legislation is the province of Congress, and one might well conclude therefore that the program Whitaker and Baxter devised for AMA would have the Congress as its primary audience. Whitaker and Baxter, however, aimed their campaign not at Congress but at the general public because they felt that Congress had to be shown that the American public was against the pending legislation. In a two-week period in October the issue was taken to the public in a $1,000,000 advertising campaign which included every daily and weekly newspaper, the principal national magazines and the electronic media in the country. Thus, to get from Point A (the AMA) to Point B (the Congress) the program was routed through Point C (the general public).

No matter what system is used in focusing on the audience(s), certain questions have to be posed:

- Who are we trying to reach?
- Which publics are most important?
- Where are they?

- Who are their opinion leaders?

- What do they read, listen to and view?

When you've found the answers to the above questions you're really just out of the starting gate in the race to reach target publics. If you hope to finish in the running you now have to uncover key facts about each group on your target list, and this means listing everything you know about them or can ascertain through research. You'll need to know what kind of people they are, their relationship to your organization, what's on their minds, why they should or could be interested in your program. In effect, what you have to do is to pose some further pertinent questions about each target audience and then, through research, find the answers.

> In its proposed Newcomer's Program for the New York Racing Association—previously cited in discussion of objectives—Silverman and Mower used the findings of focus group research to pinpoint the nature of the program's audience.

> Identifying the typical member of the target audience as being a nonuser of the thoroughbred race track, the agency cited his major concerns for nonuse as being a fear of gambling and a lack of information concerning track procedures and facilities, betting methods, and horses and riders.

> Thus, having carefully identified the attitudes, concerns, knowledge, and other attributes of the target audience, the agency then established the framework of a program geared to meet objectives. At the core of the program were ways and means of overcoming the nonuser's fears, providing him with the information he needed, and establishing the track-going experience as an enjoyable one.

ESTABLISHING A THEME

Public relations programs which involve a variety of projects—as most successful programs do—achieve a unity of purpose through the use of a basic theme or set of themes. In the continuum of public relations planning and programming a theme bears close relationship to musical and literary themes. In both music and literature a theme is the underlying tie which runs through an entire work and binds it together. In similar fashion, a theme is the underlying tie that runs through the various facets or projects in a public relations program and makes for a unified, consistent approach to public relations problems.

A theme is to public relations programming as thread is to the tailor. With thread the tailor fashions a suit; without it he's got so many swatches of cloth. With a theme the public relations practitioner fashions a campaign; without it he's got so many isolated projects. When Whitaker and Baxter were handling political campaigns in California, themes formed the basic core of all their campaigns. Before starting a campaign the husband-and-wife counseling team would work out a theme and a plan, and then with equal care they would work out another theme and plan. Both themes and plans were then matched against each other and a decision made as to which would be used in the forthcoming campaign. Every subsequent speech, poster, brochure, television and radio spot would then emphasize and develop the campaign's basic theme.

A theme can be set forth in a variety of ways. It may be expressed in the form of a summary statement or of a slogan, but its basic purpose remains that of providing unity to programming. Whatever its form, a theme should:

1. Make its point clearly

2. Be capable of being retained by those at whom it is directed

3. Be relevant and honest

The last point bears close analysis because of the glib way in which some themes are too often put into effect.

David Finn makes the case for relevancy and honesty in the following words:

> . . . It is not the slick job that does the trick, but the job that most genuinely reflects the way management feels about itself. Dapper Frank Lloyd Wright did not have a better public image than tousled Albert Einstein. Both won public respect and affection because they looked like what they were: people could feel that both of them were being honest with themselves. Above all, the way they looked was consistent with what they stood for, and this is the key to good graphic public relations.

Because catchy themes have eye and ear appeal there is often the temptation to employ themes whether they honestly reflect the organization that uses them. But on ethical, moral, and practical grounds irrelevant, dishonest, and meaningless themes should be avoided. Such themes may gain immediate approbation for the practitioner who creates them, but in the long run they serve no useful purpose, do little intrinsic good, and eventually backfire.

Today's public is too wise, jaded, and jaundiced to be taken in by superficial slogans and themes, and this conclusion is particularly true of those organizations whose products and services are sold to and used by the general public. If the product purchased by the average consumer proves to be shoddy or if the service rendered proves to be abysmal, no catchy theme or slogan is going to convince him to "put his trust" in that company's products or services. As Finn puts it: "A theme makes sense only when it is deeply felt by the people running the business. All of the company's publics then recognize that the idea or theme is genuine and not an artificial concoction of clever promoters."

INITIATING AN ACTION AND ACTIVITY PLAN OF STRATEGY: PROJECTS, TACTICS, AND TIMING

At the core of most successful public relations programs is an action and activity plan of strategy involving three major elements:

projects, tactics, and timing. *Projects* provide the vehicle whereby public relations objectives and goals are reached; *tactics* involve the mechanics in carrying out planned projects; and *timing* is often the crucial difference between success and failure.

Projects

Projects come in all shapes and forms and are limited only by the imagination and ingenuity of the practitioners who plan, create, and carry them through to completion. One veteran public relations man sees projects as "the only convenient way in which an otherwise nebulous undertaking can be analyzed, organized, and controlled," and in his opinion the more projects clustered around a theme the better.

Some projects are of such a magnitude that a single project may comprise the entire public relations program. Into such a project would go all the talent, manpower, and resources that public relations can provide. Most often, however, programs are built around a variety of projects that overlap each other and act as a series of waves cresting towards a common shoreline goal. The analogy to waves is deliberate: at times practitioners initiate and carry through projects that demonstrate activity is taking place, but unless projects build towards a common public relations objective and goal, the practitioner is merely going through the process of making waves that go nowhere.

A project may be as simple as a normal press conference announcing a new product or may be as complex as an American vice president debating with a Soviet premier in a typical American dream house set up in a Moscow exhibit to demonstrate the virtues of the American way of life (and the products in that house). A project may be local in nature, such as an Open House initiated to have residents in a plant community learn first-hand about an industrial organization, or it may be national and involve a sixteen-city tour by a well-known personality to demonstrate to a wide geographical audience the virtues of a product. A program may consist of a major, one-day event—such as a Walk-a-Thon for a disease-fighting agency—or it may entail several major events and some minor ones spread out over a months-long campaign.

Projects and public relations program activities are not easily categorized because they exist in a wide variety of guises, and new ones are constantly being initiated by imaginative and creative practitioners. However, some projects and activities have gained such widespread acceptance their utilization by practitioners justifies their listing as major types. By no means should one consider that the following project and activity categories represent the only effective ones to be used in programming. The listing is chiefly a means of setting forth some major ways in which projects and activities have been used in public relations programming.

Projects or activities that support, display, and/or dramatize an existing event, facility, or situation. Virtually every organization, at one time or anther, carries out activities or events that need public relations support, and in many instances the facilities of organizations are also the focal point of public relations activity. Some facilities, events and situations utilize public relations support on a regular, recurring basis, others as the need arises.

For example, every local United Way organization in the country conducts a yearly fund-raising campaign aimed at raising sufficient funds to support the agencies belonging to the United Way. Usually of a month's duration, these campaigns inevitably commence with a kick-off dinner or event, are followed by periodic report meetings and luncheons, and culminate in a final victory dinner or event. Throughout the entire campaign period the UW's public relations department serves a key role in devising ways and means of supporting, dramatizing, and communicating the activities and events taking place during the campaign. Some typical projects include an opening day parade; a lighted thermometer placed on top of a large building to indicate fund-raising progress; a fireworks display to demonstrate the campaign has gone over the top; a costume ball to increase attendance on the final report night.

The United Way campaign as an existing event requiring public relations support is duplicated in many ways. Colleges and universities hold convocations, commencements, Parents' Days, and Alumni Days. Cities and department stores sponsor and run the Tournament of Roses Parade, the Thanksgiving Day Parade, the Peanut Queen Festival, and the Kutztown annual Pennsylvania Dutch Folk Festival. There's the annual Westinghouse Science Talent Search, the Sealy Golf Classic, and the American Legion Boys' State and Boys' Nation. Rockefeller Center has its outdoor skating rink, major resorts have outdoor ski slopes, and a number of large cities have a variety of gas-light, take-me-back-to-the-good-old-days areas. Each of these existing events, facilities, and situations is supported and dramatized by public relations projects and activities.

Even factories and plants—not usually considered prime areas for public relations programming—have been utilized to good public relations advantage because someone with imagination figured out that wineries and breweries could attract millions of visitors if tours of their facilities were spiked with sampling of the product at the end of the tour. Designing, establishing, managing, and promoting many of these tours has become partly or wholly a function of public relations departments. In some instances the facility tour has become so successful a drawing card that the sponsoring company has split it off from the brewery operation, broadened the scope of the attraction, and run the activity as a profit center. An example is the Busch Gardens operation of Anheuser-Busch, Inc., in Tampa, Florida.

Projects or activities that support and/or dramatize communication events or actions. There is a narrow but significant difference between existing organizational events and communication events supported and/or dramatized by public relations projects and activities. By *communication events* are meant those designed as part of public relations programming rather than those that exist as part of an organization's activities. For the most part communication events are "one-shot" affairs, although they can prove so successful and integral to an organization that they become recurring affairs and thus an integral part of an organization's activities.

Criticism has been leveled against communication events for being "manufactured" and "pseudo," and the criticism has a good deal of validity. However if the communication event serves purposes other than merely being reported by the media, the argument that it is manufactured loses a good deal of its weight and substance. Practitioners can create event after event, but unless they interest the public they will inevitably fail to bring about media coverage. The test, therefore, is not in the event but in the substance of the event.

There are innumerable ways in which communication events are meshed with public relations programs, projects and activities. Some of the more common ones are seminars, forums, competitions, special awards, surveys, educational campaigns, conferences, and convocations. The best of them pass three basic tests:

1. They meet and dovetail with fundamental objectives and goals of the organization.

2. They provide a public or publics with information, knowledge, or ideas that are in the public interest.

3. They merit and secure media attention and coverage.

This three-fold test is difficult to meet. Only those created communication events that are the most thoughtful and imaginative pass with high marks. A variety of such created communication events are cited in the examples that follow, and it should be instructive to discuss, rate, and judge each event's public relations effectiveness by applying the three-fold test previously listed.

A Communications Conference

At their first meeting in October members of the Blank College chapter of the Public Relations Student Society of America decide that their major chapter project of the year will be the staging in March of the First Southwest Collegiate Communications Conference. Planning takes up the chapter's attention for the entire academic year. Two mailings are sent out to all PRSSA chapters and to journalism and public relations schools, departments, and teachers in the southwest. Speakers and panelists at the March event include two nationally known public relations practitioners and journalists from the southwest. Attendance at the two-day conference consists chiefly of public relations students of Blank College—many of them to handle classroom assignments based on conference activities—and fourteen students from four other southwest colleges and universities. Good media coverage of conference activities is given by media in the Blank College area, and brief mention of the conference is also carried in national public relations newsletters, the *Public Relations Journal,* and the PRSSA's *Forum.* The Blank College *Weekly Record,* student newspaper, runs many pre-conference stories and a long story with pictures the week after the conference.

An Automobile Competition

By arrangement with local and state automobile clubs, an international oil company which markets its products throughout the United States conducts a cross-country automobile competition. Entries are restricted to one-owner automobiles which are at least twenty years old. Local, state and regional elimination competitions are held, and the final race consists of twenty automobiles in a race from Paramus, New Jersey, to San Francisco. All entrants have to use gasoline and oil produced by the sponsoring oil company. The winner is feted at a dinner in Detroit addressed by the president of one of the major automobile manufacturers, and the automobile which won the race is put on permanent display in a new National Automobile Museum erected on the outskirts of Detroit. The winner is awarded the top of the line in a new model car of the winner's choice. Media coverage is excellent on all levels: local, state, regional, and national. The oil company "merchandises" the races and final winner in newspaper, magazine, radio, and television advertisements and commercials and by point-of-sales displays at its gas stations throughout the country.

Two for the Trees

Retained by a national association of nurserymen, a public relations counseling firm proposes two major projects:

a. Plant-A-Tree Week, to be held in August in commemoration of the sixtieth anniversary of the appearance in *Poetry* magazine of Joyce Kilmer's poem "Trees." Local nursery associations throughout the country would be provided with detailed project kits telling them (1) how to conduct a poetry contest with awards going to hitherto unpublished local poets whose poems dealing with nature are judged to best exemplify Kilmer's tribute to trees; (2) how to have the mayor of their city proclaim August 15 as Joyce Kilmer Day, and to have a ceremonious planting of a budding tree—donated by the nurserymen—by the mayor or his deputy; and (3) ways to demonstrate proper plant and shrub care on a local television show during Plant-A-Tree Week. The proposal also projects a similar set of activities on a national level to be conducted by the national nurserymen's association and subsequently publicized by the counseling firm.

b. The underwriting of a grant by the national association of nurserymen to the romantic poetry section of the Modern Language Association to support a symposium dealing with "Nature, Poetry, and Modern Man." As visualized by the counseling firm, the grant would be used to underwrite the costs of the symposium where major papers would be delivered by leading romantic nature poetry scholars. The papers would later be compiled and published in book form and the book distributed to all libraries and teachers of poetry in colleges and universities throughout the country. All costs of publication and distribution would be covered by the nurserymen's association. The only mention of the association would be a brief acknowledgment of the grant in the preface to the book. In a covering letter to the libraries and teachers receiving the book, the association would cite its sponsorship of the symposium and the group's commitment to the beauty that is inherent in nature and in poetry concerned with nature.

Projects or activities that support and/or dramatize products, sales, and services. Public relations projects and activities conceived and carried out to support an organization's products, sales, and services are so common they're often handled on a regular basis by staffers specifically assigned to this purpose. Such projects and activities are also the ones most enthusiastically supported by other functions and divisions of organizations because of the direct help they provide to these functions and divisions.

Product, sales, and service promotion comes in many forms. It can consist chiefly of press releases and feature stories sent to trade and consumer publications, newspapers, syndicates, radio, and television outlets. Sometimes it takes the form of making the product available to movie makers and television producers and subsequent viewing by millions when the film is released for distribution. Though this is a form of subliminal impact which is hard to measure, there is no doubt that some members of the movie and the television audience will be influenced by seeing the product.

Introducing a new product to the market is primarily a function of the sales department, but public relations assistance is often provided in the form of press releases, press conferences, advance showings, press showings, packaged presentations for use on morning and afternoon television shows, and a host of other devices and methods.

A common form of product promotion is to tie it up in a promotional package and take it on a tour of leading cities and markets by a personality accompanied by a public relations representative who schedules bookings and appearances and works with the media in the cities visited. Another common form is the tie-in promotion wherein the product is put to use and shown in action at some facility that draws millions of visitors. Power boats and outboard motors are an integral part of the daily shows at Cypress Gardens in Winter Haven, Florida; they may as well be X powerboats and Y outboard motors as anyone else's.

For its client, Lenox Crystal, the Ruder & Finn organization recommended that Lenox commission three young photographers to explore new ways of looking at crystal. A unique exhibit of approximately 120 photographs was organized and presented at department stores throughout the country. The program's aim was to demonstrate Lenox's interest in the art of glassmaking and in the art of photography, thereby presenting a new and different way of viewing the firm's product. (Three of the pictures with captions are shown on the following pages.)

Reflections in the Glass—The multiple lines and shapes reflected in glass characterize this photograph of stemware by *Mies Hora,* one of over eighty dramatic prints featured in "Crystal Images," an exhibit by Lenox Crystal, on display through October 26 at B. Altman, New York. The exhibit, which includes the work of three young photographers commissioned by Lenox to explore new ways of viewing crystal design, has been shown in Tampa, Detroit, Atlanta, Cleveland, and the greater Washington, D.C., area before its showing at B. Altman, New York.

Courtesy Ruder & Finn, Inc.

Glass in Glass—Two types of crystal stemware, one inside the other, are the unusual subject matter for this equally unusual photograph by *Amy Binder*, one of eighty dramatic prints featured in "Crystal Images," an exhibit by Lenox Crystal, on display through August 26 at ZCMI. The exhibit, which includes the work of three young photographers commissioned by Lenox to explore new ways of viewing crystal design, is traveling to major cities throughout the country.

Courtesy Ruder & Finn, Inc.

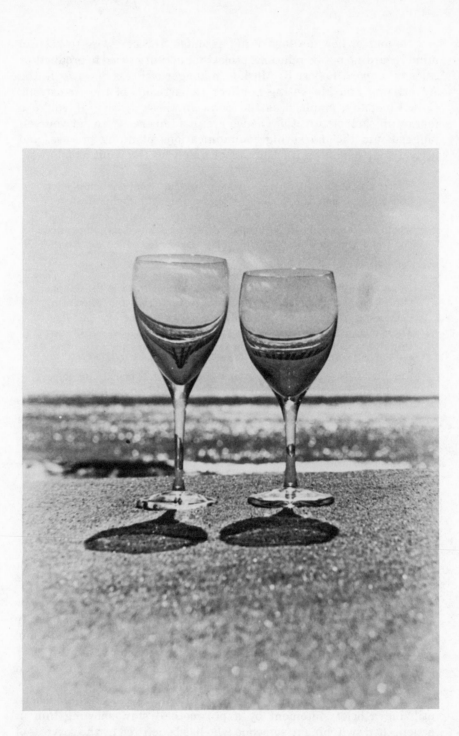

Crystal Illusions—Wine glasses appear suspended over sand in a photograph by *Jimmy Scotese,* one of over eighty dramatic prints featured in "Crystal Images," an exhibit by Lenox Crystal, on display through October 26 at B. Altman, New York. The exhibit, which includes the work of three young photographers commissioned by Lenox to explore new ways of viewing crystal design, has been shown in Tampa, Detroit, Atlanta, Cleveland, and the greater Washington, D.C., area before its showing at B. Altman, New York.

Courtesy Ruder & Finn, Inc.

No matter how developed and executed, the key word to keep in mind regarding public relations projects or activities tied to products or sales is *support*. Robert K. Marker, manager of Press Services in the Advertising and Marketing Services Department of the Armstrong Cork Company, emphasizes the point in these words: "If you're a marketing-support function, as we are, it's imperative to get yourself plugged into the marketing communications planning process, and actively participate in it." He further amplifies the point as follows:

> There are seven operating divisions in our company, and each division is responsible for forecasting its own sales and profit levels for the next five years. There's a general marketing plan developed which explains how the division expects to achieve its long-range goal; and there's a very specific plan drawn up which charts the division's course in the coming year.

> After these programs are reviewed and approved in the President's Office, each division sits down with Advertising and Marketing Services and lays out its plans and objectives for the ensuing year. These meetings take place in late summer, and that's our cue to start thinking about our own program for the next year.

> The first step is to carefully review the divisional marketing objectives, and develop from them a list of *communications objectives* — that is, a statement of what it is we want to try to accomplish through communications next year to help the divisions reach their goals. The communications objectives are written out, discussed with the marketing divisions, fine-tuned if necessary, and then ordered in terms of priority.

> Our next step is to develop written *strategies* — how we propose to accomplish the communications goals that we and the marketing people have agreed are important in the coming year. Who do we want to reach, and how often? What's the best way to reach them? What should we say to them? There's more discussion and fine-tuning, and at this point, the operating budget for our department begins to take shape.

Supporting products and sales by means of public relations projects and activities is easier to achieve than supporting services, chiefly because the former lend themselves more readily to dramatization.

An effective way of dramatizing services is to substitute things or people for services, and to utilize these in subsequent dramatization and promotion. The United Way of America did this very effectively with public service cameos on pro football television broadcasts, utilizing a brief statement by a pro football star, showing him in action, then switching to someone who has benefitted by the services of a United Way agency, and finally combining both the star and the United Way client in a wrap-up sequence.

In a similar manner, Smokey Bear was used for many years to personalize messages about the dangers of forest fires, while Reddy Kilowat was used as the symbol for services performed by an electric utility. To show the services they render to their communities, high schools and colleges often allow their athletic fields, pools, and auditoriums to be used by community groups. In times of disasters many companies have donated supplies and manpower to help those whose homes have been devastated by floods, tornadoes, and fires. Project Hope was a service project on an international scale supported by funds, manpower, and supplies provided by American companies and industries. The white hospital ship which brought medical supplies, teachers, and treatment to other countries is a fine example of a project which serves others and at the same time brings goodwill to the sponsors.

Projects or activities built around special occasions. One day may be just like another to the average person, but not to the alert public relations practitioner who builds projects around the days that are special in American life.

Holidays are special days, and many a public relations project has been tied in to Columbus Day, Independence Day, Labor Day, Ground Hog Day, and all the other days which are spelled with a capital D. The key to a tie-in is that it be intrinsic and not foreign to the day to which it is aligned. You've got to be a near genius to carry out a public relations project that connects Grandma Brown's Beans to Columbus Day, but it just takes a little forethought and planning to tie Franco-American spaghetti to that same day. Ground Hog Day is a natural for any organization that is concerned with the weather, but not to a lumber company. The latter might better try to do something with Paul Bunyan Day.

Most of us check the calendar to see how many days are left until the weekend comes, but alert practitioners check their calendars to see what important years may be in the offing. In public relations offices throughout the land plans and projects were being fashioned in 1974 and 1975 for the all-important year 1976 when the country would be celebrating its bicentennial. If you're going to produce a special movie, book, series of publications, or other means of connecting your organization with the nation's 200th birthday, you don't start it on January 1, 1976, but a year or two earlier.

To those two certitudes—death and taxes—one can add a third meant particularly for public relations people: special days and occasions lend themselves neatly to public relations projects, but the competition is fierce because this knowledge is widely shared. To capitalize on these days and occasions the practitioner has to plan wisely in advance and be more imaginative than the competition.

Two reminders are in order in summing up the subject of projects in public relations programming. First, projects should be closely related to organizational and public relations objectives and goals and should not be undertaken unless this relationship is clear.

Second, projects should provide a blueprint for public relations action and indicate clearly to management the strategy of a program; the manpower and resources needed to carry out the program; and the budget and funds needed to support the activities set forth in the program's blueprint. By setting forth a series of projects the practitioner offers management a choice of options and thus if management decides—usually for financial reasons—not to authorize the entire package there should still be sufficient projects remaining to make up a viable program.

The proposed Newcomer's Program—devised for the New York Racing Association and previously mentioned in connection with objectives and audience—ran to fifty-six typewritten pages and threfore can be but briefly capsulized here. However, it clearly centered around a basic theme and approach and was so organized as to permit flexibility.

To attract newcomers—the target audience—the Silverman and Mower agency devised a packaged "Day at the Races" which could be implemented any day, regardless of weather, and which included details about transportation, convenience, and ease of execution. The major elements were: (1) a Continental breakfast; (2) a multitheatre experience; (3) a track tour; (4) a wagering seminar; (5) lunch; and (6) between-races activities.

To tell the track story and close group sales, the program included a Newcomer's Bureau that would identify groups, set up speaking engagements, and utilize scripts, a slide-sound or film presentation, brochures, displays, and bounce-back coupons.

Stressing the flexibility of the program, the proposal noted that it could probably not be implemented all at once, but would have to evolve over a period of time.

"The first step in implementing this proposal is deciding on a timetable," stated the agency. "Two elements that must be considered are: (1) What are the most important aspects of the proposal? and (2) What can be economically and physically accomplished within a given time?

"Many elements are relatively easy and inexpensive to implement, and should be gotten up and running immediately. Some others may have to wait. The important thing is that we start going out and closing the sale by telling the exciting story of thoroughbred racing and offering a unique package at the track."

As the above example illustrates, it's to the advantage of the practitioner to offer management a choice of options. Though "A Day at the Races" was a single, unified concept, it offered management the option of accepting all elements or of selecting certain ones and phasing in the others as time and finances allowed.

Tactics

In setting forth a program composed of a series of projects the practitioner should also indicate a clear order of priorities based on a descending degree of importance. Project A, for example, should head the list because the practitioner, as the expert in public relations, considers it most important in terms of reaching objectives and goals. Last on the list should be the project considered least important.

In setting up an order and description of planned projects, more than one list may be needed. For example, a campaign may well involve actions to be taken on a national and local level, and if so there would be an order of priorities within each list of projects.

The program blueprint should also indicate the funds, talent, and mechanics necessary to carry through various projects. In dealing with the latter great care should be taken to distinguish between those which are within the control of the practitioner and those which are not. Project D, for example, may involve a sixteen-city tour by a national personality, and it is tactically within the practitioner's control to arrange contracting with the personality and setting up all the minute details of the tour. Guaranteeing that specific media will cover the event in each city and print stories about it, is *not* within the control of the practitioner and hence is tactically unwise; such a guarantee is also ethically wrong and indefensible.

One of the virtues of initial research is that it often provides clues to strategy and tactics. As has been mentioned several times in this book, public relations practitioners are problem-solvers, and research often uncovers clues, tips, and leads to solutions.

In the long run, however, it's experience, creativity, and organizational ability and follow-through that lead to success in carrying out public relations programs. Experience tells the practitioner that establishing grassroots committees will be effective in certain instances, but not in others. Creativity is the flair that distinguishes the ordinary from the unusual and that enables the practitioner to make the most of opportunities. But the most successful practitioner is the one who combines experience and creativity with the organizational ability to pursue carefully designed tactics. At times this practitioner will pursue local level tactics, and in other instances he or she will work on both the local and national level. In some cases, it will be tactically wise to operate independently, but in other cases it will be best to join forces with others. It may even be found wisest to join with one's critics rather than to fight them, as the example below testifies:

In the early seventies, the salt industry faced serious opposition to the use of its product for melting ice on winter roads. Critics claimed the salt damaged cars, pavement, and vegetation and endangered water supplies and wildlife. Though every public works agency in the 33 snow-belt states used salt to keep winter roads safe and traffic moving, the industry recognized that salt had been improperly stored or spread inefficiently in some localities, thus causing environmental problems.

Retained by The Salt Institute, the Byoir organization began its study of the problem by visiting editors and news directors in 115 key communities in 11 snow-belt states. The field research was supplemented by a mail poll of all snow-belt public works directors concerning their salting practices. The results showed that (1) salt was often misused; (2) the industry itself was guilty of poor storage practices; (3) newsmen wanted specific information about local conditions and solutions; and (4) issues varied from one community to another depending on local factors.

Byoir's approach to the problems was to establish a "Sensible Salting" program of citizen action to help communities make their own decisions about salt use. As the agency explained it, here's how the program worked:

"To augment its small staff, the Institute conducted a week-long seminar to train two dozen representatives of member companies as field men who worked in assigned territories. To correct salt misuse by public works agencies, 24 environmental seminars were conducted to teach some 1,875 snowfighters modern and efficient salt-use procedures.

"To monitor use throughout the snow belt, the Institute launched an industry-wide policing program to bring poor storage practices at industry depots to the attention of top management. To obtain prompt reports of citizen protest of salt misuse, the Institute established an alert system with quick-action forms sent to all salt company field employees. To provide accurate and useful information, a fact-filled Sensible Salting Kit was produced and distributed to 1,600 citizens and officials.

"Simultaneously, Byoir initiated a broad publicity program to counter inaccurate news accounts about salt effects and to explain ways of preventing salt pollution."

What was so unusual about the Sensible Salt program was the tactical decision to join rather than to fight the critics. According to Byoir's George Hammond, the client had asked the agency to mount one of its high-impact publicity campaigns that would overpower the environmentalists who were against salt. However, Hammond noted, "the environmentalists were right with the times. . . . and they kept coming up with studies that showed salt ruined roadside vegetation, rusted cars and damaged drinking water supplies." So the plan emerged to have the salt people and the environmentalists join in a program to "use salt smarter." That it worked was shown by the fact that three states and more than 100 communities reversed legislation that would have banned salt.

A postscript is in order at this point. The tactic used by the Byoir people worked because they had the ear of top management. "We sat, fortunately, among the highest councils of the salt industry," says Hammond. "We were able to sell this program because we were in a position to recruit the trust and excite the interest of the people who were paying for our service. . . . The program worked because the client relationship worked and enabled us to embark on an uncharted path to win this almost unwinnable battle."

Timing

Experienced practitioners know that poor timing is the fatal flaw that can upset even the most carefully designed program and project. Many aspects of timing can be anticipated in advance, and from long experience the practitioner takes these into consideration in planning. For example, it's a well known fact that Saturday morning and afternoon newspapers are the thinnest of the week. The news "hole" for such papers is meager and therefore events scheduled for Friday evening may never be covered in the next day's newspapers. Because the early evening network news shows need sufficient lead time to process film and to match sound with film, events scheduled for late afternoon have little chance of being covered. Most of the material in Sunday newspapers has to be set in type Thursday or Friday, hence a feature submitted on Saturday stands little chance of being published in Sunday issues.

These anticipated aspects of timing deal essentially with technical aspects of the mass media, but there are others which are more directly within the purview of the practitioner. Most of these are spatial in nature in that they deal with the *spacing* of events, activities, announcements, and similar aspects of programming. It's generally not wise, for example, to schedule two major activities on the same day bcause they will inevitably compete with each other for public and media attention. Scheduling an event on election day is like committing public relations hari-kari; major disasters may be able to vie at such a time with the political news, but certainly not a press conference announcing the selection of a firm's new chief executive. Taking their cue from political campaign managers, astute public relations practitioners are aware of the danger of "peaking" too soon when spacing a project over a period of time, but they are also aware of the need to be on top of a situation and to take advantage of unexpected breaks.

Unfortunately for the novice, there are no hard-and-fast timing ground rules, but there is the need to be sensitive to the ebb and flow of the tides of public interest in issues and events. An organization's private project may have solid substantive value and interest, but has little chance of gaining public attention if promoted at a time when public and media receptivity is low. How does one know when public interest is high or low? Chiefly through a great deal of reading of daily newspapers and weekly news magazines, viewing network television news shows, keeping abreast of what's going on in national, state, and local community affairs, and being sensitive to the things that are of interest to those publics which are most important to an organization.

COMMUNICATING AND EVALUATING

Lumped together as the final elements of planned programming are two areas of professional endeavor in which the average practitioner is both the most and the least adept.

Communication, particularly the use of the written word and knowledge of media to reach various publics, is the one skill common to most practitioners. The average practitioner may not know much about communication theories, but he is generally skilled in writing and communicating, and he uses these skills to inform, influence, and gain public understanding and acceptance.

On the other hand, evaluation of plans, programs, and public relations activities is often more noticeable by its absence than by its presence. Two of the reasons for this absence is the fact that a good many public relations activities and programs do not lend themselves to accurate evaluative measurement, and the fact that evaluation can be a proposition whose costs managements are unwilling to assume.

Because both communication and evaluation are such key factors in programming they will be discussed in full detail in chapters to come. For the moment, they stand as the final steps in the orderly consideration of planning and programming.

SUMMATION

Planning and programming is at the core of successful public relations practice, whether we're considering the internal practitioner or the counselor. Though this chapter has explored the facets of plans and programs at some length, it has admittedly merely scratched the surface. In the continuum of the practice of public relations there is a wide gap between the beginner and the experienced practitioner, and this gap is bridged chiefly by the degree of sophistication possessed by the two extremes.

Given the assignment of promoting reflectorized highway signs the beginner sends out releases and art publicizing the signs; the veteran organizes seminars and develops features dealing with highway hypnosis, well aware of the fact that reflectorized signs help alleviate this danger to highway safety. Given the assignment of changing the stereotype of a metropolitan Chamber of Commerce, the beginner produces self-serving advertisements extolling the virtues of the chamber; the veteran creates a Business Advisory Bank, manned by chamber members who provide assistance in eight problem areas to more than 400 small businessmen in one year. Where the beginner is most likely to program along a line that promotes the private interests of company or client, the veteran programs to reach that point where the line of self-interest intersects the line of public interest, and when there is no intersecting point he follows another line that will intersect.

In summation, the programs developed by veteran practitioners:

1. Mesh organizational objectives and interests with public objectives and interests

2. Have continuity, are not overtly commercial, and lead to predetermined and determinable results

3. Consist of units which have individuality but which join well with each other and can be packaged and "merchandised" to maximize audience exposure and diverse organizational interests

QUESTIONS AND PROBLEMS FOR DISCUSSION

1. What are the major advantages of public relations planning?

2. In what ways can "overprogramming" and "undue program rigidity" be pitfalls in planning and programming?

3. Cite and briefly explain the nature of the seven steps cited by the author as providing a blueprint for public relations action and programming.

4. What major functions are served by carrying out a preliminary study?

5. What are some of the major elements that should go into the study or background report?

6. Just what does the author mean when he says that experienced practitioners make distinctions about problems?

7. In what respects is problem identification largely a result of assumptions, and just how does this relate to the basic matter of defining the problem?

8. What are the various ways one might go about establishing an order of problem priorities?

9. Cite and explain some important criteria to apply to the establishment of sound public relations objectives and goals.

10. What are some of the ways to categorize the audience for public relations programs?

11. Under what circumstances might it be more feasible to reach a target audience indirectly rather than directly?

12. Explain some of the basic qualities which should be inherent in a public relations theme or themes.

13. Explain some ways in which projects are used to support and/or dramatize: (a) an existing event, facility or situation; (b) communication events or actions; (c) products, sales, and services.

14. What considerations are important to the practitioner in applying tactics and timing to public relations programming?

15. Why is it important to plan programs along a line where private interests intersect with public interests? To illustrate this principle, cite some situations where this intersection takes place.

16. What are the basic elements of "management by objectives"? Why isn't MBO used more extensively by public relations practitioners?

PROJECTS, ASSIGNMENTS, AND MINI-CASES

1. SETTING FORTH SOME THEMES: THREE MINI-PROBLEMS

1. Assume you have been given the assignment of setting forth two major themes which can be used as the basis for public relations programming for your college or university for the coming academic year.

   In a memorandum to your vice president for public relations explain the essence of the two themes you would propose for your institution. Do *not* use a slogan format, but explain the nature of your proposed themes in a paragraph for each.

   As a supplement to your memorandum, explain *why* you have proposed each theme. In short, justify your themes.

2. Themes can be discerned in most major advertising campaigns of national concerns and organizations. Some are astute, relevant, and honest, and some are not.

   Select and analyze one such major, current advertising campaign of a national concern or organization, and in a memorandum to your instructor explain the nature of the theme or themes you discern in the campaign; provide illustrative material from the campaign to demonstrate how these themes are used; and critique the use of said themes in terms of their effectiveness, relevancy, and honesty.

3. Select any organization with which you are familiar—it can be local, regional, or national; profit or nonprofit—and set forth two major themes which can be used as the basis for a projected public relations campaign for the coming year.

   In a memorandum to your instructor explain the essence of the two themes you would propose for the organization. Do *not* use a slogan format, but explain the nature of your proposed themes in a paragraph for each.

   As a supplement to your memorandum, explain *why* you have proposed each theme. In short, justify your themes.

2. BUILDING PROJECTS AROUND SPECIAL OCCASIONS: TWO MINI-PROBLEMS

1. You are to assume that it is early in 1976 and the National Football League has agreed to allocate to the Public Relations Society of America fourteen half-minute public service cameos which will be put on the air during games in the 1976-77 season.

   Because these are to be public service spots, the television network is not charging air time. However, the NFL stipulates that the spots should be built around a central theme involving the nation's bicentennial.

The Board of Directors of the PRSA has raised the funds needed to cover production costs for the fourteen cameos and has tentatively assigned you total responsibility for the project. However, before giving you final approval the board requests that you prepare and send it a position paper covering the following:

A. A concise statement explaining why you perceive the NFL cameo opportunity meets basic objectives and goals of the PRSA

B. An explanation of the specific central theme which you propose to be exemplified in each of the fourteen half-minute spots

C. A brief explanation describing the nature of *each* of the fourteen cameos

D. A rough video-voice script for any one of the cameos

E. A concise statement explaining your perception of how your proposed theme and the fourteen cameos you have projected will meet the basic objectives and goals you have outlined in Item 1

2. You are to assume you are vice president for public relations of Sears, Roebuck and Company. A year before the nation's bicentennial you proposed to the president and the company's board of directors that your department be given the authority and funds to carry out five major projects during the bicentennial year. You have been asked to submit a memorandum covering the following:

A. The basic objectives and goals of the year-long program

B. The major publics to be reached and the theme(s) of the program

C. A description of the five major projects in sufficient length to enable the president and board to have a clear understanding of their nature

D. A statement of reasons why the company should support and carry out the program

3. A RETIRED COUNSELOR IS ASKED TO REVIEW A PROGRAM: A MINICASE

Spotless Laundries, a hitherto privately owned commercial laundry in Wilmington, Delaware, whose chief customers are restaurants, colleges, and hospitals in the state of Delaware, was sold one year ago to a three-member group in their early thirties.

Determined to extend the operations of the firm, the new owners went "public" in order to raise more capital and for the past six months the stock has been traded on the American Stock Exchange. With the modest amount of new capital which has been accrued, the new owners built a new plant in Bethesda, Maryland, and the two plants in Wilmington and Bethesda now service customers in the two states and in the District of Columbia.

Traditionally, the commercial laundry field has consisted mainly of firms very similar to Spotless in that their business is mostly local, and in some cases regional, and serves customers within one day's driving range of the firm's trucks. To break this pattern and with the eventual goal of becoming a truly national firm, the new owners of Spotless have aimed their efforts at capturing an increasingly larger and larger share of the lucrative college and hospital linen fields. The former is served chiefly by local commercial laundries and the latter by local commercial laundries and by laundries owned and operated by the hospitals themselves.

The new owners have set up two wholly-owned subsidiaries of Spotless—College Linens of America, Inc., and Hospital Linens of America, Inc.—and are now planning to extend their operations. As the necessary finances become available, the owners hope first to build new plants anywhere in the Northeast where there is a reasonable certitude that colleges and hospitals will make use of their services, and then to move out into other geographic areas of the country. The major selling tool of both subsidiaries is a "total systems approach" which CLA and HLA have developed and which is demonstrably able to provide interested colleges and hospitals with faster, more dependable and cheaper service than they can secure from either their own facilities or from local commercial laundries.

You are to assume that you are a retired public relations counselor and a long-time personal friend of Mrs. Melissa Gordon, president of Spotless Laundries. Mrs. Gordon has written informing you that she recently had discussions with a counseling firm relative to taking on the assignment of handling public relations for CHLA. The firm, writes Mrs. Gordon, has submitted a program proposal which includes the following ten major projects, and Mrs. Gordon would be most appreciative if you would review them and let her know your reaction to them in a return letter. She also asks you to submit a bill with your critique.

1. *Case History Program:* CHLA's satisfied clients are its best press agents. We would ask you to open doors for us. Then we would go in, interview some of your customers, prepare their comments in article form, and place them for publication. Among other things, this is a very valuable way for CHLA to improve its client relations.

2. *By-liner Program:* The top executive of CHLA ought to receive a certain amount of exposure in important publications via by-lined articles. These could deal with the total CHLA service, but more likely possibilities would deal with particular aspects of the service, how it solves specific problems, etc.

3. *A Standard Logo:* Ready identification can be established for CHLA by the development of a new, distinctive, and impressive logo which can be used on everything from calling cards to signs on delivery trucks.

4. *Sales slide presentation:* Our graphics and multi-media departments will prepare an exciting slide presentation which can be

used to sell CHLA to prospective customers. We would schedule this presentation for important college and hospital industry meetings, trade shows, and similar gatherings.

5. *Survey and Report:* We can put this technique to use in several ways valuable to CHLA. We would design a telephone or personal interview survey to spotlight the views of specific audiences, and then we would report the results of the survey through appropriate media. The technique lets you know what your prospects are thinking and it provides a means for spot publicity. Subject matter can range all the way from how business leaders' view their community hospital problems—or college financial problems—to the way hospital purchasing agents view their linen problems. The material developed through surveys would also have many secondary uses: in subsequent articles, speeches, booklets, and sales manuals.

6. *Sales Brochures:* We would develop two of these to be used for a local and national program. They would stress the systems aspects of the service and show how it differs from the ordinary linen supply operation.

7. *Monographs:* We would contract with leading authorities to write a series of informative monographs dealing with various aspects of college and hospital management, and these would be given wide distribution throughout both fields to college and hospital executives. The monographs would be noncommercial in nature and the only reference to CHLA would be on the cover page.

8. *Seminars:* Here is another noncommercial way of establishing CHLA as the leader in its field. We would contract with leading authorities to take part in these seminars—to be held throughout the country—and to discuss important college and hospital problem areas. The seminars would generate local publicity in print and electronic media, while national exposure would be gained by selective mailing of seminar summary remarks to a key list of important community and professional leaders.

9. *Speaking Dates:* Another useful way of gaining valuable exposure for CHLA is to have some of your executives speak before local and regional business and professional organizations. The talks would have to be broad in nature, rather than commercial, and would help sell CHLA as the authority in the hospital and college fields.

10. *Reprints:* This is Standard Operating Procedure, but it's an excellent means of keeping your name before important individuals and groups.

4. THE OWENS-CORNING FIBERGLAS CORPORATION'S ENERGY CONSERVATION AWARDS PROGRAM: A MINI-CASE

A record number of entries—close to 200—were submitted in 1978 by architects and engineers competing in the seventh annual Owens-

Corning Fiberglas Corporation's Energy Conservation Awards program.

Refined and executed by Burson-Marsteller for its client, the Owens-Corning Fiberglas Corporation, the program was instituted in 1971 and subsequently sanctioned by the American Institute of Architects (AIA). The competition was designed to recognize architects, engineers, and building owners who have made significant contributions to energy conservation and the environment through design and construction technique.

"Through our Energy Awards program we hope to stimulate more people to address themselves to one of this country's most pressing issues," explained Charles E. Peck, executive vice-president for Owens-Corning. "The annual rise in project entries (the entries in 1978 were almost twice the number in the previous year) reflects the growing concern of professionals in the building industry over the energy problem and ways to solve it."

Five categories of buildings were covered by the competition: institutional, commercial, industrial, government, and special. The last-named category included residential structures and any building or project not covered in the traditional categories. Ineligible were speculative designs and work performed for Owens-Corning or by members of the awards jury for their firms.

Judges for 1978 were: William W. Caudill, FAIA, chairman of the board, Caudill, Rowlett, Scott, Inc., Houston, Texas; David L. Grumman, P.E., president, Enercon, Ltd., Evanston, Illinois; Frank J. Powell, M.E., manager, Insulation Program at the National Bureau of Standards, Washington, D.C.; James S. Polshek, FAIA, dean, Graduate School of Architecture and Planning, Columbia University, New York City; Jack E. Tumilty, president, Jack E. Tumilty, P.E. and Associates, Tulsa, Oklahoma; and John J. Labosky, P.E., mechanical discipline head, Energy Conservation and Research Division, Smith Hinchman and Grylls, Detroit, Michigan.

Meeting at Owens-Corning's New York office for three days in September (September 13-15), the six judges selected five winners and five honorable mentions. Cited below, in alphabetical order by category, were the awards, projects, and entrants:

WINNERS AND HONORABLE MENTIONS

Award	Project	Entrant
Commercial		
Honorable Mention	Georgia Power Company Corporate Headquarters Office Building Atlanta, Georgia	Heery and Heery, Architects and Engineers, Inc. 800 W. Peachtree St., N.W. Atlanta, Georgia 30300
Honorable Mention	South Central Bell Telephone Company Administrative Headquarters Alabama Operations Jefferson County, Alabama	Crawford, Giattina and Associates Architects, Inc. 2031-11th Avenue South Birmingham, Alabama 35205

Government

Winner	Headquarters for the State University of New York Albany, New York	William A. Hall and Associates, Architecture and Planning 42 East 21st Street New York, New York 10010
Winner	State Office Building Site 3 Sacramento, California	Benham Blair and Affiliates of California, Inc. 1901 Avenue of the Stars Los Angeles, California 90067
Honorable Mention	Police Services and Fire Administration for the City of Mountain View Mountain View, California	Goodwin B. Steinberg Associates Architects 737 North First Street San Jose, California 95112

Industrial

Winner	Regional Transportation District (RTD) East Metro Bus Maintenance Facility Aurora, Colorado	RNL, Inc. 1576 Sherman Street Denver, Colorado 80203
Honorable Mention	Advanced Wastewater Treatment Facilities Southerly Wastewater Treatment Center Cuyahoga Heights, Ohio	Malcolm Pirnie, Inc. Consulting Environmental Engineers 2 Corporate Park Drive White Plains, New York 10602

Institutional

Winner	The Museum of Science and Industry of Tampa/Hillsborough County Tampa, Florida	Rowe Holmes Associates Architects, Inc. 100 Madison Street Tampa, Florida 33602
Honorable Mention	Law School Facility University of Minnesota Minneapolis, Minnesota	The Leonard Parker Associates Architects, Inc. 430 Oak Grove Minneapolis, Minnesota 55403

Special

Winner	Pitkin County Air Terminal Aspen, Colorado	Copland Finholm Hagman Yaw Ltd., Architects P.O. Box 2736 Aspen, Colorado 81611

Announcement and presentation of the awards to winners and honorable mentions were made at an awards dinner on December 4, 1978, in the Essex House in New York City. A total of 172 attended the dinner, including 27 editors. Each winner and honorable mention received a Steuben crystal trophy entitled *Triangles,* specially commissioned and designed for the energy conservation awards program and ranging in cost from $1,500 to $2,500 each. Each editor received a thick press kit, carried in a three-ring binder, containing remarks by Peck; a listing of winners and honorable mentions citing the award, project, and entrant; individual stories about the firms and projects; and photographs of their entries. The kits and separate stories were later distributed to key trade publications in the architectural, construction, and engineering fields; to vertical publications, such as *Fleet Owner*, in appropriate fields; and to newspapers, consumer magazines, and electronic media.

> Case material courtesy of Owens-
> Corning Fiberglas Corporation and
> Burson-Marsteller

Discussion Questions

1. What's your opinion about the Energy Conservation Awards program as a public relations project? Justify your answer.

2. In what respects do the combination of elements or aspects of the Energy Conservation Awards program make it one that seems to meet the interests of the sponsor, the entrants, and the public?

3. What changes, if any, would you suggest be made in the Energy Conservation Awards program? Why?

4. If you were asked to do so, how would you go about justifying the cost of the program? Try to be as specific as possible.

Projects and Assignments

1. As a member of the account team at Burson-Marsteller, you have been assigned the task of compiling a list of trade and professional publications to which releases can be sent when members of the awards jury are selected and when the awards are announced and presented.

   Compile and present your list in a memorandum to your supervisor.

2. As noted in the fact pattern of the case, each winner and honorable mention received a Steuben crystal trophy entitled *Triangles*. This Steuben crystal has been described as a "floating sculpture that captures and reflects light from multiple triangular planes."

   It has been suggested that a different kind of award or trophy be given next year to each winner and honorable mention. In a memorandum to your instructor, cite and describe or explain *two* other kinds of awards or trophies that could be given to next year's winners and honorable mentions. You can assume a total budget of $25,000 for the awards or trophies.

3. As noted in the fact pattern of the case, announcement and presentation of the awards to winners and honorable mentions were made at an awards dinner on December 4, 1978, in the Essex House in New York City.

   It has been suggested that when the awards are announced next year a special time be set aside for media coverage on the day (or evening) of the awards dinner. In a memorandum to your instructor, explain exactly at what time of the day (or evening) and in what manner you would take care of media coverage. Try to be as specific as possible in regard to *time* and *arrangements*, and explain reasons for your decision.

4. You are to assume that you're on the account team at Burson-Marsteller and the client has asked you to suggest some changes in the Energy Conservation Awards program. In a memorandum to the client, set forth the changes you recommend be made and the reasons for your recommendations.

RECOMMENDED READING

Edward L. Bernays, *Biography of an Idea*. New York: Simon & Schuster, 1965.

_____, *Public Relations*. Norman, Okla.: University of Oklahoma Press, 1952.

J. D. Bogart, "Your Long-Range Planning Role," *Public Relations Journal*, September 1976.

John F. Budd, Jr., *An Executive's Primer on Public Relations*. New York: Chilton Book Co., 1969.

Roger E. Coleman, Jr., "Turning Critics into Helpers," *Association Management*, November 1973.

R. L. Dilenschneider, "Seven Steps to Program Planning," *Public Relations Journal*, November 1976.

David Finn, *Public Relations and Management*. New York: Reinhardt Publishing Co., 1960.

George Hammond, "Meeting Client Expectations," remarks made at seminar, East Central District, PRSA, Detroit, May 16, 1978.

J. W. Leslie, "Staff Evaluation Is a Two-Way Process," *Case Currents*, April 1977 (Council For Advancement and Support of Education).

Philip Lesly, "Analysis, Planning, and Programming," in *Lesly's Public Relations Handbook*, 2nd ed., ed. Philip Lesly. Englewood Cliffs, N.J.: Prentice-Hall, 1978

Robert K. Marker, "The Armstrong PR Data Measurement System," *Public Relations Review*, Winter 1977.

John Marston, *Modern Public Relations*. New York: McGraw-Hill, 1979.

A. N. Mavis, "How to Organize and Manage a Public Relations Program," *Consulting Engineer*, August 1976.

"Newcomers' Program Proposal," Silverman & Mower, Syracuse, N.Y., December 1977.

Jack R. Nowling, "How to Write the PR Program," *Public Relations Journal*, July 1976.

Edward J. Robinson, *Communication And Public Relations*. Columbus, Ohio: Charles E. Merrill Books, 1966.

Irwin Ross, *The Image Makers*. Garden City, N.Y.: Doubleday, 1959.

R. D. Ross, *The Management of Public Relations: Analysis and Planning External Relations*. Somerset, N.J.: Wiley-Interscience, 1977.

Raymond Simon, ed. *Perspectives in Public Relations*. Norman Okla.: University of Oklahoma Press, 1966.

———, *Public Relations Management: Cases and Simulations*, 2nd ed. Columbus, Ohio: Grid Publishing, 1977.

Leonard Snyder, "Better Problem Solving Is Possible," *Public Relations Quarterly,* March 1976.

Howard Stephenson, ed., *Handbook of Public Relations,* 2nd ed. New York: McGraw-Hill, 1971.

Anita H. Thies, "Practicing PR by Objectives," *Case Currents,* January 1978.

9

Communication: Basic Elements, Theories, and Model

In handling the five major elements of public relations in action—assessing public opinion, researching, planning and programming, communicating, and evaluating results—public relations practitioners consider that communicating presents the fewest problems. This is not because the art of communication is quickly and easily mastered, but because it is most closely aligned to the practitioner's prior professional life experience. Starting with the pioneers who commenced the practice of public relations early in this century, practitioners traditionally have begun their professional life as journalists. The basic tool of the journalist has been the word—written in the case of the print journalist and verbal in the case of the electronic journalist—and he has used it to communicate effectively with readers, listeners, and viewers. When practitioners moved from journalism into public relations they took along their skill in communicating through the word.

Newcomers to the field of public relations discover quickly that effective communication is still the core element of successful public relations practice. A few practitioners may carry out successful practice by assessing public opinion, conducting research, planning, and programming, but the biggest game in town is still communication. Practitioners must understand the nature of public opinion and must be able to counsel and plan programs, but unless they can communicate they don't last long in the field.

And so the practitioners communicate, often successfully and effectively. But don't ask too many of them to provide a rational, thoughtful description of the communication process, to discuss how communication works, or to explain *why* some communication will affect opinion change, some behavior change, and some neither. This chapter will provide some of the answers about the nature and process of communication, and at the same time will raise some questions for which there are no ready and simple answers. The following chapter will consider the practical realities of communication via media relations, publicity techniques, and public relations advertising.

Comment

THREE BASIC CONSIDERATIONS

The primary approach to communication in this chapter will be by means of a communications model, but first some observations are in order about the *purpose, form,* and *process* of communication.

PURPOSE

Idle conversation—a form of daily communication engaged in by most people—serves the purpose of passing away the time of the day, but this is not the main reason why public relations practitioners engage in communication. There's purpose behind all successful communication, and this elementary fact has to be recognized and purpose clarified *before* communication is set in motion.

Mass media section

The mass media, the major means of communication utilized by public relations practitioners, serve three main purposes: to *inform, influence,* and *entertain.* Harold Lasswell, who pioneered in the study of communication, placed these in a social context when he postulated that the three major social functions of communications are: (1) surveillance of the environment; (2) correlation of the different parts of society in responding to environment; and (3) transmission of the social heritage from one generation to the other. The connection between the two concepts is not difficult to make: providing information serves as a means of surveilling the environment; editorials, columns, and commentaries serve to correlate the different parts of society in responding to the environment; and it is through the various means of entertainment that the mass media help to transmit the social heritage.

Valuable as the three-fold division of purpose may be, it is not distinctive nor purposeful enough for the kind of professional communication tasks assigned to or undertaken by public relations practitioners. David K. Berlo suggests a more definitive role for communication when he proposes that the nature of the *response* to be sought from communication be its paramount purpose.

Berlo on purpose

"... All communication behavior," says Berlo, "has as its purpose, its goal, the production of a response. When we learn to phrase our purposes in terms of specific responses from those attending to our messages, we have taken the first step toward efficient and effective communication." (*The Process of Communication,* Holt, Rinehart, and Winston)

Berlo's suggestion that communicators concentrate on the response to be sought is highly relevant to public relations practitioners, and at the same time it is not necessarily antithetical to the three-fold purpose model. If one wants mainly to provide information, that's fine, but at least recognize that this is the purpose and the response to be sought. If one wants mainly to entertain, that's fine also so long as the communicator recognizes what response is to be achieved from entertainment.

In Berlo's opinion, the main purpose of communication is to influence or, as he puts it, "to affect with intent." In the following criticism that Berlo makes of numerous communication efforts is a valuable lesson for public relations practitioners:

> Too often, writers think that their job is to *write* technical reports rather than to *affect the behavior* of their reader. Television producers and theatrical directors forget that their original purpose was to affect an audience—they get too busy "putting on plays" or "filling time with programs." Teachers forget about the influence they wanted to exert on students and concentrate on "covering the material" or "filling fifty minutes a week." Presidents of civic and professional organizations forget they are trying to influence or affect their members—they are too busy "having meetings" or "completing programs." Agricultural extension workers forget they are trying to affect farmers and homemakers—they get too busy "giving out information" or "reporting research."

Berlo could well have added that public relations practitioners often are: so busy writing and mailing out hundreds of press releases they forget that the first purpose of a release is to be accepted and used by the mass media and the second is to be read; so busy creating stunts and activities they fail to relate them to the objectives and goals of the organization; so busy "doing" they forget that behind the doing there has to be the purpose of achieving a predetermined response.

FORM

The form that communication takes is divisible in many different ways. One can consider communication as being personal or impersonal, oral or written, private or public, visual or nonvisual, internal or external, tactile or nontactile, face-to-face or interposed, indoor or outdoor, and even hot or cold. The form that a particular communication takes may be dictated by the circumstances surrounding it or may be at the control of the communicator; it may be influenced by the social controls of the society in which it takes place; and it may be dependent on technological circumstances.

Form is more than just an idle exercise in semantics or academic gamesmanship, particularly when the communicator has to make a choice. If you're an Indian chief whose tribe is being surrounded by an overwhelming army force, do you send up smoke signals to bring help or do you send a warrior on a fast pony? If you're Samuel Adams, do you send a letter protesting the stamp tax or do you stage an event and dump tea into Boston harbor?

None of the above examples illustrates conventional forms of communication, but they make the point that communication can take all sorts of forms, many of them unconventional, in an attempt to "get the message through" and to persuade others. Symbols are a form of communication, as witness the use of the American flag at rallies of both the far right and the far left. Both sight and smell are forms of communication, as testified to in the summer of 1975 by the millions of New Yorkers who saw and smelled their piles of garbage when the sanitation-men left it there in protest of the wholesale dismissal of their union membership. Sound is a form of communication, as anyone who has ever attended a rock festival will clearly testify.

These varieties of form are a reminder that there's more to communication form than a speech, feature story, press release, or television appearance. Given the choice, the practitioner uses that form most appropriate to the situation and which seems most likely to bring about the desired response.

PROCESS

Communication involves process. Communication does not take place in a vacuum or void, and is not singular but pluralistic. Do not expect communication to ensue if you lock a person for weeks in an air-tight, totally dark, escape-proof, sound-proof, perfectly bare dungeon with walls three feet thick; that person will not only be unable to communicate, but will undoubtedly die. Put two people in the same dungeon and they may also die, but they will communicate.

How they will communicate depends on a wide number of variables—their ages, education, nationality, ingenuity, state of mental and physical health, dexterity, and so forth. What if one of the two is 10 years old and the other 40? What if one has a sixth-grade education and the other a Ph.D. degree? What if one is American and the other Hungarian? The human spirit being what it is, the two will overcome all barriers to communication. The barriers themselves are cited to illustrate that communication does not take place in a vacuum or void but in a situational context that affects it. The dual nature of those in the situation is a reminder that communication takes place only when there is more than one person involved. Wilbur Schramm, who has devoted a professional lifetime to the study of communication, summed up these two important aspects of communication in these words: "If there is one thing we know about human communication it is that nothing passes unchanged in the process, from person to person."

A BRIEF SYNOPSIS OF THEORIES

Some of the early scientific studies of the nature of communication were so simplistic they viewed the act of communication as a one-plus-one-equals-two phenomenon. One school of researchers postulated the *"hypodermic needle"* theory of communication in which the communicator sent his message through the mass media to bring about certain behavior on the part of the audience. News stories, radio, and television programs were likened to a hypodermic needle which took the messages sent by the communicator, stuck them in the minds of the audience, and produced desired effects.

A refinement of this theory was the *"two-step flow"* hypothesis which theorized that ideas flow from the media to opinion leaders and then from them to the less active elements of the population. The key study which led to this theory was conducted in Erie County, Ohio, in the 1940 presidential election by Paul Lazarsfeld and colleagues at the Bureau of Applied Social Research of Columbia University. Using the panel research technique, the researchers concluded that very few people reported being influenced by the media about voting but rather by personal contacts and face-to-face persuasion by opinion leaders. Another study, conducted among women in Decatur, Illinois, and reported in the book *Personal Influence* by Katz and Lazarsfeld, concluded that there are different levels and degrees of opinion leadership, that some women are opinion-forming influentials when it comes to movie-going, others when it comes to fashion, etc.

The fault with both theories is that they fail to recognize that communication is a process in which key elements are constantly interacting with each other. As Wilbur Schramm puts it:". . . The idea that something 'flows,' untransformed, from sender to receiver in human communication is a bit of intellectual baggage that is well forgotten. It is better to think of a message as a catalytic agent with a little force of its own except as it can trigger forces in the person who receives it. . . ."

A third theory of mass communication—the *diffusion process theory*—developed from the attempt to describe how news and information about new methods of doing things flow from certain mass media through key persons to other individuals who act eventually on the information received. Everett Rogers, considered to be the most systematic diffusion model researcher, concluded there are four stages in the adoption of innovations: the information and knowledge stage; the persuasion stage; the decision or adoption stage; and the reevaluation stage. The model was originally formulated to describe how new agricultural methods and processes come to the attention of so-called "innovaters" and then move downward to others who eventually use and adopt them as standard practice. According to diffusion theorists, the mass media are seen as important only in the information stage; interpersonal communication is viewed as predominant in the last three stages for most people.

Essentially descriptive in nature, the diffusion theory and model may be useful in explaining how innovations and inventive new methods are transmitted, but critics doubt its applicability to the transmission and use of political and social information and ideas. It is also seen as relatively ineffective when audience response to information and ideas is unpredictable and uncontrolled—which is precisely the situation in which most public relations practitioners find themselves when dealing with audiences.

A fourth theory or model of the communication process receiving much attention in recent years is the *transactional model*. As its name implies, this model explores influences from both the communicator and the audience. One researcher, W. P. Davison, cites this view of the audience:

The communicator's audience is not a passive occupant—it cannot be regarded as a lump of clay to be molded by the master propagandist.

Rather, the audience is made up of individuals who demand something from the communications to which they are exposed, and who select those that are useful to them. In other words, they must get something from the manipulator if he is to get something from them.

Leonard J. Snyder, writing in the late seventies, emphasized this new direction of the transactional model when he reviewed what has been called "the uses and gratification" approach to communication research. Rather than take the communicator as the starting point, this approach considers the media consumer as the starting point. The view of the audience is one where its members actively utilize media content to meet their own individual needs and wants. "It is increasingly evident . . .," stated Snyder, "that patterns of media use are shaped by audience needs, wants, and expectations, and that these are important determinants of media effects."

This stress on the audience's "needs, wants, and expectations"—another way of emphasizing "uses and gratifications"—will be explored further in this chapter during discussion of the message stage of a simple communications model. Readers of this text may also recall that one of Newsom's guideposts to public opinion—the identification guidepost—puts the same stress on the need to identify with the needs, hopes, aspirations, and desires of the intended audience.

A CAUTIONARY NOTE

The public relations practitioner is well advised to view communication just as he or she views public relations. Both are dynamic, and neither process has a beginning, a middle, and an ending. Both public relations and communication in action are continuous, always in a state of flux with their basic elements constantly interacting with and upon each other. Life for the practitioner would be simple if it were possible to freeze the communication process and set it off in time and space, but communication cannot be frozen.

What do we mean when we say that communication is not frozen in time and space? Simply that all communication takes place in a setting, and the setting is an important factor in determining whether communication will be effective and in trying to predict audience reaction.

Consider that you are director of public relations for a major oil company. The time is June 26, 1965, just prior to the start of the summer vacation season. It has been decided to raise the price of your gasoline three cents a gallon at the pump. You send out a press release announcing the price increase, and it is carried by the wire services and run on the inside pages of most of the country's daily newspapers. The price goes up as scheduled, people pay it, and there is little public concern.

It is now June 26, 1975, just prior to the start of the summer vacation season. There have been several years of gasoline shortages, steep price increases by the oil-exporting countries, and much national concern about the energy crisis. It has been decided to raise the price of your gasoline three cents a gallon at the pump, and this will represent an all-time high. You send out a press release announcing the price increase, and it is virtually a carbon copy of the release sent out in 1965. The story is carried by the wire services and appears on the front pages of most of the country's daily newspapers. The price goes up as scheduled and people pay it, *but*: there is a public outcry; consumer advocate groups issue statements highly critical of the action; letters to the editor denounce your company and other oil companies who also raised their prices three cents a gallon; senators and representatives issue statements demanding an immediate investigation of alleged price fixing and gouging; and subsequent public opinion polls show a sharp drop in public opinion toward your company and other gasoline companies.

The above example underscores the importance of the setting or framework within which communication operates. Even though the other elements in the process may be similar, the setting is vital in determining effects or results.

Though the setting for communication is a vital factor in the whole process of communication, it was not given much consideration by the "hypodermic needle" and "two-step flow" researchers, and unfortunately most experimenters in communication continue to err in drawing conclusions from their experiments as though they had been conducted in a milieu frozen in time and space. Because people differ and because the situations in which people find themselves differ, it is not wise to draw sweeping conclusions about human communication on the basis of what tends to be a controlled environment.

This does not, however, justify the equally sweeping conclusion that human communication experiments serve no valuable purpose at all. On the contrary, they help to underscore the important fact that communication is a process and that certain key elements are involved. Therefore, in order to understand the process and to learn lessons from it, these key elements need to be identified, analyzed, and discussed. To achieve these purposes, communication scholars have developed relatively simple—perhaps deceptively simple—communication models, and it is through such a model that the process of communication will be explained in the section that follows.

The process of communication itself is not orderly and does not work in linear form. However, the model will project the elements in linear form chiefly for the purpose of an orderly discussion of communication.

A COMMUNICATION MODEL: INTRODUCTION

A simple communication model consists of four major elements: the sender or source; the message; the channel; and the receiver or recipient. If we were to project these four elements in linear form to explain the communication process our model would work out as follows:

In its simplest form communication involves a source or sender whose purpose is to send a message through a channel in order to reach a receiver or recipient. Three other sub-elements, however, are usually present in the communication act and these involve *encoding, decoding,* and *feedback.*

Encoding is essentially a matter of translating the ideas of the source and giving them meaning. Usually this is performed by the motor skills possessed by the sender who uses his vocal mechanisms to produce oral words or his muscle system to produce written words or gestures. In simple communication situations the source and encoder are the same person, but the two are generally separate entities in complex communication situations in which an organization is involved. As an example, the organization may want to communicate with its union public but entrusts the encoding of the message to its public relations department.

Decoding represents the reverse of encoding and means a retranslation of a message into a form that the receiver can use. In face-to-face communication the encoder is the set of motor skills used by the source, while the set of sensory skills used by the receiver is the decoder. The source encodes by using speech or writing; the receiver decodes by using hearing or reading. In a more complex situation the functions of encoding and decoding are separable from the source and receiver functions.

Berlo reminds us that the concepts of source, encoder, decoder, and receiver should not be interpreted as being separate things, entities, or people, but as the names of behavior performed when communication takes place. Thus, one person may be both a source and a receiver and encode and decode messages. In complex communication patterns these functions would be carried out by different people. As an example to describe the communication behavior of a complex organization, Berlo cites the operation of a large-city newspaper:

> The operation of the newspaper involves a complex network of communication. The newspaper hires people whose prime job is decoding—reporters who observe one or more kinds of events in the world and relay them to the "central nervous system" of the paper, the "desk" or "slot" or central control office.

> When these messages are received, some decision is reached by the editorial staff. As a result of these decisions, orders are given from the control desk to produce or not produce a given message in the paper. Again, the encoding function becomes specialized. The paper employs rewrite men, proofreaders, linotype operators, pressmen, delivery boys. They are all responsible for one or another part of the encoding and channeling functions, getting the message out of the control office on to the pages of the newspaper, and thence to a different set of receivers, the reading public.

In the example cited above there is no direct linear line from source to message to channel to receiver, but rather a set of activities interrelated to each other, almost indivisible, and constantly in motion. Communication within this organization is also affected by the perceptions, attitudes, and beliefs of those involved in the process; by the standards and codes of the paper; and by the situation existing at the time the communication process takes place.

Among the factors involved in the dynamics of the communication process is the concept known as *feedback*. It operates at all levels, but is of particular importance at the source level. *Feedback is essentially a return flow from the message as it is received from the recipient.* Its impact and effect can be instantaneous and powerful—as in face-to-face communication—or delayed and weak—as in mass communication. When a skillful speaker addresses an audience he is constantly making use of audience feedback to judge the impact he is making. Because this feedback is instantaneous and immediate he is able to change his delivery, tone, and even the talk itself in order to adjust to the feedback he receives from the audience. Contrast this with communication by means of television where the audience is remote, removed, and out of sight. Here feedback is delayed, weak, and almost nonexistent. It's for this reason, among some others, that television shows are performed before specially assembled, live audiences, even though the real audience is somewhere out there in the remote land of the home receiver set. Feedback is what actors mean when they say there's a dynamic quality in the air when performing in the theatre as compared to the static quality when performing before the movie camera.

Feedback is highly important to public relations practitioners because it enables them to adjust, modify, or change messages in accordance with the dictates of the feedback. Practitioners can use all the skills at their command when sending a message through mass media channels, but without feedback they have no way of knowing the immediate impact these messages have on the intended recipient.

THE MODEL SUMMED UP

In very brief form we have examined the elements that must be present if communication is to take place. There has to be a *source*—one person, two people, or an organization—with some reason for engaging in communication. This source *encodes* to translate his or her ideas, information, or thoughts, and at the same time can be *decoding* and receiving *feedback*. He or she then *assigns meaning* to the ideas, information, or thoughts, and puts them in the form of a *message*. The message is sent through a carrier or *medium* and is thereby channeled to a *receiver*. The receiver may be one person, two people, or an organization, and the receiver *decodes* the message to give it meaning. At the same time he or she may be encoding and receiving feedback.

The entire communication act, operating within a societal environment, is a matter of a process in which the key elements overlap, interact, and feed back upon each other. Thus, as seen in the accompanying

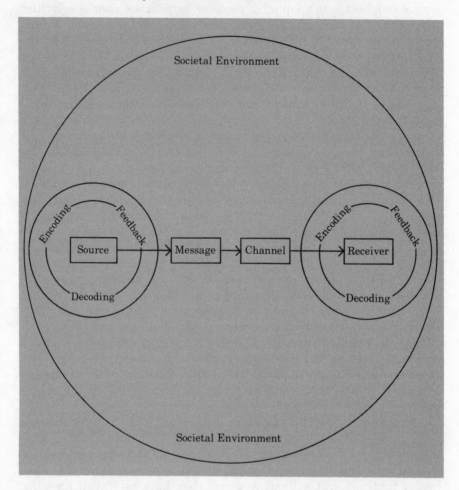

chart, the process is both linear and circular. It is not static, but is dynamic, and it takes place in the context of a societal environment whose elements affect the communication act.

THE COMMUNICATION MODEL DISSECTED

The purpose of this section is to examine each of the four major elements of our communication model from the viewpoint of possible maximum effectiveness. As hi-fi enthusiasts know, the quality of sound produced by the system is at its maximum level when there is no interference anywhere within the system. Similarly, the quality of communication produced by a communication system is at its maximum level when there is no interference anywhere within the system. To produce maximum efficiency-level communication, therefore, one must dissect the communication model and explore the *factors within the four major elements that lead to maximum communication effectiveness*.

SOURCE-SENDER

The most common role played by the public relations practitioner within the communication act or system is as the source or sender of messages. As discussed earlier in this book the practitioner is also a listener and an assessor of public opinion, but his success or failure is most often based on the way in which he communicates. A score of factors are involved in this aspect of public relations practice, but four major ones concern the communicator's degree of *empathy, credibility, situational acuity,* and *communication skills.*

EMPATHY

According to the dictionary, *empathy* is the "imaginative projection of one's own consciousness into another being," and in the communication act the other being is the intended receiver. Naive communicators send their messages "to whom it may concern" and hope they will reach someone. When the owner of a pleasure boat finds his boat is sinking he sends out a "may day" call, hoping to reach someone. When my younger daughter was three years old and inadvertently crawled under her covers and found herself stuck at the end of the bed, she howled "help, *somebody, somebody* help."

In contrast, the skilled communicator composes messages with a specific audience in mind, and when sent out these messages are directed to the specified audience. Wireless operators on large ocean vessels keep in constant touch with other ships, and if trouble occurs they know exactly where these ships are. If my younger daughter, now age 11, gets into trouble today and needs help she doesn't yell for "somebody" but for her mom or dad.

The wise communicator, therefore, develops a keen sense of empathy regarding his intended receiver or audience. He recognizes that everyone exists within a variety of systems, among which are the system of self or personality; the cultural system of ideas, beliefs, values, and symbols; and the social system of human relationships and social structures and organizations. Each of these has an important influence on the receiver's view of the world, his role and the role of others in the communication process, his reaction to messages, his use or nonuse of various channels, and so forth.

Some communicators are very good at developing empathy, others very poor. The best ones, in effect, try to step out of their own skins and into those of the audience they're trying to reach. They view communication situations not from their point of view, but from that of the audience. They are as much concerned about how a message will be perceived and received as how it is worded, written, and sent. The poor ones are either uncaring, insensitive, or oblivious to the audience they're trying to reach. They write from their point of view—or that of the organizations they represent—and are more concerned with the form of their words than they are with their impact.

CREDIBILITY

Source *credibility,* like empathy, is a key factor in establishing effective communication because of its connection with the receiver or recipient. By source credibility we mean the degree of faith and trust that the receiver has in the sender of a message, and the effect that this trust has on the receiver.

Psychological studies of opinion change conducted by Hovland, Janis and Kelley of Yale University drew the following basic conclusions about source credibility:

1. When a person is perceived to have definite intentions to persuade others, it is likely he will be viewed as having something to gain and therefore less likely to be trusted.

2. The very same presentation tends to be judged more favorably when made by a communicator of high credibility than one of low credibility.

3. When dealing with issues and problems of a highly technical nature, an individual will be especially susceptible to influence by persons who are perceived to be experts.

The above broad conclusions about source credibility were drawn chiefly from experimental studies with small groups of people under controlled conditions. In addition, they leave unanswered many questions about variations in source credibility as a factor in communication effectiveness—for example, how about an expert who does not inspire trust?—but they do underscore the fact that source credibility is an important factor in persuasive communication.

The implications for public relations practitioners are manifold because the research indicates that *cues about a communicator's intentions, expertness, and trustworthiness significantly affect the way in which communication will be received.* There is great practical value in knowing that people are likely to distrust communication when they perceive it stems from a source that has much to gain from the communication. There is similar practical value in knowing that communication from a high credibility source is more effective than one from a low credibility source, and that it is wise to use an expert when dealing with communication technical in nature.

It's not surprising that the scientific research of communication sources has documented the effectiveness of high credibility and expert sources and the ineffectiveness of communication from sources perceived as having an axe to grind. In the early days of the republic when life was relatively simple but communication difficult, people learned to accept communication from sources they considered reliable. Even though the level of education has risen, there has been such an explosion of knowledge and information, so many complex issues and activities taking place and being disseminated by so many different means and methods, that people have found it impossible to deal with them personally. In trying to cope with the flood of messages, people turn to sources they can trust: a favorite columnist; commentators;

political leaders who seem honest and forthright; the local bartender, mailman, and friends who have proven to be sagacious and wise.

Some Examples

The use of source credibility to enhance the effectiveness of ⟵ communication has long been recognized in advertising, politics, and public relations practice—though not always wisely utilized. Television commercials feature nationally and internationally acclaimed personalities to promote products. When congressmen of the same political party as the president are up for reelection they find it useful to have him make a fast stopover during the campaign or they send out photos showing them in serious conversation in the Oval office. Colonel Sanders is made to seem like a father figure as he hovers in the background of commercials for a fast-food chain; Grandma Brown seems to give her personal blessing to every can of baked beans; Mickey Mouse and his friends are stamped on almost every product sold at two vast family entertainment centers in Florida and California. The communication message is clearly the same; you can put your trust in our products because they're endorsed by the Colonel, Grandma Brown, and Mickey Mouse. The fact that the products are the end result of vast, highly organized commercial organizations recedes conveniently into the background.

There is more to source credibility, however, than simply centering communication messages around personalities who inspire trust and confidence. What is sometimes forgotten is that there has to be some relevancy between the source and the product or institution being extolled. Many people will readily identify the famous baseball player seen in a supermarket scene selling the virtues of a coffee maker, but just as many will wonder about the connection between pounding a baseball and making coffee. Having a famous sports announcer appear in auto commercials during big league baseball telecasts is a neat juxtaposition of commercial and sports, but one wonders what makes him an expert on automobiles. The credible becomes incredible when relevancy is missing.

Public relations practitioners seeking to maintain source credibility in large organizations operate on levels far above those of television commercials. There's the inner-managerial level within their own organizations where in the practitioners seek to establish responsible officials as reliable and trustworthy sources of information. There's the outer-media level where in their relationships with the mass media the practitioners seek to establish themselves as reliable and trustworthy sources of information. Between these two levels, however, there is a level not often discussed openly that causes no end of problems.

For want of a better word, let's call this level the *buffer-zone, the no-man's land in which public relations practitioners so often find themselves in trying to establish and maintain source credibility.* Managements make mistakes, but don't like to admit them. Managements have to close plants and lay off employees, but don't like to admit it. But reporters learn about these things, and they inquire. Such inquiries are directed at the public relations practitioner or they come in to management which in turn directs them at the practitioner. That's when the public relations person lands in the buffer zone.

Even children no longer believe the old chestnut about George Washington and the cherry tree, so it comes as no surprise that people lie from time to time. However, if public relations practitioners find themselves lying, obfuscating, and being disingenuous as a matter of routine, they'd better forget about establishing source credibility.

Source credibility, in summation, is so valuable a factor in the process of communication it requires careful cultivation and deserves the hard fight practitioners must put up in the buffer zone between their managements and the media and the public.

SITUATIONAL ACUITY

Although not a term commonly used in public relations circles, *situational acuity* plays an important role in determining the effectiveness of practitioners as a communication source. Given a communication situation, Practitioner A will suggest action along a certain set of lines, Practitioner B along another set of lines, and Practitioner C no action at all. It's hardly likely that all three proposals will result in the same degree of effectiveness, and hence the practitioner whose keenness of judgment about the situation—situational acuity—will be the one whose proposed action or inaction will bring about the most effective communication results.

The need for situational acuity arises in all instances where people interact with each other, but it has particular relevance in the communication process. *How* the source sizes up a communication situation will determine in large degree what he or she does about it and the results. It could be an internal communication matter involving employees; an external one involving a community public; a media matter involving an inquiry from a newspaper reporter; or any matter in which communication is involved and which forms such an important aspect of daily public relations practice.

One might well raise these questions: Why stress the need for public relations practitioners to have situational acuity? Do not other management personnel need the same sense of keenness about situations? The answer is that the need is greater for the public relations practitioner because his activities and communications involve the entire organization and affect all of its publics. As the source for most of the communication emanating from an organization to its many publics, the practitioner has the heavy responsibility of ensuring most effective communication. *Sizing up the situation—the milieu—within which communication takes place* thus becomes a matter of real concern and great importance.

Unfortunately, there are no simple ground rules—no ten easy steps—for achieving situational acuity. Public relations situations involving communication seldom duplicate themselves, and people, organizations, and times change. The men and women who run today's large businesses, colleges and universities, and the armed forces are a different breed from those who ran them thirty and forty years ago. The men and women who work on assembly lines or punch buttons in plants, who attend colleges and universities, and who serve in the armed forces are a different breed also. Today's factory and plant are a far cry from factories and plants of thirty and forty years ago, as are colleges, universities and military installations. The situation, in short, has changed and the communicator has to be keenly aware of the change and its implications.

The source has to be aware also that changes in communication situations occur not only on large but also on small scales, yet there is still the same need to be keenly tuned in to situational nuances. When your candidate for senator promises during the campaign he will conduct himself with total candor if elected, does he mean the same thing one year later when an enterprising reporter calls and says he has information about illegal contributions made to the now-elected senator? When your firm's earnings have declined appreciably and there's a dispute between you and the finance vice-president about the degree of candor in reporting it in the annual report, what does the president mean and what do you do when he suggests the two of you "work it out" so no one will look too bad?

Can one develop situational acuity to make for a more effective communication source? Experience, of course, is an answer, but one doesn't have to drown in order to handle a drowning situation. The wiser course is to learn from near-drowning experiences.

COMMUNICATION SKILLS

Communication skills are the string which wraps up the package of the three other factors—empathy, credibility, and situational acuity—which produce source effectiveness. Even though the source is empathetic and credible and has keen judgment in sizing up situations, he will be ineffective if unable to communicate thoughts, ideas, and information with a high degree of competence and skill.

The skills of the communicator are those of speaking and writing, and they're put to use every working day of the communicator's professional life. Surveys of public relations practitioners repeatedly demonstrate that their most common activities involve some form of speaking or writing: writing speeches or giving talks; writing releases and feature stories; composing memoranda, reports, and statements; conferring with management and editors. Such skills are chiefly encoding skills, but in carrying out the communication process the source also decodes, and here the practitioner puts to use the skills of listening and reading.

Entire books have been devoted to exploring the four communication skills of speaking, writing, listening, and reading, and their importance to the source is self-evident. As sources of information, public relations practitioners stake their professional careers on mastering each and all of the skills needed to make communication effective.

Within the communications model the skills associated with communication from the source deal chiefly with messages and media, and these will be discussed in detail in the sections that follow. Media or channels are so all-important, however, that they call for further amplification—hence the decision to include in this second edition a full chapter on media relations, publicity techniques, and advertising for public relations purposes. That chapter follows this one.

MESSAGES

One way to deal with the message stage of a communication model is to treat it from the standpoint of the semanticist, anthropologist, or social scientist. In doing so we would consider factors such as learning, abstraction, extensional and intensional meanings, social reinforcement, referents, language acquisition, and a score of other epistemological features, all of which might well make for confusion rather than elucidation on the part of the readers of this book. The English language translation of that last sentence is that it's the author's opinion there are some simple, key points about message effectiveness which can be presented without resorting to complicated language. This is not to gainsay the value of the semanticist's approach to the study of language—on the contrary, such an approach can have a high degree of significance for the public relations practitioner—but simply to point out that it's not within the purview of this book.

Further, there's need to stress that there are no immutable laws about messages, and it must be emphasized that messages do not have a life of their own. They exist within the context of the communication process, and the process itself can change the meaning and effect of a message.

comments on Effective message

KEY CONSIDERATIONS FOR ACHIEVING MESSAGE EFFECTIVENESS

Given these cautionary observations, there are certain key aspects to messages as they apply to public relations communication situations. Both research studies and practical experience have shown that if certain key considerations are kept in mind, practitioners will increase the possibility of communication effectiveness by obeying the dictates of these message considerations. Their presentation shall be listed and discussed in no particular order of importance but in terms of their relevance to public relations situations.

To Be Effective, a Message Must Reach Its Intended Audience

Three astute observers of the public relations scene—Earl Newsom, Edward Robinson, and Gerhard Wiebe—arrive at the same conclusion about the need for "message reach," though each phrases his ideas in a different way.

In setting forth his four public opinion signposts—described in the chapter on public opinion—Newsom prefaced his conclusions with the observation that people don't stand still to be educated. The average person, he reminds us, is preoccupied with everyday problems and personal matters which take up most of that person's waking hours and many of the hours when he or she should be sleeping. Trying to catch the attention of this average person are thousands of individuals and organizations who want to "educate" him or her about their particular area of interest. Newsom concludes that it's little wonder, therefore, that the average person, preoccupied with personal problems, not only won't stand still to be "educated" but in sheer self-preservation because of the countless educational messages beamed at him will tune himself or herself out.

Wiebe, former dean at Boston University's School of Public Communication, postulates the "gyroscopic phenomenon" to explain the public's reluctance to be educated. Like the gyroscope, says Wiebe, people spin within their own orbits and resist outside forces. He makes his point in the following perceptive paragraph:

> If you accept this image of the public, you will necessarily reject an image that has been around too long and that dies hard—the image of the public as a bunch of nice, leisurely, receptive people who will absorb your message if you just use short simple sentences and good pictures. It isn't that simple. It is more the rule than the exception that a public relations message must be so contrived that it penetrates a field of resistance, a resistance generally characterized by a massive disinterest in your company's concerns, and an avid preoccupation with what we have called the sustaining of people's own systems of dynamic equilibrium.

Robinson adds another dimension to the problem of catching audience attention, and he phrases it in terms of *nonmotivation* on the part of the audience to messages beamed at them. He describes the problem of audience nonmotivation by asking the following questions:

> Who cares if the company our ... public relations practitioner represents has been a good corporate citizen and has done its share in trying to solve a particular community problem?

> Who cares if such-and-such nonprofit health group is making progress in finding a cure for some disease that very few persons know anything about in the first place?

> Who cares if some small liberal arts college has drastically revised its educational standards and is providing good solid liberal arts education for a certain number of students, but is now in critical financial straits?

Is there an answer to the problem of audience preoccupation, disinterest, and nonmotivation? Robinson suggests you must make sure your message is available to the audience—that is, select a medium that reaches the intended audience—and you must anticipate and counteract the numerous competing factors that may intervene between source and recipient. Of course, having done this still doesn't solve the problem of audience preoccupation, disinterest, and nonmotivation, but recognizing the problem is the important first step: it forces the communicator into the realization that the audience is not breathlessly waiting for those words of wisdom which will "educate" it to his or her point of view.

The Impact of a Message Depends on How It Identifies with the Interests of the Intended Audience

Two common faults made by communicators are associated with the concept of interest-identification. One fault is to misunderstand or fail to understand the interests of the intended audience, and the other is to confuse the communicator's interests with those of the intended audience. Both failures lessen the impact of messages, and in many instances make them totally ineffective.

Identifying with the interests of the intended audience can best be achieved through *empathy, observation,* and *perception.* Fortunately for the astute communicator, these are not inherited traits but traits which can be learned, developed, and refined. In many cases the matter of interest-identification is mainly one of being careful not to operate under assumptions which are not warranted by reality.

Being careful not to confuse the communicator's interests with those of the intended audience is most often a case of being honest with one's assessment of a communication situation. It's all too easy, for example, to conclude that the audience will be interested in what we have to communicate simply because we want them to be, so we engage in a litle game of self-deception in hopes our interests will somehow coincide when we honestly know they don't.

Professor Robinson provides a valid reminder about audience-interests when he notes that reactions to messages are interwoven with the drives and needs of their recipients. "A message," he points out, "must arouse certain needs in a potential recipient and indicate how these needs can be satisfied." It's also his opinion that public relations communicators tend to rely too strongly on delivering information and not strongly enough on satisfying personal needs and motivations.

Unfortunately, such reminders too often fall on deaf ears because failures to follow audience interests and needs are strewn all over the communication landscape. Consider, for example, what happened in the summer of 1975 when the nation was in the midst of a period of severe recession coupled with serious inflation. More than seven million people were unemployed, and people were concerned about jobs, taxes, the high cost of living, rising crime rates, and the ever-increasing cost of gasoline. At such a time, when these were the main concerns of most Americans:

1. Local school boards presented their communities with record-high budgets which gave little evidence of innovative ways of cutting costs. The local boards were mainly interested in having their proposed budgets approved, but when given the chance to vote on the budgets the public turned them down in record-breaking numbers.

2. Private colleges, faced with decreasing enrollments and rising costs, continued to raise tuitions at a constantly increasing rate. The colleges were mainly interestd in attracting more students in order to stave off budget deficits, but in all but the most prestigi-

ous schools, enrollments dropped as middle-income Americans found themselves being priced out of the private college market.

3. Major oil companies, just before July 4, announced a three-cent-a-gallon increase in gasoline prices. The companies contended the increase had nothing to do with the fact that people would be doing more travelling during the summer months, but the public concluded that the timing was so coincidental as to prove that the companies couldn't care less about the public's interests.

4. The president of the United States presented to Congress an energy plan which embodied even higher prices for gasoline in 1975 and ensuing years. He said his program was the best way to cut down on gasoline consumption and would serve as an incentive to the oil companies to drill for new oil. Many people, and congressmen, said the program would hit hardest those who had trouble enough coping with inflation, and they also wanted to know why the oil companies had to be provided with incentives to do what they were supposed to be doing at a time when they were reaping record high profits without incentives.

Granted, local school boards, private colleges, and major oil companies are hit by inflation and rising costs, but they don't gain support simply by automatically raising taxes and consumer costs. At the very least they should show by their actions that they are concerned about the consumer, that they are honestly seeking ways to be more efficient and to keep costs down, and that they don't raise consumer costs by instant reflex. In far too many instances the messages the consumer receives indicate that the senders are either insensitive about the intended receiver or are self- rather than public-motivated.

Messages Should Relate to Common Experience and Meaning

This precept, like the first two already cited, stresses the vital need to tie the source to the receiver of messages and emphasizes that *common experience serves as a unifying force between sender and receiver.* When this common experience is expressed in words and terms shared and understood by the source there's even more reason to expect that communication will be well received.

There are, of course, problems concerned with the common experience precept. Very often there are no common experiences that have been shared by source and receiver, and there are many times when messages are expressed in words and terms that have lost meaning or are irrelevant to the receiver. Some communicators, however, seem to go out of their way to avoid common experience by beaming messages that are either cute or far-fetched and which might relieve life's daily tedium but do little to bring about desired communication effects.

The world of the television commercial continues to serve up intriguing examples of messages which violate sound communication precepts. They bring us white knights who ride through our kitchen waving magic cleansing potions; charming ladies who discuss their intimate underarm and "feminine hygiene" problems in the middle of cocktail gatherings; smiling gasoline attendants who not only gas up our cars but are willing to spend precious minutes discussing shock absorbers, mileage tips, oil treatment cues, and tire rotation principles.

There's one small problem with all these scenes; they have little relationship to reality. White knights don't ride through kitchens, and even if they did they'd seem very much out of place in the kitchens of the millions of blacks who have the same cleaning problems as the rest of us. The last thing in the world that charming ladies discuss at cocktail parties is deodorants. Gasoline station attendants not only do not smile very much, but if we are to judge from the growing number of self-service pumps they haven't even the time to gas up our autos, no less discuss all those other problems the commercials indicate they're so willing to talk about.

Thus, one of the first lessons for the communicator is to avoid stressing and creating uncommon experiences in fashioning messages. The second is to seek out, stress, and communicate common experiences in words and terms that have meaning and relevance to the recipient. And the third is to find ways to uncover common experiences when they don't seem to exist.

The last point requires some careful thought and a dash of creativity. When polling organizations conduct surveys in Watts or Harlem they make sure their pollsters are blacks and not whites. When colleges send representatives to College Days, they don't send the oldest members of the admission staff but those who have most recently been graduated. Although relatively small sums are collected from house-to-house canvassing, local social and health organizations continue to utilize such neighborhood canvassing because they know it brings better understanding of their activities because the canvasser and those canvassed share common experiences and talk the same language.

These examples all show the use of selectivity by large organizations in choosing the sources to put across their messages, and the common denominator in such selectivity is common experience with the recipients. The precept operates on all levels. If you want to reach the scientific community, you utilize by-lined articles by scientists within your organization because they share the same experience and use the same language as the readers of the publications in which their articles appear. If you want to have a new journalism textbook adopted for classroom use you seek endorsements from leading journalism professors. The wise communicator, in short, selects those representatives who have most in common with and talk the same language as the intended audience. Although he wasn't an expert in economics, politics, science, or the arts, Hal Boyle proved to be the Associated Press's most durable and popular columnist for more than two decades because he had the knack of writing about life's daily comedies and tragedies in a way that touched the average reader. His desk at the AP was a marvel of total disorganization and he was about as urbane as a backwoodsman, but what he wrote was read with joy and pleasure because he understood what interested people, and what interested people interested him. He would undoubtedly snort at the term, but he was a communicator in the truest sense of the word.

Messages Should Be Tailor-Made for the Situation, Time, Place, and Audience

Elsewhere in this text it has been pointed out that tailor-made suits have a distinct advantage over mass-produced suits because they fit better. They also cost more because of the time and skills involved, and of course this has to be taken into consideration, particularly if you're operating on a limited budget.

There is no doubt, however, that given the time, talent, and money necessary to cover their cost and other production aspects, tailor-made messages have a distinct advantage over other messages. Because they're crafted with care they indicate to the receiver that "this message is meant for you."

Innumerable examples can be cited to illustrate the principle of the tailor-made message. One doesn't address a street gang as one would a gathering of bank officials. Yelling "fire" in the middle of a noisy city street won't have the same effect as yelling "fire" in a crowded and hushed theater. When a father is concerned about an impending layoff he doesn't react kindly to a request for a new car, though he might listen if you hit him up just after his ten dollar bet paid off at 30 to 1 in the fourth race.

If you care to go back that far—and who does?—you might recall the kind of messages you sent out when you were between the ages of five and eight and wanted an ice cream bar on a hot summer day.

At the age of five you simply asked for an ice cream bar and if you got it, fine; if not, a few tears. At the age of six you just didn't ask for an ice cream bar, but you demanded it and as this became a test of wills you more than likely didn't get it. At the age of seven you not only demanded an ice cream bar but you pointed out quite clearly that you were the only kid on the street who wasn't allowed to have an ice cream bar. At the age of eight you began playing off your father against your mother, and if that didn't work you went out and bought the bar yourself with money from your piggy bank.

What you were doing was applying the tailor-made principle by changing your message to fit the situation, time, and audience and at the same time using feedback and peer group pressures as a wedge. The only variable remaining constant was the place, though of course that could have been a factor had you been at home one year, on vacation the next, etc.

The same principle applies in the adult world. At one period or another, a message might be tailored to fit a situation with the other three variables remaining constant. Or, it might be tailored to fit both a situation and an audience, with the other two variables remaining constant. Here are some examples:

It is August 1 and you have announced you will be a candidate for reelection in the November mayoralty election and will run on your record of having maintained full employment in your city. On August 30 the largest plant in the city announces it is closing down effective next week. The time, place, and the audience has remained constant, but the situation now calls for a new message to be beamed at the electorate.

It is August 30, same city. You are director of public relations for the firm which owns the plant which will be closed down next week. This is but one of thirty such plants in the country, and it is obsolete and hence the decision to move its operations to a more modern installation. The firm's profits are at an all-time high and the firm is in excellent shape in all respects. The story announcing the closing will be shaped one way as released locally; another way as released in the city to which the operation will be moved; and another way as released to national trade and business publications. Thus, the situation and time remain constant, but the place and audience differ and thus will require different message treatments.

Tailoring a message should not be construed as telling one story to one audience and an entirely different story to another, for this would be akin to selling one piece of goods to one customer and a cheaper piece of goods to another and charging both the same price. You can alter the fit, but you should be sure that the basic material of the message is the same.

CHANNELS

In the communication process a channel is a *passageway, pathway, or means* by which a message passes from source to receiver. Used in this way, it's clear that a communication channel can be a smoke signal; the voice in face-to-face situations; radio, television, newspaper, magazines, and books in communication by means of the mass media. It is also possible to categorize channels in terms of whether they are *interpersonal* or *mediated* (face-to-face versus a telephone conference call); *personal* or *impersonal* (a meeting of 10 people versus an outdoor gathering of 50,000 addressed by means of loud speakers); *assembled* or *nonassembled* (the same outdoor gathering versus a television audience of millions watching and litening to a political speech in their homes). Although in each instance the forms set forth above seem to be in contrast to each other, they should not be thought of as being opposed to each other or mutually exclusive. As Schramm points out, ". . . distinctions and boundaries are much less clear than that. Most campaigns aimed at teaching or persuading try to combine media and personal channels so that one will reinforce and supplement the other. Political campaigners use all the media but still arrange door-to-door visits and public meetings. Family planning, agricultural, and health campaigns maintain field staffs but support them with all the media they can afford."

The majority of communication situations involving public relations practitioners call for channels or message vehicles that are impersonal and/or mediated. This does not mean that they are more effective than other forms of channels—on the contrary, they are often less effective—but simply that the communication situation makes it impossible to use other channels. *Modern society is structured to make it an impossibility to deal with receivers or recipients of messages on a face-to-face, personal, direct basis.* For this reason the professional communicator has to rely on channels that are impersonal, indirect, and usually nonassembled.

This means in turn that there will be some intervening mediating mechanism, force, or organization occupying the channel between source and receiver. Even when the group to whom we are addressing our messages is assembled in one place, the group may be so large that the intervening, mediating mechanism has to be some method of voice amplification. When the group is out of sight the intervening, mediating mechanism or force could be in the control of the public relations practitioner—such as in the case of an internal publication, annual report, or annual meeting—or it could be out of the practitioner's control.

The channels to be considered in the discussion that follows are those that are out of the control of the practitioner but are nonetheless of the most importance and significance in the process of reaching mass audiences. These channels are the four mass media: *newspapers, radio, television,* and *magazines.* These mass media channels will be analyzed in terms of the following five questions raised by Berlo:

1. What is available?

2. Which channels are received by the most people?

3. Which channels have the greatest impact?

4. Which channels are most adaptable to the source's purpose?

5. Which channels are most adaptable to the content of the message?

After analysis of the five questions raised by Berlo, we will sum up our discussion of channels by relating them to a relatively new concept called "agenda-setting."

KEY CONSIDERATIONS ABOUT CHANNELS

In taking up these five questions we will deal mainly with newspapers, radio, television, and magazines because they are the mass media that reach people on a systematic, regular basis and are most often used by public relations practitioners as message channels. Books and films—especially the sponsored film—are important and valuable channels for public relations messages, but they are not used as frequently as the four media on a regular basis by practitioners, and in addition the sponsored book and film is within the control of the practitioner and hence outside the parameters of this analysis.

What Is Available?

For the most part when communication scholars analyze the communication process and discuss the mass media they do not dwell at length on the subject of availability. Presumably this is a nonacademic matter, but for the public relations practitioner the subject of availability is highly relevant. To what avail—other than that of making the practitioner wiser—is knowledge and understanding of the mass media channels if these media are unavailable? Obviously, availability embodies very practical considerations for the public relations practitioner.

A quick, knee-jerk reaction to the question of mass media availability might be, why of course they're available, accessible, ready for use. But are they really, and to what degree? Even the beginner knows that if you want to promote Product X or Idea Y you can't just wave a magic wand and find your story on the AP or UPI wire, the front page of the Chicago *Tribune*, or a prime time television show. Something stands between the wish and the fulfillment, and that something is most easily described by the term known as "the gatekeeper."

The mass media gatekeeper has been described in a variety of ways. The fact that the mass media are highly organized and complex means that the organization itself serves as a gatekeeper and therefore the practitioner has to understand how the media operate if he or she is to get past the gatekeeper.

> In studying the flow of Associated Press news from agency home offices to four Wisconsin non-metropolitan daily newspapers, Scott Cutlip reported that an estimated 100,000 to 125,000 words of news copy comes into the AP every news cycle. From this copy the AP editors select and send out about 238 items totaling about 57,000 words. The Wisconsin AP editors cull out and transmit 77 items totaling 13,352 words to non-metropolitan Wisconsin dailies. From this state wire, four typical Wisconsin dailies select and use about 74 items totaling 12,848 words.

The above example is but one illustration of the way in which the organizational facets of the mass media—in this case concerning the wire services and the newspapers they serve—operate as a gatekeeper. Similar organizational facets serve as controls on radio, television, and magazines, and they all emphasize the fact that the complex nature of the mass media makes them difficult to penetrate.

By definition a gatekeeper means that a person is involved in guarding the mass media gates against intrusion by outsiders, and this person is found at numerous stages in the process of transmitting information, ideas, opinions, and entertainment by means of the mass media. Some typical gatekeepers are the person who selects the guests who appear on popular late evening TV shows; the section editor of a business publication and the editor of a trade publication; the disc jockey on local radio shows; wire service editors on state and national levels; assignment editors on network news organizations and on daily newspapers; the copy desk editor on all dailies.

Each of these goes through a process of *selection* and *elimination* in

choosing from the "glut of occurrences" those items which, in the ←?
opinion of the gatekeeper, deserve to win out in the competition for
attention. In the final analysis, therefore, it's comforting to know that
the mass media are available to the public relations practitioner, but
it's more important to know that at the same time the gatekeeper is
constantly on guard to permit entry only to those messages which
deserve to reach the mass audience. What the practitioner wants and
desires is important, but more important is to understand the wants,
desires, and interests of the gatekeepers because they open the gates
only when these are met. Gatekeepers make their selection on the
basis of maximum appeal to the audience served by their medium, and
thus the most important factor in eventual use of material is the
gatekeepers' perception of what will most interest their audience.

Which Channels Are Received by the Most People?

In order to understand the nature of the mass media audience, it's
important to understand the complexities of the mass media system,
and this can best be done by setting forth pertinent data about the four
major media as of January 1978:

Newspapers. There was a total of 1,753 daily newspapers with
combined daily circulation of 61.5 million. Half of the dailies had
circulations of less than 10,000. About 125 dailies had circulations of
100,000 or more. The median-sized daily in most states had 13,000
circulation. The average adult spent 37 minutes a day reading the
daily newspaper.

Between 9,500 and 10,000 weeklies, semiweeklies, and thrice-
weeklies served small communities and suburbs. A few had circulations between 6,000 and 10,000, placing them in the ranks of small
dailies in terms of circulation.

The average daily newspaper receives its state, national, and
international news from either the Associated Press or the United
Press International, and receives its columns and features from syndicates and from the two wire services.

Television. There was a total of 996 television stations, 727 of
which were commercial and 269 of which were noncommerical. Of the
727 commercial stations, 516 were VHF and 211 were UHF.

The three major networks—NBC, CBS, and ABC—each owned
and operated five VHF stations, the maximum allowed by law. The
number of affiliates of each network was: NBC, 216; CBS, 202; and
ABC, 200. Between 80 and 90 percent of programming on the affiliates
was from the networks. State, national, and international news on the
average station stemmed from either AP, UPI, or the national news
departments of the networks.

Approximately 98 percent of American homes (73 million) had
television sets. The national television audience on any one day was
between 75 and 80 million people. Average estimated audience for a
prime-time show: 32 million people. The average adult watched
television 3 hours and 49 minutes a day.

Radio. There was a total of 8,408 radio stations; 4,508 were commercial AM, 2,986 were commercial FM, and 914 were noncommercial FM. There were four major national radio networks—Mutual Broadcasting System (MBS), CBS, NBC, and ABC—and scores of regional networks, including a relatively new National Black Network with 82 AM and FM affiliates. The largest by far of the networks was MBS, with 720 affiliates. By a large majority, most of the radio stations were unaffiliated.

With more than 444 million sets in use, radio virtually blanketed the country. Radio sets were in 99 percent of American homes, in more than 106 million automobiles, and in more than 10 million public places. The average adult listened to radio 3 hours and 27 minutes a day.

Magazines. Somewhere between 8,000 and 9,500 weekly, monthly, and quarterly magazines and journals were published. Among these were 2,500 business and trade, 600 general circulation, 1,500 religious, and 800 agricultural publications. The average adult spent 20 minutes a day reading magazines.

Dominating the field in terms of circulation was *Reader's Digest*, with a circulation of more than 18 million, and *TV Guide*, with a circulation of 20 million. *Time* led the news magazines with weekly circulation of over 4.5 million, followed by *Newsweek* and *U.S. News and World Report*, with 3 and 2 million respectively.

The vast majority of magazines were written for and appealed to special audiences.

The figures cited above should be read and analyzed with care. One way to analyze the data is to look at it from the standpoint of total numbers and size. There are almost twice as many daily newspapers as television stations, and five times as many weeklies and radio stations as daily newspapers. However, the national television audience on any one day is between 75 and 80 million while the combined circulation of all daily newspapers is just over 61 million. Both audience totals for these two media do not reach the total audience for radio, but are vastly greater than the audience for magazines.

Another way of looking at the mass media audience is to note the audience for single units within each medium. For example, the combined circulation of all *Reader's Digest* editions is more than 28 million and the audience for a prime-time television show numbers 21 million. This compares with the 4 million circulation of *Time,* the largest circulation news magazine, and the 2 million circulation of the New York *News,* the largest daily newspaper circulation in the country.

A final way of looking at the mass media audience is to recognize that it's an overlapping audience. Though there are millions of people who only look at television and who do not read a daily newspaper or magazine, there are more millions who not only view television, but also listen to radio and read a daily newspaper and magazines.

Thus, the public relations practitioner must not only know data relating to the number of radio and television sets, stations and networks; the number of daily and weekly newspapers and magazines;

the nature of affiliations; and the audience for each media; but he must also analyze the *specifics about the data as they relate to the organization he represents.* The data, in summation, have meaning only insofar as they are carefully applied to the practitioner's public relations needs and problems.

Which Channels Have the Greatest Impact?

Study after study has demonstrated the pervasive role of the mass media in American life. They show that:

Eight out of ten adults read one or more daily newspapers on the average weekday and spend an average of 35 minutes a day on them.

On any weekday evening, 75 million Americans are likely to be watching television. The average home set is in use more than 6 hours a day and individual viewing is now more than 3 hours a day.

The approximately 40 percent of Americans who read magazines regularly spend an average of 33 minutes a day on them.

The one-third of Americans who read books regularly spend an average of 47 minutes a day on them.

The audience for radio is far greater than that for any other single medium of mass communication.

There is no doubt about the profound impact that mass media make on public information, knowledge, culture, and patterns of living. There is considerable speculation, however, about the extent of *specific effects* resulting *from exposure to specific media.* On occasion, it has been possible to prove the spectacular effect that exposure to a specific medium has had on people, but these instances are few and far between.

The evening of October 30, 1938, Orson Welles and his CBS radio theatre group dramatized an imaginary invasion from Mars. The hour-long drama was prefaced by the announcement that the show was a dramatization of a novel by H. G. Wells. The show itself consisted of extremely realistic bulletins and newscasts, interspersed with music, flashes from the "scene," interviews with "experts," the police, and eye-witnesses.

The reaction was panic on the part of thousands of listeners and others who were contacted by listeners. Thousands of people called the police and agencies of the federal government; other thousands warned their friends; and still other thousands took direct action by packing up their family and belongings and driving away from the Eastern seaboard where the invasion from Mars was supposedly taking place.

Few of the effects of the mass media are as direct and sharp as those resulting from "The Invasion from Mars" radio broadcast. For the most part, the effects of the mass media are cumulative, long-term and hard to isolate. There is more or less general agreement that the mass media:

1. *Do not ordinarily have a direct effect on audiences but rather operate through a variety of mediating factors and influences.*

2. *Basically reinforce rather than convert.* Thus, most studies show that exposure to mass media campaigns solidify the attitudes and opinions of their audience but do not generally change attitudes and opinions.

3. *Serve to confer status.* The mass media focus attention on people and organizations, and they also tend to "feed on" each other. Hitherto relatively unknown people and organizations suddenly become known throughout the country because they catch the attention of the mass media and are featured in newspaper stories, on talk shows, and in magazine articles.

4. *Provide the source with credibility.* Because they're considered to be impartial and nonpartisan, mass media messages are deemed to be more credible than those stemming directly from a public relations source.

Answering the question as to which of the mass media has the greatest impact is difficult if not impossible because of multi-media exposure to the media by the public. We do know radio provides the *swiftest* means of information dissemination; that television provides the *most dramatic* coverage of events; that newspapers and magazines provide the most *in-depth* dissemination of news and information; and that all of them combined provide our basic view of the American scene and Lippmann's world which is "out of sight, out of mind." As Schramm sums up mass media effects:

> We can be confident . . . that the mass media do have a significant effect on the organization of our leisure time and a significant effect on what we know, and when and in what detail we know it. The effect on knowledge is sufficiently important to cause some troubled thoughts about what appears in the media and how what appears is determined. We have good reason to believe, also, that under certain conditions . . . the media can have a direct effect on social behavior and that under certain conditions they may function to inhibit social change. . . .

Which Channels Are Most Adaptable to the Source's Purpose and to the Content of the Message?

The two questions relating to channels are so closely related they are being taken up as a unit rather than individually. The key word is "adaptable" and it correctly implies that each medium has certain characteristics that make it more suitable than the others for specific purposes. All too often practitioners utilize a particular channel—most of the time it's the newspaper—because they're more at home in that channel's milieu. But the newspaper may not be the best medium for the source's purpose or for the content of the message, hence the question reminds us that there's a need for purposeful rather than random communication.

Marshall McLuhan, the Canadian sage who was much in vogue in the sixties, cryptically maintained that "the medium is the message." If he is taken literally he means that the nature of the medium itself, irrespective of the contents of the message, is what makes the difference in the communication process. Another way of stating McLuhan's thesis is that form is more important than substance.

Though McLuhan presents us with an intriguing view of the media and though there is validity to his contention about the unique importance of the nature of the media, his thesis is all too embracing and sweeping to be accepted at face value. The nature of the medium does affect communication, but so do the nature of the source, message, channel, and receiver. A more fruitful line of inquiry in regard to the question about the media and their adaptability to the source's purpose and the content of the message is to consider the question in terms of the three essential roles of media: to inform, influence, and entertain.

If the purpose of the source is to *inform*, one has to rate print media as being more adaptable than the electronic media for the transmission of *detailed* information. It is true that radio and television may be the first to inform us of events, actions, and activities, but the information they provide is admittedly sketchy and superficial. As a nationally known, highly respected television commentator has observed, the entire contents of a half-hour network news show would take up only one part of the front page of the New York *Times*. Furthermore, as to content of the message, the more complex and specialized the information, the more adaptable it is to newspapers and magazines.

Thus, if the source wants to get across information quickly and swiftly and is not dealing with detailed and involved material, the electronic media would best suit the source's purpose. However, if the source is dealing with information not easily digested at a glance or a first hearing, newspapers and magazines would be more suitable both for the source's purpose and for the contents of the message.

If the purpose of the source and the message contents are meant to *influence*, we are faced with a situation where no one medium has a singular advantage over all the others. Radio and television have the advantage of *immediacy* in terms of influencing people, but there is no evidence to support the view that this influence has long-range, carry-over effects. Television's unique ability to take its audience right into the middle of an event or activity with both sight and sound provides that medium with vivid impact value, but again there is no evidence to support the view that this influence has long-range, carry-over effects. Highly respected print media—particularly columnists with large followings and publications that influence others through their editorials and investigative reporting—have immediate and also carry-over impact when their ideas and thoughts are picked up by others. But again, there is no conclusive proof of their long-range effects.

Equally important in the context of the relationship among source purpose, message content, and adaptability is the problem of *entry* and *control*. The three network evening news shows reach an audience of between forty and forty-five million homes, but getting past the gatekeepers on these shows is a very difficult task. Getting past newspaper and magazine gatekeepers is also difficult, but not as difficult as with television because the total "news hole" is larger on print media. Of course, control of the material is always in the hands of the media except in the case of paid advertising.

Because it is paid for and its composition is in the hands of the practitioner, public relations advertising surmounts both the entry and control problem and has been used often by practitioners by way of the print media. Such advertisements can be targeted to specific publics and later "merchandised" to other audiences for maximum exposure. There have been instances where they've had considerable impact—two that come to mind are the Byoir advertisements in behalf of the A&P and the Whitaker & Baxter advertisements in behalf of the AMA—but there has been no proof about the effects of the vast bulk of such public relations advertising.

If the purpose of the source and the message contents is to *entertain*, there is no doubt that television is the prime medium. People receive a good deal of their information about the world and are influenced in many respects by what they view on television, but the major strength of the medium is in its ability to entertain. Further, if we consider entertainment in the broadest sense we find that television also has the ability to meet Lasswell's concept of the media as transmitters of culture and the social fabric. Through its combination of sound and picture, television brings us the world of dance, music, drama, manners, dress, living patterns, and the many other aspects of our national life. Print media entertain and transmit culture through features, comics, essays, columns, and long articles, but they come in a poor second to television—and one might say, even a second to radio in terms of popular music—when it comes to entertainment.

Summing up, in considering adaptability of the various media to the source's purpose and message content, the practitioner has to understand and recognize the major assets and deficits created by the nature of the individual medium. In most instances, this will result in the use of all media by the practitioner, but with careful attention to the specific reasons for communication by the source.

Channels as Agenda-Setters

The *agenda-setting* function of the mass media is of major interest to the practitioner who uses research as a tool in the public relations process. By agenda-setting we mean *the ability of the media to influence the public's perception of the important topics and issues of the day*.

The concept of agenda-setting can be traced back to Walter Lippmann, when he noted more than half a century ago that the press is a major factor in forming "the pictures in our head" of the unseen world around us. Neither Lippmann nor Bernard Cohen, who analyzed the role of the press in shaping foreign policy in the sixties, called the concept "agenda-setting," but they perceived it as such nonetheless. As Cohen said:

... the press may not be successful in telling its readers what to think, but it is stunningly successful in telling its reader what to think *about*. And it follows from this that the world looks different to different people, depending not only on their personal interests, but also on the map that is drawn for them by the writers, editors, and publishers of the papers they read. ... The editor may believe he is only printing the things that people want to read, but he is thereby putting a claim on their attention, powerfully determining what they will be thinking about, and talking about, until the next wave laps their shore.

It was in the seventies that Maxwell McCombs, Donald Shaw, and their fellow mass communication researchers started to carry out the first formal empirical tests of the agenda-setting hypothesis. Through their many field studies these researchers explored the different ways in which the mass media as channels tell us *what to think about*. These studies, which are continuing at time of this publication, concern themselves with the manifold ways in which the media "set the agenda" for public knowledge, attitudes, and opinions. As McCombs puts it:

Through its patterns of selection and play of the daily news, the press presents the public a continuous stream of cues about the relative importance of various topics and events. Newspapers clearly communicate salience through page placement, headline size, and the amount of space accorded an item. Television news formats also provide cues about the relative salience of news events.

... Agenda setting is a relational concept specifying a positive relationship between the emphases of the news media and the perceived importance of these topics to the mass audience.

... Effective public relations requires lead time, and opportunities to communicate before an issue is approaching its zenith.

The agenda-setting role of the mass media in the communication and public relations process is a vital one. By carefully watching the media and by keeping up with communication research studies, the practitioner can track issues and events as they become part of the "public agenda." In so doing he or she should be able to deal with issues when they first appear rather than after they've reached their apex.

RECEIVER-RECIPIENT

Just as Banquo's ghost hovered in the background to haunt Shakespeare's Macbeth, so does the receiver-recipient hover in the background of the communication process to haunt the source. As has been noted, the receiver is all-important, although all too often he is neglected or given insufficient thought by the source-sender when messages are conceived and transmitted.

Big league pitchers don't simply throw baseballs to big league batters and hope their good old fast ball or change-up will smack in the strike zone. They study the line-up before the game, picking out the weak and the strong hitters and planning their general pitching strategy. When they face the batter they take note of the particular situation existing when the batter comes to plate; study his stance; try to figure out what the batter knows about the pitcher's delivery and whether he's a sucker for a fast ball, curve, or knuckle ball. Then, after an exchange of signals with the catcher and some tugging at his cap, the pitcher slams one over.

Public relations practitioners would do well to emulate successful big league pitchers. This calls for a careful study of the receiver from many different angles and perspectives, the most important of which are the *receiver's knowledge, communication skills, predispositions and group membership,* what Schramm has termed the *"fraction of selection,"* and *opinion leaders.*

THE RECEIVER'S KNOWLEDGE

In considering the receiver's knowledge we are thinking of two forms of knowledge: general knowledge and knowledge about the source.

General knowledge provides a clue about the receiver's ability to absorb information or ideas transmitted by the source. For the most part, communicators err when they operate on the assumption that the average person is well informed simply because he's bombarded on all sides with information from a wide variety of sources. Despite the advanced stage of media in the United States, the widespread ownership of radio and television sets, the millions who read newspapers and magazines, the fact remains that only a fraction of information and ideas get through the invisible net that people seem to cast about themselves.

Study after study has proven that people are ignorant about such elementary facts as the name of their congressman and senators, vice presidential candidates, the secretary of state, etc. Little wonder, therefore, that even after repeated exposure to mass media identification messages millions of people don't know whether it's Goodrich or Goodyear that sponsors those blimps; whether it's Westinghouse or General Electric in whom you can put your trust; and whether it's Vantage or True that has the lowest nicotine and tar content. If there's so little knowledge about high officials and oft-repeated slogans—and there is—then a wise course is to assume that most people have less knowledge about your organization than you think they have. Better yet, rather than draw assumptions conduct a study to ascertain for certain the degree of knowledge held by the publics you're trying to reach. Readership studies provide tangible evidence of reader knowledge as well as opinions about employee publications, and public opinion surveys provide similar input about public knowledge and opinions about organizations.

THE RECEIVER'S COMMUNICATION SKILLS

Communication skills are important factors for the source, but they are equally as important for the receiver although they involve a different set of skills. When dealing with the receiver's communication skills we are concerned mainly with the skills of reading, listening, and viewing (and tangentially with the skills of writing and speaking as they relate to feedback). When we're writing for an employee public we need to know the *decoding skill levels* existing within that public, and we should be cognizant of the probability that a management audience will be more highly educated than an hourly employee audience and hence can understand and absorb a higher level of language, expression, and thought.

Similarly, in dealing with the television audience we should recognize that the decoding level of the audience at 7:30 p.m. will differ from that of the audience at 11:30 p.m., not merely in terms of educational levels but in terms of sophistication and insight.

In short, there's need to understand there are different decoding communication skill levels that operate within, as well as between and among, media audiences. With some exceptions, one shouldn't expect to find the same decoding communication skills among readers of the median-sized daily newspaper of 13,000 circulation and among the reader of the New York *Times*; among the vast radio audience and the readers of *Scientific American;* among readers of the *Reader's Digest* and readers of the *Atlantic*. Preparing communications for these disparate audiences entails recognizing the varying decoding communication skill levels existing within each audience and then tailoring messages to match these levels.

> Although hourly employees do not generally have as high a level of language, expression, and education as management personnel, they should not be treated and viewed condescendingly.

> A major flaw of much employee communication is the tendency of the source to "talk down" to the receiver. The average hourly employee may not have the skills needed to decode messages about the international balance of payments, but he certainly has the skills needed to decode messages relating to *his* job, *his* paycheck, and *his* union. In matters affecting him closely and personally, he can decode company propaganda and "snow jobs" better than a cryptographer can decipher enemy messages.

AUDIENCE PREDISPOSITIONS AND GROUP MEMBERSHIP

Within every audience there exist certain *predispositions* that govern the way in which members of the audience will react to messages. In part these predispositions are individual in nature and tied to an individual's basic personality, early upbringing, and education. To a great extent—as noted by the Yale psychologists Hovland, Janis and Kelley—these predispositions result from conformity tendencies induced by group membership. They are based on the individual's perception of the behavior expected of him by the group to which he belongs and often govern the manner in which he will react to messages from the source. Hovland states the point this way:

> An analysis of the influence of groups upon the attitudes of their members is of obvious importance to the general problem of changing opinions through communications. Communicators often use these social incentives to facilitate acceptance of the opinion they advocate. For instance, community leaders frequently assert that group approval will follow upon the adoption of their recommendation or that disapproval will be the consequence of failure to accept it. On the other hand, a specific recommendation may encounter resistance because a group provides strong incentives for holding original opinions. Certain methods of persuasion entail lowering the importance of the incentives delivered by the group . . . or increasing the incentive value of competing groups.

The concept of group membership affecting reception of messages is a reaffirmation of the point made earlier in this chapter about the modification of the old "hypodermic needle" theory. That theory, as may be recalled, postulated that each individual is directly needled by the message sent through the media. However, everyone is part of a network of family, occupational, and social groupings and these influence an individual's opinions and reactions to messages. How an individual is affected by messages transmitted by the source is shaped in large part by the groups to which the individual is attached.

Thus, when the statement is made that public relations practitioners should be applied social scientists, this means that practitioners have to understand and be sensitive both to individual predispositions and to group membership because of the important role they play in the reception to messages. Members of the mass audience may be anonymous to the communicator but they are not inert. Rather, they are part of an active social environment, and it's the wise communicator who acknowledges, understands, and keeps that environment in mind when he fashions and transmits messages.

> One of the differences between the journalist and the public relations practitioner is that the journalist takes data and facts and fashions them into a story without too much concern for other factors. In dealing with facts and data the practitioner must be constantly aware that both she and her intended receiver are members of their group environments with all the pressures that such environments may exert. The message that passes from source to receiver is inevitably affected by the groups to which *both* are linked—hence the need for the practitioner to recognize not merely her group allegiance, but also that of the source.

SCHRAMM'S "FRACTION OF SELECTION" HYPOTHESIS

As a rule-of-thumb way of explaining the chance of an individual selecting any given communication, Wilbur Schramm devised an interesting formula which he calls the "fraction of selection" hypothesis. His formula is stated as follows:

$$\frac{\text{Promise of reward}}{\text{Effort required}} = \text{Probability of selection}$$

The promise of reward, as Schramm sees it, refers chiefly to the content of messages and the likelihood that they will satisfy needs as felt at any given time. The effort required refers to the availability of media and the ease of using a particular medium.

Thus, notes Schramm, people select an easily available television show rather than entertainment which they have to go out of their homes to see or hear. In short, there is little effort required of the recipient in choosing television entertainment over other forms. At the same time, perhaps from past experience from viewing a particular show, the recipient seeks out those shows which have rewarded him in the past.

"Over the years," says Schramm, "a person tends to seek the kinds of communication that have rewarded him in the past—his favorite television programs, a built-in expectation of reward developed from looking in certain places. Beyond that, he tends, other things being equal, to select the cues of information which are close at hand and easy to find in the glut of communication."

Schramm is well aware that his fraction of selection approach is a generalized one because he warns that at some time and in some situations, some information is so important a person will go to almost any effort to secure it. As an example, he notes that we may be willing to spend years studying to get a Ph.D. even though the easier path is to be satisfied with an undergraduate degree.

OPINION LEADERS

The role that opinion leaders play in the communication process has been studied chiefly by sociologists and political scientists and has resulted in field studies carried out in both small towns and cities. These studies have assayed the manner in which political decisions are made and influenced by opinion leaders; the manner in which decisions on selected issues have filtered down from small groups of influentials to the mass public; the manner in which influentials use the mass and specialized media to influence their information-input patterns and in turn influence selected publics; and similar patterns of selectivity, leadership and influence by key persons. From the many studies which have focused on selected field situations have come some generalized concepts of opinion leadership as they apply to the communication process. These are summarized briefly below:

Opinion leaders and the people they influence are often very much alike and typically belong to the same primary groups.

What this concept means is that we not only find so-called elite opinion leaders, but we find opinion leaders operating within groups and sub-groups. There is seldom a group of leaders who influence everyone in all groups on all issues, but rather leaders who influence—to name some examples—union members, political clubs, social organizations, ethnic groups, educational bodies, and so forth. The problem for the practitioner is in ascertaining who are the opinion leaders in each group considered important to the communicator. If this can be done, then the communicator can key messages to these leaders in the expectation that the leaders in turn will transmit them to a wider sub-public.

Opinion leaders are more exposed than others to contact with the outside world by means of the mass media.

A study relating to the use of hybrid seed corn showed that it took fourteen years to gain widespread adoption of the new seed corn by farmers. The study showed there were five stages to adoption: awareness, interest, evaluation, trial, and adoption. The leaders in adoption—those who first demonstrated awareness—were the most widely read. However, one should not automatically assume there is a simple two-step flow from media to opinion leaders to followers. Opinion leaders rely on *many* sources for their information and ideas, and they are also influenced by others whom they consider to be leaders.

Opinion leaders utilize a variety of media and means in relating their groups to relevant parts of society.

The study carried out in Decatur, Illinois, and reported in the book *Personal Influence* by Katz and Lazarsfeld, showed that large city newspapers served to relate fashions to the fashion leaders. A study of doctors showed that out-of-town meetings were important sources of information about new medical ideas. The hybrid seed corn study showed that contact with the city and with farm bureaus of agricultural colleges were important for the farm innovators. Thus, general media, meetings, colleges, specialized media, and a wide variety of sources are used by opinion leaders in gaining information and ideas.

In summation, opinion leaders are important as they relate to the receiver in the communication process, but once again we must remember that we are talking about a process in which an almost limitless number of factors are involved. Being aware of these factors and their roles in the process is only the first step in achieving real understanding of the complex nature of communication between and among people.

QUESTIONS AND PROBLEMS FOR DISCUSSION

1. Of what relevance to public relations practitioners is David K. Berlo's suggestion that communicators concentrate on the response to be sought through communication?

2. Name and explain some of the forms that communication can take.

3. What does the author mean when he states: "Communication does

not take place in a vacuum or void, and it is not singular but pluralistic?"

4. Explain the "hypodermic needle" and the "two-step flow" theories of communication. What are some criticisms that can be leveled against both theories?

5. Explain what is meant by encoding, decoding, and feedback, and cite some examples to illustrate each.

6. Exactly how does source-receiver empathy serve to bring about effective communication?

7. What is meant by "source credibility" and how does it operate?

8. What does the author mean when he states that practitioners often find themselves in a buffer zone or no-man's land between management and recipients when trying to establish and maintain source credibility?

9. Exactly how does situational acuity serve the source in bringing about effective communication?

10. What are the chief communication encoding skills needed by the source?

11. Explain the connection among Newsom's idea that people don't stand still to be educated, Wiebe's concept of the gyroscopic phenomenon, and Robinson's thought about nonmotivation as each of these applies to reaching audiences with messages.

12. Cite some examples to show how interest-identification with an audience improves the impact of messages.

13. What are some of the problems faced by the source in trying to relate messages to common experience and meaning between source and receiver?

14. Cite some examples to show how messages have been tailor-made for the situation, time, place and/or audience.

15. Explain or illustrate the difference between channels which are: interpersonal or mediated; personal or impersonal; assembled or nonassembled.

16. What is meant by "the gatekeeper" in communication through mass media channels? Why is the gatekeeper important to the communicator?

17. Cite some data to illustrate the extent of the mass media picture in terms of newspapers, television, radio and magazines.

18. Cite some data to illustrate the pervasive role of the mass media in American life as they impact on the audience of mass media.

19. What does Marshall McLuhan mean when he says that "the medium is the message"? What criticism can be made of this concept?

20. In rating the various mass media in terms of their adaptability to

the source's purpose and to message content, how would you rate each medium as it relates to providing information? To influencing the receiver? To providing entertainment?

21. In what way is communication effectiveness influenced by the receiver's knowledge? By the receiver's communication skills? By the receiver's predispositions and group membership?

22. Explain Schramm's "fraction of selection" hypothesis as a way of judging the chance that an individual will select any given communication.

23. Explain some key concepts about opinion leaders and the way they influence the reception of messages.

24. What is meant by the agenda-setting function of the mass media?

PROJECTS, ASSIGNMENTS, AND MINI-CASES

1. A LESSON IN INTELLIGENCE OPERATIONS: A MINI-CASE

In his book, *The Man Who Never Was,* Ewen Montague tells how British Intelligence used a dead man to pull off an intelligence coup in World War II prior to the invasion of Italy. They took an unknown dead man; provided him with a complete life history and identity as a major in the Royal Marines; packed him in ice; shipped him off on a submarine after planting a letter and some documents on him; dumped him into the sea in the dead of night near Huelva on the southwest coast of Spain. These elaborate procedures were followed to give the impression that the "officer" had gone down in a plane crash and washed up on shore in an area where the British knew a German intelligence person was operating. The hope was that the Germans would be fooled into believing that the Allies did not intend to invade Sicily (which they did) and would draw away their troops and vessels. In describing the "vital document" which was the means by which he hoped to fool the Germans, Montague cited the problem as follows:

> If the German General Staff was to be persuaded, in face of all probabilities, to bank on our next target being somewhere other than Sicily, it would have to have before it a document which was passing between officers who *must* know what our real plans were, who could not possibly be mistaken and who could not themselves be the victims of a cover plan. If the operation was to be worthwhile, I had to have a document written by someone, and to someone, whom the Germans knew—and whom they knew to be "right in the know."

> So I put up the proposal that General Sir Archibald Nye, the Vice-Chief of the Imperial General Staff, should write the letter and that he should write it to General Alexander (who commanded an army in Tunisia, under General Eisenhower) at 18th Army Group Headquarters. . . . The letter should be what we junior officers called "the old boy type" . . . and the sort of friendly letter which can give information and explanations that can't be put into an official communication. That sort of letter, and that sort of letter only, could convey convincingly to the Germans the indication that our next target was not Sicily, and yet could be found in the possession of an officer and not in a bag full of the usual documents going from home to our army abroad.

> I was aiming high, and I had to. I expected something of an explosion, and I got it. For many of even the most able and efficient people failed to appreciate what was wanted for this sort of job; for to realize that needed a particular sort of approach and a peculiar sort of mind that could look at the same puzzle from several different angles at the same time.

You are a British Intelligence Officer; you have an opposite number in the enemy Intelligence, say in Berlin; and above him is the German Operational Command. What you, a Briton with a British background, think can be deduced from a document does not matter. It is what *your opposite number*, with his German knowledge and background, will think that matters—what construction *he* will put on the document. Therefore, if you want *him* to think such-and-such a thing, you must give him something which will make *him* (and not *you*) think it. But he may be suspicious and want confirmation; you must think what inquiries will *he* make (not what inquiries *you* would make) and give him the answers to those inquiries so as to satisfy him. In other words, you must remember that a German does not think and react as an Englishman does, and you must put yourself into his mind. . . .

> from Ewen Montague, *The Man Who Never Was*, Lippincott, 1954, p. 43

Questions for Discussion

1. In what specific respect does the above case and excerpt illustrate and exemplify some of the major key points made about communication in this chapter?

2. What lessons does the case teach you about the communication process?

3. Can you cite any personal communication experiences or observations of your own to illustrate the same points?

2. A TEST OF SITUATIONAL ACUITY: A MINI-CASE

You are 27 years old and the coordinator of external publicity of a profitable division of a large industrial corporation. The division sells information services rather than a hard product, and its customers are other business firms. The time is January, 1976, and your salary is $18,500.

Head of the communication department to which you belong is a director whose background has been chiefly in advertising. Reporting to him are two managers, one of whom is your immediate superior.

Your division has recently had a change of presidents, switching from an outgoing, affable, publicity-conscious chief executive to a more reserved president whose background is technical and who is very wary of the press. One of the new president's first moves is to schedule a meeting with the director and the two managers of the communication department, but due to an unavoidable conflict in his schedule the manager to whom you report is unable to make the meeting. He is to be gone a week, and the director agrees that you can substitute for him at the briefing which is scheduled a week from today.

Before leaving, your superior calls you into his office to warn you that the new president does not believe in interviews with the press "particularly because the post-Watergate glorification of investigative reporting has even filtered down into the ranks of the business and trade press." He further says: "In no circumstances say that interviews with him are necessary or desirable because his philosophy is that he won't grant interviews."

These remarks disturb you because your job is to get favorable publicity for the division. Both of you are aware that you were given a relatively free hand to arrange interviews with the previous president and the record shows that the ones you scheduled resulted in excellent coverage by the trade and business press. However, because your superior is obviously in a rush to take off on his trip you don't press the point.

A half hour before the scheduled morning briefing with the president—and as a result of a good deal of spade work on your part over the previous weeks—your contact on a leading national business publication calls to inform you that he has been assigned to handle a cover story the two of you had been discussing. The story will deal in depth with the information service field, and as your division is a leader in the field the writer would like to interview your new president. You tell him you will see what you can do, and it is agreed you will call back that afternoon.

Because the call came in just prior to the meeting you have no time to discuss it with the director of the communication department. You are well aware, though, that he reports directly to the president and has remarked more than once that whoever signs his paycheck is entitled to deal with the press in any manner he chooses.

When your turn comes to make your presentation you do a very good job, and you know it's good because the new president nods warmly at its conclusions and says something like "very impressive" to the director of the communication department. The president then turns to you and says: "What do you think of my policy against personal interviews?"

Questions for Discussion

1. What would you say in response to the president's question? Do not generalize, but state exactly what you would say. (The instructor may want to set up a role-playing situation here.)

2. Explain *why* you would respond in the manner you have answered the president. In short, how do you see the situation as it relates to you; to you and your immediate superior; to you and the department director; to you and the president?

3. What questions might you want to raise about the situation which may, in your opinion, have a bearing on your response? Given the answers to these questions, in what way might they change the nature of your response to the president's question?

3. A TEST OF SOURCE CREDIBILITY: A MINI-CASE

For several years, at an appropriate time and without indicating he was testing a hypothesis, the author has submitted the following quotation to groups of people and then asked the members to indicate their opinion of the statement in a space below it provided for remarks:

> ... But all agree, and there can be no question whatever, that some remedy must be found, and quickly found, for the misery and wretchedness which press so heavily at this moment on the large majority of the very poor.

> ... By degrees it has come to pass that working men have been given over, isolated and defenseless, to the callousness of employers and the greed of unrestrained competition.

> ... And to this must be added the custom of working by contract and the concentration of so many branches of trade in the hands of a few individuals, so that a small number of the very rich men have been able to lay upon the masses of the poor a yoke little better than slavery itself.

Each time the above statement was distributed and opinions asked of it, the group surveyed—unknown to its members—was divided in half. At the top of the statement above given to half the members was the notation: "The following statement was printed recently as an editorial in the official publication of the Socialist Workers Party of America." At the top of the statement above given to the rest of the members was the notation: "The following statements are taken from encyclical by Pope Leo XIII in 1891."

In short, the statement remained the same; the only difference was the attribution to sources.

Questions for Discussion

1. What effect, if any, do you think the two differing notations as to the source of the statement would have on receiver reaction to it?

2. What connection do you think might exist between the statement, source credibility and probable receiver reaction when we consider the receiver's religion? Economic status? Social status? Job or profession? Educational level?

3. What conclusions do you draw from this example about source credibility?

4. First, for those who are curious, the statement is from the encyclicals of Pope Leo XIII in 1891. Second, you might care to try the experiment on a group of colleagues not in this class. Simply duplicate the statement and on half the copies use the notation from the Pope and on the other half the notation from the SWPA.

RECOMMENDED READING

David K. Berlo, *The Process of Communication*. New York: Free Press, 1960.

Jay G. Blumler and Elihu Katz, eds., *The Uses of Communication: Current Perspectives On Gratification Research.* Beverly Hills, Calif.: Sage Publications, 1974.

W. P. Davison, "On the Effects of Communication," *Public Opinion Quarterly* 23, 1959.

Dorothy Douglas, et. al., "An Information Campaign that Changed Community Attitudes," *Journalism Quarterly*, Autumn 1970.

G. M. Gelb, "The Uses and Misuses of Feedback," *Journal of Organizational Communication* 3, 1976.

C. I. Hovland, I. L. Janis, and H. H. Kelley, *Communication and Persuasion.* New Haven, Conn.: Yale University Press, 1953.

Elihu Katz and Paul Lazarsfeld, *Personal Influence.* New York: Free Press, 1964.

Joseph T. Klapper, *The Effects of Mass Communication.* Glencoe, Ill.: Free Press of Glencoe, 1960.

Sidney Krauss and Dennis Davis, *The Effects of Mass Communication on Political Behavior.* University Park, Pa.: The Pennsylvania State University Press, 1976.

Melvin L. LaFleur, *Theories of Mass Communication,* 2nd ed. New York: David McKay, 1970.

Otto Lerbinger and Albert J. Sullivan, *Information, Influence, and Communication: A Reader in Public Relations.* New York: Basic Books, 1965.

Maxwell McCombs, "The Agenda-Setting Function of the Mass Media," *Public Relations Review,* Winter 1977.

Maxwell E. McCombs and Lee B. Becker, *Using Mass Communication Theory.* Englewood Cliffs, N.J.: Prentice-Hall, 1979.

Harold Mendelsohn, "Some Reasons Why Information Campaigns Can Succeed," *Public Opinion Quarterly*, Spring 1973.

Edward J. Robinson, *Communication and Public Relations.* Columbus, Ohio: Charles E. Merrill Books, 1966.

Everett M. Rogers and W. Floyd Shoemaker, *Communication of Innovations.* New York: Free Press, 1971.

Wilbur Schramm, *Men, Messages and Media.* New York: Harper & Row, 1973.

Wilbur Schramm and Donald Roberts, eds., *The Process and Effects of Mass Communication.* Urbana, Ill.: University of Illinois Press, 1971.

Donald Shaw and Maxwell McCombs, *The Emergence of American Political Issues: The Agenda-Setting Function of the Press.* St. Paul: West Publishing, 1977.

Leonard J. Snyder, "Uses and Gratification to Implement a PR Program," *Public Relations Review,* Summer 1978.

Phillip J. Tichenor, George A. Donohue, and Charles N. Olien, "Community Research and Evaluating Community Research," *Public Relations Review,* Winter 1977.

David Weaver, Maxwell E. McCombs, and Charles Spellman, "Watergate and the Media: A Case Study of Agenda-Setting," *American Political Quarterly,* October 1975.

10

Communication Techniques: Media Relations, Publicity Techniques, Institutional and Advocacy Advertising

In the previous chapter various communications theories and the concept of communication as a process were examined. We also explored a communications model involving four elements: the sender, the channel, the message, and the recipient. In an earlier chapter concerned with public opinion, we dealt at length with the recipient in analyzing the public, attitudes, opinions, and the nature of public opinion and opinion formation.

This chapter is concerned chiefly with so-called downward communication, communication that comes from the communicator and moves through the media which serve as channels for messages. As with all elements of the public relations process, the downward communications stage deals with relationships—in this instance the relationships between the practitioner and the media. At no time static, these relationships are constantly changing and in motion. They can mean the difference between communications success or failure.

But the state of practitioner-media relations is but one part of the process. A second part of the process relates to the degree of skill with which the practitioner fashions messages and sends them through media channels—hence the chapter's concern with publicity techniques. That these techniques are ever-changing is demonstrated by the relatively recent emergence of advocacy advertising, a communications tool examined in the concluding section of this chapter.

MEDIA RELATIONS

UNDERSTANDING THE MEDIA'S ROLE

In the so-called "good old days" when life often depended on a king's whim, being a messenger to the king was a hazardous calling. The messenger who brought good news was rewarded for his efforts; the messenger unfortunate enough to be the bearer of bad news lost his head.

We're more civilized today. We don't behead messengers, but we often excoriate them. Modern managers tend to vent their wrath on the messengers—the mass media who carry the news of the day—rather than deal with the contents of the messages the media carry. Any issue of a daily newspaper or weekly news magazine provides numerous illustrations to prove the point.

When the wire services carry stories reporting government inefficiency, the reaction of government officials is to charge that they're the victims of a media vendetta. When prestigious daily newspapers carry reports of price collusion or the distribution of bribes by representatives of American companies in overseas markets, the reaction of the concerned businesses is to charge that the media are the reason why the public has a low opinion of business. Not enough of the executives who manage our organizations seem to recognize that they should be more concerned with the content of the messages than with the messengers who report them.

The source of the problem lies in the fact that too few executives understand the role of the mass media in American society. In a free society such as ours, the mass media are independent entities whose main functions are to report the news of the day, provide entertainment, reflect cultural changes, and, in the proper place, comment and editorialize. In carrying out these basic functions, the media are supposed to be responsible, but responsibility is difficult to measure, is open to interpretation, and is often uncontrollable. Thus, we find differences of opinion about the media's role and about the media's degree of responsibility.

A daily newspaper runs a front-page story reporting that the city's largest employer has laid off one-third of its work force (previously unannounced) and is scheduled next week to lay off another one-third. The story is factually correct, but the paper is accused of being irresponsible.

Another daily newspaper in another city carries a similar story about a reduction in force by the city's largest employer. The story is accurate, brief, and is run on an inside page of the second section of the paper. The executives of the company, though not happy to have the news reported in the paper, are pleased that the paper has shown responsibility.

To what degree have the above-mentioned newspapers been responsible, and to whom should they be responsible? It's obvious that there are serious economic and other consequences when a city's major employer lays off a sizable share of its work force. Reporting and printing such news also brings consequences, and although some media critics may doubt it, most editors are keenly aware of these consequences when they make decisions about news coverage and placement. It's therefore wise to recognize that although few managers like to read, hear about, or view negative news about their organizations, the primary responsibility of the mass media is to *report* the news—whether the news is good, bad, or indifferent.

In dealing with the mass media one must understand this primary responsibility of the mass media. A few simple precepts should help to clarify such understanding:

1. We live in a society whose members are more inclined to be interested in conflict than in harmony. It is not newsworthy when a company concludes ten years without labor strife. It is news when a strike is called and the labor force walks out.

2. Most people and most organizations pursue their destinies in a decent, lawful fashion. That's not newsworthy. But when someone robs a bank; when an executive is found guilty of misappropriation of funds; when a company is adjudged to have carried out unlawful acts—that's news, and the media will report it.

3. The all-important wire services—AP and UPI—which supply the bulk of the state, national, and international news appearing in our daily media, try to present a balanced report of news events, and this is especially true when the event concerns differences between two or more sides or groups.

   However, media can't provide balance when one side makes itself unavailable for comment, and this happens all too frequently when large organizations find themselves in trouble. In such cases hitherto available executives play a game of musical chairs in an effort to be seated when the music stops. He who is left standing becomes the goat.

This musical chairs routine was nicely illustrated when Lee A. Iococca resigned as president of the Ford Motor Company on July 13, 1978, after a fallout with Henry Ford II, chairman of the company. The action was a major source of news and comment throughout the country, and it made many front pages, including that of the *New York Times*. After citing the resignation in its lead, the *Times* said the resignation followed two days of heated debate within the company's board of directors. The third paragraph of the story provided a graphic illustration of the musical chairs game played by business leaders when conflict news is carried by the mass media. It read as follows:

Neither Mr. Ford nor Mr. Iococca could be reached for comment. The company did not announce the resignation immediately, and the public relations executives at its offices could not be reached for comment.

What should one do when a major internecine dispute erupts between the top executives of an organization? There are no simple answers. Silence may well be golden. Certainly, you can't put your foot into your mouth if you keep your mouth shut. But if you can't be reached for comment when it's obvious that press inquiries will be forthcoming, you're sure to confirm a media precept about public relations people: they're the media's best friend when the going is easy, but they're seldom around when the going is tough. Whether the precept be fact or fancy depends on the special kind of relationship existing between the practitioner and the media. That multifaceted relationship is discussed in the next section.

IT'S A MARRIAGE, FOR BETTER OR WORSE

Some marriages seem made in heaven and some in hell, but most seem to exist in between these two extremes. In the latter category one could well place the forced marriage between public relations practitioners and the media.

As has been noted in the second chapter of this book, public relations is often referred to pejoratively by the media. Whereas journalism is considered to be a noble calling protected by the First Amendment to the Constitution, public relations is considered to be a less than noble activity protected only by the wits of those who practice its alleged black arts. Journalists see themselves as independent writers who present only the truth and who are beholden to no one. They perceive public relations practitioners to be hired hands who bend the truth for unseen clients and companies who employ them to deceive the public.

As with most perceptions, reality is clouded by the dark glasses through which perceptions are filtered. Remove the glasses, and this picture comes into focus:

1. There are very few truly independent journalists today who are totally free to write as they please. However, journalists are certainly more free and impartial than are public relations practitioners, because the latter are advocates and journalists are not. This sense of unfettered writing freedom—though illusionary at times—enables the journalist to sneer at his public relations cousin. The sneer may be small comfort to the journalist, whose monetary rewards are so much lower than those of the practitioner, but it's a comfort nonetheless.

2. Though the journalist doesn't like to acknowledge or admit it, the newspaper, radio, or television station for which he works is a business entity. As such, it is guided by unwritten ground rules that affect what is written and what is left unwritten. The smaller the entity—and the *average* newspaper, radio, or television station is a small business—the more likely the unwritten ground rules apply. So, although journalists are more pure than public relations practitioners, they are certainly not so pure as they profess or imagine themselves to be. However, no one likes to face up to the truth when it mirrors a reality less salutary than illusion. Therefore, if the journalist is

pleased to consider himself pure and the public relations practitioner impure, allow him that small luxury.

3. Reality dictates that the journalist and the practitioner cohabitate despite their differences. If one were to take the average daily newspaper and the newscasts of the average radio and television station and eliminate from them all the stories that stemmed in some fashion from public relations sources, the end product would be an emaciated version of the original. It could be done, of course, but at a cost that the owners of these media are unwilling or unable to bear. It would mean larger staffs, bigger payrolls, and smaller or few profits.

So the media grudgingly, not too happily, use the material, ideas, and help offered by the public relations practitioner. Some media use a great deal of the material, help, and ideas, and often use the material without editorial changes. Some media use some of the materials, help, and ideas, and often change the material in the process. Some media use public relations material some of the time, use little material at other times, and always make considerable editorial changes in what they eventually use. Virtually no media use no public relations material at all.

4. In the game of wits between the media and the practitioner, some ground rules are set by the media and some by the practitioner, but unfortunately there is no universal rule book and no referees to resolve disputes. Perhaps that's what makes the media-practitioner game so interesting, and perhaps that's why it requires skill, imagination, and a certain amount of luck to play it. A few examples:

- Newspapers don't take kindly to seeing the same story in two different parts of the paper. Ground rule: don't send the same story to two different section editors.

- Editors know full well who is advertising in their papers, and they don't take kindly to reminders of this from practitioners seeking to have their news releases printed. Ground rule: by all means advertise, but don't use your ads as a bludgeon.

- Practitioners who want to give all media an even news break embargo releases for use at a specific future time. But editors often feel free to ignore embargoes, and some will print stories ahead of the specified release time. Ground rule: embargo if you must, but do so sparingly.

- Practitioners will often favor large circulation papers with their best news releases in order to secure maximum exposure. To assuage the anger of the smaller papers, they'll throw an occasional release sop their way. Ground rule: dole out your goodies, but share them.

As the game of wits is played between the media and the practitioner, the hardened, experienced practitioner recognizes that he will win some and he'll lose some. He learns quickly that to promise that a story will surely be carried in a particular medium is to gamble with the fickle finger of fate. Every editor knows that although he and

310

the practitioner are bound together for better or for worse, in reality the practitioner is but a guest in the house. Fortunately for the practitioner, he recognizes that if matters really get too bad he can always move to another house—to another medium—where he will be more welcome.

SOME ELEMENTARY GROUND RULES

"I spent two days working on this talk. It was very important that we warn our employees that if they don't improve productivity their jobs are in jeopardy. It cost the company a lot of money to stop work for an hour so I could talk to all of them, on our time, and impress on them the gravity of the situation. I praised them for their hard work, gave them the facts of foreign competition, said we all have to work harder. What did I get for my troubles? The lead story in the lousy newspaper said I threatened the work force. That's what I got for all the trouble I went to."

> —Comment from the chief operating officer of a national company after giving a talk to the work force of a local plant of the company.

"More than 500 people put countless hours of time and effort into this year's campaign. We raised more money than we've ever raised before, and we almost reached our goal but just couldn't put it over the top. I just can't understand why a newspaper which depends on the support of the community would use a headline stating that the 'UNITED WAY FAILS TO REACH ITS GOAL.' "

> —Comment from the campaign chairman of a local United Way drive.

"When we had this important announcement about a new product we went to great trouble to accommodate the two local television stations. Instead of making the announcement at company headquarters in Chicago we set up a press conference at our plant here, and we timed it to give TV plenty of leeway to develop their film for the evening news. What did we get? Nothing, absolutely nothing. They said something about two fires and some lousy auto accident in which a family of six were killed."

> —Comment from the vice-president of marketing of a national company.

Three separate comments from three separate sources were all harping on the same theme: the media can't be trusted to tell their stories the way they ought to be told. This sound and fury from disgruntled executives is heard daily throughout the land. What it really signifies is a failure to understand the rules of the media game.

As has been noted, there is no universal rule book, and some of the problems stem from this fact. However, veteran public relations practitioners have learned to play by the rules without benefit of a rule book. This section aims to set forth some of the ground rules that need to be mastered if one wants to succeed at the media game.

Space Is Limited, Time Inexorable

Only the *New York Times* would dare to claim it runs all the news that's fit to print, and even the *Times* knows that it can't possibly measure up to an impossible standard. Getting out a daily newspaper and a weekly news magazine; producing a half-hour newscast; publishing a monthly magazine; airing a five-minute radio news broadcast— each of these involves a drastic process of *elimination* and telescoping of information. Finished diamonds aren't plucked raw from the bowels of the earth, but are the end result of a sifting out process involving tons of raw material. The news stories we read in our daily newspaper and hear and view on radio and television are the end result of a similar sifting out process.

This sifting out process takes place on all media. Whether they're local, regional, or national, all media receive and process far more news than they use, The so-called "glut of occurrences" is a flood of news and information that inundates the newsrooms of the nation.

It has always been so with news in America, but today space demands are more severe than ever before. Chiefly for reasons of cost and economy, the news hole on the average daily newspaper is limited. It is even more limited on radio and television. Only about twenty news stories make up the half-hour network nightly news program, and the longest of these runs less than three minutes. Stories are cut to the bone, and a journalistic version of the Social Darwinian theory of the survival of the fittest rules the selection of news.

Social Darwinists theorized that only the most fit and sturdy of a species will survive. The journalistic version of this theory adds a time dimension to the survival process. It simply means that Story A may be more newsworthy than Story B, but if Story A arrives first in the newsroom it may well be dummied into the paper early and survive the winnowing process because Story B arrived too late for inclusion.

Thus we must add time to space demands when dealing with the media. An entire newspaper becomes a finished product in the short period of several hours. Deadlines for print and electronic media are inflexible. Both the journalist and the practitioner must meet these deadlines in order to survive.

Editors Determine What Is News

Beginning journalism textbooks define news in many different ways, but in reality each editor determines what is news and what isn't news. Richard M. Detwiler, public relations consultant, explains it this way:

Importance in news is important only to the extent that the editor thinks it is important, and what the editor thinks is important is not necessarily important.

Detwiler's explanation may sound like something out of *Alice In Wonderland*, but it makes sense to every editor and should make sense to every practitioner. Editors determine newsworthiness on the basis of long years of experience in sizing up what will interest their readers. Most of them have a very keen understanding of what will interest readers, listeners, and viewers, and there is a surprising amount of agreement among editors on this score. One of the major reasons why former newsmen are good at handling the media is that they've been part of the media and understand how editors view potential news items.

However, there are many variables affecting the actual coverage and eventual publication of news. It is therefore dangerous to try to predict how a potential news item will be treated by individual editors. Consider, for example, some of these questions:

- *What day of the week is it?* The same news item will get one kind of coverage on a light news day and another on a heavy news day.

- *What time of the day is it?* If you run a press conference at 10:30 a.m. you'll have a better chance of making the evening news than if you run the conference at 4:30 p.m.

- *What news are you competing against?* You can have a perfectly good news item considered newsworthy on almost every score, but if several other major news stories break at the same time, you may well find your item either not carried or else relegated to an inside page.

- *Does your news item fit the standards of the medium?* If your news release is single-spaced and takes up four pages, don't be surprised to find that it's been cut to three paragraphs. If your story involves abstract, nonvisual material, don't be surprised to find that television is not interested in it.

- *How much will it cost the medium to cover your event?* Travel takes time and is costly, so don't expect coverage if your news site is miles from town.

Each of the above deals with the mechanics of covering and handling potential news. Mastering the mechanics is essential to success. Once you know the mechanics you are at least assured of having editors pay attention to your story. Whether they'll print it or put it on the air is another matter, but you'll have a fighting chance rather than no chance at all.

Media Need Cultivation

If it's true that each editor determines what is and what isn't news, then it makes good sense to know each editor with whom you have to deal. The same principle applies to key reporters and to those who make assignments for print and electronic media.

If you're in the habit of sending out mass mailings to hundreds— sometimes thousands—of media, it's impossible to be personally acquainted with all those who handle your news. As a general rule, however, every practitioner finds that there are a limited number of media and media personnel who are of special importance to him. Determining who these are is not a particularly difficult task:

Step 1: Decide which public or publics are most important to your organization.

Step 2: Ascertain which media are important to this public or to these publics.

Step 3: Determine which reporters, editors, and others working for these media are important to you.

Step 4: Get to know these reporters, editors, and others.

Applying the above four-step process becomes an individual matter for each practitioner. The process is applicable whether one works in the internal public relations department of an organization or is a counselor serving clients.

Example 1

The practitioner is a counselor. The client is listed on the New York Stock Exchange and is headquartered in Des Moines, Iowa, where it has a manufacturing plant that produces aluminum castings. Its three major publics are the Des Moines community; the financial and business community; and firms that use aluminum castings. The important media for this practitioner are the Des Moines newspapers, radio and television stations; financial and business publications; and the trade press in the aluminum field and in those fields that utilize aluminum castings in their manufacturing processes. Editors, news directors, and reporters of these media are the ones who should be cultivated by the practitioner.

Example 2

The practitioner is director of public relations for a hospital in Atlanta, Georgia. Its major public is the Atlanta community and various subpublics within that community. The important media for this practitioner are the Atlanta newspapers, radio and television stations. Editors, news directors, and reporters of these media are the ones who should be cultivated by the practitioner.

How does one "cultivate" media personnel? As a first step, if this is a new relationship, the practitioner should visit each important medium and get acquainted with its key personnel. A second step is to hand-deliver important stories when the occasion warrants such delivery. A third is to avoid taking up a news person's time when he or she is near a deadline. A fourth is to be available when called. A fifth is to provide news tips and ideas for features that are keyed to the needs and interests of particular media. A sixth is to gain respect by knowing one's business, knowing the special needs of each medium, and by being a reliable source of news and information about the organization one represents.

The perceptive reader will note that the relationship described above seems to indicate a state of affairs in which the practitioner gives and the journalist takes. In most instances, this is what happens. But there will be certain important, crucial days when the "taker" gives. Such a day arrives when a reporter calls the practitioner first to get his side of a negative story; when an editor decides to run a negative story on an inside page or to downplay it on a newscast; and when a trade publication producing a major roundup story seeks out the practitioner in order to cite him as one of the reliable and authoritative sources in the field.

Credibility Isn't Gained By Chance

Handling media inquiries that put the practitioner on the spot is one of the most difficult tasks of the public relations practitioner. Such inquiries don't occur daily, but they happen often enough to be a source of concern. They're especially important if the practitioner hopes to maintain a respected relationship with the media. Credibility and reliability are the practitioner's stock in trade. He has little or no stock left if he loses one or both of these attributes. Consider these suggestions about the kind of response to give media or the kind of action to take when the telephone rings and the journalist poses some tough questions:

Don't react too hastily or without careful thought. A hasty, ill-conceived response can get you into trouble. You gain time for thought and for a response by asking for the journalist's deadline and by promising to get back to her before that deadline. This is a perfectly sound reaction on your part, and especially so when the inquiry concerns a matter about which you have little or no knowledge. Even if the inquiry concerns a matter about which you do have knowledge, time provides you with the opportunity to come up with a reasonable response.

When possible, try to anticipate inquiries. If you've ever worked as a newsperson—or if you can think like a newsperson even though you haven't any news experience—you should be able to know or sense when an inquiry will be forthcoming about certain kinds of situations. If you can anticipate the inquiry, you should be able to figure out an appropriate response *before* it is made, not when that telephone rings.

> You're director of public relations for a college. Today is Wednesday, and you get word that the weekly student newspaper, due out on Friday, will carry a front page editorial demanding that the president of the college resign. Will the media be calling? You may just as well ask if Friday will follow Thursday, and you had better anticipate inquiries and the response you will make (or be allowed to make).

Visualize your response in print or on the air. As many a practitioner has learned to his dismay, skilled journalists can have a field day with some of the dodges used to avoid answers to questions. The English language at the command of some practitioners—most often those who practice their art in the political or business world—is sometimes used like a foil in a fencing match. The answers, ranging from the simple to the complex, all end up as a nonresponse to the question. There's the simple "No comment," and then there's the more complex "I can neither confirm nor deny that." Another variation of the nonresponse is the delaying ploy: "We are investigating that." A fourth variation takes the form of the disappearing practitioner: "So-and-so could not be reached for comment," or "So-and-so was unavailable for comment," or "So-and-so was out of town." At times so many practitioners are so often "out of town" in tight situations one wonders if there exists a permanent convention of unavailable practitioners who meet regularly so as to be out of town when they should be answering media inquiries.

But journalists are used to such nonresponse dodges, and they can utilize them in such a way as to make the practitioner rue the use of a nonresponse when he sees it in print or hears it on the air. Just one nonresponse in print or on the air raises the public's suspicion that the practitioner is trying to hide something. The practitioner may have a short-run gain, but in the long run the practitioner who gets the reputation for dodging questions loses credibility and invites a rapidly deteriorating relationship with the media.

Keep Up with the Times

The successful public relations practitioner who professes to be an expert when it comes to dealing with the media must keep up with the times, and this means more than just the *New York Times.* As noted earlier in this book, reading, listening, and viewing are essential tools for the practitioner. One learns best about media needs, wants, and interests by keeping abreast of the media. You gain first-hand knowledge about the *Times, Time, Newsweek,* and about general, business, and trade publications by reading them. Similar first-hand knowledge about radio and television news, talk, and entertainment programs comes from listening and viewing.

However, because there simply isn't enough time in the work day or evening hours to monitor all media or even a fraction of them, the practitioner must rely on professional publications devoted to news about the media and about the public relations field. Richard Weiner, veteran public relations counselor, has compiled a list of newsletters and of weekly, monthly, and quarterly periodicals of particular importance to public relations practitioners. The list, cited in Figure 10.1, testifies to the wide variety of publications of value to all practitioners.

Figure 10.1
A Periodical List for All Seasons

The following list of newsletters, weekly, monthly, and quarterly periodicals of particular value to public relations practitioners was compiled, with brief notations, by Richard Weiner, veteran public relations counselor. It appeared in the *Public Relations Journal* in August 1977, and the subscription prices cited were as of that date.

AIM Report, Accuracy in Media, Inc., 777 14th St., N.W., Washington, DC 20005. $15. Accuracy In Media, a nonprofit organization, monitors publications and programs for fairness and accuracy. Orientation is decidedly conservative. . . .

Atlanta's PR/News World, Southeastern Press Relations Newswire, 161 Peachtree St., Atlanta, GA 30303. Free. Four-page newsletter, published sporatically several times a year, with news and comments about media in the Southeast, primarily Atlanta. . . .

Business Wire Newsletter, 235 Montgomery St., San Francisco, CA 94104. Free. . . . Four-page monthly newsletter includes promotional material, but it is one of the most up-to-date, comprehensive regional media publications in the country. . . .

Columbia Journalism Review, 700 Journalism Bldg. Columbia University, NY 10027. $12. Articles have broad popular appeal. . . .

Communique, Box 2226, Hollywood, FL 33022. Free. Coverage includes marketing, advertising, media and public relations in the Carolinas, Georgia, Alabama, Louisiana and Texas. . . . Focus is the advertising industry. . . .

Contacts, Larimi Communications Assocs., 151 E. 50 St., NY 10022. $90. Four-page weekly newsletter for publicists about print and electronic media opportunities. . . . Larimi also publishes two directories, *Television Contacts* and *Radio Contacts.*

The Corporate Communications Report, 112 E. 31 St., NY 10016. $65. A 12-page bimonthly newsletter designed "to help the chief executive officer and his key advisors communicate effectively with stockholders and the financial community." . . . Articles generally not oriented to public relations. . . .

Editor & Publisher, 850 Third Ave. NY 10022. $15. Weekly bible of the daily newspaper field. Features data about new publications, syndicates, supplements and other print media, editorial personnal changes and other news about the fourth estate. . . .

editor's newsletter, Box 243, NY 10021. $20. Four-page, monthly compilation of news and comments about trends and techniques of business communications. Of greatest use to house organ editors. . . .

The Gallagher Report, 230 Park Ave., NY 10017. $60. Confidential letter to marketing, sales, advertising and media executives. Covers public relations only peripherally, but is extremely valuable for its data and comments about media and advertisers. . . .

in black and white, Associated Editorial Consultants, Box 2107, La Jolla, CA 92038. $25. Four- to eight-page, biweekly newsletter "for those who write, report and edit for publications." . . .

Jack O'Dwyer's Newsletter, 271 Madison Ave., NY 10016. $50 Competes with *pr reporter* and *Public Relations News* by taking a totally different approach. Independent, entertaining, easy to read. . . . Also publishes two directories on public relations agencies and public relations departments.

Journal of Communication, Annenberg School of Communication, U. of Penn., Philadelphia, PA 19103. $15. Quarterly journal with scholarly articles on theory, research, policy and practice of communication.

Media Industry Newsletter, 150 E. 52 St., NY 10022. $58. News, features, research, reports, predictions and candid opinions about publishers and broadcasters crisply reported in eight-page weekly newsletter. Primarily of interest to advertising, marketing and media people, and not specifically oriented to public relations.

Media News Keys, Television Index, Inc., 150 Fifth Ave., NY 10011. $50. . . Weekly, four-page compilation of leads, contacts, changes and other data about all media of interest to publicists . . . Greater amount of space devoted to broadcast than print media. . . .

PR Aids' Party Line, PR Aids, Inc., 221 Park Ave. So., NY 10003. $60. One 8½ x 11 sheet (both sides) published weekly. Worth more than its weight in gold to publicists. Succint roundup of current placement opportunities in all media.

Figure 10.1 (Cont.)

Includes descriptions of new syndicated columns and magazines, information about needs of free-lance magazine writers and changes in contacts for radio and TV programs. . . .

pr reporter, PR Publishing Co., Inc., Box 66, Exeter, NH 03833. $60. Weekly, four-page newsletter with . . . comments on broad aspects of public affairs and communications. Supplements include one-sheet, bimonthly summary of articles in social science and other journals. . . . Company also publishes two directories, *Who's Who in Public Relations* and the *PR Blue Book.*

The Perry Letter, Perry Corporate Communications, Box 91247, Atlanta, GA 30344. Free. Four-page, monthly newsletter states that the annual subscription price is $50, but actually it's sent free to annual report producers and other prospective customers of this graphics firm. Each issue consists of descriptions of over a dozen annual reports and other publications. . . .

Practical Public Relations, Box 3861, Rochester, NY 14610. $60 . . . Often contains publicity tips and practical advice rarely found in most of the newsletters. Easy-to-read, attractive format justifies its slogan, "the practical newsletter for professional Communicators."

Public Relations Journal, Public Relations Society of America, 845 Third Ave., NY 10022. $7.50 of annual PRSA membership dues is for subscription; nonmember subscription, $12. Only monthly magazine in the public relations field, has the largest circulation (12,500) of any public relations publications. . . . One of the most useful features is collection of monthly columns on relevent topics.

Public Relations News, 127 E. 80 St., NY 10021. $79.50. Four-page newsletter with largest circulation of any newsletter in the public relations field. First half of each issue is devoted to news and comments about public relations events, accounts and people. Second section consists of a case study, with details about materials and results of recent campaigns, projects and special events.

Public Relations Quarterly, 44 W. Market St., Rhinebeck, NY 12572. $12 . . . PRQ

often publishes in-depth articles with detailed advice and comments, and is a useful component of the public relations library. . . .

Public Relations Review, College of Journalism, University of Maryland, College Park, MD 20742. $10. The PRSA-sponsored Foundation for Public Relations Research and Education, Inc. started this quarterly journal to build a bridge between public relations and social and behavioral science. Articles, generally by social scientists, often report or comment on research. . . . Definitely the journal of research in the public relations and communications field. . . .

Publicist, PR Aids Inc., 221 Park Ave. So., NY 10003. Free. Snappy-looking tabloid newspaper sent free to just about every working publicist in the country. Sponsors are eight major companies (including PR Aids mailing service) who sell to publicists. Between the ads is an amazingly good collection of well-written, easy-to-read, how-to-do-it studies, case histories, personality profiles and other articles. . . .

Publishers Weekly, 1180 Ave. of the Americas, NY 10036. $25. Bible of the book publishing industry, Includes section on media, with information of value to all publicists. . . .

The Quill, 35 E. Wacker Drive, Chicago, IL 60601. $10. Published since 1912 by Sigma Delta Chi (The Society of Professional Journalists). Popular (circulation 30,000) monthly magazine with news about members and chapters, as well as articles about print media. . . .

The Ragan Report, Lawrence Ragan Communications, Inc. 407 S. Dearborn St., Chicago, IL 60605. $50. Four-page weekly newsletter, with each issue supplemented by a two- to four-page commentary by outside contributor. Potpourri of news and views, mostly about employee magazines and other special-interest publications. . . .

Writer's Digest, 9933 Alliance Road, Cincinnati, OH 45242. $7.95. Primarily for beginning and professional free-lance writers. Most articles not likely to be of value to publicists. However, descriptions of new and offbeat media often include material not found elsewhere. . . .

PUBLICITY TECHNIQUES

THE PUBLICITY RELEASE

The publicity release is to the publicist what the wrench is to the plumber and the drill to the dentist. Sometimes called a *handout*, the publicity release is a special tool used to convey information, news, and feature material from the publicist to the media. Professionals who handle it skillfully find that it gains them entry to print and broadcast outlets. Amateurs who mishandle the publicity release find that it ends up in the circular file.

Format

There are many varieties of release form, but the basic publicity release follows these simple rules:

- It should be typed on plain white paper, 8½ x 11 inches. Fashion publicists sometimes use colored stock, but this is not considered advisable for the average release.

- Identity of the sender should be carried in a block of copy single-spaced in the upper left-hand corner of the page. Identification should include the name and address of the organization; the name of the publicist; the office telephone number; and a number to call after 5 p.m.

Counseling firms also list the client's name by noting the release has been prepared for such-and-such a client. A counselor-client identification block would look like this:

John Peters and Associates
4654 Lawrence Avenue
Pittsburgh, PA 15222
Contact: Steve Charming
(412) 263-1102
After 5 p.m. 263-1506

For: The Pryramid Company
  Gateway Center
  Pittsburgh, PA 15222

- Release date information should be about an inch below the identification block, but on the right-hand side of the paper. This information is usually underlined.

If the material is to be used when received, it will contain notation to this effect. Common forms used are "For Immediate Release" and "For Release on Receipt."

If the material is to be used at or after a specific time, it should specify day of the week, the month, and the date. Do not include the year (since the year is obvious). Some common examples include: "For Release Thursday, October 21, or Thereafter;" "For Release PMs, Thursday, October 21, or Thereafter;" and "For Release 12 Noon, Thursday, October 21, or Thereafter."

If the release is directed to one publication, this information should be indicated in a line double-spaced directly under the release time line. An example:

For Release On Receipt

Exclusive To The Pittsburgh Post

The above notation means that the release has been sent only to the *Pittsburgh Post*. A variation of such notification is to indicate that the release is *"Exclusive In Your Circulation Area."* A third is to state that the release is being sent *"Special To The Pittsburgh Post,"* and the implicit understanding is that the release is not exclusively or only for the *Post* but that other papers in its circulation territory have not received the same release.

- The release proper should start about one-third down from the top of the page. It is advisable to try to leave about one-and-a-half to two inches between the release date information and the start of the release. This permits room for editorial notations or for small headlines that can be machine-set.

- The release itself should be double-spaced. Single spacing makes it difficult for the editor to make corrections or changes in copy.

- The word "more" should be placed in brackets at the bottom of the page if the release is to run more than a page.

- At the top of the second page, on the left, put an identifying slug-line followed by several dashes and the number 2.

- At the end of the release put a "30," centered immediately after the last sentence of the release.

- For filing purposes, a file number and the date the release is sent out should be carried at the bottom of the last page of the release. This date should include the month, day, and year and should run flush left.

Headlines?

The use of headlines on releases is a matter of debate. Some organizations always run a headline with their releases, placing it in the white space between the release date information and the release proper. Those who use headlines argue that they provide editors with a quick summary of the most important aspects of the release. Further, they note, there's always the possibility that an editor may use the suggested headline and if this is done the publicist can score twice—both through the headline and through the release itself.

Others argue that there are so many different sizes and families of headline type it is impossible to come up with a headline that will fit the space specifications of all media to whom the release is sent. Editors will therefore have to edit out the headline, so why use it in the first place? Further, the nonusers contend, editors resent the use of headlines because they feel it's an unwarranted intrusion of editorial prerogatives.

If decision is made to use a headline, use capital letters, write two lines, and if possible flush left and flush right.

Datelines and Time

Because an editor may not have the time nor the inclination to check a possible time ambiguity in a release, it's important that the publicist be absolutely clear when he uses "today," "tomorrow," or "yesterday." For example, when a story states that it is "For Release On Receipt" and the lead mentions "today," what day is today?

One way to clear up the ambiguity is to put the date in brackets immediately after "today." This may not be the proper form usually utilized by the medium, but it is expected that editing will take care of form. Here's an example:

For Immediate Release

The Worthington Company revealed today [October 21] that it will build a new $12 million plant on a site ten miles outside Excelsior, Ohio.

Another way to clear up ambiguity is to use a dateline to lead off the first paragraph. An example of this form would read as follows:

For Immediate Release

Excelsior, Ohio, October 21—The Worthington Company revealed today that it will build a new $12 million plant on a site ten miles outside of this city.

Recognizing that the media place much store in timely news, publicists often use the fact of an announcement as the peg for timeliness. They do this by citing the news in the lead clause and having the announcement with its "today" appendage as the end of the lead sentence. The same item would then read as follows:

For Immediate Release

The Worthington Company will build a new $12 million plant on a site ten miles outside of Excelsior, Ohio, it was announced today [October 21] by President Jonas Worthington.

GETTING MAXIMUM COVERAGE

Thousands of press releases are sent out daily to the media in this country, but only a small percentage of them get into print or on the air. Securing maximum coverage for your organization calls for careful attention to details and attention to the special needs of the various media that make up the mass communications mix. This section focuses on the following key elements of this communication mix as it relates to maximizing publicity efforts:

- The Media Distribution System

- Don't Take the "A" Train, Take the Local

- Orchestrate When Possible

- The Press Conference

- Comes the Technological Revolution

The Media Distribution System

The media distribution system in the United States, which was discussed in the previous chapter in the section on channels, has an important bearing on the effectiveness of publicity output and efforts. Consider the following aspects of this system:

- The bulk of international, national, regional, and state news and feature material appearing in daily newspapers and on radio and television broadcasts is supplied by two major sources, the Associated Press and the United Press International. Additional sources are various syndicated services.

- News and features transmitted over the wires generally emanate from state bureaus, move on to regional distribution points, and finally to the national A wires. Editing occurs at each point in the distribution system, but for the most part the starting point for publicists is the state bureau(s).

- If you can make the A wire with your story or feature, you've reached virtually every daily newspaper, radio and television station in the country. One six-inch AP story, for example, might appear in more than 1,000 daily newspapers and be read by more than 40 million people.

- A few media have an importance far beyond their readership, listenership, and viewership. It was the *Washington Post*, for example, that first broke the Watergate story, and it was the *New York Times* that first ran the Pentagon Papers. Both papers are important because they're read by other editors and because they're also read by so-called opinion leaders and organizational executives. Although each of the three network evening news shows carries only twenty-two minutes of news and features, each relatively brief in nature, they're seen and heard by millions of Americans.

- News and feature assignment editors are often imitators rather than innovators. *Times* editors read the *Washington Post*, and vice versa. *Time* editors read *Newsweek* and vice versa. The AP runs a story on a new teenage craze, and suddenly dailies all over the country discover the same craze in their own communities. As noted earlier in this chapter, editors determine what is important, and this determination often occurs because some other editors have deemed it important.

- In every field, business, profession, and organization there exist specialized publications that may not be known to the general public but that are vitally important to those who read these publications. One story in such a publication may be worth hundreds of stories in the nontrade press.

It is mainly through experience that the publicist learns to work within the media distribution system of the country. The system seems simple, but it's complex because of the multiplicity of media and the media networks within which news and features are transmitted. These networks are both national and regional in scope, and on the very large individual media highly specialized functions exist. Thus, for example, one finds numerous departments and department heads on publications such as *Time* and *Newsweek*; on wire services such as the AP and UPI; on newspapers such as the *New York Times*, *Chicago Tribune*, and *Los Angeles Times;* on business magazines such as *Business Week*; and on the three network television news shows. Contacts become vital, but equally vital is knowledge about how the media operate. Today's contact becomes tomorrow's retiree, but knowledge about how the media operate transcends contact with personnel.

Don't Take the "A" Train, Take the Local

The "A" Train, immortalized in song by Duke Ellington, is an express that runs between 125th Street and 57th Street in Manhattan without an intermediate stop. It's a very fast subway ride, bypassing in a quick blur the many local stops between the two points on the line.

Taking the express is a very efficient way to get from 125th Street to 57th Street. It's an inefficient way to move publicity material from publicist to daily newspapers. Therefore, if you want to reach and interest editors of daily newspapers, don't take the "A" Train—take the local.

A crucial fact about media in America is that they are local rather than national. Most countries have national newspapers that circulate in the entire nation. There is no national daily newspaper in the United States. The closest we have to a national paper is the *Wall Street Journal*, but its focus is on business and financial news. (As a side point, this is one reason why business and financial organizations are pleased when their news is carried by the *Journal*. Because the *Journal* is printed and distributed throughout the entire country, it reaches a national business and financial public.)

The average daily newspaper in America carries four kinds of news: national, international, regional/state, and local. As already noted, this paper secures the first three kinds of stories from one or both of the wire services and from syndicates. Its local news comes from its own staff and from public relations and publicity sources. This same newspaper will generally carry as much local news as the other three kinds of news combined, and very often it will carry *more* local news than the other three combined.

The same situation exists among broadcast media. The average radio and television station receives its national, international, and regional/state news from the two wire services. Station personnel either read this news or else the station puts it on the air as broadcast by the networks or the audio services of the wire services. The local news results from the efforts of the station's own staff or comes in from public relations and publicity sources.

Local news means exactly what it says. It is local in nature and is considered of interest to readers or listeners because it concerns what's happened in their town, city, or area. It's usually the kind of news that would have little interest elsewhere because it is so local in nature, but it's one of the main reasons why people buy the local newspaper and read and listen to the local broadcast media.

That sounds simple, doesn't it? Yet thousands of press releases are mailed from public relations sources every day to the country's dailies and broadcast stations, and the great bulk of them are quickly discarded because of one major reason: they have no local interest. An occasional release will slip by because of its intrinsic human interest, and sometimes a release will be printed and put on the air because it fits an open slot and nothing else is available at the moment. For the most part, however, these nonlocalized releases are a waste of time, money, and talent.

Therefore, whenever possible, think local when you're dealing with the raw material of release matter. Ask this simple question: Is there anything about this material that would have local appeal to a particular medium? Ask another question: Is there any way I can shape the material so that it will have local appeal to a particular medium? Ask a third question: Is there any way I can underscore local appeal to certain media in a release that is otherwise general in nature? The answers, surprisingly enough, aren't difficult to come by.

Example 1

A national concern with many distribution centers throughout the country makes an announcement concerning one of its products. It sends a release from its headquarters in Chicago to all 1,762 dailies in the country. Very few get printed.

Another national concern with many distribution centers throughout the country makes an announcement concerning one of its products. It tailors a release so that attribution of the story is applied to the local manager at each distribution center. Most of the stories get printed in dailies serving the localities of the distribution centers.

Example 2

After an intensive national competition, a major educational foundation selects fifty high school seniors as winners of four-year college scholarships. It sends out a national release to all United States dailies summarizing the total amount of scholarship money granted and listing the names of the winners at the end of the release. Pickup by the newspapers is minimal.

The next year, following another competition and selection of winners, the foundation sends out another release. Instead of simply listing the names of the winners at the end of the release, the foundation appends a listing of winners arranged by states and localities and citing winners by name, age, and local address. A note to editors advises them of the appended list, and, where applicable, each name is circled whenever it matches a local newspaper printed in the winner's town or city. Pickup is excellent.

It's obvious that not all releases can be localized. It's just as obvious that many which aren't localized have the possibility of localization. The lesson is clear: think local, and you'll find your story used more often than you thought possible.

Orchestrate When Possible

Having your story carried by one medium is an achievement, but it's a more effective achievement if the story is carried by many media. Bringing about this desired result calls for careful orchestration of your basic release.

The key to orchestration is to recognize that different media have different deadlines and to work within these deadlines when transmitting your release. As an example, assume that your release is meant for use in a community that has an afternoon daily newspaper; a weekly newspaper that goes to press on Wednesday and is distributed on Friday; several radio stations; and a television station. If you want to give all media an even break, then you should peg your release for use on Friday, see that it gets to the weekly by Wednesday, the daily newspaper by Friday morning, and the radio and television stations before noon on Friday. Although the weekly will receive the story two days before the stated release time, the weekly won't use it until publication day (Friday). The afternoon daily will have to have the release Friday morning if it wants to get it into print that afternoon. The radio and television stations will be able to air the news by noon, but it is generally considered fair to give the broadcast media a few hours lead time over print media. (If a story is meant to be used by a morning newspaper, then it is considered fair to release it to broadcast media the evening before, either for their early or for their late evening newscasts.)

Orchestrating a release in the above manner should only be attempted when the release time is within the control of the publicist. It should not be attempted when you're dealing with a spot news event, because the event itself will determine release time. Thus, if you're handling an activity that takes place on a Tuesday, you can't very well set your release time for Friday simply because you're trying to get maximum coverage. An activity taking place on Tuesday should be released on Tuesday.

However, if you have the option of setting release time—such as occurs when you are making an announcement—you may as well make the announcement on a Friday as on a Tuesday if a Friday suits your orchestration plans. Or, as often happens, you can schedule the activity for Friday if you have the option of so doing.

The Press Conference

Every college professor has had to face that moment of truth when, in the midst of what he considers to be the lecture of the academic year, he looks closely at a student in the back row and sees sheer glaze. Professors teaching a course in public relations have learned to recognize the glaze as the Walter Mitty Look. It's the look that indicates clearly that the student is dreaming he's a public relations Walter Mitty orchestrating a stupendous press conference attended by hundreds of media representatives busily taking down every word of the student's client, the president of one of the country's largest companies.

Who can blame the student for dreaming about his moment of professional glory? A press conference is a much more exciting affair than is a classroom lecture. There's real satisfaction in bringing off a successful press conference after long hours of careful preparation and hard work, and the payoff in resultant media coverage can be eloquent tribute to the competence of the initiator. But for every successful press conference there's one that didn't quite succeed, and there's also the ultimate horror: the press conference that bombed. The difference between the successful and the unsuccessful press conference is usually found in one or more of the elements discussed below.

What's the Subject? Long before you hold a press conference, you have to decide whether you have a subject worthy of a conference. Your decision will be based on the answers to several crucial questions, and the most important of these is whether the media will be interested enough in your subject to attend the conference. For certain kinds of press conferences there's no problem judging probable media interest: a presidential press conference is a sure media draw. If the chairman of the board of a major corporation fires the chief operating officer and calls a press conference to announce and discuss it, that's another sure media draw. If your company plans to build a multimillion-dollar plant and calls a press conference to announce details, that's another sure media draw.

Those are easy. Assume, though, that your company is in Chicago and it calls a press conference to announce details about the promotion of ten middle management people. Or assume that you're in charge of sports publicity for a small college and you call a press conference to announce the hiring of a new varsity swim team coach. Or assume you're director of publications of a small midwestern tool company and you've brought your new president to New York City to introduce him to the media at a press conference. Will the media show up in sufficient force at these conferences? Will it rain two weeks from Tuesday? What team will end the season in your conference with a .500 season average? No one can really supply the answers to these questions, and that's what makes long-range weather predictions, conference standing predictions, and press conference media coverage predictions a gambler's choice.

Your reputation as a practitioner requires that you be right more often than wrong when calling a press conference. Although you can never predict accurately the kind of media turnout for a conference, you can be more often right if you call a conference only when you're reasonably sure of success. Use the conference route sparingly—make reasonably certain that you've got a subject that will interest media reps.

Choose Your Site and Time Carefully. Selection of a press conference site is dependent on many variables, but the most important consideration is convenience. The site should be one that is most convenient to the bulk of invitees. In a large city, this usually means a downtown location. This could be a well-known dining establishment (which is usually glad to have its facilities used in the morning hours), a club, or a large hotel. In every large city, each of these establishments usually has the facilities and the experience in handling press conferences. If, on the other hand, you decide to hold the press conference at your own location, then you have to take care of transportation of the media to and from the conference site. When possible, bring the conference to the media, a technique that saves media time, trouble, and expense.

> Judging by the way they announce the acquisition of new baseball players, the New York Yankees have their own rules about site selection. The more they pay for a free-agent, the fancier the site selection.
>
> When the Yankees signed Luis Tiant they held the press conference in the press room, which is in the stadium basement. Rich Gossage and Tommy John, who cost the Yankees much more money than Tiant, were unveiled at conferences held in a suite on the club level at the stadium. The signing of Don Gullett and Reggie Jackson, whose compensations were among the highest in baseball, were announced in mid-Manhattan at the Americana Hotel.

The exact time for holding the press conference is the time that's most convenient to the media. Generally this means a midmorning, midweek conference. Some press conferences are tied to the lunch hour and therefore include lunch as part of the program. The midmorning conferences generally include light refreshments.

Take Care of Details. Veteran press conference sponsors often work from checklists of things-to-do, checklists that contain scores of items. Among the many details that have to be covered are the following:

- *Invitations* are usually sent out anywhere from one to two weeks before the conference. They should be brief, incite interest, be clear about details, and include a return card or envelope.

- A *telephone check* of invitees is usually made a day or two before the conference to serve as a reminder to those who have indicated attendance and to elicit attendance from those who have not responded.

- The *conference program* should be carefully designed so that the conference runs smoothly according to plan. Decision has to be made in advance regarding the person who will be running the conference; the people who will speak; what they will talk about; how long they will talk; and how questions will be handled.

  Provision has to be made in advance for the special needs of the various media. Television, in particular, has specific equipment needs, but at the same time television equipment proves bothersome to print media. One way to handle this problem is to provide for prearranged television interviewing in an adjoining room before the conference begins.

- *Press kits* should be prepared in advance, should include the kinds and amount of material most likely needed by the media covering the conference, and should be distributed to those who attend.

  At a minimum, the press kit should contain a basic press release summarizing the subject of the conference; some sidebar releases about ancillary features of the subject; photographs relating to the subject; and a basic data sheet relating to the subject if it is scientific or complex in nature. (Figure 10.2 shows two publicity photos.)

  Careful tab should be kept of those who do *not* attend the conference. When the conference ends, press kits should be transmitted to those who did not attend, and sometimes this calls for immediate delivery by messenger service. Kits should be mailed to others who don't need immediate service, but who may be likely to use the material.

- *Tabulating media pickup* calls for arrangements to be made in advance to record the amount and kind of coverage given by television, radio, and print media. There are organizations that monitor and report electronic coverage, and clipping services do the same for print media. A post-conference report should include a summary of media coverage and should include examples of coverage by television, radio, and the print media.

- A *post-mortem report* to yourself should provide details about what went right and what went wrong. Score one for your side if you had far more "rights" than "wrongs," and make sure you right the wrongs the next time you set up a press conference.

Comes the Technological Revolution

Of major significance for public relations practitioners has been the swift development of new methods of electronic printing and airing of news. By the end of the seventies, this electronic revolution was firmly established at major newspapers and television stations and it brought with it major consequences for publicists.

328

Publicity photos, with accompanying captions, show imaginative use of photography by the Carl Byoir organization on behalf of two clients: Detroit's Renaissance Center and the Borg-Warner Corporation. (Pictures and captions reproduced with permission of Carl Byoir & Associates.)

Figure 10.2

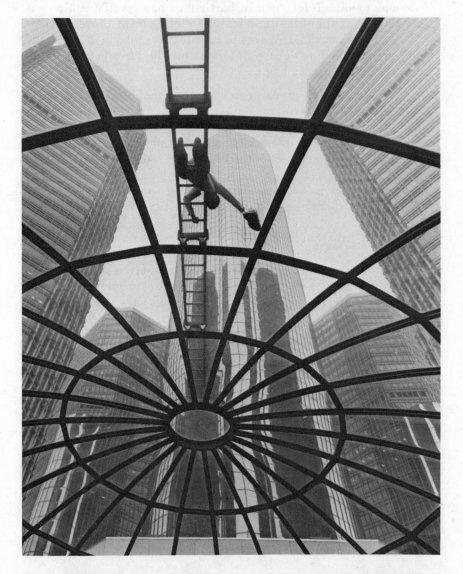

Towering Refractions of Renaissance Center shimmer through the dome of the Detroit Plaza Hotel swimming pool as a workman tackles part of the world's largest window washing job. The five towers contain nearly two million square feet of glass, three times the window area in the New York World Trade Center. The center, which opened last year on downtown Detroit's riverfront, consists of the 73-story hotel, four 39-story office towers and a four-level podium structure covering 14 acres.

Figure 10.2 (Cont.)

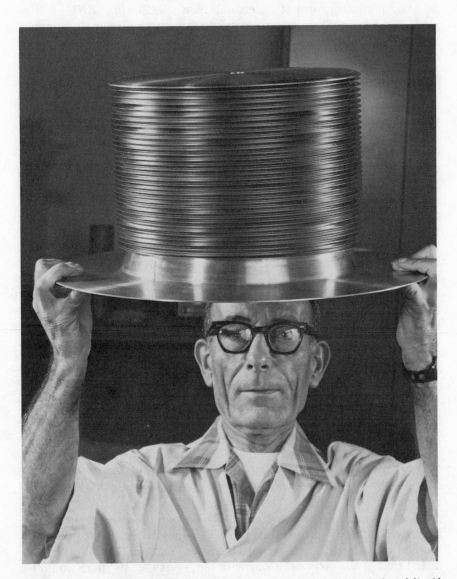

"ABE LINCOLN TOPPER" is a flexible metal bellows used on valves aboard liquid natural gas (LNG) tankers. Accordian-like construction is used to sense slight variations in line pressure and also to open and close valves. Flexible metal bellows are made in sizes ranging from 7/8 to 22 inches at the Mechanical Seal division plant of Borg-Warner Corporation in Temecula, Calif.

ENG (Electronic News Gathering). As previously noted in this chapter, television newscasts do not provide many opportunities for the use of material from public relations sources, and the main reason is the brevity of the newscasts and the individual items being aired. Even in those localities where television stations have developed hour-long and two-hour-long newscasts, there are limitations on the kind of news being broadcast and on the length of individual items. Thus, for the most part, the publicist finds himself concerned with television news mainly when it has some visual element, is of major importance, and is especially timely.

One significant change that took place at the end of the seventies was the increasing use of Electronic News Gathering (ENG) equipment, consisting of minicams and microwave transmission. In common use for many years by the national network news teams, ENG usage took firm hold at stations in the nation's largest markets. This means that ENG equipment could be found mainly in the biggest cities in the country—but, of course, that's where much of our population is centered and so it is why ENG is of interest to public relations practitioners.

Because conversion from film equipment and techniques for ENG equipment and techniques is a very costly proposition, it is not by any means certain that ENG will become standard equipment at local stations throughout the country. However, as costs come down, there's a good likelihood that ENG may become the prevalent mode of television news gathering and airing. What ENG certainly means for the practitioner of the eighties is that the television stations in our major markets and largest cities have the equipment, capability, and techniques for covering news swiftly, on-the-spot, and for putting it on the air immediately.

Thus, though the practitioner may not be able to do anything with ENG, he should certainly be aware of the implications that ENG can have when his organization becomes the focus of coverage by local stations or networks using ENG equipment.

> Assume, for example, that a major fire breaks out in your plant, or that a major disaster occurs at your installation. The local television station, using ENG equipment, can transmit pictures and narration directly from the scene and put the story on the air as it happens. You no longer have the "luxury" of time (as you now have when film is taken and has to be delivered back to the station for processing). If you have anything to contribute to the story, you had better be prepared to do it at the scene or else just forget about it.

In a *Special Report* in mid-1978, *Broadcasting* magazine predicted that ENG, despite its escalating cost, would become the prevalent method of collecting and airing the news. The publication also predicted that at the larger stations with longer newscasts there would be more coverage of those stories that are difficult to cover, including political and investigative stories. If such prediction becomes reality, the need for practitioners to react swiftly to all kinds of stories covered by ENG is obvious.

VDT, the computer, and the newspaper. VDT (Video Display Terminal) is to the newspaper what ENG is to the television station. Though the technological revolution came to newspapers later than it did to other elements of our national life, when it finally reached fruition it arrived with a bang. By the end of the seventies newspaper after newspaper—and not merely in the major cities—had discarded the typewriter and the linotype machine and replaced them with video display terminals and the computer. The all-electronic newspaper had finally arrived, and it has wrought a major change in the way newspapers handle the writing and printing of the news.

In the all-electronic newsroom *paper* is an anachronism. Reporters still use a keyboard to type their stories, but instead of appearing on paper the stories appear on a video screen connected to the electronic keyboard. When completed, the stories are fed into a computer after they are edited by editors who "call up" the stories on their VDTs. Wire service copy, processed at the rate of 1,200 words a minute in 1979, is also fed into the computer because it is compatible with—and hence a part of—the all-electronic system.

What does this mean for the publicist? Simply that all stories except wire service or public relations wire copy have to being typed by reporters and fed into the system via the VDTs. On nonelectronic newspapers a well-written, properly angled news release needs but some brief editing before being sent through pneumatic tube to the composing room. Because all copy on the electronic newspaper needs to be retyped on a VDT, the likelihood is greater that it will either be rewritten, drastically reduced, or not used at all. The electronic newsroom therefore poses a real challenge to the competency of the practitioner. Copy has to be very tight, well written, and to the point. Only the very best material is likely to get through the electronic screen and the reporter's natural aversion to being a typist merely copying someone else's material.

The public relations wire services. Helping to meet the challenge of the all-electronic newsroom are the press relations wire services. These wire networks transmit press release information over their own private line circuits directly into the newsrooms of major print and broadcast media. Cost of the service is borne by the clients of the service, who usually pay a membership fee plus a charge for each release transmitted. The services act essentially as middlemen between the sponsors of releases and the media to whom they are sent. Their basic value to the practitioner is that they transmit releases swiftly, simultaneously, and directly to the media after editing for news style, attribution, and accuracy.

The original public relations wire service is PR Newswire (PRN), now a subsidiary of Western Union, which went operational in 1954. Other public relations wire services, mostly local or regional in nature and coverage, are the Business Wire, San Francisco; PR News Service, Chicago; Newswire Central, Minneapolis; Southeastern Press Relations Wire, Atlanta; Southwestern Press Relations Newswire, Dallas; and services in Detroit, Washington, and Philadelphia. Because it provides national and international coverage and is the major such service in the country, PR Newswire will be discussed in detail in this section.

In marking its twenty-fifth year of operation, PRN in 1979 initiated its "second generation" wire service and put into full operation a computer-based system geared to complete compatibility with the automated editorial newsrooms of America's print, broadcast, and wire service media. PRN's sophisticated computer system enables it to deliver copy at speeds up to 1,200 words per minute in upper- and lower-case using joint AP/UP copy style. This copy is transmitted directly to PRN's high-speed terminals at the media or into the media's own computers, which are linked to the media's automatic typesetting equipment. Just as do the AP and UPI, PR Newswire flashes news simultaneously to all (or any) points served by its system; generates copy indexes or "abstracts" for immediate retrieval and review by editors on teleprinters or VDTs at their desks; and stores, retrieves, changes, transmits, or repeats in seconds any copy issued over its system (see Figure 10.3).

Stories and releases moving on the PR Newswire reach 220 news points and leading financial institutions in more than 75 cities. A total of 60 of the news points are in the New York metropolitan area and in 30 of the largest newspapers in the country. An average of 125 releases is transmitted each day, and on some days the number reaches 300.

David Steinberg, president of PR Newswire, reported in 1979 that PRN serves more than 5,000 news sources. Hundreds of major corpora-

Figure 10.3

PR Newswire's editorial headquarters in New York City, where press releases are professionally handled for immediate processing and transmission over the service's nationwide press communications system.

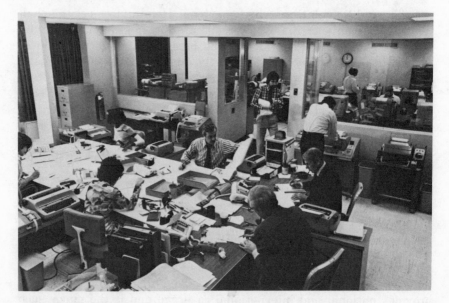

Courtesy of PR Newswire.

tions and public relations firms are frequent users of the service, releasing financial information, press conference notices, personnel change announcements, photo tips, obituaries, memos to editors, feature stories, and general news information to print and broadcast media, the wire services, and financial institutions. Seventy-five percent of the volume carried by PRN consists of business news, and the remainder is entertainment, travel, and other news and features.

"Immediate Release" financial news transmitted over PRN's *Basic News Line* is automatically issued 15 minutes later over the system's *Investors Research Wire*. By so doing, PRN thus carries financial news not only to the media—thus helping clients meet Security and Exchange Commission requirements—but also to the brokerage and investment community and to leading stock exchanges. Among nonpress points served by PR Newswire are the New York, American, and Pacific Stock Exchanges; banks; insurance companies; mutual, trust, and pension funds; brokers; and underwriters. Headquartered at 150 East 58th Street, New York, New York 10022, PR Newswire has offices in Boston, Los Angeles, Miami, and San Francisco.

INSTITUTIONAL AND ADVOCACY ADVERTISING

INSTITUTIONAL AND CORPORATE IMAGE ADVERTISING

Corporate use of advertising as a communication tool has been commonplace for several decades, and, as with most forms of communication, it has gone through distinct phases. For our purposes, it should be made clear that such advertising differs significantly from the usual product or service advertising. Instead of promoting or selling products and services, advertising used for public relations purposes aims to "sell" a corporation or a point of view. As with product advertising, this form of advertising can either be soft-sell, hard-sell, or neutral in tone and scope.

Such public relations advertising has been called by various names, and the names tend to indicate the phases in which they occurred. Most of the early public relations advertising was called *institutional* or *corporate image* advertising, and its aim was to build up the public image of the corporation, creating for it the image of a good citizen and institution in our society. By no means extinct, institutional advertising is still used as a means of communicating to the public the activities, growth, and strength of the corporation and to serve as a bridge between the corporation and its publics. Corporate image or institutional advertising is generally noncontroversial and nonargumentative. Some critics consider it a waste. As described by a scholarly observer, S. Prakash Sethi of the University of Texas, "institutional advertising is expensively and beautifully produced; is generally dull, bland, and self-serving; and is seldom taken seriously by anyone."

Perhaps a major reason institutional/corporate image advertising is not taken seriously is that its effects are so difficult to measure.

Particularly difficult to measure have been the various attempts to "sell" the free enterprise system and the virtues of American business and industry. At various times in our recent past American businessmen have launched campaigns to promote our economic system through institutional advertising. It has been felt that by proclaiming the virtues of the system, business can "educate" the American public to appreciate and better understand the system. Billions of dollars have been spent on such advertising, but there is little evidence that it has had much of an effect or that it has been needed. Commenting in the early fifties about the attempt to sell the free enterprise system through advertising, William H. Whyte, Jr., came to this conclusion: "The free enterprise campaign is psychologically unsound, it is abstract, it is defensive, and it is negative. Most important, in a great many of its aspects it represents a shocking lack of faith in the American people, and in some cases downright contempt." Of interest is the fact that Whyte's comments were made in an article in *Fortune,* a magazine sympathetic to business and to the American enterprise system.

Despite the criticisms leveled against it, institutional or corporate image advertising is still considered of value as a communication tool. Among major users are the large conglomerates that, since they have absorbed so many different corporate entities, feel it's important to establish in the public mind some understanding of what they represent. Under headings such as "Who We Are," these companies describe themselves and explain some of the diverse companies and subsidiaries that come under their corporate wing. A very large, diversified corporation could with justification find reason to believe it is important to run a series of corporate image advertisements, each carrying several paragraphs describing the parent corporation and the remaining paragraphs describing an individual offspring company. Properly packaged, an entire campaign can be reprinted and "merchandised" in numerous ways to specific publics.

In similar fashion, some very large universities in metropolitan centers have found it useful to use institutional or image advertising to describe the many individual components that make up the university. The same can be done for any organization or institution that is so large that it feels it necessary to demonstrate that it still cares about its employees, its customers, and other publics. (See Figure 10.4.)

ADVOCACY ADVERTISING

Although it is often considered synonymous with institutional advertising, *advocacy advertising* is significantly different from the older form of advertising and can be viewed as a separate means of corporate communication. Unlike most institutional or image advertising, advocacy advertising is usually argumentative, deals with controversial subjects, and is directed at either specific or general targets and opponents.

Advocacy advertising, says Sethi, presents facts and arguments that "project the sponsor in the most positive light and opponents'

Figure 10.4

A message from Nursing Home Professionals.

Don L. Brewer, President

Roger Lipitz, First Vice President

David E. Meillier, Treasurer

Fred Beene, Secretary

Health care abuses. Profit abuses. Bureaucratic fumblings. These and other attacks leveled at nursing homes have always appeared as front page news.

When these stories appear, we are just as outraged at the shame and the scandal. We abhor the tales of unsafe facilities, inadequate diets, patient neglect.

Perhaps, unwittingly, we have built a serious communications gap. A gap between what most critics believe to be the facts and what actually are the facts related to the nursing homes in our nation today.

Nursing home care is a relatively recent development in this country. From the early community-sponsored shelters that served as poor houses, the nursing home was born. Usually a small family-run home that planted the seeds for today's modern facility.

But as human life spans continued to increase, so did the problems of aging and the care for the aged and the chronically ill. So that by the early 1950's, the need to improve conditions and facilities was critical. A major growth took place, not only aided by public awareness, but by the private investment of billions of dollars for land, construction and qualified personnel.

Suddenly, the number of long-term facilities tripled from 6,500 to 25,000.

Suddenly, from 172,000 available beds in 1953, the number of beds became 1.2 million by 1973.

Today, there are 20,000,000 Americans aged 65 and over. But, as many as 600,000 need nursing care and can't get it. Because for all the growth, for all the improvements, the number of Americans needing professional health care has skyrocketed.

Where can these people go? As fast as new, modern, professionally staffed facilities are built, just as quickly the waiting lists multiply. Many remain residents of boarding houses, independent homes, some inadequate, too many unsafe.

The incidents that have stigmatized the entire health care industry are mainly focused on those homes.

But these stories mask the progress of the vast majority of AHCA members who provide a wholesome, enriching environment for their residents. We are constantly improving both the social and physical environment; we are working to build individual dignity to its highest level; we are recruiting more qualified full-time specialists, searching for methods to train and re-train doctors and nurses in geriatric care. The nursing home profession has outgrown the county poor farm. Certainly the story of progress in health care is just as valid as the story of abuse. Let's report them both.

ahca
American Health Care Association
1200 15th Street N.W. Washington D.C. 20005

Reprinted with permission

Theodore Carcich, Jr.
Immediate Past President

arguments in the worst." John E. O'Toole, president of Foote, Cone and Belding, sees two major forces—the system and the adversary culture—involved in an increasing number of issues. Advocacy advertising, he says, is a legitimate and appropriate way for the system—industries, businesses, and financial institutions—to counter the adversary culture, which he describes as "those in intellectual and academic pursuits, some political activists, and 'consumer interest' groups who seek basic changes in the system."

In brief, advocacy advertising is directed at an opponent—at times a specific opponent and at times an unspecified one—which is considered to be "the enemy." The target can be political activists, the media, competitors, consumer groups, or government agencies. As used by its sponsors, advocacy advertising has been utilized to "set the record straight"; to gain adherents; to counteract public disapproval of business; to stress the value of the free enterprise system; and to provide "facts" that counteract alleged bias in news reports or in the opposition's advocacy advertising.

One of the earliest examples of advocacy advertising—described in the mini-case at the end of this chapter—was the campaign devised and carried out several decades ago by the Byoir organization on behalf of the Great Atlantic and Pacific Tea Company when that company was faced with threatened antitrust action by the government. More recent users of advocacy advertising have been Mobil Oil, American Telephone and Telegraph, Exxon, General Motors, Allied Chemical, Union Carbide, the American Petroleum Institute, American Electric Power Company, and Texaco.

Illustrative of more recent advocacy advertising campaigns was the one mounted in the seventies by the American Electric Power Company against environmental groups, against the Environmental Protection Agency, and against other private and government groups. Another energy-centered example was Mobil's advocacy advertisement campaign, which was critical of the Federal Energy Administration, environmental groups, and other government agencies. Mobil has also taken on the media for alleged bias in newspaper and broadcast coverage of energy matters. Herbert Schmertz, Mobil vice-president responsible for the company's aggressive advocacy advertisement campaign, believes there's a good deal of unfair coverage of corporate activities and news by both print and broadcast media. Under his direction, the company has not been hesitant to tackle the media when it feels the media deserve it.

Although the preponderance of advocacy advertising campaigns aim their attacks at groups outside the corporate world, take-over and merger situations sometimes produce internecine advocacy advertisement warfare between two opposing corporate bodies. One such print battle was waged in late 1978 by United Technologies of Hartford, Connecticut, and the Carrier Corporation of Syracuse, New York, when the former made a tender offer to purchase the latter's stock and merge Carrier into UTC. Figure 10.5 is a reproduction of one of the full-page ads UTC ran in the Syracuse and other papers to present its case to the general public and to Carrier's stockholders.

Figure 10.5

The Proposed Merger:

Everyone Will Benefit

Ever since we proposed a merger of Carrier Corporation and United Technologies, concern has been expressed about the potential effects of such a merger on the Syracuse community.

Scare talk has been rampant. Fears have been raised about a drying up of jobs . . . about a loss of small businesses in Central New York dependent on Carrier . . . about a lessening of Carrier's role in the economic, civic, and cultural life of this community.

These fears are all groundless. There's no valid reason for concern. There is no justification for anxiety. United Technologies is a responsible, sensitive, sensible corporation. We will not act irresponsibly. We will not hurt Carrier, or its employees and their families, or the community.

We know how much Carrier means to this community. We want to contribute. We respect Carrier. We want to help strengthen it as a business enterprise, as an employer, as a supplier, and as a productive corporate citizen of Syracuse.

We've been operating in New York State since 1853. That's when our wholly owned subsidiary, Otis Elevator Company, was founded. Our newest affiliate, Ambac Industries, which joined us in July, is also headquartered in this state.

We already contribute to the economy of New York State. We'd like to play a larger part. We have about 2,500 employees in the state now. This year, we'll pay them more than $50 million in wages and salaries. We'll spend more than $1 million in New York state and local taxes. We'll buy more than $250 million worth of goods and services from New York businesses.

A merger with Carrier would be yet another step in the continuing expansion of our business operations in New York State. We believe a Carrier-United Technologies affiliation would be good for the state and its people, particularly in the Syracuse area. We believe a merger would benefit Carrier employees and their families.

We sincerely believe we can help bolster Carrier's business. This would bring expansion of Carrier's operations, increased job opportunities in its plants, and greater job security for its people. We reaffirm what we have already told Carrier's management in our invitation to negotiate a merger: We will protect the pension and other employee-benefit plans of its people.

Carrier is a superb company, with competent management. We want to keep its organization intact.

In a merged organization, we intend to have Carrier continue to operate under its present management at its present locations. Carrier headquarters would remain in Syracuse. And Carrier would continue to draw on this community for its employees. We will continue our historic emphasis on local management of our facilities . . . and our long-standing policy of hiring within the communities where our plants are located.

We're sorry about the unwarranted anxieties aroused a few days ago by a published prediction of the loss of some small companies in Central New York through what was alleged to be a planned shift of Carrier purchases to Connecticut under a so-called "centralized purchasing system."

We don't have a centralized purchasing system at United Technologies, and we have no plans to establish one. We're not going to disturb Carrier's existing supplier relationships. Each of our operating units makes its own purchasing decisions. That's how each subsidiary can really control its own profits. Each chooses its own suppliers. Carrier would do the same when merged with us. It would continue to buy from the same companies, large and small, with which it now does business.

Carrier is an exemplary corporate citizen of Syracuse. The company and its people contribute generously to the quality of life here.

Like Carrier in Central New York, United Technologies and its people in Connecticut take part in a broad range of community and civic activities. If the two companies are merged, we'll encourage Carrier to build on its fine record of corporate citizenship. So there is absolutely no justification for concern that there would be any weakening of Carrier's involvement and participation in community life as a result of the merger we have proposed.

Our philosophy at United Technologies is that the responsibilities of business go beyond the balance sheet; that a successful company must apply its resources, both human and financial, to community needs.

That's a philosophy we practice in our home state of Connecticut, where we give about $1.5 million a year in support of health, education, social welfare, recreation, and the arts. It's a philosophy that Carrier carries out so well in Syracuse.

We hope that we'll be allowed, through a merger, to expand our contributions to the economy of New York State and to participate, with Carrier, in the life of Syracuse. Everyone will benefit.

UNITED TECHNOLOGIES.

Pratt & Whitney Aircraft Group • Otis Group • Essex Group • Sikorsky Aircraft • Hamilton Standard
Power Systems Division • Norden Systems • Chemical Systems Division • United Technologies Research Center
United Technologies Corporation, Hartford, CT 06101.

This advertisement appeared in the Syracuse, New York POST-STANDARD and HERALD-JOURNAL on October 5 and 6, 1978, and the HERALD-AMERICAN-POST-STANDARD on October 8, 1978.

Reprinted with permission

Proponents of advocacy advertising contend that it has the following major advantages over other forms of communication:

1. Control of the message is in the hands of the sponsor.

2. Complex issues can best be handled within the context of an advertisement.

3. Messages can be directed to specific audiences.

4. An entire campaign can be best mounted through a series of advertisements.

Such arguments have a good deal of validity to them. Once a press release is distributed, for example, the sponsor loses control of its contents and its final appearance in print media or on the air. There is no way of knowing how much of the release will be used, when it will be used, and how it will be used. Because it is paid for, however, an advertisement appears as it is written. It can be scheduled for a specific time, and there is even the opportunity to schedule the place of its appearance. Mobil Oil, for example, contracted for placement of advocacy ads on the Op-Ed page of the *New York Times*, and that's where they've appeared every week because the company has been willing to pay for this preferred space. As of 1979, Mobil advocacy ads were also running weekly in the *Washington Post, Washington Star, Wall Street Journal, Boston Globe, Los Angeles Times,* and *Chicago Tribune*.

There is also no doubt that complex issues can best be handled within the context of an advertisement, that messages can be directed to specific audiences by means of advertising, and that an entire campaign can best be mounted through a series of advertisements. Thus, although advocacy advertising is costly, it certainly has built-in advantages for those willing to bear the cost.

On the other hand, there are also disadvantages to advocacy advertising. When a press release, for example, is processed through the media machinery, it tends to lose sponsor identification and is seen by the recipients as news rather than as a special pleading. Advocacy advertising, however, bears the sponsor's identification and is recognized as representing the point of view of the sponsor. Very often it is looked upon as corporation propaganda, and thus it bears the stigma associated with the term *propaganda*.

Advocacy advertising can also incur a backlash unless handled with extreme care. When the courtroom advocate presents his or her case, no one expects him or her to be *fair*, but rather to make the best possible presentation for the client. However, when the corporation presents its case through advocacy advertising, the reader expects a fair presentation; unfortunately, the reader does not always get one. If the reader perceives that she is being lied to or if she perceives that the corporation is dissembling, then that corporation loses the very credibility that is needed to make advertising effective.

When the target of advocacy advertising is one or more of the media, there is special need for the sponsoring corporation to be on solid ground in presenting its case. Responsible publications, for example, do not react lightly to charges that they are biased in their presentation of news. The corporation that charges the media with bias—as some corporations have done—should be able to document its charges and should certainly not be guilty in its presentation of the very kind of tampering with facts it claims for the media it is attacking. News personnel have long memories and many ways of retaliating. Those who challenge the media through unfair advocacy advertising may well find they win some battles, but end up losing the war.

One of the major "battles" won by advocacy advertising proponents was achieved on April 26, 1978, when the Supreme Court ruled by a 5-4 vote that a corporation has the right to speak out on public issues, regardless of whether such issues are germane to its business interests. The case—*First National Bank of Boston* v. *Bellotti*—dealt specifically with the right of a corporation to take sides on an upcoming referendum, but the ruling applied to other public issues and to the corporation's right to speak out about them. The major exception is that corporations are still barred from endorsing or opposing candidates for public office in their advertising.

The Bellotti ruling was a major decision, and should provide impetus for those who view advocacy advertising as an important corporate communications tool. As Mobil's Schmertz notes:

> In practical terms, the Supreme Court decision means that business managers who see some aspect of public policy leading to undesirable ends—for their company, for their state, or for the nation—have the legal right to comment on such policy, even if they seem to be out of step with the public at large. . . .

> The Supreme Court decision seems, at first glance, to open new vistas for corporate managers who believe their companies should participate in public debate whenever a matter of concern confronts the nation or the community. These vistas are real. At the same time, the court ruling seems to reaffirm and clarify a fragile right.

Though Sethi and Schmertz have often disagreed on aspects of advocacy advertising, they both recognize—as did the Supreme Court in the Bellotti ruling—inherent dangers in such advertising. A major danger relates to the point that corporations, because of their economic power and wealth, may dominate public debate on crucial societal issues.

"Through constant repetition," states Sethi, "a corporation is able to shape the minds of its publics regardless of the inherent accuracy or objectivity of the message. Advocacy advertising campaigns, therefore, when pursued over a period of time, can overwhelm the information mix received by the public."

Though not as concerned as Sethi about the ability of corporations to "overwhelm the information mix," Schmertz understands that "rights carry responsibilities, and the American legal tradition has never been very tolerant of those who use economic bulldozers to get their way." He warns against excesses in the following statement:

> All rights carry with them heavy responsibilities, and corporations should not take them lightly. The dividing line between First

Amendment rights and potential violation of corrupt practices acts can be razor thin. And while the letter of the law applies equally to obscure individuals and prominent corporations when such violations occur, such transgressions will cause far greater embarrassment to companies with a high profile. . . .

Inherent in Schmertz's remarks is the recognition that there is both a political and an economic base to advocacy advertising. An advocacy advertisement is a corporate statement to the world. As such, it is bound to be subject to careful scrutiny and to criticism. Though it advocates a point of view, it must be fair in fact and reasoning. Because it is often aimed at a hostile or indifferent audience, its message must be credible. Because it forms only a small part of the total impressions the public has of its sponsors, it must be compatible with company actions and policies. Sethi sums up these imperatives about advocacy advertising in the following statement:

"Unless corporate activities are congruent with the public image it wishes to promote," he says, "there will be a spate of other images about the corporation, carried through alternative communication forms, that will be incongruent with the image the corporation intended to develop through its institutional advertising program. Advocacy advertising can play a healthy role only if a company is making other efforts to bring its performance in line with public expectations."

Summed up, advocacy advertising—as with public relations—can only be effective if words and actions are synonymous and compatible with each other.

QUESTIONS AND PROBLEMS FOR DISCUSSION

1. What are some of the major complaints that business leaders have about media coverage of business activities and actions? Are they justified?

2. What are some of the major complaints that the media have about business leaders and their relationships with the media?

3. Explain the meaning of the following statement by Richard M. Detwiler: "The executive generally fails to understand that the news system is a relentless process of simplification and over-simplification."

4. What does the text mean when it states that there's a "forced marriage between public relations practitioners and the media"?

5. What does the text mean when it states that "the journalist and the practitioner cohabitate despite their differences"?

6. What are some actions the practitioner can take to "cultivate" media personnel?

7 .What are some things a practitioner can do in handling media telephonic inquiries that put him on the spot?

8. Cite some basic technical aspects of a proper press release.

9. Cite some arguments in favor of and against writing headlines on news releases.

10. Discuss some aspects of the media distribution system that are of importance for publicists.

11. What are some ways of "localizing" a news release?

12. Cite some of the major details that must be taken care of in a press conference.

13. Explain how Electronic News Gathering (ENG) and Video Display Terminals (VDTs) affect publicists.

14. What advantage does the PR Newswire provide publicists?

15. What are the chief differences between institutional or image advertising and advocacy advertising?

16. What are some of the major advantages and the major disadvantages of advocacy advertising?

17. In the *Saturday Review* of January 1, 1978, S. Prakash Sethi and Herbert Schmertz debate the merits of advocacy advertising. One member of the class should be assigned the role of Sethi and one the role of Schmertz. In a forthcoming class session the two should argue the merits of advocacy advertising as viewed by the two experts.

PROJECTS, ASSIGNMENTS, AND MINI-CASES

1. BYOIR AND THE A&P: A MINI-CASE

When the Great Atlantic and Pacific Tea Company (the A&P) was threatened by national legislation aimed at breaking up and divorcing the company's retail outlets from its manufacturing and distribution operations, the company turned to Carl Byoir & Associates, its public relations counsel, for assistance in meeting the governmental challenge. A wide variety of approaches were available to meet the threat to the company, but the Byoir organization decided to rely chiefly on institutional advertising.

With as much care as though they were writing a literary masterpiece, the Byoir people prepared a series of full-page institutional advertisements, each one aimed directly at the vast American public. The messages stated that government bureaucrats were trying to destroy "your" A&P; cited the A&P's long service to the buying public, and suggested that readers support the A&P by rallying to its support because to do so was in the public's interest. Cost of the advertising campaign, which ran to hundreds of thousands of dollars, was covered by replacing the usual A&P full-page product advertisements with the institutional advertisements every second week for a period of weeks. The end results were a series of endorsements of the A&P's position by a wide variety of national organizations, an outpouring of favorable letters from the general public, and the dropping of the threat to break up the company's manufacturing, distributing, and selling operations.

Whereas advertising and public relations practitioners at times find themselves in an internal organizational conflict, in the A&P antitrust case the division of responsibility was clearly established to avoid such conflict. The Byoir people, considered to be skilled in communicating institutional messages, were given responsibility for conceiving and writing the advertisements. Preparing the graphics and placement of the advertisements in the media became the responsibility of the advertising men.

Cited here in its entirety is the first full-page advertisement prepared by the Byoir organization for the A&P. The ad was carried in more than 1,000 daily newspapers across the United States in place of the usual full-page A&P product advertisement.

Analyze and discuss the advertisement in regard to its basic theme, tone, writing style, content, editorial approach, probable reader reaction, and overall public relations effectiveness.

2. MOBIL OIL TAKES ON THE NEW YORK TIMES: A MINI-CASE

This mini-case concerns a New York *Times* article and the reaction to it three weeks later by the Mobil Oil Corporation in an

Do You Want Your A&P Put Out Of Business?

Last Thursday in New York, the anti-trust lawyers from Washington filed a suit to put A&P out of business.

They asked the court to order us to get rid of most of our stores and also the manufacturing facilities which supply you with A&P coffee, Ann Page products, Jane Parker baked goods, and other quality items we produce.

This would mean higher food prices for you. It would mean less food on every dinner table and fewer dollars in every pay envelope.

It would mean the end of A&P as you know it.

This poses a basic question for the American people: Do they want to continue to enjoy lower prices and better living? Or do they want to break up A&P and pay higher prices, and have lower living standards?

What do *you* want?

Why Destroy A&P?

This suit was brought under the anti-trust laws. These are good laws. They were passed about fifty years ago to prevent any company, or any group of companies, from getting a monopoly in a field and then raising prices to the public.

A&P has never done any of these things.

> Nobody has ever shown that we have anything even approaching a monopoly of the food business anywhere. As every housewife knows, the retail grocery business is the most competitive in the country and we do only a small part of it.
>
> Nobody has ever said we charged too high prices — just the opposite. This whole attack rises out of the fact that we sell good food too cheap. We would not have had any of this trouble if, instead of lowering prices, we had raised them and pocketed the difference.
>
> Nobody has ever said that our profit rate was too high. During the past five years our net profit, after taxes, has averaged about 1¼¢ on every dollar of sales, which is less than almost any other business you can think of.

The American people have shown that they like our low-price policy by coming to our stores to do their shopping. If A&P is big, it is because the American people, by their patronage, have made it big.

Obviously, it is the theory of the anti-trust lawyers that the people have no right to patronize a company, if their patronage will make that company grow; and that any big business must be destroyed simply because it is big, and even if the public gets hurt in the process.

Do You Want Higher Prices?

There is much more involved in this case than the future of A&P. The entire American system of efficient, low-cost, low-profit distribution which we pioneered, will face destruction and the public will suffer.

A&P was the first chain store in this country. For more than ninety years we have tried to build a sound business on the simple formula the founder gave us: "Give the people the most good food you can for their money." Year after year we have tried to do a better job, make our business more efficient, and pass the savings on to the consumer in the form of lower prices.

Our efforts along these lines have led other grocers to keep their costs and profits down.

In the old days before A&P, food that cost the grocer 50¢ often sold as high as $1.00 at retail.

Today, food that costs the grocer 50¢ generally sells to the public at less than 60¢.

The methods we pioneered have been adopted not only by other grocers, but by merchants in other lines. There are today literally hundreds of chain stores, voluntary groups and individual merchants operating with the same methods and in the same pattern here under attack.

If the anti-trust lawyers succeed in destroying A&P, the way will be clear for the destruction of every other efficient large-scale distributor.

Who Will Be Hurt?

There has never been any question in our mind that it is good business and good citizenship to sell good food as cheaply as possible. As Fortune Magazine said about A&P some time ago, "It is firmly attached to the one great principle — the selling of more for less — that has made the desert bloom and the nation wax great."

> We sincerely believe that we have helped the American people eat better and live better.
>
> We believe that the hundreds of thousands of farmers and manufacturers who have voluntarily sought our business have profited by our fast, low-cost distribution of their products.
>
> We know that our 110,000 loyal employees enjoy today, as they always have, the highest wages, shortest hours and best working conditions generally prevailing in the retail food industry; and that these men and women have found in A&P good opportunities for security and progress.
>
> We know that thousands of businessmen — the landlords who rent us our stores, the haulers who operate our trucks, the people who supply us with goods and services — have a big stake in our operations.

Obviously, all these people will suffer if this company is put out of business.

What Shall We Do?

We admit that the interests of the owners of A&P are of little importance.

Frankly, they could make an enormous amount of money by breaking up A&P, as the anti-trust lawyers wish, and selling off the parts.

But is this what the American people want? Do they agree with the anti-trust lawyers that our food prices are too low, and that we should be put out of the picture so other grocers can charge more?

Frankly, if this were the case, we would not want to continue in business.

But we seriously doubt that this is the case. Twelve years ago, an effort was made to tax this company and other chain stores out of business. The public rallied to our support. They said they liked our quality foods and our low prices. As a result of their opposition, the tax was defeated.

Now we are faced with this new attack through the courts. We are faced with the heavy costs and all the trouble that lawsuits involve.

But we believe this attack is a threat to millions of consumers who rely on us for quality foods at low prices; to farmers who rely on us for fast, low-cost distribution of their products; and to our loyal employees.

We feel that it is our responsibility to all these people to defend, by every legitimate means, this company and the low-price policy on which it was built.

THE GREAT ATLANTIC & **A&P** **PACIFIC TEA COMPANY**

Reprinted with permission

advertisement by the company on the Op-Ed page of the *Times*. (The *Times* story is summarized below; students may prefer to check their library for the complete story.)

On Thursday, August 7, 1975, the New York *Times* carried a 23-paragraph story, with a Washington, August 6, dateline, written by David Burnham. The story was 26-column-inches in length and ran on an inside page under a three-column headline which read:

2,300 Scientists Petition U.S. To Cut
Construction of Nuclear Power Plants

"In a petition presented to the White House and Congress," the *Times* lead stated, "more than 2,300 scientists warned today that the dangers of nuclear power were so grave that the United States should make a 'drastic reduction' in the construction of new reactors.

"Calling for a major program of research on reactor safety, plutonium safeguards and nuclear waste disposal, the scientists said that 'the country must recognize that it now appears imprudent to move forward with a rapidly expanding nuclear power plant construction program.' "

Noting that the country has 55 operating reactors which generate about 7 to 5 percent of the nation's electricity, the story said that government planners hope there will be 830 reactors producing more than 50 percent of the country's electricity within 25 years. It pointed out that the petition was presented to the President and Congressional leaders on the 30th anniversary of the dropping of the atomic bomb on Hiroshima.

"The petition," stated the fifth paragraph of the article, "was presented by the Union of Concerned Scientists in the debate over the potential dangers of nuclear reactors as an electric power plant engineering concern—Ebasco Servics, Inc.—made public a national poll it had sponsored indicating that about two-thirds of those interviewed favored the building of more reactors."

The article quoted Dr. Henry Kendall, physics professor at M.I.T. and a founder of the Union of Concerned Scientists, as declaring the petition was significant because it destroyed the industry argument 'that no reputable scientists had doubts about the safety of reactors.'

"Among the 2,300 biologists, chemists, engineers, physicists and other scientists who signed the petition," the article noted, "were James Bryant Conant, the retired president of Harvard University; George D. Kistiakowsy, professor of chemistry, emeritus, and Victor Weisskopf, former chairman of the M.I.T. physics department, all of whom were intimately involved in the World War II effort to develop the nuclear bomb.

"Another signer was George Wald, professor of biology at Harvard and one of the nine Nobel laureates who endorsed the petition . . .

". . . To gain the signatures for its petition, the Union of Concerned Scientists sent the statement last June to 16,000 persons, most of whose names were drawn from the mailing lists of the Federation of American Scientists and the Bulletin of Atomic Scientists.

"Dr. Kendall said that the 2,300 scientists who responded represented about 20 percent of the 12,000 scientists and engineers on the two mailing lists. The physicist said this was a far better response than the 1 to 2 percent reply rate that he said mailing experts had told him to expect. The union itself has less than 100 members."

The petition, noted the article, said there are three major problems connected with the widespread use of nuclear power. The article went into detail about each of these three problems as cited in the petition. It then cited the scientists as calling for "a greatly enlarged national effort to conserve the use of energy and to develop techniques for using coal without polluting the atmosphere and for harnessing the energy of the sun, the wind, the tides and the heat of the earth's crust."

Paragraph 16 of Burnham's story stated that a public opinion survey taken last spring by the polling firm of Louis Harris and Associates showed that 63 percent of those interviewed in a nationwide survey favored the building of more nuclear power plants while 19 percent were opposed. (This is the survey sponsored by Ebasco.)

The remaining eight paragraphs of the story cited data from the survey by the Harris organization showing more people in favor of than opposed to speeding up construction of the Alaska oil pipeline; increasing efforts to produce oil shale in Western states; starting off-shore drilling for oil off the Atlantic, Pacific and Gulf coasts, and allowing more strip mining of coal.

Questions for Discussion

The Mobile Oil advertisement—reprinted on the following page—appeared on the Op-Ed page of the *New York Times* on August 28, 1975. After reading it, answer and discuss the following questions:

1. Do you feel the criticisms of the *Times* story cited in the Mobil advertisement are justified? In expressing your conclusions, cite specifics to prove your point of view.

2. What do you perceive to be Mobil's public relations objectives in writing and running the ad in the *Times*? What's your opinion of these objectives? Do you think the advertisement will achieve these objectives?

3. What's your personal opinion of the ad? Your professional opinion?

Assignment

Assume that you are public relations counsel to Mobil. A draft of the ad has been sent to you on August 14 with this notation: "Following is a draft of an ad we are thinking of running in the *Times* on August 28. We would appreciate your professional opinion of the ad and our intention to run it on the Op-Ed page."

Write a memorandum to the vice-president of public relations of Mobil, giving your reaction to the proposed ad and Mobil's intention to run it on the Op-Ed page on August 28.

The people speak.
But the message gets lost.

From time to time we have criticized Congress for its tardiness in enacting sound national energy policy. But how can our elected representatives know the facts needed for sound legislation when the energy information they see in the press gives a misleading impression of how Americans feel on this issue?

Consider, for example, *The New York Times* article on August 7 headlined, "2,300 Scientists Petition U.S. to Reduce Construction of Nuclear Power Plants."

The hasty reader gained the impression that a survey of the scientific community showed scientists solidly opposed to the new plants. No such thing. In reality, the 2,300 were those who indicated by mail their support of a position of the Union of Concerned Scientists. And they represented only about 20 percent of the 12,000 professionals polled.

Was this an impressive response, even so? Far from it, says Hugh Hoffman, who heads three opinion research organizations and is a recognized expert in the field. "If the petition's viewpoint were strongly held in the scientific community, a 60 percent return wouldn't have been surprising, given the fact that these were articulate, concerned individuals."

The Times did, in the same article, report a public opinion survey showing that 63 percent of the people <u>favor</u> building new atomic plants, while only 19 percent are opposed and 18 percent undecided. Among those living near existing nuclear plants, the same majority—63 percent— favor new A-plant construction.

But that survey, unfortunately, wasn't mentioned until the fifth paragraph and support-ing detail was relegated to the last part of th 23-paragraph story. *The Times* had "balanced the news. But had it, really? Many reader we suspect, never got that far down in th article.

We were sorry, too, that *The Times* did n cite—as the *Washington Post* did in its story the petition—another petition of scientists whic strongly <u>supported</u> A-plants. (Signers include 11 Nobel Prize laureates, six of them in physic the science most associated with nuclear deve opment.) In the *Post* article, a Nobel Prize lau reate was quoted as comparing opposition nuclear power to earlier-day opposition to th advent of airplanes and railroads.

We were disappointed, too, that *The Time* chose to overlook another recent poll, by Opinio Research Corporation, which found that 56 pe cent of a cross section of American enginee believe nuclear power should receive immediat priority. Sixty-three percent of this group fe present atomic-safety regulations are basicall adequate.

Why is an oil company worried about nuclea power? Obviously, because the atom can lift great deal of the burden from oil and gas. Bu also because this case clearly tells why Congres and other officials aren't getting their constitu ents' thinking about energy. Why the messag isn't getting through.

Isn't it time both sides of energy issues wer presented more objectively? So that everybod can understand what's really happening, and ho people really feel? So that the country can ge the facts needed to formulate a sound energ program? We think so.

RECOMMENDED READING

Louis Banks, "Taking on the Hostile Media," *Harvard Business Review*, March-April 1978.

Richard Detwiler, "The CEO and the Practitioners," *Across the Board*, May 1977 (New York: The Conference Board).

David W. Ewing, "The Corporation as Public Enemy No. 1," *Saturday Review*, January 1978.

David Finn, "Truth or Consequences," *Saturday Review*, January 1978.

"Industry Fights Back: The Debate over Advocacy Advertising," *Saturday Review*, January 1978 (S. Prakash Sethi and Herbert Schmertz debate the merits of advocacy advertising).

Kerryn King, "Corporations, Free Speech and the Public's Right to Know," *Public Relations Journal*, November 1978.

William A. Latshaw, "Target Group Research: New Tool for Advocacy Advertising," *Public Relations Journal*, November 1977.

"Local TV Journalism in 1978, Special Report," *Broadcasting*, August 28, 1978.

John E. O'Toole, "Advocacy Advertising Shows the Flag," *Public Relations Journal*, November 1975.

J. Poindexter, "The Great Industry-Media Debate," *Saturday Review*, July 10, 1976.

Joseph C. Quinlan, "Sixteen Ways to Stretch the Product Press Release Budget," *Public Relations Journal*, November 1977.

Bernard Rubin and Associates, *Big Business and the Mass Media*. Lexington, Mass.: D. C. Heath, 1977.

Herbert Schmertz, *Corporations and the First Amendment*. New York: American Management Association, 1978.

S. Prakash Sethi, *Advocacy Advertising and Large Corporations*. Lexington, Mass.: D. C. Heath, 1977.

————, "Alternative Viewpoints: Should Business Aid the Opposition?" *Public Relations Journal*, November 1978.

George Seldes, *The Big Business Press*. Secaucus, N.J.: Lyle Stuart, 1976.

Raymond Simon, *Publicity and Public Relations Worktext*, 4th ed. Columbus, Ohio: Grid Publishing, 1978.

John F. Steiner, "The Business Response to Public Distrust," *Business Horizons*, April 1977.

J. B. Strenski, "Tips for Better Press Briefings," *Public Relations Quarterly*, Fall 1976.

348

"The Techniques of Communication," chapters on publicity by Herbert Baus, Martin Cooper, Philip Lesly, and Jeanne Young in *Lesly's Public Relations Handbook,* 2nd ed., ed. Philip Lesly. Englewood Cliffs, N.J.: Prentice-Hall, 1978.

Richard Weiner, *Professional's Guide to Public Relations Services*, 3rd ed. New York: Richard Weiner, 1975.

_____, *Professional Guide to Publicity*, 2nd ed. New York: Richard Weiner, 1978.

11

Feedback: Reporting, Measurement, and Evaluation

In considering the communications model, feedback was described as a key factor in the source and receiver stages. Feedback as discussed in this chapter is the factor that closes the public relations process circle that began with public opinion and progressed through research, planning/programming, and communication. Composed of three parts—reporting, measurement, and evaluation—feedback has three major functions:

1. It tells management *what* has been achieved through public relations activities and actions.

2. It provides management with a quantitative means of *measuring* public relations achievements.

3. It provides management with a means of judging the *quality* of public relations achievements and activities.

As a general rule, most human and organizational activities and performance are subject to reporting, measurement, and evaluation. Salesmen send back weekly sales reports to the home office. Corporations mail quarterly and annual reports to their stockholders and hold annual meetings where reports are given. The president of the United States delivers an annual State of the Union message in which he reports to the Congress and to the entire country.

Competitive athletes and teams are measured by their ratio of wins to losses. Students are measured and evaluated by grades; professors by student evaluations; deans by presidents; and presidents by boards of trustees. Beginning in kindergarten and lasting throughout his or her entire working life, the individual is the subject of reporting, measurement, and evaluation via a wide variety of forms. Some are rigidly organized, some informal; some are quantitative, some qualitative; some are intuitive and personal; some are precise and impersonal.

The public relations field bears witness to the plethora and variety of forms used for reports, measurements, and evaluations, and this chapter will deal with them in orderly fashion. Because reporting is more prevalent than the other two, it will be discussed first.

REPORTING

Reports are the means whereby the practitioner details public relations activities, actions, and results achieved over a specified period of time. The report is another way of stating: this is what we have accomplished. It can be a series of brief statements; it can be pegged to previously stated goals and objectives (in which case it provides a form of measurement); and it can include work that remains to be done.

The report is an excellent way of stating accomplishment in quantitative terms. It can state, for example, how many releases were prepared and mailed out; sum up the column inches of copy resulting from use of the releases by the print media and the minutes of air time resulting from use of the releases by the electronic media; cite the circulation and audience of the media where the material appeared.

The report enables management to keep tabs on the public relations function and the people responsible for carrying out that function. It provides valuable input and serves to provide the intelligence data needed for managerial decisions relating to public relations activities. When presented regularly and in accordance with predetermined patterns, it enables comparisons to be made over a period of time.

On the other hand, the report is generally a poor way of stating accomplishment in qualitative terms. Reports seldom deal with the *quality* of the work accomplished or with the *results* of such accomplishment. To mention, for example, that a specific release was carried by the Associated Press or by the United Press International is one thing. To sum up the number of newspapers that actually printed the story is a more difficult matter, and to draw definite conclusions about the *impact* of such coverage is an almost impossible task.

For example, consider the following extracts from a monthly public relations report:

1. Gave two talks to Rotary and Kiwanis in _____.

2. Release on taurine eliminate carried by the _____ Gazette, the _____ Observer, and the _____ Daily Press.

3. Taurine eliminate brochure delivered by the printer and mailed to our A-B-C lists.

It's possible to add up the number of people who heard the talks, the circulation of the three papers which carried the taurine eliminate story, and the number of people who received the brochure. What *effect* the talks, news stories, and the brochures had is open to conjecture.

FORMS OF REPORTS

Reporting of public relations results is done both informally and formally.

INFORMAL REPORTING

A good share of the reporting of public relations activities is done through informal means, at irregular intervals, and as part of the normal operations of an organization. One should not assume, however, that informal reporting has little or no value. On the contrary, such reporting can be of more value than the formal type of reporting since it is carried out without much advance warning.

Large counseling firms with a sizable number of account executives operating under the supervision of a small number of executive vice presidents are frequent users of informal reporting. The author spent an entire working day sitting in the office of an executive of such a firm noting what transpired. A good share of that executive's day was spent going over the status of various accounts with the account executives responsible for activities on behalf of the clients. In effect, what the executive was doing was to touch base with the account men under his jurisdiction, asking questions about what had been done, what was being done, and what was planned for the future.

Similar informal reporting is also carried out in the public relations departments of organizations. Where the department is actually a single public relations person, he or she keeps in touch informally with the executive to whom he or she is responsible. Where the department is of some size, the head of the department follows the same procedure used by the counseling firm executive by touching base informally with those in the department who are responsible for various public relations activities.

Time—or the lack of time—is one of the main reasons executives rely on informal reporting as a means of checking on the work of those under them. Formal systems of reporting which require meetings and conferences take up sizable chunks of valuable time, both on the part of the executive and those reporting to him. An informal accounting takes no more time than is required for a short inter-office call or visit. The following comment made to the author by the head of a large public relations department emphasizes the problem of time:

> One reason for abandoning it (a formal audit) was that I have been too busy. . . . Now, as best I can, I follow what each staff member is doing, note areas of improvement, and from time to time broaden a discussion on a specific phase of work into a general review, with my criticisms and suggestions. A less formal approach, but more successful too.

FORMAL REPORTING

There are four major ways in which public relations results are formally reported: *memoranda and reports* provided at regular intervals; *plans board, group, and committee* meetings; *briefings and presentations;* and *year-end annual reports.*

Memoranda and Reports

Probably the most common form of reporting by formal means is through the use of memoranda and reports submitted at periodic intervals, and these can range from the simple to the elaborate. Depending on the circumstances, such memoranda and reports are provided weekly, semi-monthly, or monthly and portray a picture of account activity as described *by the person responsible for the activity*. (For this reason, one seldom finds failure writ large in said reports.)

The most common form of such reports is a simple listing of activities in the period covered by the report. No attempt is made to cite activities in order of importance, nor does the report state the degree of difficulty and time involved in carrying out the activity. A stark recital of factual reporting, the memorandum or report simply sets forth work accomplished, partly accomplished, and/or still to be put into motion. In most cases the report or memorandum is a single copy sent to a superior; where circumstances warrant it, copies are sent to others.

In counseling firms account executives often send a monthly activity report to the client with a copy to the executive vice-president supervising the account executive. In addition, counseling firms often require that account executives, particularly those handling several accounts, send reports to their superiors in the firm summarizing activity on all the accounts being handled.

An example of a bimonthly report delineating the activities of a one-person public relations office is that prepared by the director of community relations for the Psychiatric Institute of Washington, D.C. The report, in the form of a memorandum, follows:

MEMORANDUM

To: Allan Weissburg   **Date:** May 22

From: Benay Leff

Subject: Activity Report of the Community Relations Office for March and April

- Completed all production work on new PI nursing recruitment brochure—blue line recieved May 21; brochure will be ready approximately June 1.
- Arranged the following speaking engagements, radio and TV appearances:
- Jeanne Mitchler-Fiks spoke at Catholic University;
- National Town Meeting—WETA%FM radio—3 PI staff members;
- Dr. Fram on WRC-TV (Channel 4) news feature;
- Clare Foundraine on "Everywoman."
- Coordinated publicity and tours for Black Nurse Recruitment Day, Tuesday, March 4.
- Prepared and distributed letters notifying students' parents of Developmental School change to foundation status.

- Served as member of Afro-American Day Planning Committee; coordinated publicity and arranged for hostesses; wrote memoranda of appreciation to kitchen staff and hostesses.

- Served as member of the D.C. Mental Health Association Planning Committee for May 15 Annual Meeting Day; attended approximately six meetings; designed, prepared, and arranged for printing of advance promotional flyer and program and did other publicity work.

- Met with Tineke Haase, *Montgomery County Journal* reporter, to discuss PI programs and services for article to appear in the *Journal*.

- Met with Rev. Duke Lundeen to discuss Augustana Mental Health Center PR efforts and relationship to other PI services.

- Made initial contact with Dr. Elizabeth Schoenberg for appearance at April's Combined Clinical Conference.

- Met with the Park Manager of Glen Echo Park to discuss their programs for children and adults; explored potential relationships with PI's Personal Resource Center.

- Initiated new monthly coffee social in March; assumed responsibility for coordinating on regular basis.

- Met with Helen Burr, PI Gerontology Consultant, to plan and design Gerontological Consultation Service brochure.

- Met with Bart Kraff, Allan Weissburg, and Kaja Brent to discuss PR impact of PI admission policies.

- Designed and arranged for printing of the Admission's Office "Aftercare Planning Form."

- Met with representatives of Mailtech to compare costs and services with current bulk mailing fees incurred by PI.

- Arranged for reprinting of Children's Unit family information guide and for the printing of five PI staff members' business cards.

In addition to the aforementioned activities, the Community Relations staff maintained its publication of the BULLETIN, completed several questionnaires, responded to innumerable inquiries regarding PI's programs, attended regular staff meetings, and answered routine correspondence.

Reprinted with permission

It should be noted that the above report is a straightforward listing of activities and work accomplished by the director of community relations. The report does not group activities and work under appropriate headings, nor does it attempt to distinguish such work and activities by degree of relative importance and value. It does, however, demonstrate a wide-ranging scope of work and accomplishments, and it clearly shows that the director of community relations hasn't been sitting on her hands during the two-month period.

A variation of the report which contains a straight listing of activities is one which lists accomplishments under appropriate headings. In this way the report details work done with media, for example, or with community groups, executives, and the like. Another break-down commonly used groups activities under the title of projects. Another method is to cite predetermined objectives and match results to the objectives. (Such a method provides the means for a comparison between objectives and results and thus sets forth the raw materials for evaluation.)

Computers have been put to good use by practitioners to provide the data for the reporting of public relations results, though chiefly where a large amount of publicity is being generated. A common practice in the past, and one which is still relied upon today, is to take clippings as they come in from the clip services, paste them neatly in bound books or reproduce them in a variety of fancy print form, and send them along to management. At annual meetings of trade associations or large organizations there are often several large standing panels on which are pasted large amounts of press clippings. The obvious conclusion is that the public relations department or counseling firm has been busy and productive, the releases have resulted in loads of press clippings, and somewhere "out there" people have been influenced.

The computer has modernized this "bushel basket" method of measuring results, has channelized and systematized the reporting, and has made it possible to draw comparisons between periods and years. A good example of how this is done is shown by the way the computer is used by Armstrong Cork Company.

Product publicity output at the Armstrong Cork Company—described in the chapter on planning and programming—is closely aligned with marketing and communication objectives. Insofar as it is possible, product publicity disseminated by the company's Press Services Department contains specific "messages" aimed at target audiences to achieve agreed-upon communication objectives.

To keep track of Armstrong's press results, the department uses the services of PR Data Systems of Rowayton, Connecticut, which utilizes a computerized system of media reporting and analysis. Armstrong's Robert K. Marker describes the system as follows:

> The computers are programmed at the beginning of each year with our complete message list, organized by division, and then by the applicable communications objective. In other words, we tell the computer what we want to do that year, and it analyzes each piece of publicity that comes in from our clipping services to determine how well it met the objective for which it was intended.

> This analysis is done four times a year, always from published material which appeared during the previous quarter. . . . Shortly thereafter we receive an analysis which gives us an up-to-date reading on two things: Quantitative, we know from quarter to quarter just how we stand in relation to the previous year on total number of stories in print or on the airways; total column inches of print space or minutes of broadcast time logged to date; dollar value of the space or time if purchased as advertising; and the number of photographs published. We get this information for each division of the company, and the figures are totaled during the quarter to give us a picture of how the company's overall program is doing in relation to the comparable period a year ago.

Secondly, the PR Data reports tell us qualitatively how we're doing with respect to message delivery—in other words, what information is actually getting across to our target audience. Each clipping is analyzed to see what message it contains, and this tells us how well, and how thoroughly, we're pursuing the objectives we establish at the beginning of the year.

The information received from PR Data is used by Armstrong's Press Services Department to monitor the department's activities and also for internal reporting. The latter is done twice a year by means of summary reports prepared for each of the marketing divisions and for the office of the company president.

There is no doubt about the effectiveness of the computer in compiling publicity results and for comparison purposes with previous periods and years. However, pertinent questions can be raised about the *evaluation* of such results. Computer printouts showing the number of clips, column inches, and appearances in publications certainly do sum up where the stories appeared, how many were used, and how they were used. But they leave unanswered questions about *actual readership, impact,* and *effectiveness.*

Plans Board, Group, and Committee Meetings

Operating on the premise that several heads are better than one, many counseling firms and public relations departments—especially the larger ones—utilize plans board, group, and committee meetings for the purpose of reporting public relations activities. Such meetings serve other purposes—they are particularly valuable for exchanging ideas for programming—but one of their major purposes and the one discussed here is to bring all concerned up to date on what is happening.

In the majority of cases those attending report meetings will have a common interest or central administrative tie that binds them together. In attendance at any such meeting might be the operating heads of the various units that make up the central public relations department of a company, or the account executives who report to an executive vice-president in a counseling firm, or all professional staff members of a public relations departmental unit or of a service unit in a counseling firm.

Achieving full attendance at report meetings poses more problems for counseling firms than for internal public relations departments. Client demands take precedence over report meetings of counseling firms, and such demands often mean that the counseling staffer cannot attend a scheduled meeting because duty calls for him to be elsewhere. Obviously, serving the client is more important than reporting about the client.

Briefings and Presentations

Where there seems to be a felt need for formal reporting of public relations activities, counseling firms and internal departments rely on briefings and presentations. The chief public relations officer of Client X may request that the counseling firm make a presentation as part of an annual meeting or conference of the chief executives of the client organization. Where no counseling firm is involved, the public relations department may be called upon to brief the firm's chief executives or make a presentation about public relations activities.

Annual sessions of this kind are tightly organized affairs which deal with the most important facets of corporate and organizational life. Public relations is just one small part of the corporate entity and is usually given a proportionately small amount of the available time. Because they will be in the spotlight for a brief amount of time, public relations executives wisely prepare their presentations with great care. Knowing that an oral presentation may be quickly forgotten they use such devices as slides, large charts and graphs, transparencies, and film. In some instances a presentation has been made in the form of a specially commissioned film, although it's wise to keep in mind that there's such a thing as over-kill; money-conscious corporate executives may question whether a film showing the results of public relations activity is worth the expenditure of corporate monies for what is generally a one-shot showing. One way of forestalling or countering this criticism is to be prepared with a plan to use the film not only at the annual meeting or conference but subsequently at other suitable and appropriate affairs. Thus, in effect, the filmed presentation can be likened to a "premiere" with other showings scheduled later.

Year-end and Annual Reports

The annual report, which is often the responsibility of the public relations department, is basically the means by which the corporation sums up its financial affairs. Prepared in coordination with the financial department, the annual report consists of financial tables, charts, and descriptive material. In recent years the report has been expanded to include four-color printing and art work as well as brief reports about all activities of a company. Public relations, as an important staff function, sometimes reports its activities in the annual report along with those of other functional areas of the company.

Some public relations departments prepare and print their own individual annual report to sum up the year's activity. This is particularly true where the department is a large one engaged in a wide variety of tasks and assignments. As with the use of a specially-commissioned film presentation, one has to use judgment in deciding how much money to spend on a report showing the results of spending money for public relations activities.

INFORMAL AND FORMAL REPORTING SUMMED UP

As this section has demonstrated, there are numerous ways of reporting public relations activities and all of them serve the useful purpose of informing management what public relations personnel are doing. Compiling reports takes time, and it can be argued that time might be more usefully spent carrying out rather than reporting activities. However, the management that is ignorant of the activities of its public relations people and department may have little respect for the function. Reporting thus not merely serves to keep management informed but builds support for the function and the activities carried out by the practitioner responsible for the function.

MEASUREMENT AND EVALUATION

Methods used to demonstrate and/or prove the *effectiveness* of public relations personnel and activities are what is meant by measurement and evaluation. The difference between *reporting* public relations activities and results and *measuring* and *evaluating* public relations activities and results is qualitative rather than quantitative. One measures and evaluates to assess the quality and value of public relations counsel, actions and activities, and this inevitably means that some *standards* are being used in the process of measurement and evaluation. These standards may be implied or they may be stated in explicit terms. They may be set forth to stand on their own or they may be compared with others. Standards are yardsticks, and whether implied or explicit they form the means of judging effectiveness.

Having accepted the public relations function as a legitimate and valuable one, the managements of both profit and nonprofit organizations want to know the *value* accruing from public relations. Increasingly, public relations practitioners are being pressed by their managements to account in a meaningful way for the worth of their activities. This value-oriented view is emphasized in observations made by three communications veterans: James F. Tirone of the American Telephone and Telegraph Company; Marker of Armstrong Cork; and Burns W. Roper of the Roper research organization.

Tirone contends that public relations managers are ill-advised to claim that public relations is "different" and therefore can't be judged the same as other functions are judged.

"The corporation," says Tirone, "is better served, and I think so is our profession, when public relations deliberately attempts to fit itself into the standard procedures of the corporation by meeting the same tests of performance as other functions and other managers."

For this reason, Tirone adds, the Bell companies implemented various measurement systems in 1978.

"The Bell companies," he reports, "have started down the road of measurement, and the results already seem productive. We are not likely to turn back."

In telling the following story about his experience with management, Marker of Armstrong shows that other companies share the same view as the Bell companies:

I was asked by a marketing executive at Armstrong to inform him, as succinctly as possible, just what he was *getting* for what he was *spending* on PR. . . . I came prepared with a considerable volume of newspaper clippings, magazine features and case histories that we had produced in support of his product line that year.

I laid all this out in front of him, along with an impressive circulation summary, and watched intently as he scanned the headlines, photos and copy. . . . I could see he was impressed.

"I had no idea you fellows were generating all this press coverage for us," he said, looking appreciative. I leaned back in my chair, feeling confident that the day was won. And then it came, the question no one had ever asked before: "But what's all this *worth* to us?"

I stammered for a moment and said something to the effect that I thought the material spoke for itself. After all, this was highly coveted editorial space we were talking about, chock full of credibility and dripping with third-party endorsement. I said it would be difficult to attach a specific value to it.

He smiled. "My boy," he said, "I have to attach a value to *everything* in this operation, or else I'm not doing my job. Why don't you go back and write me a memo outlining clearly what this function does for us, and then we'll talk about your operating budget for next year."

Marker says he had a difficult time writing the requested memo because the public relations people felt they knew what they were doing but weren't taking the time to analyze it, to spell it out, and to report back to the people who were providing operating funds. The conversation, he reports, eventually led to the formalized system the Armstrong press department has been using for the past decade to set communication objectives, monitor activities, and measure and interpret results.

Roper, the third member of our trio of communications veterans who recognize the need to prove the value of public relations activities, explains management's views as follows:

There is a degree of skepticism on the part of managements who are users of public relations—even managements that employ large public relations departments of their own and outside public relations counsel as well. As a concept, modern management is aware of the value of public relations—or at least they are not sure enough that it is valueless to ignore public relations activities. At the same time, doubts are frequently voiced as to whether or not a particular public relations campaign is really working, as to whether or not the sponsoring organization is getting results.

This skepticism is natural, because public relations operates in the field of ideas, attitudes and men's minds. There are no laboratory tests that will measure whether a public relations campaign works or does not work. You can't put a campaign in a test tube. But management nevertheless wants concrete proof of the value of public relations, just as it wants concrete proof of its other activities.

How does management secure concrete proof of the value of activities other than public relations? In some cases, very easily; in other cases, the task is difficult. Almost all *line* areas of organizations—that is, those which are engaged in producing the product or service—are measured and evaluated against a set of standards. If the organization is one that manufactures and sells automobiles, the manufacturing department is measured and evaluated on the basis of the number, cost, and quality of the cars produced in a given period; in similar fashion, the sales department is measured and evaluated on the basis of the number of cars sold in a given period. Obviously, measuring the number and cost of cars produced is easier than measuring the quality of cars, but nonetheless number, cost, and quality are all measured and evaluated. If the number, cost, and quality do not measure up to predetermined quotas and standards, management takes action to bring about desired results. Processes and procedures may be changed; personnel may be shifted around, demoted or moved out.

But, say public relations practitioners, we are *staff* people who counsel, advise, and initiate actions and activities designed to assist the line and we can't be measured as easily as line people. True, but other staff functions are also measured and evaluated. The legal department, for example, takes cases to court and these are either won or lost. If the box score shows two cases won and ten cases lost, you can be sure that changes will be effected in the legal department. The financial department sets up tax shelters and systems of financial reporting, and if the box score shows that the Internal Revenue Service has disallowed ten and allowed two or that the Securities and Exchange Commission has successfully levied sizable fines, you can be sure that changes will be effected in the financial department.

There is validity to the argument that the activities and counsel of staff personnel can't be measured as easily as those of line personnel, and certainly public relations practitioners are also correct in claiming that their activities are more difficult to measure and evaluate than those of other staff functions. As Roper rightly points out, public relations operates along lines that are extremely difficult to measure and evaluate, and in addition public relations campaigns are not like laboratory experiments. One might very easily design and carry out two public relations campaigns along identical lines, but with dissimilar results because of circumstances beyond the control of the practitioner. It's with good reason that Roper, whose professional life has been devoted to survey research, concludes that "measuring public relations effectiveness with research techniques is only slightly easier than measuring a gaseous body with a rubber band."

Difficult as measurement and evaluation may be, nonetheless the attempt should be made whenever it's possible to do so. The function that can prove its effectiveness is the function that will be most valued by management. The function that can't be measured or evaluated is most likely to be cut back or dispensed with when there is a need to cut costs. For its own sake and also because measurement and evaluation are important elements in the dynamics of the process, public relations must make best use of the measurement and evaluative tools at its disposal. Such tools and methods are discussed, described, and analyzed in the sections that follow.

TOOLS AND METHODS OF MEASUREMENT AND EVALUATION

The tools and methods used in measuring and evaluating public relations counsel, actions, and activities range from the primitive to the sophisticated with various way stations in between these two extremes. In all cases where public relations is being evaluated certain value judgments are made, and these are made by people. Thus, the fact that a value judgment is based on a relatively primitive method—for example, a judgment made through personal observation rather than by means of a computer printout—does not imply that the evaluation or judgment is faulty. In the end, evaluation depends as much on the perception and wisdom of the judge as it does on the tools and methods available to him and used by him in forming judgments. For this reason, the listing of tools and methods described and discussed below are presented in no particular order of intrinsic value and importance.

PERSONAL OBSERVATION AND REACTION

Judgment of public relations performance based on personal observation and reaction by a superior is one of the most common, albeit primitive, methods used in evaluating public relations effectiveness. At all levels in all types of organizations public relations personnel and their performance are judged and evaluated by those to whom they report.

Kal Druck of Harshe-Rotman & Druck describes one level of evaluation as being *intuitive judgment*, and if we follow the dictionary definition of intuitive he means judgment made without the conscious use of reasoning. Thus, the public relations practitioner proposes an activity and management's intuitive response is "this is a good thing to do," or the practitioner takes actions and carries out an activity and management's response is "that was well done." Pinning one's professional hopes on such intuitive judgments entails a good deal of reliance on faith and charity, and where these cease to be forthcoming management's reaction could very well be "this is not a good thing to do," or "that was not well done."

Faith, hope, and charity being practiced more in the breach than in the observance these days, practitioners wisely provide their managements with tangible evidence of their performance and, as has already been noted, such evidence most often takes the form of reporting practices that have previously been discussed. Management, of course, can form its judgment by personally observing and reacting to *discernible* activity or results ensuing from public relations programming. Thus, if one aspect of the public relations program of an internationally known department store is the staging of an imaginative parade on Thanksgiving Day, the executives of that store need only observe that parade in progress to form some judgment about its effectiveness.

MATCHING OBJECTIVES AND RESULTS

As has been noted in the chapter dealing with planning and programming, public relations activity without a clearly designed purpose is not uncommon. Clearly, however, setting objectives is vital to successful programming. Even a generalized set of objectives is better than none at all, though objectives presented in *specific* terms are the most meaningful because they provide direction and also lend themselves to accurate measurement and evaluation.

When the specific terms set forth by objectives relate to actions, activities, or media coverage there is little problem in measuring and evaluating results. Thus, if a program's stated objective is to set up 1,000 "coffee houses" in order to increase the use and consumption of coffee by young people, it's not difficult to count the number of such houses established over a period of time and even to measure coffee consumption by those frequenting such establishments. If a program's stated objective is to write and place a series of feature stories about such coffee houses in at least 1,000 daily newspapers, reaching x number of people, it's not difficult to count and measure newspaper pick-up and circulation.

Much more difficult, however, is to set forth objectives in terms of specific attitudes and opinions changed or modified as a result of public relations programming. Here we are not dealing with actions or activities which are tangible things or objects, but rather with intangibles relating to points of view, frames of reference, mind-sets, and other aspects of attitude and opinion. Little wonder, then, that objectives relating to men's minds are not often couched in specific terms and not too often measured and evaluated when a program has ended and results are in.

If it's any consolation to public relations practitioners, their advertising brethren do not fare much better. Steuart Henderson Britt, nationally known professor of marketing and advertising, analyzed "proofs of success" for 135 campaigns by 40 advertising agencies and he concluded that almost none of the agencies really knew, or even could know, whether or not their campaigns were successful. Britt reported that 99 percent of the agencies did not state campaign objectives in quantifiable terms; most of the agencies did not prove or demonstrate the success of the campaigns that they themselves had publicly stated were successes. Concluded Britt:

Advertising of a product or service must prove its success as advertising by *setting specific objectives*. Such general statements of objectives as "introduce the product to the market," "raise sales," and "maintain brand share" are not objectives for advertising. Instead, they are the objectives of the entire marketing program. And even when considered as marketing goals, such statements still are too general and broad to be used to determine the extent of a plan's success or failure.

Advertising goals should indicate (1) what basic message is to be delivered, (2) to what audience, (3) with what intended effect, and (4) what specific criteria are going to be used to measure the success of the campaign.

When the advertising campaign is over, the advertiser can best judge the results by comparing them with the intended results, as expressed in the campaign objective. Only when he knows what he is intending to do can he know when and if he has accomplished it.

If we are dealing with a public relations campaign, we can justifiably substitute public relations for advertising in Britt's above-mentioned conclusion. And if we do we will find that items one and two relating to goals—indication of the message and audience—will usually be covered in public relations programming, but items three and four relating to *intended effect* and *criteria to be measured* will most often be noticeably absent.

The Team Approach

Communications researcher Harold Mendelsohn suggests that one way to achieve attitude and behavior modification through public information campaigns is to involve the evaluators (communications researchers) in the campaign. Mendelsohn rightly points out that public relations practitioners and the communications researchers live in different worlds. As an alternative, he proposes that teams of practitioners and researchers work together in the development of information campaigns that utilize research principles rather than work separately. Further, he advises, the teams can then evaluate the campaigns' effectiveness in terms of actual rather than assumed intent and effect. If this is done, says Mendelsohn, such public information campaigns will have a high potential for success provided:

1. The campaigns are based on the recognition that most of the target audience will either be only mildly or not at all interested in what is communicated.

2. The campaigns seek to achieve carefully delimited goals.

3. Specific target audiences are delineated according to their life-styles, value and belief systems, and personal and psychological attributes.

Mendelsohn cites as one example of his thesis a television safety program devised by the National Safety Council, the Communication Arts Center of the University of Denver, and the Columbia Broadcasting System. The target audience were so-called "bad drivers," and the aim was to reach three middle-range objectives: (1) to overcome public indifference to traffic hazards caused by bad driving; (2) to make bad drivers aware of their faults; and (3) to call attention to community social mechanisms designed to correct bad driving faults.

To implement the objectives a team of communications researchers, traffic safety experts, and television production personnel devised "The CBS National Driver's Test." A massive promotional campaign was instituted to attract a vast national audience to the program, which was subsequently aired just prior to a Memorial Day weekend. Both during the airing of the program and afterwards, evaluation research was carried out to determine the success of the program in meeting the specific objectives it had set up for itself.

Results? Approximately 30 million people watched the program. CBS received mail responses from 1.5 million viewers. Nearly 40 percent of the licensed drivers who participated in the broadcast test failed it, and 35,000 drivers enrolled in driver improvement programs nationwide following the telecast. States Mendelsohn:

> The lessons learned from this exercise suggest that innovative information-giving formats, abetted by strong prior promotion, can overcome preexisting so-called public apathy to a great degree. Second, it is clear that reasonable middle-range goals, narrowly defined and explicitly stated, are amenable to successful accomplishments.

Management By Objectives

Mendelsohn's formula of practitioner-researcher team efforts is one way to achieve successful campaign results and to evaluate their effectiveness. Another is through the technique of *management by objectives,* which was discussed when we considered public relations planning and programming. The process is basically a method whereby an executive and each major subordinate manager under the executive work out together the identification of common goals, clearly define the subordinate's major area of responsibility in terms of expected results, and then use these measures as guides for operating the unit and evaluating the work of the subordinate and the unit.

The important elements of the process are joint agreement between superior and subordinate about goals that are agreed upon in advance. At the end of a time period the subordinate's performance and that of his unit are reviewed and evaluated, usually by joint participation of superior and subordinate in the review and evaluation process. If necessary, during the specified time period adjustments are made and inappropriate goals are discarded. If there are gaps between goals and performance or results when the final mutual review is made, then steps are taken to ascertain what might be done to overcome the problems.

The major advantage of the management by objectives process is that it involves mutual commitment to goals and objectives, a clear charting of objectives, mutual review of results and evaluation. In effect, the process provides a map or chart to be followed in setting forth objectives, an order of priorities, and a method of review and evaluation. It can be used very effectively where objectives and activities to achieve them lend themselves to measurement and evauation; it's difficult—as it is under almost all other systems—to use the management by objectives chart process as a means of measuring and evaluating programs and activities expected to lead to changes in attitudes and opinions.

The system used at Howard Community College (HCC) in Columbia, Maryland, provides a good example of a Management by Objectives program. At HCC goals are established for the entire college
staff, and objectives for the college are set forth in terms of one-year
and five-year objectives. Each unit in the college—and this includes
the Office of Community Information—is then required to compile an
annual "MBO Performance Plan." This plan is reviewed by each unit's
appropriate supervisor and, as approved, it provides a tangible means
of evaluating and measuring the activities of the unit for the academic
year.

The accompanying chart (Figure 11.1) lists seven of twenty-six
specific activities advanced by the Director of Community Information
for approval by the unit's supervisor in one academic year. As noted,
the chart sets forth each activity, type of objective, plan of attack,
means of measuring or judging achievement, criteria for measuring
achievement, and degree of priority. Not included in the plan are such
routine objectives and activities as serving on committees and attending public meetings.

PUBLIC OPINION SURVEYS AND PANELS

Survey research in the form of public opinion surveys and survey
panels is a major method used in gathering empirical evidence to
measure and evaluate public relations performance.

Public opinion surveys are utilized in two ways: either by means of
a single survey taken at the end of a campaign or after a specified
period of time, or by means of a before-and-after set of surveys. In both
instances use is made of the survey techniques described in the chapter
on research techniques: objectives of the survey and the universe are
set forth; a random probability sample is drawn; a questionnaire is
designed and administered; data is collected, and a report is written
and delivered to management. The major objective of public opinion
surveys as used in evaluation is to ascertain measurable results
stemming from public relations performance and/or programs in
regard to people's knowledge, attitudes, and opinions. The single
survey makes no attempt to measure attitudes, opinions, and knowledge in advance of programming, but does so after the program has
been carried out for a period of time.

Company Y, a leading manufacturer of chemicals, has scores of
plants throughout the country. One such plant, the Zulch Plant, is
located on the banks of a heavily polluted river in the mid-West. In
the late 1960s and early 1970s pollution of this river became so bad
that citizens formed an anti-pollution committee that campaigned for
clean-up of the river. Media supported the drive with numerous
editorial campaigns, and one of the chief targets was the Zulch Plant.

Called in by the plant management to give counsel and advice and to
propose action was the central public relations department of Company Y. An independent outside agency was retained to conduct a
study of the river's pollution, and its results showed that the Zulch
Plant was but a minor contributor to the pollution. By means of

meetings with concerned citizens and opinion leaders, a press conference announcing the results of the study of the river's sources of pollution, and other measures the public relations department told the story which exculpated the Zulch Plant.

A public opinion survey conducted shortly thereafter showed that 88 percent of those surveyed considered the river to be dangerously polluted; 58 percent knew who were the main polluters; and 63 percent felt that the Zulch Plant went to much trouble and expense to avoid polluting the river. In almost all respects, the Zulch Plant was given high marks and considered in favorable terms by the respondents.

Thus, by the use of public opinion surveys the public relations department of Company Y was able to cite favorable survey results to measure the effectivenes of its campaign. Instead of merely reporting counsel given and action taken and then concluding that the program had been a success, the public relations department went directly to the public concerned, measured its knowledge and opinions, and cited results of the survey to prove effectiveness.

There is one single, but important flaw to the above illustration. Because no survey of public knowledge and opinion had been taken *before* the program was instituted it was impossible to show that the program had changed lack of knowledge to knowledge and/or had changed unfavorable attitudes and opinions to favorable ones.

Before-and-After Survey

The *before-and-after survey* technique is a means of correcting the flaw cited in the above-mentioned case. As its name implies, this technique consists of two public opinion surveys, one taken *before* a campaign or program has been instituted and one taken *after* it has run for a period of time or has been concluded. The technique thus enables the practitioner to show numerical and percentage changes in public knowledge, attitude, and opinion taking place before and after public relations action and activities had been instituted, thereby enabling the practitioner to cite more reliable effectiveness proof than could be cited by means of the single public opinion survey.

The before-and-after survey technique is not often used in actual practice for several reasons. For one thing, it is expensive. Most managements are unwilling to incur expensive obligations for the sake of measuring effectiveness, but would rather put their money into actual programming. Another reason is that public opinion surveying requires a special expertise not generally found in public relations departments or counseling firms. A third reason is that the circumstances about many public relations programs do not lend themselves to precise before-and-after measurement and evaluation because there are too many variables involved. A fourth reason is that when dealing with a large universe, those surveyed before and after will inevitably be different samples of the universe and even though these will be probability samples they are really different groups of people. A fifth and final reason is that before-and-after surveys could

Figure 11.1

MBO Performance Plan: Office of Public Information

Howard Community College, Columbia, Maryland

Specific Statement of Outcome	Type of Objective*	Plan of Attack (What actions will you take to get the planned results?)	How Will Achievement Be Measured or Judged?	Measures of Achievement (Criteria can include quality, quantity, cost, time, completeness, accuracy, currency)			Priority E-Essential I-Important D-Desirable
				Minimum	Average	Maximum	
Prepare and release news and feature articles to appropriate media to maintain a constant flow of information about HCC to the public.	R	A. Circulate "Newsfinder" forms monthly to encourage staff and faculty to identify news possibilities. B. Meet with faculty, staff and students to develop publicity for special programs. C. Write and distribute 3-4 releases per week. D. Suggest story ideas to editors and reporters. E. Arrange for photo coverage of significant college events.	The Community Information Office will maintain a clipping file and tabulate year-end results.	150 releases 500 published articles	175 releases 550 published articles	200 releases 500 published articles	E
Revise, update and maintain adequate supply of all brochures for instructional programs.	R	A. Meet with division chairmen to assess existing and new publication needs. B. Rewrite and/or edit content where needed. C. Supervise graphic design and production.	Publication of revised brochures by established deadlines; ratings of publications in student services and staff evaluations conducted by Office of Institutional Research.	Jan. 1980 revision date 2.5 rating	Dec. 1979 revision date 3.0 rating	Nov. 1979 revision date 3.5 rating	E
Publish college catalog to meet all legal requirements for document and to provide necessary information to students and accrediting institutions.	R	A. Develop schedule for production to be distributed to college deans for submission of revisions. B. Obtain bids and select printer. C. Create improved format.	Publication by specified date. Judged by student and staff Services Evaluation.	June 1 2.5 rating	May 1 3.0 rating	April 1 3.5 rating	E

Objective	Type	Activities	Measurement				Class
Update Speakers Bureau brochure and coordinate and promote usage by the community.	R	A. Develop form for staff to indicate interest in participating in Speakers Bureau. B. Publish revised brochure by April 1. C. Develop mailing list and distribute to community groups.	Publication by specified deadline for usage by community.	5 engagements annually	10 engagements annually	15 engagements annually	I
Serve as advisor to the student newspaper.	PS	A. Provide professional guidance to students on content, design and journalistic ideals. B. Assist editorial staff in dealing with management and fiscal issues. C. Attend regular meetings of college newspaper staff.	Attendance at meetings. Publication of predetermined number of issues.	70 percent attendance 11 issues annually	80 percent attendance 12 issues annually	90 percent attendance 13 issues annually	D
Develop program of sports information to increase coverage of HCC intercollegiate athletics.	PS	A. Will meet with athletic director to define needs for program literature and pres coverage. B. Will produce brochure on athletic program. C. Will distribute stories on sports events and athletes.	Production of articles on athletic programs and HCC's "Sports Stars".	60 percent coverage of inter-collegiate events 3 features	70 percent coverage of inter-collegiate events 5 features	80 percent coverage of inter-collegiate events 8 features	I
Recruit and supervise intern for community information.	PS-I	A. Contact area schools with journalism and/or public relations programs. B. Supervise intern	Recruitment of intern.		One intern per year	Two interns per year	D

R-Routine
P/S-Problem Solving
I-Innovative
P/G-Professional Growth

Reprinted with permission

be the "moment of truth" for the practitioner by revealing that his carefully prepared and executed campaign produced either no change in public opinion or a change along negative lines, and certainly no one relishes that prospect.

The Survey Panel

The *survey panel* is used in measuring public relations effectiveness because it doesn't have the disadvantages of the single public opinion survey or the large cross-section samples used in before-and-after surveys. The panel is a sample of the same people interviewed more than once over a period of time. It is usually much smaller than the samples used in general cross-section public opinion surveys. Care is taken to ensure that the panel remains constant when the group is used to measure knowledge, attitudes, and opinions before and after a campaign has been instituted. Because the panel is small, its use as a measuring device is far less expensive than the larger cross-section sample. When the panel remains relatively constant it's possible to secure realistic measurement of campaign results as they affect the same group of people.

On the other hand, the survey panel poses another set of problems. When the panel is small—and most are small when compared to the larger samples used in normal cross-section surveys—any diminution of panel members changes the basic nature of the sample used before the campaign and the sample surveyed after the campaign. When the survey sample is as large as that used in normal cross-section samples there is an inevitable mortality that occurs in any population over even a brief period of time. Second, the smaller the survey panel the more likely it will not be truly representative of the universe. Finally, because most panelists become aware that they are being used for measurement purposes they become unduly conscious of their role and thus cannot be considered typical of the universe from which they were drawn. Despite these drawbacks, the survey panel offers the practitioner a relatively inexpensive, reliable, and simple means of measuring program effectiveness when used properly and with awareness of its methodological pitfalls.

INTERNAL AND EXTERNAL AUDITS

The process of auditing, which is most commonly identified with the field of accounting, has been used increasingly in recent years in public relations. The accounting audit entails an examination of records and accounts to check their accuracy. The public relations audit is most often used not so much to check accuracy but to check and improve the effectiveness of programs.

The *internal audit* takes the form of evaluation by one's peers and/or superiors within a public relations department or within a public relations counseling firm. The focus is usually on three areas summed up by three questions: what have you been doing and with what results; what are your problems; and what do you plan to do?

Sometimes the internal audit is a one-on-one evaluation of a staffer by his or her superior, but most often it's an evaluation by a "team" or committee selected for the sole purpose of conducting the evaluation. When the evaluation is completed, the team or committee is disbanded. Departmental audit teams are generally made up of the public relations department head and two or three middle-level or section heads. An audit of the account executive within a counseling firm is generally handled by a team composed of an executive vice-president who does not directly supervise the account executive and two or three other account executives.

When a staffer or account executive is being audited, he or she is inevitably given advance notice and, in many cases, is requested to prepare an advance-audit memorandum summarizing account or program activity, problems, and future plans. This enables the audit team to focus on specifics and has the added advantage of pushing the auditee into self-analysis. The audit itself is most often informal in nature, provides the auditee with valuable inputs from colleagues and superiors, and gives the auditors insights into account activities and programs they knew little about prior to the audit.

There are certain practical and psychological negative aspects to internal audits. An audit takes time, and time is precious in departments and counseling firms. Within departments public relations staffers have their own functional problems and committee meetings to attend, and the same applies to counseling firm account executives and supervisors. Those whose perceptions and judgments are excellent for audit team purposes are usually using these perceptions and judgments to handle accounts and important departmental tasks, and hence they cannot be called upon too often for an audit. Obviously, this problem can be taken care of by spreading auditing assignments, but not in small departments or in small counseling firms.

The psychological barrier can be a serious one because relatively few creative people react with equanimity to criticism, and there is a tendency for an auditee to be defensive. Thus, the audit team must use a good deal of tact as well as judgment when an audit is being conducted.

The practical and psychological problems involved in internal public relations audits are summed up succinctly in the following excerpt of a letter sent to the author by the head of a large public relations department:

> There are two reasons why we abandoned the audit: I have been too busy, and the method was not successful—psychologically.
>
> Had I time, we could probably remedy the latter defect and resume the audit. The method was to sit down regularly with each section head and one of his staff peers for a discussion of his work. Objectives were re-examined, progress was discussed, and suggestion made for improvement. The difficulty with this procedure was that the co-auditor frequently did not have sufficient background for his task, and some section heads were defensive in their reaction. . . .

The author had the opportunity to spend several weeks one summer at Hill & Knowlton where account audits are conducted regularly within the firm. At H & K audit teams are called into being from within the organization, each team usually being unique and existing for the purpose of one audit. After the team has been selected, the account executive whose account is being audited prepares a memorandum describing the main aspects, objectives, plans, and programs of the account. Distribution of the memorandum is made to the team, following which the account executive and members of his staff (where there is a staff) meet with the team to discuss the items in the memorandum and to be critiqued by the auditors.

The author's interviews with various H & K people indicate that the audit brings out new ideas that can be put to valuable use. At the same time, those on the audit team gain from the process because they get insights about accounts unfamiliar to them. The chief executives of the firm do not sit in on audits, but they receive every audit correspondence and thus the system not only brings about an evaluation of program effectiveness but also provides better all-agency service to clients. A more or less typical H & K pre-audit memorandum is described in the case at the end of the chapter.

The External Audit

The *external audit* differs from the internal audit in one obvious, major way: it is conducted by those outside of the organization being audited. In some cases the organization may contract with an outside expert or a panel to come in and conduct a one or three-day audit of practices, procedures, and programs, and to make recommendations for improving effectiveness. More common, however, is the comprehensive audit service now being offered by an increasing number of public relations counseling firms.

In many respects the external audit is similar to the preliminary study undertaken by counseling firms when they first take on a new account. Through research, interviews, and analysis a thorough study is made of the organization's goals, publics, products and services, public relations objectives, short and long range plans, etc. The major difference between the preliminary study and the external audit is that in the former case the counseling firm usually carries out its analysis prior to establishing and carrying out a public relations program; in the latter case the analysis is usually made of an existing public relations program and is therefore an analysis and measure of the public relations effectiveness of the program. Most external audits go beyond measuring effectiveness and provide suggestions and/or a blueprint for future public relations activity. The audit is considered here chiefly as a tool for measuring public relations effectiveness.

The axiom that "you get what you pay for" applies to the external audit as well as to the purchase of most products and services. An audit may be completed in five or six weeks or it may take six months; it can deal with only one aspect of a public relations program or it can encompass the entire program; it can be carried out entirely by the counseling firm's own staff or the firm may call in national research organizations. Properly handled, the external audit is an effective means of practical research that provides management with another tool to measure public relations efforts.

QUESTIONS AND PROBLEMS FOR DISCUSSION

1. According to the author, *reporting* public relations activities and performance is more commonplace than measuring and evaluating activities and performance. Why do you think this is so?

2. In what ways is the report of public relations activities and performance of value to management?

3. Why is the report considered a "poor way of stating accomplishment in qualitative terms"?

4. The author says that lack of time is one of the main reasons why public relations executives rely on informal rather than formal reporting as a means of checking on the work of those under them. Is this a justifiable reason?

5. Cite and explain the essential nature of the three major forms of formal reporting used in public relations.

6. What are the major advantages and disadvantages of these forms of formal reporting?

7. According to the author, the computer is now being used to report publicity results, but it leaves unanswered questions about actual readership, impact, and effectiveness. Do you think the computer might well be used for these purposes? If the answer is yes, *how* do you think this might be done? If the answer is no, why do you think it can't be done?

8. To what extent do you consider management justified in asking for concrete proof of public relations effectiveness?

9. To what extent do you consider public relations practitioners justified in contending that such concrete proof is impossible to present?

10. Why may it be advantageous or disadvantageous for the practitioner to rely on the intuitive judgment of management in evaluating his or her performance?

11. What kind of problems can be anticipated when trying to match specific objectives with specific results?

12. What are the major reasons why before-and-after public opinion surveys are not used too often in public relations practice?

13. What are the main advantages and disadvantages about using the survey panel as a means of measuring public relations effectiveness?

14. What are the main advantages and drawbacks to the internal public relations audit? The external audit?

PROJECTS, ASSIGNMENTS, AND MINI-CASES

1. SOME REFLECTIONS ABOUT EVALUATION: A MINI-CASE

In its mid-sixties *EXECUTIVE REPORT*, "Inside Public Relations," Prentice-Hall quoted Charles Prout, at that time director of public affairs for Mead Johnson & Company, as stating:

> The great deficiency of public relations as it is practiced today is the lack of means of measuring the effectiveness of its efforts. . . . We are still forced to rely too much on subjective judgments—which are neither totally reliable for our own guidance nor readily communicable to others for their evaluation of our efforts.
>
> It is my belief that the public relations profession will reach full maturity and full productivity only when it devises adequate measurement techniques which can weigh costs against results in a meaningful balance sheet which both practitioners and management can read clearly.
>
> We deal in public attitudes rather than in things. We're concerned with the subtle question of what people believe. This involves two very basic problems from the standpoint of measurement: (1) What people believe is not as easily quantified as what they buy or how fast they can insert a rivet in the side of an assembly line component and (2) changing people's beliefs is a lengthy and delicate process which often is not defined with a clearly marked beginning and end.
>
> . . . The essential challenge here remains: How do we in public relations equate the value of these services with dollars and cents? How do we know for our own planning that 'X' dollars is a good investment in a particular public relations program, but 'Y' dollars is too much? And how do we let others know that same thing?

Questions for Discussion

1. What is your opinion about Prout's conclusions about "subjective judgment" as a means of measuring effectiveness?

2. Do you consider any of the methods for measuring and evaluating public relations effectiveness which have been described in this chapter as an answer to the need for the adequate measuring techniques mentioned in Prout's second paragraph?

3. Do you see any conflict between the ideas expressed in Prout's third and fourth paragraphs? If your answer is affirmative, explain the nature of the conflict. If your answer is no, explain why you think there is no conflict.

4. Assume that you are on Prout's staff and that he has advised you that his superior in the management structure of Mead Johnson &

Co. has posed to him the three questions cited in the last paragraph. Prout has asked you to send him a memorandum which suggests answers to the three questions. Write the memorandum.

2. ANNUAL REPORT OF THE AMERICAN TRUCKING ASSOCIATIONS: A MINI-CASE

The American Trucking Associations, Inc., the national organization of the trucking industry, is a federation of state trucking associations with a Washington, D.C., headquarters staff of several hundred employees headed by a president selected by the ATA's Executive Committee. Each year the ATA headquarters office prepares and publishes an Annual Report which summarizes activities for the year and is addressed primarily to the ATA Executive Committee composed of more than 100 trucking company executives. Following is the section of an ATA Annual Report describing the activities of the Public Relations Department:

> The energy shortage and the resultant strikes and slow-downs by independent truck owners and drivers multiplied the problems, as well as the opportunities, for the ATA Public Relations Department. . . .

> While the trucking industry, as represented by ATA, was not a participant in the strikes and slow-downs, nevertheless, the news media focused attention on ATA, resulting in more numerous contacts with press relations staff, as well as specialists throughout the organization. During the year the Press Relations Section of the Public Relations Department was brought up to its current authorized strength and developed the most active campaign of contacts with the media in the history of the department.

> This fully-staffed operation issued more than 400 news releases this past year and prepared many special articles and features, on request, for newspapers, magazines and industry publications.

> Special attention was given to furnishing material to state associations, including feature articles on driving safety and other topics for re-issuing from their own association headquarters.

> The press section also developed a special manual on improved press relations for the specific use of state trucking associations.

> As a special project, a 16-page industry background insert, run as an advertisement, and developed through the ATA Foundation and one of its members, was mailed with a letter from the press section to the editor of every daily newspaper in the United States. This mailing also offered the services of the press relations staff and precipitated requests for additional information on some of the topics covered in the 16-page insert.

> A special kit of material for the news media on National Transporta-

tion Week was prepared and distributed, with press relations members conducting the major part of the operation.

Other members of the Public Relations Department staff also participated in the promotion of National Transportation Week and a kit of promotional ideas as well as news releases, speeches and radio copy was provided to the trucking industry. Indications point to wide use of this material.

This project won for ATA a special award for its work in promoting National Transportation Week by Traffic Clubs International during its annual convention in September in Phoenix, Arizona.

The Driver of the Year program was a signal success. The Public Relations Department arranged for the Driver of the Year and his wife to be presented with his trophy . . . in ceremonies at the White House. This and other Driver of the Year activities received wide press coverage including nearly 10 minutes on the full NBC television network during the popular "Today" program. This nationwide exposure occurred at the height of the strike by independent drivers and did much to present the organized industry's position in a favorable setting, and to offset unfavorable publicity.

Cargo theft and hijacking also attracted PR interest. As the attention of government officials, the public and the news media to this problem increased, the Public Relations Department in cooperation with the Trucking Industry Committee on Theft and Hijacking (TICOTH)—in a project funded by a member of the ATA Foundation—produced two motion pictures dealing with cargo protection. One film, directed to trucking industry and law enforcement audiences only, had its premier this spring in Washington before an impressive audience of government and law enforcement officials, as well as the Washington press corps. A second film, designed for public audiences, shows what the industry is doing to reduce cargo theft, and the role the public can play in discouraging the selling and buying of stolen goods.

The Officer Pressley "Safety Circus," sponsored by ATA, completed a most successful year . . . and now has begun a tour of the Southeastern, Southern and Southwestern states for the current school year.

Mail received from state highway and safety officials, law enforcement officers, and educators, as well as the audiences of young people, proves the solid public relations benefit of this safety program. In addition, in every city and town, Safety Circus, Officer Pressley, and the trucking industry received much press attention as well as television and radio exposure which more than offsets the cost of operating such a project. Millions of young people have been taught their earliest lesson in safety through the courtesy of the American trucking industry and the various state associations which help sponsor the show.

The Public Relations Department gave increased emphasis to the ATA National Truck Roadeo—held this year in Minneapolis—and with good result. In addition, one of ATA's regular advertisements in *U.S. News & World Report* was devoted to the truck Roadeo winners and the industry's safety programs as a follow-thru to Roadeo activity.

More than 600 tape-recorded radio interviews and more than 100 TV news films were distributed from Minneapolis during the Roadeo. Also, some 50 "live" newscasts were made direct to radio stations via telephone circuits.

Photographs from the Roadeo were sent to newsrooms across the nation via wirephoto, while local working press and trade press covered the event from press facilities provided and set up by ATA. . . .

In the field of radio public service, ATA has continued to send sets of tape-recorded public-service messages to approximately 4,000 radio stations. A steady response from stations indicates good usage. Many stations notify ATA of the equivalent advertising value of these trucking industry messages.

As a follow-up to this activity, and as part of the Public Relations Department's expanded services to state trucking associations, the department has issued scripts for public service announcements to state associations for distribution on their own letterheads to stations within their state.

Motion pictures, available through the ATA Public Relations Department, play an important part as one of the public relations tools put to use on behalf of the trucking industry.

During the past year there were more than 1,500 film showings to a total audience of nearly 11 million. There were 619 telecasts of ATA-sponsored films, and 887 showings to special audiences as well as trucking industry groups.

The Public Relations Department also added a new service—the furnishing of "stock" artwork of trucks to trucking industry communicators, editors, and state associations. This new art service has been well received and will be continued and expanded.

Since the trucking industry is so dependent upon public understanding for its operations, advertising placed by ATA during the past year centered on the themes of safety and essentiality.

In its drive for increased productivity through weight or size increases, the industry has continually reminded influential segments of the public that it operates in a safe and efficient manner over the highways shared with motorists. The ATA advertising program has emphasized this vital factor.

By the end of the calendar year, ATA will have received some 35 million advertising exposures in the pages of *U.S. News & World Report, Newsweek* and *Atlantic* magazines. With a combined circulation of almost six million, these particular magazines were selected to carry our story after extensive evaluation to provide a national audience of business leaders and other individuals active in civic and community affairs—those vitally concerned with the transportation problems and needs of the nation. . . .

During the past year, a great amount of career literature was mailed out as a follow-up to career promotions carried out by members of the ATA Foundation.

Nearly 15,000 requests for a new career booklet were received and the majority of other requests to the Department were for vocational guidance materials. . . . More than one million publications were distributed . . . with more than 680,000 going to schools, for both students and teachers, and more than 387,000 going to the trucking industry and the general public. It is important to note that all of ATA's educational material is sent out only upon request.

There were in excess of 37,000 requests from teachers and 36,000 from students and young people. This included nearly 6,000 individual requests from boys who wanted information on the Boy Scout Merit Badge on trucking. There were another 7,000 requests from trucking companies.

One of the major objectives of ATA's public relations program has been to explain and demonstrate that trucks pay for the roads they use and are not subsidized.

The ATA truck tax signs help promote this concept. The truck tax sign project was reorganized and new signs were sold to carriers to place on the back of trailers. More than 10,000 such signs were distributed to motor fleets during the past year and the program will receive active promotion in the year ahead.

Telling the story of the American trucking industry to so many audiences on a continual basis, while at the same time responding to constant challenges, is fulfilling and rewarding for ATA's public relations professionals.

Reprinted with permission

Questions for Discussion

1. What's your opinion of the report format, tone, wording, and contents?

2. What does the report tell you about the work assigned, assumed and/or delegated to the Public Relations Department and carried out by its members?

3. Cite instances in the report whereby the Public Relations Department not merely reports but tries to provide a means of evaluating activities.

4. After citing the distribution of public-service messages to radio stations, the report states: "Many stations notify ATA of the equivalent advertising value of these trucking industry messages." What's your reaction to this statement?

5. As mentioned in the preface to the case, the report is distributed to the ATA Executive Committee. Would you also distribute the report to the media? Why or why not? Cite reasons for your decision.

3. A MANAGEMENT BY OBJECTIVES CHART: A MINI-CASE

There are a variety of forms which can be used in charting objectives, action plans, and results achieved by means of the management by objectives process. In applying the process to the public relations department, the United Way of the Greater Utica Area (Utica, N.Y.) set up the flow-chart on the following page to cover the first six-month period; as will be noted, "Results Achieved" and "Rating" have not yet been completed. (Note: a total of ten objectives were listed but only seven are cited here.)

Questions for Discussion

1. What is your opinion of the five-item flow chart devised by the Greater Utica Area United Way? Cite any problems you feel may occur in utilizing and implementing the chart.

2. What is your opinion about each of the seven objectives, the priority of objectives rating given to each, and the action plans devised to achieve the objectives?

3. Can you suggest any ways to modify or improve the chart? Justify your suggestions.

4. THE CINCINNATI UNITED NATIONS CAMPAIGN: A MINI-CASE

In a world of swift-moving change, what happened just yesterday seems to be ancient history. Therefore, the educational campaign conducted in Cincinnati in 1947 must seem like medieval history. Yet that campaign and the surveys associated with it remain a classic case of before-and-after measurement and evaluation. The case is classic chiefly because it has seldom been duplicated in the years since; therefore, it deserves our attention.

What was involved here was an information campaign designed to make Cincinnati residents better informed about the United Nations and world affairs. What makes the case of interest and importance to public relations students and practitioners is that sufficient funds were provided through a grant to carry out independent before-and-after surveys to determine the effectiveness of the six-month campaign. The "before" survey consisted of interviews in September with a random/probability sample of 745 persons; the "after" survey consisted of interviews in March with a random/probability sample of 758 persons, 592 of whom had been interviewed in September. (The last 20 percent of the original sample either refused to be interviewed a second time or could not be located.)

Between the two surveys a massive educational campaign was conducted in Cincinnati to make its residents more intelligently informed about world affairs and about the United Nations. A total of 14,000 children in the Weekday Church Schools held a World Community Day program; training courses were given to 150 leaders in the Cincinnati Council of Church Women; close to 13,000 people were

PR WORK PLAN

-1-

UNITED WAY OF THE GREATER UTICA AREA, INC. MANAGEMENT BY OBJECTIVE WORKSHEET

First six months

Objective	Priority of Objective	Action Plans To Achieve Objectives	Results Achieved	Rating
Produce Annual Report/Annual Meeting Program for Thursday, Feb. 6	1	Develop slide series and accompanying script to be narrated by _____. Presentation will double as the annual report and will include a review of significant activities. Other agenda items are recognition of retiring officers and directors and election of new officers. A list of all employee groups cited will also be prepared and distributed at the meeting.		
Prepare, mail United Way Communications Report and packet by Jan. 24	2	Write report, select materials to accompany it, package and mail.		
Publish Rainbowgram on at least an every-other month basis	1	Gather information, write, print, mail. Each issue will highlight a specific area of activity. For example, the Jan. Rainbowgram will feature an explanation of the United Way reorganization.		
Revise/update directory of Agency Services by April 1	2	Review current edition, determine where changes are needed, select printing process, publish. Include service statistics by employer.		
Develop and distribute an Editor's kit for all weeklies and all in-plant publications.	2	Prepare general news stories and photos relating to UW services, campaign, etc. Include repro artwork of UW logo and theme. Distribute kits to appropriate editors. Continually update media list adding in particular all union publications.		
Have Campaign brochure ready for printers by July 1	1	Create, design, write copy, take photographs, and deliver to printer.		
By June 1, recruit and organize manpower for both the Publicity and Campaign Activities subcommittees; and develop a written workplan for both groups	1	Work with Public Relations Chairman in selecting and asking local communication professionals to serve on the respective committees. Devise an outline of projects and action plans for each subcommittee, based on items recommended as priorities by the PR Director and PR Chairman. Submit workplan for appropriate committees for additional input and subsequent initiation.		

Priority of Objective:

1. Primary
2. Secondary
3. Least-important

Rating of Accomplishment:

4. Consistently exceeds job requirements
3. Fully satisfactory—meets all job requirements
2. Satisfactory-some improvement needed
1. Unsatisfactory

reached through programs on world understanding put on by the Parent-Teachers Association; UN literature was given to every school child; radio stations and newspapers aired and printed UN news and information during the entire six-month period; and a total of 60,000 pieces of literature were distributed, 2,800 clubs reached by speakers, and hundreds of documentary film presentations were made. The slogan, "Peace Begins with the United Nations, the United Nations Begins with You," was shown everywhere and repeated in every conceivable manner.

The effectiveness of this massive informational campaign was measured by the results obtained by the two surveys, and they showed relatively few changes in public knowledge and attitude. A total of 65 percent in September and 66 percent in March were of the opinion the United States should take an active part in world affairs rather than keep out of them; 76 percent in September and 73 percent in March were of the opinion that the United States should join with other nations to establish an international police force to maintain world peace. In September 30 percent could not tell the main purpose of the United Nations, and by March the number had dropped to 28 percent. In September 55 percent knew that one job of the UN was to see that all people get equal rights and 50 percent knew another UN job was to improve health conditions everywhere; by March the comparable figures were 60 percent and 55 percent respectively. By March people blamed or praised the UN for the very things they had blamed or praised it earlier and by virtually unchanged percentages.

Questions for Discussion

1. What is your opinion of the before-and-after design of the surveys as a means of measuring the campaign's effectiveness?

2. What is your reaction to the survey results? Can you cite reasons why there was so little change in public knowledge and opinion after such an extensive educational campaign?

3. After consulting appropriate sources to ascertain the nature of international and UN relationships between September-March, 1947, explain the connection you see between these relationships and the survey results.

4. What lessons do we learn from this case?

5. AN INTERNAL AUDIT MEMORANDUM: A MINI-EXAMPLE

Preparatory to an internal audit at Hill & Knowlton, the account executive responsible for Account X wrote and disseminated the following pre-audit review memorandum which was sent to those on the audit team:

Background

The client manufactures a wide variety of products which are sold through independent wholesalers. The account was relatively dormant until a new president was installed and the client switched from a fee-plus-staff time basis to a monthly minimum that provides a specific service for every dollar spent.

PR Objectives

H & K's main efforts are focused on getting maximum exposure in all media for those products and brand names of the client listed under Item A on the attached list. The company's internal p.r. staff also is helped to service routine financial news. The management and its public relations department were advised on strategy to fight off possible tender offers a few years ago. . . .

Problems

The overriding concern is to give the client satisfactory performance and results without pricing ourselves out of the market. Staff charges for creative talent are expensive compared to the salaries paid the internal publicity department which is located in a non-metropolitan area. Another complication is that H & K's system of hourly charges does not make it practical to assign a writer permanently to develop ideas and news outlets for the client's products. We do not specialize in the area represented by these products and the publicity department would need to gear up to placing articles in trade magazines important to the account.

A serious situation within the company is the lack of liaison between public relations and advertising and sales promotion. This impedes sales promotion from capitalizing on later publicity placements to dealer organizations.

The new president of the company has been avoiding interviews with financial and business publications until he has established, as he says, a track record, an obstacle which may be surmounted as he gains confidence in his position.

Recommendations

Since the client's internal public relations staff is fairly competent, H & K charges can be kept within reasonable bounds by feeding his people ideas which they can proceed to develop. Such suggestions can be given more impact by uncovering new outlets for product publicity unexplored by the client. We can also bring the client to the attention of influential groups and audiences he is not now reaching.

A fertile, untapped field for the client is the real estate section in local newspapers. The product publicity managers are greatly impressed by circulation figures tabulated and analyzed by PR Data. These figures, in turn, are presented enthusiastically to the Division managers who underwrite the public relations program. Anything that can be done to boost the circulation totals will fortify our position.

This suggestion can be expedited by getting two or three other H & K clients with related interests to participate in a monthly clip sheet directed to special editors and sections of newspapers. Done properly, the project would go far beyond a mat sheet beamed only to weeklies and small dailies.

The client's conservative approach to publicity must be changed by generating stories with popular appeal. Pollution is a subject that is in the news, and as the client's products effectively reduce pollution this can be brought to the public's attention in a variety of ways. Service features can be developed pointing up areas where use of the client's products can be most advantageous, and publicity can also be developed to demonstrate unusual product applications. TV can be exploited profitably by developing a traveling show for interview programs, with a company representative demonstrating the various ways in which client products are useful to the consumer.

Reprinted with permission of Hill & Knowlton

Questions for Discussion

1. What is your opinion of the tone, format, and contents of the above pre-audit memorandum?

2. What questions would you ask about the problems cited in the memo? At this point, without knowing the answers, what advice—if any—would you give to help solve the problems?

3. What is your opinion of the recommendations cited in the memorandum?

4. If you were on the audit team, what points in the memorandum would you want to explore further?

5. If you were the H & K executive to whom the writer of the memorandum reports, in what ways has the memorandum influenced your evaluation of the writer?

RECOMMENDED READING

John E. Bowes and Keith R. Stamm, "Evaluating Communication with Public Agencies," *Public Relations Review*, Summer 1975.

Steuart H. Britt, "Are So-Called Successful Advertising Campaigns Really Successful?" *Journal of Advertising Research* 9:2.

Glen M. Broom, "Coorientational Measurement of Public Issues," *Public Relations Review*, Winter 1977.

Robert O. Carlson, "The Role of Research in Public Relations," in *Lesly's Public Relations Handbook*, 2nd ed., ed. Philip Lesly, Englewood Cliffs, N.J.: Prentice-Hall, 1978.

Robert C. Grass, "Measuring the Effects of Corporate Advertising," *Public Relations Review*, Winter 1977.

Noel L. Griese, "Feedback: The Vital Link," *Public Relations Journal*, December 1977.

James E. Grunig, "Evaluating Employee Communications in a Research Operation," *Public Relations Review*, Winter 1977.

Donald W. Jugenheimer, "How to Evaluate Corporate Advertising," *Public Relations Journal*, November 1975.

Sidney Kraus and Dennis Davis, *The Effects of Mass Communication on Political Behavior*. University Park, Pa.: The Pennsylvania State University Press, 1976.

Otto Lerbinger, "Corporate Use of Research in Public Relations," *Public Relations Review*, Winter 1977.

————, "How Far Toward the Social Audit?" *Public Relations Review*, Summer 1975.

Robert K. Marker, "The Armstrong/PR Data Measurement System," *Public Relations Review*, Winter 1977.

"Measuring and Evaluating Public Relations Activities," an AMA Management Bulletin, American Management Association, 1968.

Harold Mendelsohn, "Some Reasons Why Information Campaigns Can Succeed," *Public Opinion Quarterly*, Spring 1973.

Wilbur Schramm and Donald F. Roberts, eds., *The Process and Effects of Mass Communication*, rev. ed. Urbana, Ill.: University of Illinois Press, 1971.

Keith R. Stamm, "Strategies for Evaluating Public Relations," *Public Relations Review*, Winter 1977.

Phillip J. Tichenor, George A. Donohue, and Clarence N. Olien, "Community Research and Evaluating Community Research," *Public Relations Review*, Winter 1977.

James F. Tirene, "Measuring the Bell System's Public Relations," *Public Relations Review*, Winter 1977.

Rene D. Zentner, "Measuring the Effectiveness of Corporate Advertising," *Public Relations Journal*, November 1978.

PART IV
PERSPECTIVES AND PROSPECTIVES

This final section and chapter deal primarily with views: the view of the veteran practitioner who looks inside himself and at his or her practices, and the view of the prospective public relations practitioner, currently a student, who would like to know what kind of education, abilities, and qualities are needed to enter and succeed in the field.

The view of the insider, the veteran, is colored by both practical and philosophical overtones and is focused on ethical and moral questions. As in every field, the veteran finds conflicts between personal values and organizational-societal values, and these are highlighted by considerations dealing with professionalism.

The view of the outsider seeking to become an insider is basically practical in nature. The outsider raises questions about the kind of education he or she should pursue and the kind of activities that will complement formal education. The outsider also questions ways in which to secure the all-important first-entry position and the type of work to be expected in that first job.

Whether viewed by the insider or the outsider, the issues raised in this chapter end ultimately in discussion of those ethical, moral, and practical questions and answers that are raised in every field and calling. They deserve careful attention, and it is hoped they achieve this attention on the part of those who use this text.

12

Personal, Professional, and Educational Considerations

In practicing a new craft, most practitioners are so busy establishing themselves and their field that they have little time for such seemingly philosophical matters as ethics, right and wrong, and professionalism. As a relatively new field of professional activity, public relations has followed the pattern of older, more established fields.

The concerns of public relations practitioners in the decades between World War I and the end of the Vietnam War were mostly of a practical nature. Their actions and activities were governed chiefly by concern about what was permissible, legal, possible, and accepted by the public. As they entered the eighties, public relations practitioners and their professional associations and societies showed increasing concern about the ethical aspects of their actions and their calling.

In so doing, the practitioners reflect a similar concern on the part of young people who are studying public relations in our colleges and universities and who hope to enter the field upon graduation. It is appropriate, therefore, to first examine in this last chapter the kinds of ethical and moral concerns that face the veteran practitioners today and are likely to face the neophyte tomorrow. Having done so, we will then turn our attention to topics considered of special interest to students: public relations education, the first job, and daily work routines.

PERSONAL ETHICS AND STANDARDS

Writing the final chapter of this book has not been an easy task. The subject of ethics is a very personal one, and the last thing in the world the author wants to do is to impose his standards on others.

However, the author knows from three decades of teaching public relations that many students have serious reservations about the public relations field because of ethical questions, and these questions deserve a full airing and should be faced squarely and honestly. It's the author's hope that the approach he has taken to the subject will allow for a free and open discussion.

To be meaningful, any discussion of ethics requires an understanding of the term itself. When we talk about ethics, we don't mean only acting within the requirements of the law. To obey the dictates of the law is necessary, but not sufficient, because ethical behavior and actions *transcend* the law. Furthermore, the law is impersonal and clear—or at least, relatively clear—whereas ethics is unclear, generally murky, and usually highly personal. This should be quickly evident as we come to grips with the term.

The dictionary definition serves as a reasonable guide when it describes professional ethics as *"conforming to professional standards of conduct."* Thus, when we talk about ethical behavior in public relations we mean responsible professional behavior as applied to both group standards and individual morals.

Frank Wylie, 1978 president of the Public Relations Society of America, adds another dimension to the professional standards concept when he says that ethics includes a *concern for others*. "The ethical person," he declares, "acts and communicates in ways which express a concern for others. Acting in a concerned manner is the first part of the job. The second part is communicating that action."

Admittedly, ethics by the dictionary definition seems to allow one's imagination almost full rein in galloping down the road towards a public relations Valhalla guided only by "professional standards of conduct" and a "concern for others." However, there *are* certain standards of conduct followed by public relations professionals, and it shouldn't be difficult to know when one's actions show a concern for others and when they are strictly hedonistic. One might, of course, deal with ethics by setting forth a detailed set of rules of acceptable behavior, but such an impossible task would be fore-doomed to failure. Therefore, although the boundaries of ethics set forth by the concepts of conformity to professional standards of conduct and concern for others are admittedly broad, hopefully they are sufficient to serve as a guide for meaningful dialogue within the areas that follow.

ETHICAL PROBLEMS EXIST IN ALL FIELDS

For a variety of reasons public relations students seem to need assurance that ethical dilemmas are not the unique province of public relations practitioners, and perhaps this is the place to provide such assurance.

In no field or profession is there a magical Land of Oz somewhere over the rainbow where its practitioners live the ethical pure life undisturbed by questions of right and wrong. Doctors, lawyers, Indian chiefs, dentists, jurists, and outright thieves, all face ethical dilemmas in which their personal ideas of right and wrong may clash with the practical demands of their working lives. In some fields and professions this clash is weak and in others strong, but it is nonetheless all-embracing, occurring wherever men and women practice their craft, profession, and calling.

To explore ways in which lay people could analyze the ethical problems they meet in their occupations, the Department of the Church and Economic Life of the National Council of Churches sponsored a project in which people in six different fields met over a period of time to discuss ethical decision-making in their areas. Here are some conclusions cited by observers who attended the meetings of four of the groups:

Bankers

After a year of monthly meetings it can be affirmed that bankers are profoundly concerned over the conflict between their business role and their personal ethical standards as derived from their roots in church and family training. Not a session of the group was without reference to this dilemma and in some of the sessions it received attention exceeding even the practical aspects of banking.

Building Contractors

There seemed to be a consensus that for them the responsible position was somewhere in between complete cynicism and ideal or absolute integrity. There was a frank recognition that so long as we continue to live in a world that is involved in corruption and sin it is not possible entirely to avoid participation in evil; if one intends to stay in the construction business then one must on occasion do things that violate one's own standard of ethics. At all costs the tension must be maintained between what one's standard of honesty and integrity demand and what is possible and necessary in a particular given situation.

Personnel Men (and Women)

There is a strong tendency within economic organizations to "translate" questions of ethics into questions of expediency. This tendency was apparent throughout the discussions. ... It should be emphasized that there is nothing wrong in itself with expediency. Every organization with a certain purpose (even a religious one) will have to think of what is expedient for this purpose and what is not. But expediency is not ethics. It should also be stressed that ethics need not always be in conflict with expediency. Reasonable men will always hope for a modus vivendi between the two. ...

Public Relations Practitioners

Ethical issues are no less complex in the public relations field than elsewhere. It is easy to speak in absolute terms about truth, for example, but there is no simple "rule of thumb" canon which will be universally helpful to a counselor involved in the day-to-day practice of his craft.

Thus bankers, building contractors, personnel men and women, and public relations practitioners face ethical problems of varying degrees of magnitude and frequency. If, as Spinoza notes, it is a comfort to the unhappy to have companions in misery, then the ethical purist might take comfort in knowing there are countless like him in fields other than public relations. The realist seeks ways in which he can best come to terms with the kinds of situations that may face him in life. This can best be achieved by first considering ethics from a personal point of view.

PERSONAL STANDARDS

Codes of ethics set forth certain standards that members of groups are expected to follow in their professional lives, yet ethical behavior still remains personal in the sense that every individual—whether consciously or unconsciously—is responsible for his own actions. John C. Merrill, a journalism professor, sums up the personal nature of ethics in the following words:

> Ethics is truly a personal matter, personal in the sense that it arises from a personal *concern* for one's conduct. It is also personal in the sense that one's conduct is self-directed and self-enforced; the person voluntarily follows a code of conduct because he feels it is the thing to do . . . It might be said that a person's ethics is: (1) personal, (2) directive or predictive, and (3) rational. It is personal in the sense discussed above; it is predictive in that it serves as a guide for conduct and indicates pretty well what one can be expected to do in a certain situation, and it is rational in that *reason* dictates its acceptance.

The idea of a personal ethical threshold has been advanced by various writers concerned about ethics, and the concept is worth serious consideration. David Finn applies the threshold concept to companies when he says that "each company has its own threshold of what it is comfortable in doing from an ethical standpoint." He further notes that each of us also has—or should have—our own individual threshold. As he puts it: ". . . Each of us has a breaking point beyond which we would not go because it would make us too uncomfortable, too conscience stricken. And this is our point of no compromise."

Finn also suggests that public relations when functioning well, acts as "the anvil against which management's moral problems can be hammered." However, this assumption presumes that: (1) public relations personnel have a set of ethical standards, (2) are willing to put them to the test when circumstances call for it, and (3) managements are receptive to ethical testing by their public relations subordinates.

There is certainly no unanimity among practitioners about Finn's moral anvil concept. John Cook, a Phoenix, Arizona, counselor contends that the corporate conscience role is both pretentious and illogical. In terming such a role a myth, Cook declares:

> . . . There is no more in the makeup, background, training or experience of the average PR practitioner to qualify him to establish or monitor morality than there is in the makeup, background,

training or experience of, for example, the engineering or sales vice president or the corporate legal counsel. Corporate social and moral responsibility is an expression of management policies and actions: PR isn't the corporate conscience, but the conveyor, interpreter and advocate of whatever conscience the corporation has . . .

Students may properly point out that they are not at the point of life when an ethical threshold has practical professional relevance, and certainly they are not now in a position to act as any kind of an anvil or conscience for hammering out managements' moral problems. However, the best time to develop an awareness of and sensitivity to ethical and moral dilemmas is when one has the option of open discussion without the need to worry about the hard realities of decision and actions. Thus, the student may start this process by debating this proposition: "With whose thesis—Finn's or Cook's—do you agree, and why?

TWO SPECIFIC AREAS OF PERSONAL CONCERN

The broad question of the practitioner's role vis-a-vis ethical and moral dilemmas can be narrowed by consideration of specific areas of personal concern.

ADVOCACY

The question of advocacy is a question of role, and it's succinctly phrased in these terms: To whom is the public relations practitioner responsible? There is virtual unanimous practitioner agreement that the primary responsibility of the practitioner is to employer or client. Admittedly, public relations practitioners are advocates.

However, just what is the extent of advocacy? To what degree is advocacy justified when the course of action that practitioners are supposed to advocate is contrary to personal convictions? And what should practitioners do when the course of action they are advocating is *not* in the public interest?

The dilemma that advocacy poses became apparent in the previously mentioned discussion among public relations practitioners who participated in the sessions sponsored by the National Council of Churches in the sixties. Here are some of the comments revealing the range of opinion about advocacy and personal convictions, and they provide appropriate raw material for student analysis and discussion:

"The professional public relations man's job is to serve as a mouthpiece for the client, regardless of his personal views."

"One should decline jobs that run counter to one's personal views."

"Ethical considerations are usually not so sharply drawn that a clean choice of staying vs. quitting is posed."

"I can work with clients holding opinions at variance with my own *as long* as these don't affect my particular task with the client. If they do it becomes an ethical issue."

"If you have done everything possible in an effort to change the client's opinion on a certain issue and you have been unsuccessful, there may come a point at which you *have* to get out."

The above comments related primarily to the conflict that results when advocacy clashes with personal beliefs. But advocacy, as already noted, can also clash with public interest. The problem here is more complicated. Everyone knows, or should know, what his or her personal beliefs are, but there is widespread disagreement about what constitutes the public interest (as noted in Chapter 3). There are very few instances where an action or activity will clearly be contrary to the interests of *all* people. The more common circumstance is one where the action or activity will be contrary to the interests of one group of people, but in the interests of another group of people. The practitioner, in effect, likens his role to that of the lawyer, and like the lawyer is an admitted special pleader for one side and not for both defense and plaintiff. However, actual situations turn his seemingly simple proposition into difficult questions, as noted below:

What should the practitioner do when it is clear that the cause, action, or activity he is supposed to advocate is absolutely contrary to the interests of the broad spectrum of the people and only in the interests of the narrow group he represents?

Is the "court of public opinion" the same as the "court of law" in that everyone and every organization is entitled to representation by an advocate?

What should the practitioner do when the cause, action, or organization he represents starts out to be in the public interest but then changes in ways that are not in the public interest?

Two previously cited practitioners—Cook and Wylie—summarize different views of advocacy in the following words, cited here for your analysis and reaction:

Cook: "PR should provide its specialized input as to how various publics are likely to respond to a potential policy, statement or action. *But the PR man has as much to do with morality as a lawyer does with justice; counsel's role is to represent and advocate.* And just as the responsibility for seeing that justice is done resides in the judge and jury, responsibility for corporate morality resides in the board of directors, top management, and, ultimately, the law of the land."

Wylie: "In public relations you serve as an advocate. If you are good at it, you are a dual-advocate: representing the public to your management, and the management to your public. I suggest . . . insist . . . that you should be extremely careful in your choice of clients and of the concepts which you advocate."

TRUTH AND CREDIBILITY

It is most common for moralists and theologians to deal with truth in absolute terms—thou shalt not lie; thou shalt not steal—and it is not difficult to agree with these admonitions about moral and ethical conduct and behavior. Virtually no one, in any field or profession, would disagree with such standards, and this includes public relations practitioners. However, the problems connected with the dissemination of truth—or falsehoods—do not generally concern outright lies and falsehoods, but rather with *degrees* of truths, the *setting or circumstance* in which communication exists, and the factor known as *credibility*.

Telling outright untruths, issuing false statements, and lying can be quickly taken care of by concluding that such actions are unethical, immoral, and unwise. Watergate and its subsequent massive cover-up is a perfect example of the precept that lies and falsehoods lead to jail sentences in courts of law and to universal public condemnation in the court of public opinion. Ironically, Watergate was attributed in part to the machinations of public relations personnel and practices when in reality the leading figures in the Watergate cover-up were lawyers, former advertising executives, and government leaders. Watergate is also a prime example proving a basic premise cited throughout this book: actions speak louder than words, and when actions are taken to insure private interests at the clear expense of the broader public interest, they will eventually backfire and be seen for what they are.

Thus, from both an ethical and practical point of view, it's unwise and wrong to lie, to communicate untruths and falsehoods. If your college's year-end budget shows a deficit, you don't report a surplus. If your social agency falls short of its fund-raising goal, you don't report the goal was reached. If your company recalls thousands of one of this year's models, you don't say no recall has been made.

But you are still an advocate and, as Wylie indicates, you may be a dual advocate. Often, within your own organization, you will find yourself arguing for dissemination of information when others will be arguing for silence. You will find yourself urging a course of action and frank communication that others may not want to take. You may win some of these internal arguments and you may lose some, but ultimately you will be the person who presents your organization's face to the outside world of publics.

In being an advocate, no one really expects you to tell only the whole truth and nothing but the whole truth because so very few people do this except under oath in a court of law. Even journalists, who look with jaundiced eye on public relations pronouncements and who are presumably dedicated to telling the whole truth, seldom, if ever, get at or reveal the whole truth. Although public relations practitioners should not tell outright lies and untruths, they do try to put their best foot forward. While reporting that your college has had a deficit, you may want to point out that it represents only one-tenth of one percent of the total budget and is the first deficit in the 100-year-old history of the institution. While reporting your agency fell short of its goal by $100,000, you may want to point out that your area has had the highest unemployment rate of the past ten years and that the total sum raised this year exceeded last year's sum by $50,000. While reporting that your company has recalled one of this year's models, you may want to point out that the full cost of such a recall is being borne by the company.

At all times, you should keep in mind that credibility is your stock in trade, takes years to build, can be lost in a moment, and once lost is hard to regain. You want to put your best foot forward, but there are times and circumstances when nothing positive can be said. You are not a miracle worker who can turn red into bright blue, a deficit into a surplus, and a Watergate cover-up into some minor burglary. As Wylie puts it: "The foundation of communication is credibility. If we wish to be heard, we must first be believable. We gain such public credibility by our actions, and secondly by our words."

SUMMATION

A summation of the various major ethical and moral considerations discussed in this section leads to the following conclusions:

1. Those who practice their craft in all fields and professions are faced at one time or another with ethical and moral dilemmas involving their personal convictions and beliefs.

2. In order to deal effectively and rationally with such dilemmas it seems wise for individuals to be aware of and sensitive to such conflicts and to have their own ethical thresholds.

3. Public relations practitioners have to be especially attuned to the need for ethical thresholds because they are advocates and are most often called upon to represent the face their organizations present to the outside world.

4. For most of their professional life public relations practitioners will be dealing with activities and actions in which there may be little concern or connection with ethical and moral values.

5. There are, however, certain "gray areas," as David Finn terms them, "in which one person feels comfortable about telling certain kinds of untruths or engaging in certain kinds of moderately deceitful practices, while another person feels entirely different about it . . ."

6. Therefore, to deal with these gray areas, it seems wise to be clear in our own minds about that point beyond which we are unwilling or unable to go and where we will not compromise.

7. Finally, keep constantly in mind that credibility underscores all effective communication. It is difficult to attain, more difficult to sustain, and once lost hard to regain.

PROFESSIONAL ETHICS AND CODES

The two-sided coin that passes for legal tender in the land of ethical standards bears the likeness of self on one side and represents the personal, self-imposed code of ethical behavior governing the individual. The other side of the same coin carries the imprimatur of the craft, field, or profession within which the individual operates and represents the impersonal, written, and unwritten codes governing those working in the craft, field, or profession. We have already examined the personal side of the ethical coin; it's time now to examine the back side of the same coin.

AN OVERVIEW

There has been considerable discussion over the years as to whether public relations is a profession, craft, calling, or trade. In the generally accepted sense of the term it's difficult to sustain the argument that public relations is a profession because it fails to meet all of the standards by which recognized professions—such as law and medicine—are judged. Both law and medicine, for example, require licensing preceded by specified education, examination, and experience, whereas anyone can enter the practice of public relations without meeting such prescribed standards.

On the other hand, public relations practitioners meet many of the other standards by which one judges whether a field is a profession. Education for public relations is now widespread; practitioners engage in a constant exchange of information by means of their journals, newsletters, institutes, and professional organizations; those in the field restrain their use of self-promotion; practitioners provide a good deal of service in the public welfare; and there is a serious concern with ethics and standards.

On balance, therefore, in weighing the pros and cons relative to the generally recognized hallmarks or professions, one would have to conclude that public relations is not a profession but that many of its practitioners are professional and that most of them follow and adhere to many of the benchmarks by which a profession is recognized by the public.

THE PRSA CODE

One of the benchmarks that denote a profession or professionalism is a written code of professional standards governing those within the field. The American Bar Association "Code of Professional Responsibility and Canons of Judicial Ethics" contains nine canons covering a lawyer's responsibilities and actions. A lawyer found guilty of misconduct can be dropped from ABA membership, and in addition a state appellate court can exercise final disciplinary authority by suspending a lawyer from the practice of law for a length of time and even disbar him or her.

Public relations practitioners are not licensed nor are their activities and practices under state control. Only 9,000 of the approximately 36,000 to 50,000 public relations practitioners are members of the Public Relations Society of America—the largest organization of public relations professionals—but the PRSA has a strong code of professional standards and rules of procedure for professional grievances very similar to the ABA.

The document that embodies ethical standards of behavior for PRSA members is the fourteen-point Code of Professional Standards for the Practice of Public Relations. The Society's first Code was adopted in 1954 and revised in 1959, 1963, and 1977. (The Code and official interpretations of various points in it are cited in their entirety in the Appendix.)

In revising the Code in 1977, the Society revised one provision and deleted another that had been questioned by the Federal Trade Commission on the grounds that they regulated prices (fees) and were in restraint of competition. The two provisions, applying mainly to counselor members of the Society, barred contingency fees and encroachment by one counselor on another's clients. They were worded as follows:

13. A member shall not propose to a prospective client or employer that the amount of his fee or other compensation be contingent on or measured by the achievement or specified results; nor shall he enter into any fee agreement to the same effect.

14. A member shall not encroach upon the professional employment of another member. Where there are two engagements, both must be assured that there is no conflict between them.

In its 1977 revision, the Society replaced the above-cited Article 13 with a new one that reads: "A member shall not guarantee the achievement of specified results beyond the member's direct control." The old Article 14, also cited above, was deleted entirely.

As with many codes, the fourteen-point PRSA Code contains some clauses that embody pious generalizations. Its basic strength is found in clauses that prohibit undisclosed or "false" fronts, the intentional dissemination of false or misleading information, practices that tend to corrupt the integrity of channels of communication or the processes of government, and the guarantee of the achievement of specified results beyond a member's direct control.

Point 6 of the Code, which prohibits a member from engaging in any practice that tends to corrupt the integrity of the channels of public communication or the processes of government, is particularly important. Its importance is found in the fact that it covers a key area of public relations practice in which there is a good deal of ambiguity. To clarify this ambiguity the Society provided the previously mentioned "official interpretation," spelling out in more detail the kind of practices, involving the mass media and government, that are prohibited. These include payment to secure preferential or guaranteed news or editorial coverage, undisclosed retainers to media employees to serve the private purposes of a member, vacation trips provided to media representatives where no news assignments are involved, and similar dubious arrangements between journalists and practitioners.

The fact that such specific prohibitions have been spelled out in some detail indicates that there have been instances of arrangements between media representatives and practitioners that involve unethical behavior, and also indicates that it takes two partners to dance the unethical tango. Thus, in every instance where a member might provide a vacation trip where no news assignment is involved there's a journalist willing to take that trip. The Society, of course, can control only the unethical behavior of its members, but journalists who criticize public relations practitioners might well consider that where there's a giver there's also a taker.

Enforcement machinery for the PRSA code is in the hands of ten district judicial panels with power to hear complaints relative to violations of the code. In 1962 the Society established a Grievance Board with responsibility for investigating instances where no individual complaint is made but where there are indications that the code may have been violated. James E. McKee, Jr., a former chairman of the Grievance Board, explains the enforcement system in these words:

> Stated simply, panels act as courts of law. A member may complain about another member and accuse him of a breach of the Code before a panel. The Grievance Board, on the other hand, performs the dual role of the grand jury and prosecutor. Where no complaint is lodged by a member, but where PRSA or the public may be harmed by non-conforming actions of another member, the Grievance Board must investigate the case and, if it finds good reason for prosecution, bring the accused before a panel.
>
> . . . When a case is brought before a panel, the Grievance Board and its attorney—acting for the PRSA—conduct the prosecution. The accused member, of course, is the defendant or respondent. The panel as a group sits in judgment in the role of a court . . . After the close of the hearing the panel submits a report to the Board of Directors of the PRSA in which it recommends disciplinary action or exoneration . . .
>
> There are six forms of discipline: 'To warn, admonish or reprimand, or to censure, suspend or expel.' The Board in its discretion may give notice to the membership in case of warning, admonishment or reprimand; it must give notice to the membership in case of censure, suspension or expulsion. Of course, where there is an acquittal, the matter is closed and no notice ever goes to anyone. Thus, in cases of acquittal, or where the Board gives no notice to the membership in cases of warning, admonishment or reprimand, only the defendant is notified of the final decision.

Membership in the Society is on an individual basis. Only the practitioner, not his firm or organization, can be a member of the Society, and thus the code relates only to the conduct of the individual member and not to the firm or organization with which he or she is affiliated. Furthermore, though the ultimate form of discipline is expulsion from the Society, this has no bearing on the practitioner's ability to continue to practice.

LICENSING AND OTHER ALTERNATIVES

As has been already noted, public relations practitioners are not licensed, but the idea of licensing—or some alternative close to it—has been a live issue of debate among the professionals as far back as 1953 when Edward L. Bernays proposed that practitioners be licensed. Various study commissions and members of the PRSA have presented reports and White Papers on licensing, but as of 1979 (when this chapter was written), the Society itself had never taken an official stand on the matter of licensing.

Recent surveys of practitioners and teachers demonstrate, however, that those against licensing are in the majority. In its annual survey of practitioners, the *pr reporter* noted in 1978 that almost two-thirds of those surveyed by the newsletter favor either a system of "open practice" (25 percent) or "voluntary accreditation by professional societies" (39 percent). Only one out of ten said they favor licensing, either by the state (6.8 percent) or by the federal government (3.6 percent).

Public relations teachers have also indicated that they do not favor licensing. Results of a survey carried out in 1977 by Professor Frank Tennant of California State Polytechnic University showed that the teachers are against government licensing by a 2.5 to 1 ratio. However, close to 80 percent of those opposed to licensing believe that public relations practices should be monitored to achieve professionalism.

As might be expected in considering such an important step, there are as many arguments against licensing as there are in favor of licensing. Readers can make up their own minds by considering the pros and cons cited below.

Arguments For Licensing

Those who favor licensing of public relations practitioners usually cite the following arguments to support their views:

1. Licensing is a key and indispensible ingredient of a profession.

2. Licensing would safeguard the public and the competent practitioners against the charlatans and incompetents.

3. A grandfather clause would protect those now practicing in the field.

4. If those now in the field do not regulate themselves, then outside agencies—usually the government—will take on this task.

5. Licensing will ensure that only qualified people will be permitted

to practice and will thereby raise the entire level of the field and the view held of it by the public.

6. The PRSA is only able to control and police its own membership whereas licensing would enable society to police all who claim to be public relations professionals.

Arguments Against Licensing

Those who are against the licensing of public relations practitioners usually cite the following arguments to support their views:

1. Because of the difficulty in defining public relations it would be difficult to fashion a meaningful law.

2. Licensing poses serious constitutional questions relating to freedom of speech and press and would probably be in violation of the First Amendment.

3. Licensing does not automatically guarantee that the public will view the activity licensed as a profession, and one finds charlatans and incompetents in fields that are now licensed.

4. If, as is most likely, licensing would be by states, then what about reciprocity and differing state laws?

5. Licensing will inevitably mean control by outside agencies, and no one knows where that can lead.

6. Malpractice can be controlled by such existing laws as those relating to libel, fraud, dishonesty, misrepresentation, and breach of contract.

Since licensing is usually sought by the group to be regulated and inasmuch as there has been no real groundswell of practitioner sentiment for licensing, there has been much talk but little action in the direction of licensing. Alternatives to licensing, however, are brought forth from time to time, and one such alternative is the *creation of an independent body composed of practitioners and representatives of the public.* Jack O'Dwyer presented this alternative in a commentary in his newsletter in 1974 in the following manner:

> The PR industry is lagging far behind the news media and the advertising industry in responding to new standards of accountability that the public is imposing on all institutions.
>
> In other words, you can now make a complaint about an individual reporter, or coverage of a story by a magazine, newspaper or TV station, and have that complaint considered by a panel whose members are not just from the media. A public hearing may be held on your complaint.
>
> Or, you can criticize an ad, and find your criticism and a reply described in a monthly bulletin that is sent to the press. The panel that considers your complaint will have members of the public on it.

But if your criticism involves PR, or something that a PR man has said or done, your only recourse in the industry is Public Relations Society of America. It is almost certain that your complaint will lead to no publicized action on the part of PRSA. Its grievance committee has a remarkable record—not a single negative word uttered about a PRSA member in ten years. . . .

Distinguished members of the PR field should form a bona fide grievance panel that will also include representatives of the public.

O'Dwyer didn't specify the panel that he says considers complaints about the mass media, though he may have been referring to the National News Council, which had been recently activated for the purpose of hearing complaints about certain disseminators of national news. Nor did he mention that some of our most distinguished national news organizations refused to recognize or cooperate with the National News Council. However, his suggestion about a similar body for the public relations field was echoed in the spring of 1975 by Neil A. Lavick in an article in the *Public Relations Quarterly*.

In calling for the establishment of a national public relations council Lavick described it as similar in nature, scope, and function to the press councils which have had established track records in countries such as Great Britain and Sweden. As he explained his proposal:

The council's purposes would include maintaining the character of the public relations practice in accordance with the highest professional and commercial standards, keeping under review developments likely to lead to abrogations of those standards, considering complaints about the conduct of PR practitioners and that of organizations relating to their public relations, and dealing with complaints in a systematic, orderly manner.

A group of concerned citizens and practitioners or a public interest group could draw up a constitution and select members to sit on the initial council . . . Councils would be established locally, statewide, regionally, or nationally. . . .

A grievance committee would screen complaints, which would have to be in writing . . . If no accord were reached, the grievance committee would investigate and hear the case. . . .

Neither the grievance committee nor the council would have punitive or enforcement powers, other than those of admonition, moral suasion, and public opinion. All decisions of the committee and council would be presented to the media for dissemination to the general public . . .

Nothing much came of O'Dwyer's and Lavick's proposals for the establishment in the United States of a watchdog council to set standards and consider complaints against public relations practitioners. However, the proposals sparked interest elsewhere.

As its alternative to licensing, The Institute of Public Relations—recognized as the sole professional body for the public relations profession in the United Kingdom and composed of 3,500 members in

1975—suggested the formation of what it termed a "Public Relations Registration Council."In a Memorandum to a Royal Commission on Standards of Conduct in Public Life, the British practitioner group said it was concerned about the activities of individuals who call themselves public relations persons but who are not members of the Institute and hence not subject to its code of conduct and disciplinary procedures. Noting that any individual—however unqualified or unscrupulous—could claim to practice public relations the Institute recommended the *establishment of a statutory register* and described it as follows:

> An initial statute would set up a Public Relations Registration Council establishing and maintaining a register of practitioners, together with an educational board to recommend appropriate qualifications, and an admission committee. The normal route to registration could be by membership of the Institute of Public Relations, which has already established standards and discipline. The Institute would have a continuing role both in the composition of the Council and as the representative body for individual practitioners. No doubt the statute would provide for membership of the Council also to include nominees of the Public Relations Consultants' Association and of the Government.

> After a stated interval, during which registration would be voluntary, a further statute would prohibit the practice of public relations as a profession by anyone not on the register.

If a licensing system for public relations practitioners is ever established on the North American continent, it may well get its start in Canada rather than in the United States. Walter Herbert, chief accreditation examiner for the Canadian Public Relations Society, told the *pr reporter* in 1978 that he believes licensing for Canadian practitioners is "inevitable." Herbert was quoted by the weekly newsletter as predicting that "the provinces, in due course, will enact legislation saying you can't call yourself a counselor or consultant unless you have established certain skills and knowledge." At the time he made his prediction, licensing legislation had been drafted in Quebec, Alberta, and Nova Scotia.

A FEW FINAL WORDS

Whether or not licensing or its alternatives—a grievance panel or a statutory register—becomes a reality, the fact remains that the actions and activities of all those who practice public relations—and this includes non-PRSA as well as PRSA members—ultimately decides the kind of reputation the field will have in the mind of the public. For this reason, as they come to the end of this text, students seeking a career in public relations should recognize that the public view of the public relations field will depend on their personal role and conduct as future professionals. How they handle this role and how they conduct themselves poses a personal challenge to all individuals who practice public relations. This challenge was clearly set forth by an executive who was named in 1974 to *Time* magazine's list of 200 emerging leaders in America. Here, in an article he wrote for the *Public Relations Journal*, is the way Luther Hodges, Jr., chairman of the board of the North Carolina National Bank of Charlotte, N.C., delineated the nature of the role-and-conduct choice for the practitioner and the future of his and her calling:

> Let's consider the qualities I look for in a public relations executive. And I must note for the females that my use of the masculine line simply refers to all.
>
> I'll begin by describing what the public relations professional is not. He is not a yes man.
>
> If the boss says newspapers are no damn good, the yes man agrees. If the boss says to tell the reporter "no comment," he does so without question or argument. If the boss says let's stonewall it, he does just so . . .
>
> Nor does the good professional take the other extreme of disagreeing with everything and everybody all the time. The type of person who does this is the one who forgets that his salary is being paid by the company he works for—and not the local newspaper or television station. He forgets that he is hired, after all, as an advocate for a given business, industry, government agency or whatever . . .
>
> The really good professional stands somewhere between these extremes. He realizes that his function is not to run the company, but to provide input to those who do run the company, so that they can base policy decisions on public relations factors in addition to all other factors. In this role he often must play the devil's advocate—and he should.
>
> He has the ability and the knowledge to tell management in advance what the predicted public relations reaction to a given action or policy decision will be. He has the ability and knowledge to make positive suggestions about how to change these actions or decisions, if necessary; and above all he has the self-confidence to argue convincingly for his beliefs.
>
> At the same time, this public relations professional is pragmatic enough to realize that management decisions are based on many inputs—not just his own—and that his total wishes may not always be reflected in the final decision. He then has the duty of supporting that decision—and helping implement it, or, in fact, of resigning from the company if the decision is one that seriously violates his professional ethics and standards of conduct.

PREPARING FOR A PUBLIC RELATIONS CAREER

As noted in the preface, this book's major purpose is to provide an effective teaching tool in the introductory course in public relations. The purpose therefore indicates the author's belief that a college education including course work in public relations is an effective and sound way in which young people can prepare themselves for a career in the field of public relations. This is not meant to contend that such a college education is *the* only way in which to prepare for a public relations career, and studies have shown that the vast number of practitioners now in the field did not study public relations while in college. This is not surprising inasmuch as public relations curricula and degree programs are relatively new phenomena on the American educational scene; although one or two courses in public relations were first taught in colleges in the early twenties, it's only been in the last two decades that the proliferation of courses and degree programs has taken place. Thus, the public relations veterans of today are mainly college-educated, but their college work did not include public relations courses. Most of these veterans entered the public relations field through either journalism, advertising, marketing, or that catch-all called "happenstance."

For the past two decades as graduates of public relations degree programs have sought their first public relations jobs they've run into the same road blocks that faced journalism school graduates trying to enter the newspaper field a few decades ago. Managing editors who had entered the newspaper field as copy boys and who had never themselves gone to college couldn't understand how a college education could possibly prepare one for a journalism career. The idea that such an education would also include work in journalism was considered even more outlandish, but this tunnel-vision view gradually gave way to a broader understanding as the world became more complex and the need for college-educated newspapermen and women became more obvious. In similar fashion, now that public relations degree programs have become more established and graduates of such programs have proved their value and become established in the field, there is growing recognition of the worth, value, and capability of these public relations graduates.

EDUCATION FOR PUBLIC RELATIONS

Students using this book will probably be taking a public relations course that either is required in a degree program, is required or an elective in a public relations or other sequence within a journalism degree program, or is an elective course within some other degree program or sequence. The educational "home" for such a course—and for other courses in public relations—is shown by Figure 12.1 and 12.2 in a study conducted by Dr. Ray Eldon Hiebert for the Foundation for Public Relations Research and Education.

Dr. Hiebert notes that public relations instruction is now offered in institutions of higher learning in 47 states and the District of Columbia, with California leading the way with 27 colleges or universities, New York with 25, Ohio with 21, Pennsylvania with 13, and Illinois with 11. The tables show that the total number of institutions offering degree or special sequences in public relations has more than doubled from 1964 to 1970 (43 to 89). Although the number of degree programs has declined from 1964 to 1970, the number of special

Figure 12.1

Number of Colleges and Universities Offering Public Relations Instruction

	1964	1970
Degree Programs in Public Relations		
Doctoral Degrees	0	0
Master's Degrees	5	7
Bachelor's Degrees	14	7
Special Sequences in Public Relations		
Doctoral Level	0	8
Master's Level	12	28
Bachelor's Level	29	75
Elective Courses in Public Relations		
Two or More Courses Available	37	46
At Least One Course Available	200	172
Total Number of Programs in Public Relations	297	343
Total Number of Schools Offering Programs	280	303

Figure 12.2

Placement of Public Relations in Academic Structure

Universities offering sequences or degrees in public relations:

	—1964—		—1970—	
	Schools	Percent	Schools	Percent
Within a liberal arts sequence	17	39.5	48	53.9
Within a professional school	24	56.0	33	37.0
Combination of the two	2	4.5	8	9.1
Total	43	100.0	89	100.0

All universities offering courses in public relations:

	Schools	Percent	Schools	Percent
Within a liberal arts structure	72	53.0	73	51.4
Within a professional school	54	40.0	41	28.8
Combination of the two	7	5.0	23	16.2
Junior College	3	2.0	4	2.8
Other			1	.8
Total	136	100.0	142	100.0

sequences in public relations within other degree programs has almost tripled.

Public relations and journalism educators hold similar views when considering the relationship of required public relations and journalism courses to the total number of courses and hours needed for graduation. With few exceptions, schools offering public relations degrees or sequences require from 20 to 30 percent of total course work in public relations and/or journalism and the remainder in electives in other disciplines. The problem facing students is in deciding what courses will round out their college education.

SUGGESTED ELECTIVES

There is no end to the number and kind of elective courses that well-intentioned practitioners suggest students take to prepare for a career in public relations. These range anywhere from the generalized statement "get a liberal arts education" to lists of courses that add up to as many as 201 credit hours. The usual practice in giving advice is to recommend courses which the practitioner has found useful in his or her own career, but the problem for the student is that no two careers will ever really duplicate each other. The wiser approach, it seems, is to consider as electives those courses that will most likely be of value no matter what special area of public relations is pursued, plus courses that may prove valuable for special purposes.

First, as to general courses, there seems to be agreement that courses in the social sciences—sociology, psychology, anthropology, political science, history, and economics—are sound fundamental courses to be taken. Courses in literature, the humanities, speech, and some of the fundamental areas of business administration—such as accounting, finance, organization, management, and marketing—are also considered wise educational investments. If available, students should take as many writing courses as possible.

Second, if the student knows in advance the area of public relations in which he or she hopes to pursue a career, it's advisable to take courses most closely related to the designated specialty. Thus, if you intend to handle public relations work in the social or health agency areas, take courses in the social work and health disciplines in your institution. If you hope to make your public relations career in education, take some education courses as electives. If you intend to seek public relations work in business or industry, the obvious choice of electives would be in the business area.

Third, be flexible enough to recognize that today's interest may be temporary and that you may start your career in one area of public relations and then move into another. For this reason it's wise to become as broadly educated as possible within the boundaries of your college's curriculum requirements.

Summed up, a sensible college education "package" for those intending to pursue a public relations career would include 20 to 30 percent of course work in public relations and journalism, and the remainder in electives in a broad range of disciplines and in a limited concentration within one discipline. The graduate of such a program should have knowledge of basic public relations principles and practices; a modicum of public relations and journalism skills; and a liberalizing, mind-broadening education.

A Recommended Curriculum

In a report issued in mid-1975, the Commission of Public Relations Education (group composed of three PRSA members and four educators from the Public Relations Division of the Association for Education in Journalism) recommended an undergraduate public relations curriculum of three major groups of courses. The report pictured the curriculum as made up of a series of three concentric circles: "The smallest, central circle would enclose those subjects specifically concerned with public relations practice. The second circle, somewhat larger, would encompass related subjects in he general field of communications. The third and largest circle would represent the general liberal arts and humanities background expected of all students. Additionally, one might envision a satellite or 'moon,' outside the largest circle, representing a secondary area of concentration for the student (a 'minor,' so to speak) representative of some special area of public relations practice. Thus, the 'minor' might be in the field of business administration for the student who plans to enter corporate public relations; or it might be in the field of public administration for the student who plans to enter government public relations, etc. . . ."

1. General Education Courses

The report recommended there be at least four semesters of *English* (writing and literature); introductory courses in the *social sciences*; a "sprinkling" of courses in the *humanities*; one or two introductory courses in the *natural sciences*; at least one *foreign language* or *area studies* courses; a course in *statistics*; and a course in *organizational structure and behavior*.

2. Communication Studies

This part of the program would encompass the following areas: *theory and process of communication; news reporting and writing; copy editing;* and *graphics of communication*.

Suggested are one or more of the following types of courses: *advertising principles and practice; media law and ethics; feature writing; introduction to survey research;* and *communication media analysis*.

3. Public Relations Core Courses

Recommended as an absolute minimum: *introduction to public relations; publicity media and campaigns; public relations case problems; internship or practicum*.

4. Electives

One or more of the following electives: *management communications; propaganda and public opinion;* and *magazine editing*.

5. "Satellite" Studies

Students interested in a "minor" or secondary area of emphasis should take at least two courses in a field related to their special area of public relations interest.

SUGGESTED EXTRA-CURRICULAR ACTIVITIES

There are several reasons for suggesting that the undergraduate's four years of course work be accompanied by a reasonable degree of involvement in extra-curricular activities. Properly selected, such activities provide the closest approximation to "on-the-job" training and experience available in a college setting. They enable the graduate to present to prospective employers not merely a record of academic but also practical experience. Finally, they're a testing ground for ascertaining personal abilities, weaknesses, and strengths.

The college newspaper, whether a daily or weekly, is highly recommended as the best extra-curricular activity for the kind of experience most closely aligned to public relations work. Students who work on a college newspaper will not only improve their reporting and writing skills, but will also gain valuable experience working with and managing others. The college newspaper also enables students to compile a sampling of stories and features that can be useful in demonstrating their competence when seeking a first position in the field.

Other valuable extra-curricular activities include work at the campus radio or television station, participation in student government, and—if available on campus—a role in the local unit of the Public Relations Student Society of America. The last-named group, first organized in 1968, now has more than 3,000 members in chapters on 82 campuses and sponsors both regional meetings and a national conference usually held in conjunction with the annual conference of the parent Public Relations Society of America. The special pre-associate membership category of the PRSA, available at a greatly reduced membership fee for graduates who have been PRSSA members, is a quick and simple entry into the parent body.

In following the dictates of an academic program or sequence in public relations and the extra-curricular options open at the average college or university, the student should keep in mind the kind of skills generally considered important for success in the field. The PRSA sums up these needed skills and attributes in the following terms:

> Because public relations involves many kinds of tasks, many different qualifications are needed. Probably the "ideal," or at least popularly conceived, public relations man or woman is the highly articulate and imaginative individual with more than a little salesmanship in his or her make-up.
>
> On the other hand, many public relations executives stress judgment as the most important single qualification that the worker must possess. Public relations practitioners are "counselors," and their services are often sought out when an organization is in trouble. Hence skill in practical action, based on reflective analysis, is an important part of the equipment of the able public relations worker. In addition he (and she) should have:
>
> - Imagination, which is an important attribute for coping with new problems and commanding the attention of others.
>
> - Verbalizing skills, which underlie competence in writing and speaking—combined with training in these arts.
>
> - Extroverted traits, sufficient to make possible successful frequent face-to-face contacts with other individuals and groups.
>
> - Sensitivity to other people. To profess a liking for people will not help a candidate get a job. However, both diplomacy and a more than ordinary ability to place oneself in the shoes of another is important in public relations work.
>
> - Organizing and planning skill, leadership and administrative ability. As with many other occupations, managerial skills are invaluable assets for successfully climbing the public relations career ladder.

GETTING THE FIRST JOB

The recession that began in 1974 and saw total United States unemployment rise to more than seven million came as a rude shock to college graduates who had been accustomed to easy entry into the job market. In previous years the job market had been wide open, but suddenly the picture changed drastically for would-be teachers, engineers, business trainees, journalists, and others. The public relations function was affected just as other functions, and this has meant that graduates seeking an entry position in the public relations field need patience, diligence, and a carefully designed search plan in order to uncover that first all-important job.

The reason why graduates need to follow a carefully designed *search* plan is that, with some few exceptions, college placement offices are not regular stops for recruiters with public relations job offers. In this respect, the public relations and the journalism graduate have had to face the same problem of going out after the first job rather than finding the first job coming to campus. Entry positions are out there and at salary ranges equivalent to those offered in such fields as accounting and similar high-demand areas, but they tend to be awarded to those who are best prepared and who seek them out. Although there are many roads leading to success in securing the first job in public relations, the following route has proven to be a sound one to travel:

1. *Prepare a portfolio* that can be easily scanned and that will provide evidence of your work and abilities. Include in it news and feature stories you've written; brochures and flyers you've produced; research and other assignments you've completed in various courses. The portfolio need not be fancy but should be well organized, easy to carry to interviews, and self-explanatory.

2. *Prepare and have printed a resume*, one page long, which will include personal, educational, extra-curricular, and work experience data. This material should be organized under the four appropriate headings. If there's room on the page, include the names and addresses of two or three references. Otherwise state that references will be supplied upon request.

   There is no single "right" form for the resume, but the resume cited in Figure 12.3 indicates the basic form to use and should suffice as an example. Note particularly that the resume does not use complete sentences and avoids the use of the first person singular.

   A final note: This is the resume of a recent graduate. Once a job record has been achieved, work experience will move to the fore on the resume and education will move into the background. After several years of work and professional experience, the applicant's major strength will be his or her previous positions and responsibilities.

Figure 12.3
A Sample Resume

Robert Vincent Ryan

Box 154, South Hall
Utica College
Utica, New York 13502
Telephone: (315) 792-3296

698 Windsor Road
Uniondale, New York 11553
Telephone: (516) IV-1-1285

Personal Data

Date of Birth: 4/1/57
Height: 5'11"
Weight: 180 lbs.

Marital Status: Single
Military Status: 1-H

Education

Utica College of Syracuse University, Utica, New York 13502
Degree: Bachelor of Arts, May 1979
Dual Major in Journalism and Public Relations
Overall Grade Point Average: 3.2 of 4.0
Average in Major: 3.4 of 4.0

Courses Taken in Major: Newswriting, Reporting, Introduction to Mass Communications, Introduction to Public Relations, Reporting on Public Affairs, Graphics, Editing, Writing and Announcing for Radio/Television, Publicity, Magazine Article Writing, Cases and Problems in Public Relations, Teacher's Assistant, Independent Study

Honors

Tau Mu Epsilon, National Honorary Public Relations Society; Student Speaker, First Utica College Convocation; Regents Scholarship

Interviewer, Telephone Conference Call Program with Reuven Frank, former president of NBC NEWS and executive producer of WEEKEND; Osborn Elliot, editor of NEWSWEEK; Jack O'Dwyer of O'DWYER'S NEWSLETTER; Skip Weiner, editor of WRITER'S DIGEST; and Babette Ashby, articles editor of FAMILY CIRCLE

Activities

Utica College Press Club; Public Relations Student Society of America; Utica College Student Newspaper, TANGERINE; DORMWEEK, Utica College Weekly Dormitory Newspaper, Founder and Editor

Employment (All part-time while attending college)

1/79 to 5/79 Utica College of Syracuse University, Utica, New York 13502
Resident Living Advisor, in charge of the 300 students in South Dormitory

1/79 to 5/79 Journalism Fieldwork: Course includes moderating four public service radio shows for WRUN in Utica and free-lancing to the local daily and weekly newspapers
Supervisor: John Behrens, Professor of Journalism, Utica College

5/78 to 12/78 Rome Air Development Center, Griffiss Air Force Base, New York, 13440
Writer—Office of Information
Information Officer: Capt. Juventino R. Garcia, USAF

8/76 to 1/79 Utica College of Syracuse University, Utica, New York 13502
Resident Assistant, in charge of one floor of students in South Dormitory
Dean of Students: Richard Caulk

5/77 to 5/78 The Student Press in America Archives
Utica College, Utica, New York 13502
Editorial Assistant
Curator: Prof. John Behrens

References

Raymond Simon, Chairman, Business Administration Division
Utica College
Utica, New York 13502

John Caponera, Writer/Editor
Office of Information
Northern Communications Area
Griffiss Air Force Base, New York 13440

John C. Behrens, Professor of Journalism Studies
Utica College
Utica, New York 13502

3. *Compile a list* of organizations where job openings might exist. If you intend to write directly to the person heading the public relations function, the best single source of names and addresses is the annual *Register* of the Public Relations Society of America, which lists the more than 9,000 members of the society. Each member receives a copy of the Register and it may be possible to borrow a copy from a PRSA member who is nearby. Appropriate lists can be compiled by referring to the annual membership directories published by groups such as the American Hospital Association, the United Ways of America, the Boy and Girl Scouts of America, the Council for the Advancement of Education (college public relations and fund-raising directors), etc.

4. *Prepare a brief cover letter* individually typed and sent out with each resume mailed. Concentrate your mailing to organizations within a 200 to 300 mile radius of your location. Even though they may be interested in your application, organizations will not set up a personal interview if you're in New York and the position is in Los Angeles.

5. *Try to establish contact* and arrange for a personal interview with professionals in areas where there are a large number of public relations people. Even though the person who interviews you may not have a position available, he or she may know of openings elsewhere or may be able to direct you to someone who will in turn direct you to an opening.

6. *Do no get too easily discouraged.* Finding the right kind of position can easily take months of search, so explore all possibilities by reading the classified section of metropolitan papers, *Editor and Publisher,* the *Public Relations Journal*, and similar sources and by sending out letters and resumes and arranging for personal interviews. If a media job opens up, by all means consider it seriously because it will provide you with the kind of experience still considered invaluable by practitioners who themselves moved into the public relations field through this route.

SALARY AND OTHER EXPECTATIONS

Any discussion of salary levels for the first job in public relations has to be red-flagged by the notation that spiraling inflation has made figures outdated almost as soon as they're reported. Thus, in mid-1972 Dr. Frederick H. Teahan, education director of the PRSA, reported that a study of a sample of pre-associate (newly graduated) members of the society showed that their starting salaries ranged from $6,000 to $14,000 with the median salary at $7,500 and the average at $8,823. By mid-1979, when the author surveyed his school's May public relations graduates, he found that their salaries ranged from $8,800 to $14,000 with the median salary at $10,500 and the average at $11,500.

Several general observations can be made about entry salaries. First, they have consistently ranged between $1,000 and $3,000 above those of graduates who have taken newspaper jobs. Second, the highest starting salaries in public relations have been in business, industry, and counseling while the lowest have been in the social and health agency and hospital fields. Third, women's salaries have lagged behind men's salaries, though this gap is constantly being narrowed in public relations as in all fields.

As to expectations, all indications point to a continuance of two of the above three trends. The bulk of entry positions in the newspaper field continue to be on small town and small city dailies while the bulk of entry positions in public relations are in large organizations situated in metropolitan areas; thus, salary levels of beginning newspaper positions will continue to be lower than those of beginning public relations positions. Entry-level public relations jobs in business, industry, and counseling will continue to offer higher salaries than similar entry-level public relations positions in other areas. However, because of governmental, legal, and activist pressures the gap between women's and men's entry salary levels in public relations, as in all fields, will become a thing of the past and will be covered over and deservedly buried.

What about salary levels of experienced practitioners? Figures compiled by *pr reporter* showed that the median salary of top-level public relations/public affairs practitioners was $30,000 in 1978, an increase of $2,200 over the median salary for 1977. The range for these top-level practitioners indicated a wide gap between the lowest and the highest, with a $20,700 median at the low end for nonprofit organizations and a $40,000 median at the top end for top-level practitioners in conglomerates and other industrials. Figure 12.4 provides details about top-level salaries for 1978.

DAILY WORK ROUTINES

Entry-level jobs in public relations tend to be involved with writing rather than with counseling for the simple reason that there are many writing but few counseling tasks that can be assigned to a relative newcomer to the field. Furthermore, the very act of counseling calls for the degree of maturity and experience that comes with age and time spent in the field. The young graduate may aspire to doling out sage advice, but he's generally not going to be asked nor paid for it until he or she gets a little older, a little wiser, and a bit more experienced.

We thus find the Public Relations Society of America describing "The Day" of the newcomer to the field in the following words:

> The junior employee will answer calls for information from the press and the public, work on invitation lists and details for a press conference, escort visitors and clients, help research and write brochures, deliver releases to editorial offices, work up contact and distribution lists, scan newspapers and journals, paste scrap books of clippings, brief his superiors on forthcoming meetings, help write reports, speeches, presentations, articles and letters, research case

Figure 12.4

Comparison of 1978 and 1977 Median Salaries of Top-Level Public Relations/Public Affairs Practitioners* in the United States and Canada and by Industry Groups

	Median Salary 1978	1977	Change	1978 Salary Range
All U.S. Organizations	$30,000	$27,800	+$2,200	$10,100-140,000
All Canadian Organizations	27,500	27,500	0	18,500-77,000
Industry Groups:				
PR Firms	36,000	39,000	−3,000	14,000-80,000
Advertising Agencies	31,000	24,800	+6,200	18,000-61,000
Banks and Insurance	27,300	26,000	+1,300	17,000-45,000
Conglomerates and Other Industrials	40,000	32,500	+7,500	20,000-140,000
Consumer Product Companies	35,000	31,500	+3,500	15,000-97,000
Utilities	35,500	30,000	+4,500	19,600-70,500
Educational Organizations	25,000	24,500	+ 500	13,300-50,000
Hospitals	22,000	20,000	+2,000	10,100-75,000
Trade and Professional Associations	27,000	23,750	+3.250	14,200-60,000
Other Nonprofit Organizations	20,700	17,100	+3,600	10,700-53,500
Government: Federal	31,200	30,000	+1,200	23,000-40,000
State	24,000	22,800	+1,200	12,500-32,000
Local	22,700	22,150	+ 550	10,800-30,000

*Presidents(in public relations firms), senior vice presidents, vice presidents, directors, managers, and supervisors of public relations.

Source: Statistics are based on sample of 493 practitioners from *pr reporter* subscriber list and PRSA and CPRS directories.
Reproduced with permission of *pr reporter*

histories, help produce displays and other audio-visual materials, do copy reading, select photographs for publication, arrange and guide plant tours, perform liaison jobs with advertising and other departments, arrange for holiday or other remembrances, conduct surveys and tabulate questionnaires, work with lettershops and printers. The telephone, the typewriter, the mimeograph and addressograph machines, telegraph, postal and other message services are communication tools that are familiar features of the public relations man's (and woman's) work environment.

On their first jobs graduates obviously won't be doing all things set forth by the PRSA occupational guide, but rather can be expected to do any one of them at some time or another. Much depends on the nature of the organization for which one works. In large organizations, public relations functions and activities tend to be compartmentalized; the beginner may well find himself or herself spending the work week writing for the employee publication or perhaps writing news releases, but not doing both. In small organizations, public relations functions or activities tend to be shared by a smaller number of professionals, and there is the opportunity to get involved in a variety of tasks. Finally, where the public relations function is the sole responsibility of one professional, this person will have to be versatile enough to handle graphics, write releases and features, deliver talks, hold press conferences, deal with printers, and counsel. Thus, although salary scales in social and health agencies and in hospitals are lower than in business and industry, the responsibilities assigned to the beginner tend to be greater and provide the opportunity to develop a wider range of skills and talents than is possible in large organizations with large public relations departments.

Next year, the year after that, or three years from now students who have used this text will be starting their first jobs in public relations. These jobs will be so varied that it's difficult to state explicitly the kind of tasks they'll be asked to handle. In concluding this last chapter, the author has selected at random excerpts from letters he has received from recent graduates. Here's what those graduates had to say:

1. From a graduate who's taken a government position:

Hope this letter finds you in good health and spirits. I am proud and happy to inform you that I have been employed by the City of _____ as a Communications Coordinator.

I am very pleased with the job. At this time I am simply handling basic publicity work and at other times filling in as a "temporary administrator" in hopes of restructuring some mismanaged departments.

The salary and benefits are excellent. My boss is very intelligent with very interesting plans for my talents. Suffice it to say, I am extremely happy with my new position.

2. From a graduate working for a public relations/advertising agency:

The work here has been interesting. I was sent to Chicago in January to talk to the editors of a new magazine that is the result of the merger of the to, two publications in the research/development field. The agency's biggest client did a lot of advertising in both of these magazines, and is hoping to get a lot of press releases in the new one.

For two days at the end of February I attended the Pittsburgh Analytical Symposium which, for some strange reason, is held in Cleveland. I was able to meet some more of the agency's clients and some important editors. One of my most trying tasks here is following up press releases on the phone with selected magazines. I think meeting some of these editors face to face will improve my communications with them in the future.

3. From a graduate working in college public relations:

Well, my college education in public relations has paid off. I have just finished my first week of work as assistant to the director of public relations. My starting salary is an even $10,000, and I am quite delighted with it. My responsibilities run the entire range of public relations from writing press releases to suggesting new ideas. I have my own office, desk, secretary, and so on. Everything I do has to be approved by my boss and then by the president of the college before it goes out. There is a lot of work to do because we have several branches, and my boss and I are responsible for public relations for all of them.

P.S.: This is the first letter I've written since graduation, and no matter what grade you give me, it won't matter now.

4. From a graduate working for a trade association:

Since I changed jobs six months ago, the scope of my responsibilities and my employer's expectations of me have increased 500 percent. My title is public relations administrator, and I'm responsible for the entire $300,000-a-year public relations program for the association.

Here I get a chance to do it all—making a film; running a press room at the world's largest trade show; writing and placing institutional ads, television and radio public service announcements; interviewing and hiring freelancers and film producers and ad agencies; spending $10,000 to promote a single annual meeting; attending all board meetings to give public relations advice; setting up features with the largest circulation magazines in the business; running a national journalism awards contest; and, most importantly, advising our president.

I've never enjoyed a job more than I have this one. I work late and often go in on Saturdays, but that's only because I like it and can see a good chance to move up in the organization by doing so.

PROJECTS, ASSIGNMENTS, AND MINI-CASES

1. PRACTITIONERS DISCUSS AN ETHICAL SITUATION: A MINI-CASE

To sharpen perceptions about ethical problems, staff members at Ruder & Finn met in a series of seminars with a group of theologians and philosophers to pursue the question of ethics and public relations. Following is one of the cases discussed, the question asked, and Finn's summary of the points of view expressed by the practitioners and scholars.

The Case

Company A decided to build an image of one of its major products as being purer than its competitors'. This was actually so. However, advertising claims of purity had been used and abused so heavily in the past by other companies that it decided to undertake a public relations program to get the story across. Accordingly, a complicated scheme was invented involving the development of an "independent" research report that was to provide the basis for newspaper and magazine articles.

The trouble was that the research was engineered; in fact, it was not even to be paid for unless the publicity appeared in print. To ensure the success of the project, the man who arranged all this had some editors on his payroll as consultants for the research, thus almost guaranteeing eventual publication. It was a neat scheme—effective for the company and profitable for researcher, editor, and middleman.

The Question

Is this a responsible method of communicating the image of purity to the public?

Summary of Discussion Reported by Finn

In support of the argument was the fact that the image was accurate; the product was a pure one. The public was not being deceived. It was being told the truth. And there was nothing specifically "wrong" with the plan. No one was being bribed to do something he should not do. The research was being done by qualified scientists.

Against the plan was the fact that it short-circuited the usual checks and balances which protect the public against deception. Normally, if the product was touted as being pure, the public could have the claim checked by truly independent editors, who would publish it only if it seemed valid to them. But if the cooperation of these two intermediaries could be secured by special payments, then the way would be clear to present false images to the public . . .

In our discussion, the temptation to endorse the plan was very strong, since there was very little doubt that it would accomplish legitimate public relations objectives . . . One of the scholarly consultants at our seminar paraphrased Plato to point out that if we make the choice to live in this world where each person primarily looks out for his own gain, we have to be prepared to find some form of deception everywhere . . .

And yet, after a great deal of analysis, the risk of possible exposure of the whole scheme emerged as the most important consideration of all . . . Our conclusion was that if research could be conducted on a truly independent basis—and there was no reason to feel it could not— there would be no danger whatsoever, and results would be just as effective . . . Everybody who participated in the seminar discussion of this case history felt that the conclusion was based upon practical considerations (that is, to avoid risk of exposure), rather than upon ethical considerations . . .

----

from "Struggle for Ethics in Public Relations"

Questions for Discussion

1. Do you consider the research project plan described in the case to be a responsible and ethical method of communicating the image of purity to the public? Why or why not?

2. What is your opinion of the "pro" arguments reported by Finn?

3. What is your opinion of the "anti" arguments reported by Finn?

4. What is your opinion about the conclusion arrived at by the seminar participants?

5. Finn reports that one of the scholarly consultants participating in a series of seminars suggested as a "piece of litmus paper" that one should never do anything he or she would not want to see published in tomorrow morning's newspaper. What's your opinion of this suggestion as a test of ethical behavior?

2. A DAY IN THE LIFE OF THREE PRACTITIONERS: A MINI-CASE

At the request of the author of this textbook, three former students selected an arbitrary date and recorded their work routine for the day. At the time in their professional careers the three were: Mrs. Linda Schmidt, director of public relations for the United Way of Broome County, Binghamton, New York; Robert O'Gara, manager of public relations, The Koppers Company, Pittsburgh, Pennsylvania; and James Leach, director of public relations, Eisenhower College, Seneca Falls, New York. Following are the "logs" they compiled and transmitted, along with a few explanatory remarks:

LINDA SCHMIDT
Director of Public Relations
United Way of Broome County

Friday, August 24

8:30 a.m. ... Arrived in office. Scanned morning newspaper.

8:45 .... Typed rough draft of minutes from last PR Committee meeting; minutes will be duplicated and sent to volunteer committee. (Prefer typewriter, rather than dictaphone, to transcribe notes and draft letters for secretary)

9:30 .... Went out to pick up metal printing plate I had a rush order on; plate will be used for in-house printing of campaign bulletins on small offset.

10:00 .... Read mail; checked bills for campaign suppliers; wrote notes to two volunteers asking for comments on draft letters I had prepared.

10:15 .... Coffee with rest of staff.

10:40 .... Telephone calls:

... checked on permit we need to hang a banner over a downtown street for campaign, wrote letter to state for permit approval.

... talked to member agency staffer who called to ask my help in getting publicity for the enrollment of their 10,000th member.

... talked with a volunteer sub-committee chairman on plans for campaign Kickoff.

11:20 .... Talkative rep from local firm dropped in to chat. Couldn't be rude to him, as his firm provided some volunteer service designing our campaign information brochure.

Noon .... Called to set up appointment with TV station film editor for later in the afternoon. Conferred with secretary on pending work.

12:20 .... Lunch.

1:10 .... Telephone calls:

... talked to several volunteers who are handling distribution of 1,000 posters advertising campaign Kickoff.

...talked with PR Committee vice-chairman about plans for showing campaign film on Cable TV in fall.

... called assistant city editor of newspaper to see if he'd be interested in a photo-feature on the agency's

10,000th member. He said "yes" and I followed up with agency. Called TV news director to see if he'd be interested in same. He said "yes." Also set up appointment with him for next week to discuss the possibility of a fall TV show on United Way.

... made several other calls, but couldn't reach anyone.

2:30 .... Researched, verified and wrote items for the first academic year issue of the campus weekly news bulletin.

3:30 .... Read recent committee reports from budgeting and planning division of United Way.

3:45 .... Went to TV station to preview a print of film we had shot; called film lab to give the go-ahead on making final prints.

4:30 .... Talked to newly-hired United Way staff member to orient him on my functions and PR committee operations.

4:45 .... Instructed a publications assistant in the preparation of the weekly news bulletin for distribution the following day.

5:00 .... Interviewed the director of the college community orchestra about his first rehearsal of the year.

5:40 .... Left to go home.

Excerpt from cover letter: 'It was kind of interesting to see the log when I finished it (yes, it's completely honest). It was surprising how much time I spent making phone calls, for instance! All in all, it seems to be a fairly "average" day—there are some that last till 8 or 9 p.m., but some that finish at 5 on the dot. And, there are some more hectic, and others that drag by ..."

ROBERT O'GARA
Manager of Public Relations
Koppers Company, Inc.

Thursday, September 13

8:00 a.m. ... Reviewed and edited two product publicity feature stories done by staff member.

8:30 .... Informal coffee session with advertising manager to discuss future publicity campaign.

9:00 .... Morning mail ... penciled notes for routine inquiries. Put aside two letters for formal replies, skimmed *Wall Street Journal* and *Industry Week*.

9:30 .... Dictation: four letters, three memos.

10:00 .... Inquiry from *Wall Street Journal* on capital spending. Set up phone interviews with comptroller.

10:15 .... General reading: *Wall Street Journal, Business Week, Newsweek,* articles from *Conference Board Record* and *Business & Society Review.*

11:00 .... Annual Report meeting with vice president, public relations and advertising, and manager, investor relations. Discussed format and copy.

11:45 .... Luncheon with United Fund representative. Discussion of campaign.

 1:30 .... Phone contact local press to arrange feature story on United Fund.

 1:45 .... Wrote Annual Report outline.

 2:30 .... Discussion with vice president/marketing on interview with *Business Week,* other activities.

 3:00 .... Meeting with manager/architectural promotion and supervisor/product information. Subject: How to publicize regional architects' seminars in major cities.

 3:30 .... Informal discussion with staff members on product publicity stories edited early in day ... discussed placement, timing, writing, etc.

 4:00 .... Informal discussion with supervisor/product information on his upcoming trip plans to cover product case histories.

 4:30 .... Prepared rough draft of release announcing new order for Environmental Systems.

 5:30 .... Left for home.

Excerpt from cover letter: "The log is not really a good indication of an 'average' day's activity because most days are really quite different. There seems to be a tendency to get involved in projects which may take a considerable amount of time, and to do this on a fairly sporadic basis. As an example—I am probably spending half of my time right now working on the United Fund. After October 30, I won't even think about the United Fund until next September. Another example: If we are working on a major story with the *Wall Street Journal* or *Business Week*, this could conceivably tie up a full week of time with little opportunity to do other things ... Another very important consideration is that a good manager owes a certain amount of time to the people who work for him. With two brand new people in our department I spend a lot of time, on an informal basis, supervising their work. Time spent this way will hopefully save the public relations manager from putting out fires six months from now ..."

JAMES LEACH
Director of Public Relations
Eisenhower College

Thursday, June 29

8:00 a.m. ... Mail

8:15 .... Reviewed details of 1978 commencement. Working from notes and files, prepared checklist that will assist in subsequent commencement preparations.

8:45 .... Completed draft of a descriptive article about Eisenhower College for a new Saudi Arabian magazine. (The college recently named a Saudi sheikh to its Board of Trustees. The article is to be submitted at the request of the publisher.)

10:30 .... Wrote letters to a new Trustee (a public relations counselor who is interested in background on student attitudes) and to the editor of the local daily newspaper (regarding Eisenhower faculty who are developing curricular materials in Egypt this summer).

11:15 .... Held briefing sessions with a new work/study photographer and with a student writer employed for the summer to produce hometown news stories.

11:30 .... Finalized arrangements for a campus tour and meetings for a visiting administrator from the University of the West Indies.

Noon .... Lunch, including a stop at the local weekly (on my way) to deliver a news release.

1:00 p.m. ... Contacted alumnus to discuss response to a recent op-ed opinion in the *New York Times* (topic: liberal arts education). An earlier piece written by this alumnus is adaptable to the response. Support material sent.

1:15 .... Received and reviewed final catalog galleys from printer's representative. Discussed new art, cover changes, timetable for production.

2:00 .... Review session with President regarding stories on new Trustees, Saudi magazine article, catalog.

2:30 .... Wrote draft story on appointment of five new coaches.

3:30 .... Met with Director of Admissions to discuss changes, updating, and rewriting of recruiting materials.

4:30 .... Began work on draft of article for special Seneca Falls supplement to the local daily newspaper. Article emphasizes importance of Seneca Falls residents in founding the college, and college contributions to the region.

Excerpt from cover letter: "The enclosed log from last Thursday typifies the days I've been spending here during the past year. It's typical because there are very few days given exclusively, say, to writing, meetings, planning, and so on, except in the case of special events such as convocations or commencements. Frequently my evenings provide the uninterrupted time needed for the preparation of longer reports, proposals, special publications, or just plain getting even with smaller jobs on short deadlines. . . . It might help your students to understand the log if they know that the public relations office here is staffed with one professional with responsibilities for public relations, publications, alumni relations, public information, and parent relations. Work/study students assist in the writing of some stories and in handling photo assignments. . . . The pace is sometimes hectic, generally stimulating, and never boring . . .

Questions for Discussion

1. What similarities do you perceive in the daily activities of the three practitioners? What do you consider to be significant differences? What conclusions do you draw about these perceived similarities and differences?

2. How would you summarize the major areas of activities of the three? What kind of specific skills and attributes would you consider necessary to carry out these activities most effectively?

3. What is your reaction to the remarks made by Schmidt, O'Gara, and Leach?

4. Did these descriptions of daily activities measure up to your expectations of what you might be doing four to six years after graduation? Explain.

RECOMMENDED READING

A Design for Public Relations Education. Report of the Commission on Public Relations Education, cosponsored by the Association for Education in Journalism and the Public Relations Society of America, 1975.

An Occupational Guide to Public Relations. New York: Public Relations Society of America, 1972.

Chester Burger, "Trends Affecting Future Skills," *Public Relations Quarterly,* Summer 1976.

John Cook, "PR Without the BS," *Public Relations Quarterly,* Spring 1974.

"The Corporate Image; PR to the Rescue," Special Report, *Business Week,* January 22, 1979.

"Education and Placement of PR Practitioners," Special Report, *Public Relations Journal,* July 1978.

David Finn, "Struggle for Ethics in Public Relations," *Harvard Business Review,* January-February 1959.

Cameron P. Hall, *On-the-Job Ethics.* New York: The National Council of the Churches of Christ in the U.S.A., 1965.

John W. Hill, "The World of Tomorrow," *Public Relations Quarterly,* October 1976.

Luther Hodges, Jr., "The New Challenge for Public Relations," *Public Relations Journal,* August 1975.

Institute of Public Relations, *Memorandum to the Royal Commission on Standards of Conduct in Public Life.* London: The Institute of Public Relations, 1975.

Neil A. Lavick, "Public Relations Council: An Alternative to Licensing," *Public Relations Quarterly,* Spring 1975.

James E. McKee, Jr., "The PRSA Grievance Board," *Public Relations Journal,* June 1971.

John C. Merrill, *Media, Messages and Men.* New York: David McKay, 1971.

Gerald Prout, "On Expecting Corporate Ethical Reform," *Public Relations Review,* Summer 1978.

Theodore V. Purcell, S.J., "Institutionalizing Ethics into Top Management Decisions," *Public Relations Quarterly,* Summer 1977.

Leonard Silk and David Vogel, *Ethics and Profits: The Crisis of Confidence in American Business.* New York: Simon & Schuster, 1976.

Frank A. Tennant, "Survey of Public Relations Division/AEJ Members on Licensing Public Relations Practitioners," paper presented at AEJ annual conference, Madison, Wisconsin, August 25, 1977.

APPENDIX

PUBLIC RELATIONS SOCIETY OF AMERICA
Code of Professional Standards
For the Practice of Public Relations

This Code, adopted by the PRSA Assembly, replaces a similar Code of Professional Standards for the Practice of Public Relations previously in force since 1954 and strengthened by revisions in 1959, 1963 and 1977.

DECLARATION OF PRINCIPLES

Members of the Public Relations Society of America base their professional principles on the fundamental value and dignity of the individual, holding that the free exercise of human rights, especially freedom of speech, freedom of assembly and freedom of the press, is essential to the practice of public relations.

In serving the interests of clients and employers, we dedicate ourselves to the goals of better communication, understanding and cooperation among the diverse individuals, groups and institutions of society.

We pledge:

To conduct ourselves professionally, with truth, accuracy, fairness and responsibility to the public;

To improve our individual competence and advance the knowledge and proficiency of the profession through continuing research and education;

And to adhere to the articles of the Code of Professional Standards for the Practice of Public Relations as adopted by the governing Assembly of the Society.

ARTICLES OF THE CODE

These articles have been adopted by the Public Relations Society of America to promote and maintain high standards of public service and ethical conduct among its members.

1. A member shall deal fairly with clients or employers, past and present, with fellow practitioners and the general public.

2. A member shall conduct his or her professional life in accord with the public interest.

3. A member shall adhere to truth and accuracy and to generally accepted standards of good taste.

4. A member shall not represent conflicting or competing interests without the express consent of those involved, given after a full disclosure of the facts; nor place himself or herself in a position where the member's interest is or may be in conflict with a duty to a client, or others, without a full disclosure of such interests to all involved.

5. A member shall safeguard the confidences of both present and future clients or employers and shall not accept retainers or employment which may involve the disclosure or use of these confidences to the disadvantage or prejudice of such clients or employers.

6. A member shall not engage in any practice which tends to corrupt the integrity of channels of communication or the processes of government.

7. A member shall not intentionally communicate false or misleading information and is obligated to use care to avoid communication of false or misleading information.

8. A member shall be prepared to identify publicly the name of the client or employer on whose behalf any public communication is made.

9. A member shall not make use of any individual or organization purporting to serve or represent an announced cause, or purporting to be independent or unbiased, but actually serving an undisclosed special or private interest of a member, client or employer.

10. A member shall not intentionally injure the professional reputation or practice of another practitioner. However, if a member has evidence that another member has been guilty of unethical, illegal or unfair practices, including those in violation of this Code, the member shall present the information promptly to the proper authorities of the Society for action in accordance with the procedure set forth in Article XIII of the Bylaws.

11. A member called as a witness in a proceeding for the enforcement of this Code shall be bound to appear, unless excused for sufficient reason by the Judicial Panel.

12. A member, in performing services for a client or employer, shall not accept fees, commissions or any other valuable consideration from anyone other than the client or employer in connection with those services without the express consent of the client or employer, given after a full disclosure of the facts.

13. A member shall not guarantee the achievement of specified results beyond the member's direct control.

14. A member shall, as soon as possible, sever relations with any organization or individual if such relationship requires conduct contrary to the articles of this Code.

OFFICIAL INTERPRETATIONS OF THE CODE

Interpretation of Code Paragraph 2 which reads, "A member shall conduct his or her professional life in accord with the public interest."

> The public interest is here defined primarily as comprising respect for and enforcement of the rights guaranteed by the Constitution of the United States of America.

Interpretation of Code Paragraph 5 which reads, "A member shall safeguard the confidences of both present and former clients or employers and shall not accept retainers or employment which may involve the disclosure or use of these confidences to the disadvantage or prejudice of such clients or employers."

> This article does not prohibit a member who has knowledge of client or employer activities which are illegal from making such disclosures to the proper authorities as he or she believes are legally required.

Interpretation of Code Paragraph 6 which reads: "A member shall not engage in any practice which tends to corrupt the integrity of channels of communication or the processes of government."

1. Practices prohibited by this paragraph are those which tend to place representatives of media or government under an obligation to the member, or the member's employer or client, which is in conflict with their obligations to media or government, such as:
   a. the giving of gifts of more than nominal value;
   b. any form of payment or compensation to a member of the media in order to obtain preferential or guaranteed news or editorial coverage in the medium;
   c. any retainer or fee to a media employee or use of such employee if retained by a client or employer, where the circumstances are not fully disclosed to and accepted by the media employer;
   d. providing trips for media representatives which are unrelated to legitimate news interest;
   e. the use by a member of an investment or loan or advertising commitment made by the member, or the member's client or employer, to obtain preferential or guaranteed coverage in the medium.

2. This Code paragraph does not prohibit hosting media or government representatives at meals, cocktails, or news functions or special events which are occasions for the exchange of news

information or views, or the furtherance of understanding which is part of the public relations function. Nor does it prohibit the bona fide press event or tour when media or government representatives are given an opportunity for on-the-spot viewing of a newsworthy product, process or event in which the media or government representatives have a legitimate interest. What is customary or reasonable hospitality has to be a matter of particular judgment in specific situations. In all of these cases, however, it is or should be understood that no preferential treatment or guarantees are expected or implied and that complete independence always is left to the media or government representative.

3. This paragraph does not prohibit the reasonable giving or lending of sample products or services to media representatives who have a legitimate interest in the products or services.

Interpretation of Code Paragraph 13 which reads, "A member shall not guarantee the achievement of specified results beyond the member's direct control."

This Code paragraph, in effect, prohibits misleading a client or employer as to what professional public relations can accomplish. It does not prohibit guarantees of quality or service. But it does prohibit guaranteeing specific results which, by their very nature, cannot be guaranteed because they are not subject to the member's control. As an example, a guarantee that a news release will appear specifically in a particular publication would be prohibited. This paragraph should not be interpreted as prohibiting contingent fees.

AN OFFICIAL INTERPRETATION OF THE CODE AS IT APPLIES TO POLITICAL PUBLIC RELATIONS

Preamble

In the practice of political public relations, a PRSA member must have professional capabilities to offer an employer or client quite apart from any political relationships of value, and members may serve their employer or client without necessarily having attributed to them the character, reputation or beliefs of those they serve. It is understood that members may choose to serve only those interests with whose political philosophy they are personally comfortable.

Precepts

1. It is the responsibility of PRSA members practicing political public relations as defined above, to be conversant with the various statutes, local, state, and federal, governing such activities and to adhere to them strictly. This includes, but is not limited to, the various local, state and federal laws, court decisions and official interpretations governing lobbying, political contributions, disclosure, elections, libel, slander and the like. In carrying out this

responsibility, members shall seek appropriate counseling whenever necessary.

2. It is also the responsibility of members to abide by PRSA's Code of Professional Standards.

3. Members shall represent clients or employers in good faith, and while partisan advocacy on behalf of a candidate or public issue may be expected, members shall act in accord with the public interest and adhere to truth and accuracy and to generally accepted standards of good taste.

4. Members shall not issue descriptive material or any advertising or publicity information or participate in the preparation or use thereof which is not signed by responsible persons or is false, misleading or unlabeled as to its source, and are obligated to use care to avoid dissemination of any such material.

5. Members have an obligation to clients to disclose what remuneration beyond their fees they expect to receive as a result of their relationship, such as commissions for media advertising, printing and the like, and should not accept such extra payment without their clients' consent.

6. Members shall not improperly use their positions to encourage additional future employment or compensation. It is understood that successful campaign directors or managers, because of the performance of their duties and the working relationship that develops, may well continue to assist and counsel, for pay, the successful candidate.

7. Members shall voluntarily disclose to employers or clients the identity of other employers or clients with whom they are currently associated and whose interests might be affected favorably or unfavorably by their political representation.

8. Members shall respect the confidentiality of information pertaining to employers or clients even after the relationships cease, avoiding future associations wherein insider information is sought that would give a desired advantage over a member's previous clients.

9. In avoiding practices which might tend to corrupt the processes of government, members shall not make undisclosed gifts of cash or other valuable considerations which are designed to influence specific decisions of voters, legislators or public officials on public matters. A business lunch or dinner, or other comparable expenditure made in the course of communicating a point of view or public position, would not constitute such a violation. Nor for example, would a plant visit designed and financed to provide useful background information to an interested legislator or candidate.

10. Nothing herein should be construed as prohibiting members from making legal, properly disclosed contributions to the candidates, party or referenda issues of their choice.

11. Members shall not, through the use of information known to be

false or misleading, conveyed directly or through a third party, intentionally injure the public reputation of an opposing interest.

AN OFFICIAL INTERPRETATION OF THE CODE AS IT APPLIES TO FINANCIAL PUBLIC RELATIONS

This interpretation of the Society Code as it applies to financial public relations was originally adopted in 1963 and amended in 1972 and 1977 by action of the PRSA Board of Directors. "Financial public relations" is defined as "that area of public relations which relates to the dissemination of information that affects the understanding of stockholders and investors generally concerning the financial position and prospects of a company, and includes among its objectives the improvement of relations between corporations and their stockholders." The interpretation was prepared in 1963 by the Society's Financial Relations Committee working with the Securities and Exchange Commission and with the advice of the Society's Legal Counsel. It is rooted directly in the Code with the full force of the Code behind it and a violation of any of the following paragraphs is subject to the same procedures and penalties as violation of the Code.

1. It is the responsibility of PRSA members who practice financial public relations to be thoroughly familiar with and understand the rules and regulations of the SEC and the laws which it administers, as well as other laws, rules and regulations affecting financial public relations, and to act in accordance with their letter and spirit. In carrying out this responsibility, members shall also seek legal counsel, when appropriate, on matters concerning financial public relations.

2. Members shall adhere to the general policy of making full and timely disclosure of corporate information on behalf of clients or employers. The information disclosed shall be accurate, clear and understandable. The purpose of such disclosure is to provide the investing public with all material information affecting security values or influencing investment decisions. In complying with the duty of full and timely disclosure, members shall present all material facts, including those adverse to the company. They shall exercise care to ascertain the facts and to disseminate only information which they believe to be accurate. They shall not knowingly omit information, the omission of which might make a release false or misleading. Under no circumstances shall members participate in any activity designed to mislead, or manipulate the price of a company's securities.

3. Members shall publicly disclose or release information promptly so as to avoid the possibility of any use of the information by any insider or third party. To that end, members shall make every effort to comply with the spirit and intent of the timely disclosure policies of the stock exchanges, NASD, and the Securities and Exchange Commission. Material information shall be made available to all on an equal basis.

4. Members shall not disclose confidential information the disclosure of which might be adverse to a valid corporate purpose or interest and whose disclosure is not required by the timely disclosure provisions of the law. During any such period of non-disclosure members shall not directly or indirectly (a) communicate the confidential information to any other person or (b) buy or sell or in any other way deal in the company's securities where the confidential information may materially affect the market for the security when disclosed. Material information shall be disclosed publicly as soon as its confidential status has terminated or the requirement of timely disclosure takes effect.

5. During the registration period, members shall not engage in practices designed to precondition the market for such securities. During registration the issuance of forecasts, projections, predictions about sales and earnings, or opinions concerning security values or other aspects of the future performance of the company, shall be in accordance with current SEC regulations and statements of policy. In the case of companies whose securities are publicly held, the normal flow of factual information to shareholders and the investing public shall continue during the registration period.

6. Where members have any reason to doubt that projections have an adequate basis in fact, they shall satisfy themselves to the adequacy of the projections prior to disseminating them.

7. Acting in concert with clients or employers, members shall act promptly to correct false or misleading information or rumors concerning clients' or employers' securities or business whenever they have reason to believe such information or rumors are materially affecting investor attitudes.

8. Members shall not issue descriptive materials designed or written in such a fashion as to appear to be, contrary to fact, an independent third party endorsement or recommendation of a company or a security. Whenever members issue material for clients or employers, either in their own names or in the name of someone other than clients or employers, they shall disclose in large type and in a prominent position on the face of the material the source of such material and the existence of the issuer's client or employer relationship.

9. Members shall not use inside information for personal gain. However, this is not intended to prohibit members from making bona fide investments in their company's or client's securities insofar as they can make such investments without the benefit of material inside information.

10. Members shall not accept compensation which would place them in a position of conflict with their duty to a client, employer or the investing public. Members shall not accept stock options from clients or employers nor accept securities as compensation at a price below market price except as part of an overall plan for corporate employees.

11. Members shall act so as to maintain the integrity of channels of public communication. They shall not pay or permit to be paid to any publication or other communications medium any consideration in exchange for publicizing a company, except through clearly recognized paid advertising.

12. Members shall in general be guided by the PRSA Declaration of Principles and the PRSA Code of Professional Standards for the Practice of Public Relations of which this Code is an official interpretation.

Index